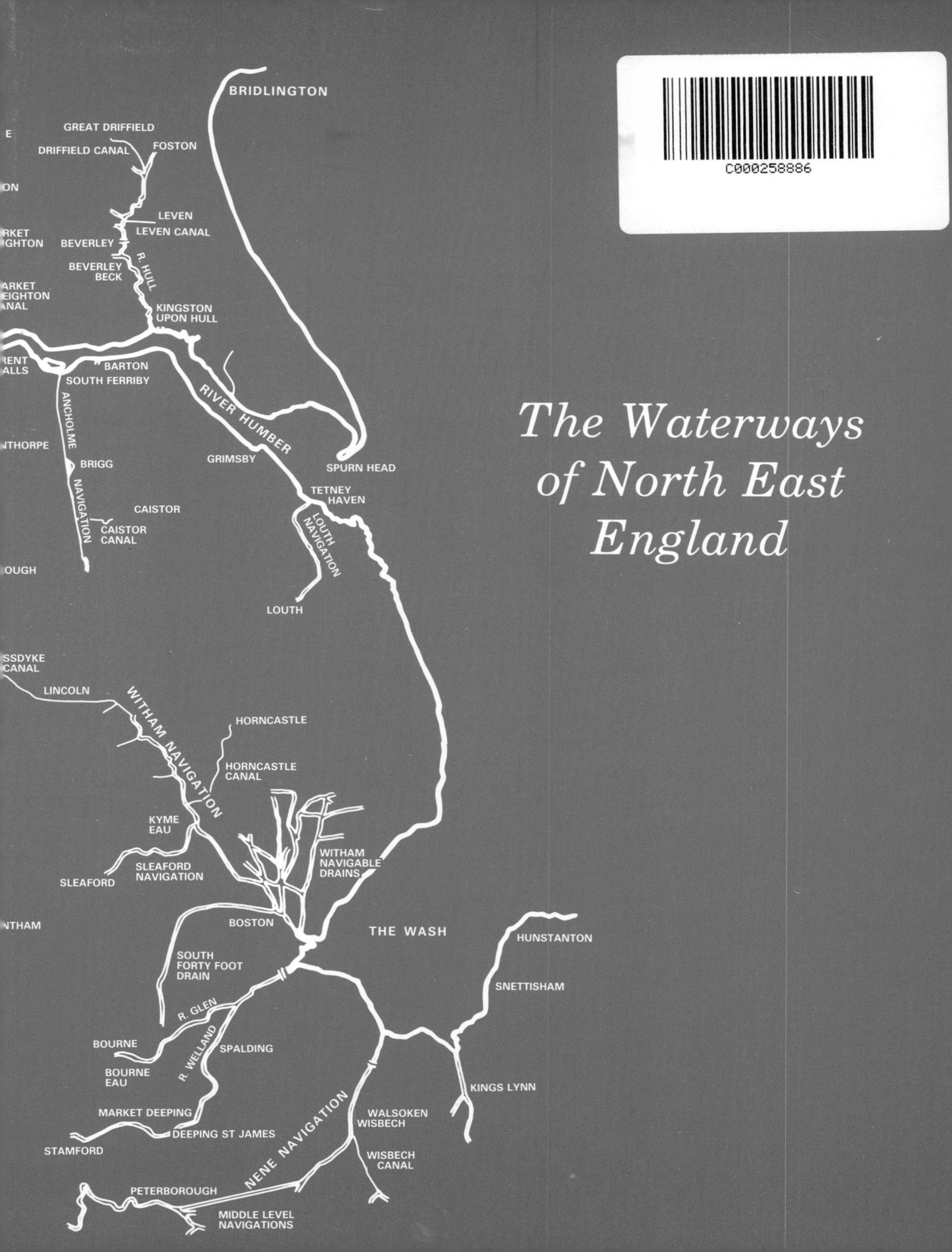

The Waterways of North East England
BRIDLINGTON
GREAT DRIFFIELD
DRIFFIELD CANAL
FOSTON
LEVEN
LEVEN CANAL
BEVERLEY
BEVERLEY BECK
R. HULL
KINGSTON UPON HULL
BARTON
SOUTH FERRIBY
RIVER HUMBER
ANCHOLME NAVIGATION
BRIGG
GRIMSBY
SPURN HEAD
TETNEY HAVEN
CAISTOR
CAISTOR CANAL
LOUTH NAVIGATION
LOUTH
LINCOLN
WITHAM NAVIGATION
HORNCASTLE
HORNCASTLE CANAL
KYME EAU
SLEAFORD
SLEAFORD NAVIGATION
WITHAM NAVIGABLE DRAINS
BOSTON
THE WASH
HUNSTANTON
SOUTH FORTY FOOT DRAIN
SNETTISHAM
R. GLEN
BOURNE
SPALDING
BOURNE EAU
R. WELLAND
KINGS LYNN
MARKET DEEPING
WALSOKEN WISBECH
DEEPING ST JAMES
STAMFORD
NENE NAVIGATION
WISBECH CANAL
PETERBOROUGH
MIDDLE LEVEL NAVIGATIONS

HUMBER KEELS

AND KEELMEN

Overleaf: *The keel* Annie Maud *on the Stainforth and Keadby Canal at Thorne in 1930. Captain Schofield is seen on the hatches, having just cast off the lee shrouds ready for lowering the sail to pass under the railway bridge carrying the Great Central line from Doncaster to Grimsby. At the tiller is Jack Williamson, Captain Schofield's regular purchase-man.* Michael Ulyatt collection

HUMBER KEELS AND KEELMEN

FRED SCHOFIELD

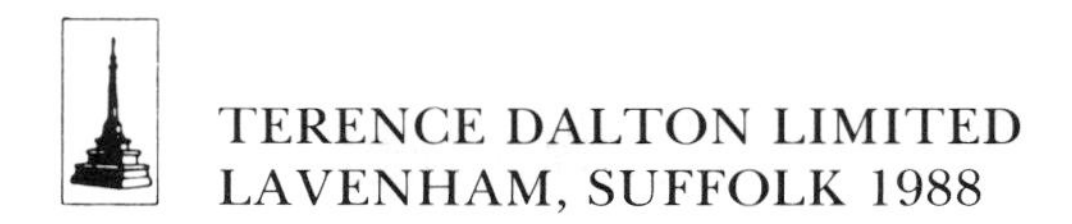

TERENCE DALTON LIMITED
LAVENHAM, SUFFOLK 1988

Published by
TERENCE DALTON LIMITED

ISBN 0 86138 059 2

To my wife Lilian

Text photoset in 10/11pt Baskerville

Printed in Great Britain at
The Lavenham Press Limited, Lavenham, Suffolk

Contents

Foreword		vi
Preface and Acknowledgements		vii
Chapter one	Keels and their Rig	1
Chapter two	Life Aboard	25
Chapter three	The Schofields	47
Chapter four	Stainforth	59
Chapter five	Hull to Sheffield before 1914	75
Chapter six	Working as Mate	93
Chapter seven	Beverley and Elsewhere	115
Chapter eight	Aboard in the Twenties	131
Chapter nine	Captain	159
Chapter ten	Keel Owner	191
Chapter eleven	Cedric Lodge	209
Appendix one	Cargoes and Destinations	223
Appendix two	Sloops	237
Appendix three	Billyboys	241
Appendix four	Steam Keels	245
Appendix five	Weights and Measures	249
Appendix six	Schofield Family Ships	250
Appendix seven	The Schofields of Stainforth	252
Appendix eight	Steel Keel Specification	254
Glossary		259
Bibliography		273
Plans of Keel *Comrade*		274
Index		277
Index of Ships		281

Foreword

by

Frank Carr, CB, CBE
Chairman of the World Ship Trust

THE Humber keel is beyond all challenge a craft of outstanding interest and importance, and it is astonishing that until Captain Fred Schofield compiled this record no book had ever been published about her. The gap has now been filled with brilliant success by an author uniquely qualified to do so. There are three reasons for this statement.

First, in a long life of over eighty years he has both sailed in them and been familiar with them from early childhood, with the whole of his working life spent serving in them first as mate and then as master and owner. There is nothing about their design, construction or handling with which he is not completely familiar.

Secondly, he has a truly astonishing memory. Having sailed over all the waterways, he is able to recall every cargo he has ever carried, not merely by type, such as myrobalans (used for tanning), but by quantity, destination, and date. It should not, however, be thought that this gives his book the character of a catalogue—far from it. Such information is kept apart without impinging on the excitement of the story; but it is there for reference by all who may be interested, and this information is not to be found anywhere else.

Thirdly, Fred Schofield has the extremely rare quality among practical sailors of being able to write. He does this with direct effect, a wide command of language, and the imaginative genius required to secure and retain the interest of the reader, both the general and the specialist.

Full marks must also be awarded to Edward Paget-Tomlinson, than whom there is no-one more knowledgeable on inland craft in all their wide variety, and whose delightful illustrations and plans both illuminate and adorn the text. No partnership could have produced more harmonious results.

To sum up, this book is so complete, so well presented, and so fully illustrated that, with nothing left out, it completely fills the long-felt need referred to above. I have no hesitation in emphasizing that in my belief it will remain for all time as the standard work on this subject.

Preface and Acknowledgements

ALTHOUGH I was not actually born on board a keel I made my first voyage with my father's keel *Fanny* when only three weeks old. That was more than eighty years ago, and since then the whole of my working life has been concerned with keels; I began work with my father at the age of thirteen years and eight months.

When John Hainsworth suggested that I ought to write about my life afloat I was not sure that anyone would want to read of my experiences. I have him to thank not only for the initial suggestion but for his continuing encouragement and advice. I have also to thank the clients of the Hull Rehabilitation Centre for help with the typing of my original manuscript.

A great many other people have also helped since I began writing ten years ago, particularly Edward Paget-Tomlinson who has made a number of superb and accurate drawings of keels to illustrate my book and has done a great deal of work in preparing my writing for publication. So many people have helped in all sorts of ways that it is quite impossible to remember them all.

I would like to thank Edward Paget-Tomlinson and Terry Robertson for producing the maps, Cedric Lodge for drawing the plans of *Comrade*—and for having established the Humber Keel and Sloop Preservation Society in the first place—and Ann Sweeney for typing the final draft. Thanks are also due to Miss E. A. Shirtliff for the photographs of Stainforth; John Wain for the map of Stainforth and for the use of his photographs; Brian Roustoby for producing from the Humber Keel and Sloop Preservation Society archives my photographs which had been handed over for safe keeping; Michael Ulyatt; Chris Ketchell; E. Fowler; C. Hutchinson; Arthur Credland of the Hull Town Docks Museum; the staff of Hull Public Library; Mrs Jean Woods for researching my family tree; Malcolm Wilson, who made the model of the keel *Guidance* which is now in the Town Docks Museum; and all who have sought to ensure that memories of the Humber keel will be preserved.

Nor must I forget to thank Colin Screeton and Jim Thompson, who willingly gave so much of their time to sail with me on *Comrade* and so made it possible for me to stay on as sailing master long after the normal retirement age. By doing so I was able to pass on much knowledge and skill to a younger generation. My thanks also to Cyril Harrison and David Robinson for sailing and caring for *Amy Howson*.

Beverley,
January, 1988

Keels and their Rig 1

THE antiquity of the vessels now known as Humber keels was first brought to my notice in 1941, when a paragraph in the *Hull Daily Mail* caught my attention. It was a review of a book called *Curiosities of Town and Countryside*. In the book the square-rigged keel was described as our greatest curiosity in shipping because she was still using the same rig as the thirteenth-century ships of the Cinque Ports which had laid the foundations of Britain's maritime power.

Curiosity or not, she is certainly the most historic commercial craft using square sail to have survived into the twentieth century, and she made a worthwhile contribution to the country's transport needs from the days when roads were non-existent until the age of the heavy motor lorry and container transport.

The word "keel" is also of great antiquity, coming from the Anglo-Saxon *ceol*, meaning a ship. In Anglo-Saxon times this would have been a vessel setting a single square sail on a single mast, and this is the definition of a keel today. The square sail must have been one of the first inventions of early man; it was used by the reed ships of the early Egyptians, by the Phoenicians and the Romans. Bearing in mind the limitations of draught on the early river navigations before they were improved, the early keels would have been small clinker-built vessels able to load thirty or forty tons of cargo. Clinker means built with planks that overlap, as opposed to planks that are set edge to edge. One of the last fully clinker-built keels was the *Blessing*, owned by William Porter of Driffield; her deadweight tonnage was eighty-six, and she would trade from the South Yorkshire coalfield to any place as far south as the Thames, according to Captain Ernest Porter of Beverley.

My father Arthur Schofield's keel *Fanny* was the first that I embarked on, at the tender age of twenty-one days in 1906. She was part clinker and part carvel, 57 feet 6 inches in length, 14 feet 8 inches in beam, with 6 feet 6 inches depth of hold amidships. She had a carvel bottom of elm and seven clinker strakes of English oak to the binds, of which there were two, four and a half inches thick each, followed by a nine-inch top strake. Her decks were of Memel redwood and her coamings and headledges of American oak. She carried a full keel rig of mainsail and topsail. She was built in 1866 at Barugh (pronounced "barg") Locks on the Barnsley Canal near Barnsley by Joshua Turner for Henry Pauling of Hull.

About that time there seems to have been a change, so far as

Opposite page: *A Lincoln keel with a stump mast on the Fossdyke Navigation about a mile west of Saxilby. She is loaded to maximum draught and appears not to be steering very well, as a stower is being used from the after deck to aid the steering.* Yorkshire Post

keels were concerned, from clinker to carvel construction, which had been used in England for larger ships since the days of Henry VIII. Later in the nineteenth century iron was employed, then steel. The *Fanny's* kelsey or keelson was American oak thirteen inches deep by twelve inches wide. All her beam knees were made out of grown crooks. By the start of the twentieth century all wooden keels were being built by the carvel method, steel girders were being used for keelsons and the beam knees were being made by the yard blacksmith out of bar iron.

A length of 57 feet 6 inches, a beam of 14 feet 8 inches and about 6 feet 6 inches depth amidships was a profitable size for a keel in the mid-nineteenth century, with plenty of coal from the Barnsley coalfield freely available. When new the *Fanny* could load about one hundred tons of coal. Towards the end of the nineteenth century many keel owners began to favour the Sheffield-size keel, 61 feet 6 inches long by 15 feet 6 inches wide and 7 feet to 7 feet 6 inches deep amidships. With a vessel this size they could not use the Dearne and Dove Canal and would have to load their coal cargoes at Kilnhurst, Denaby or Roundwood coal staithes. The advantage here was being able to take a few more tons to Sheffield and to load up to about 110 tons of coal down, as well as having a larger cubic capacity hold for when a lighter, bulkier cargo might be on offer. In the mid-nineteenth century there was some coal

Keels and other shipping in Queen's Dock, Hull, about 1880. A number of the keels that can be seen are clinker-built craft. Hull Town Docks Museum

traffic from the Barnsley area to the Horncastle Canal by a few purpose-built keels 54 feet long by 14 feet 4 inches wide, vessels with a low profile because of the limited headroom through the bridge at Lincoln, which also limits the draft to a little over four feet.

The 57 feet 6 inches clinker-built and semi-clinker (sides only) keels such as the *Fanny* were fine seaworthy craft with bows not so bluff as latter-day vessels'. Their underwater lines showed a slight entrance and a long clean run, and they were fast sailers and could be handled easily.

They should not be confused with the 57 feet 6 inches "West Country" keels that were built in the West Riding above Wakefield, which had a few inches less beam with fuller lines, round bows and not much run at all. They were built to suit the local navigations, to carry the most tonnage on the least draft. Only a few carried any sails; they were usually towed by steam tugs below Wakefield and were horse hauled on the Calder and Hebble Navigation and the Rochdale Canal. They went over the Pennines to Manchester and Liverpool and could be considered canal craft. Albert Wood of Sowerby Bridge, the junction of the Calder and Hebble with the Rochdale, was a major owner of this type of vessel; his craft had a distinctive yellow livery. Such vessels were of the general family of West Yorkshire keels, distinguished from Humber keels in that they had less depth of hold, six feet six inches as opposed to the seven feet six inches of their Humber sisters. Some of these "West Country" boats would be classed as non-tidal Yorkshire keels, restricted to non-tidal waters; those that did venture into tidal waters were rigged but not necessarily fitted with leeboards; their sails would not be as big as a Humber keel's, and their sides were notably rounded, more barrel shaped. Keels up to about seventy-four feet long could trade on the Barnsley Canal and on the Trent and Ouse, but their beam was restricted by the width of the narrowest lock.

The Trent "catches" or ketches, while using the same square mainsail and topsail as the keel, were of different construction altogether. They were built of wood, carvel planked, double-ended with sharp bows and stern and flat bottomed with a hard chine bilge like a Thames spritsail barge. The stern was so narrow that the tiller had to work over the top of the rail. In addition to the square sails they would at times set a standing lugsail on a mizzen mast, unshipped when not in use, hence the term "catch" or "ketch". They were about 74 feet long and 14 feet 4 inches beam, not more than 6 feet deep.

Trent craft have had a complex history. Eighteenth-century vessels were often rigged as keels but open holded with canvas cloths instead of hatches; some, apparently with two holds, had a

Two clinker-built keels, one of them laden with a stack of barrel staves, in Queen's Dock, Hull.
Hull Town Docks Museum

Upper Trent boats, which worked up the Soar, the Grantham Canal and the Trent and Mersey Canal to Burton, being towed by one of the Trent Navigation tugs, which were named after Robin Hood and his followers. Newark was the transshipment point between Humber keels and Trent catches, as we could not pass through Newark Lock until 1926 and Newark Town Lock until 1952. Newark District Council Museum

capacity of 51 tons on a draught of 3 feet 3 inches, measuring 68 feet long by 13 feet 11 inches. Not dissimilar were Upper Trent craft, which handled traffic above Nottingham, up to Burton, on the Nottingham Canal, on the Soar to Leicester, and on the Grantham Canal. For canal work they put their sailing gear ashore, the rig being similar to a keel's but without a topsail and generally without leeboards. They too could carry up to fifty tons, measuring some sixty feet by fourteen feet.

Keel design was governed by the sizes of locks on the various navigations they were expected to work. To make maximum use of the limits imposed by the lock chambers hulls were built as full as possible, with bows almost flat across and sterns full above the waterline. More thought, however, was given to the underwater lines aft because they would affect both the steering qualities and the ability of the keel to work to windward aided by the leeboards. Keelmen spoke of the "run" aft, the inward sweep of the hull towards the sternpost. It began about a third of the vessel's length forward of the sternpost and developed a concave curve before meeting the latter. Athwartships, keels were given rounded bilges between vertical sides and flat bottoms, the bilge rounding in to the stempost, with no flare of the bow timbers to throw off seas or anything like that.

Wooden keels continued to be built into the nineteen-twenties, wood and metal carrying on alongside each other. Timber sizes were generous. First came the keel, of oak, twelve or fourteen inches across but only six deep, three inches projecting below the planking as an external keel; more massive and the real spine of the ship was the keelson or kelsey, of pitch pine, twelve inches by twelve or fourteen. Passing between keel and keelson and bolted through both were the oak floor timbers, each four by four inches, the same size as the frames, although thickening to five inches at the bilge. The frames, spaced at nine-inch centres, were built up as follows: first the floor timbers butted up to the side frames, then were strengthened at the bilge by overlapping futtocks of naturally curved timber. To stop rot down the end grain the tops of the frames were capped by a covering board, while their inner sides supported knees, on which rested the deck beams. The beams across the hold were also supported by horizontal knees, oak until iron came into general use. The deck beams or carlins, two and a half inches by two and a half, sprang from each frame, but in way of the hold they extended only some two feet, the width of the side decks, being bound together by the coaming plank three inches by six. There were two fixed beams across the hold, the main beam and the middle beam, as well as the portable half hatch beam and the fixed beams under the headledges.

Planking and framing at the bows of a short-stemmed wooden keel. Because of the sharp turn of the planking inwards to form the bluff bow, the first four frames were set at right angles to the side frames.

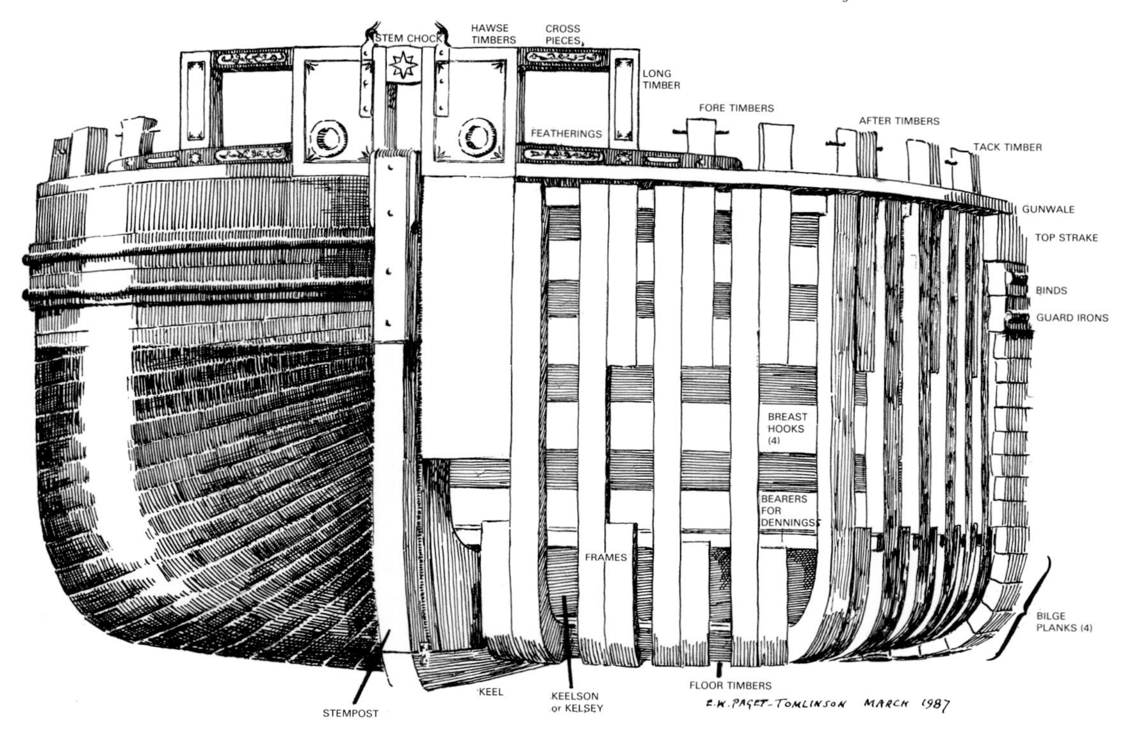

Stem and stern post were reinforced by apron pieces, and the frames at the bow, strengthened by breasthooks—as were those at the stern—were ranged at right angles to the side frames because of the acute turn of the planking to meet the stem. The breasthooks were made from natural oak crooks, selected because of their shape. The carvel planking, oak, was two inches thick by six inches across, except at the turn of the bilge where it thickened to three inches. The bottom planking was of elm. The deck planking was redwood or pitchpine, three inches by three inches across, plus a six-inch waterway inside the covering board and a six-inch coaming plank. Finally there were ceilings and shutts in the hold, with removable limber boards alongside the keelson to check the limber holes in the floor timbers through which the water drained to the pumps by the bulkheads forward and aft. In the ceiling each

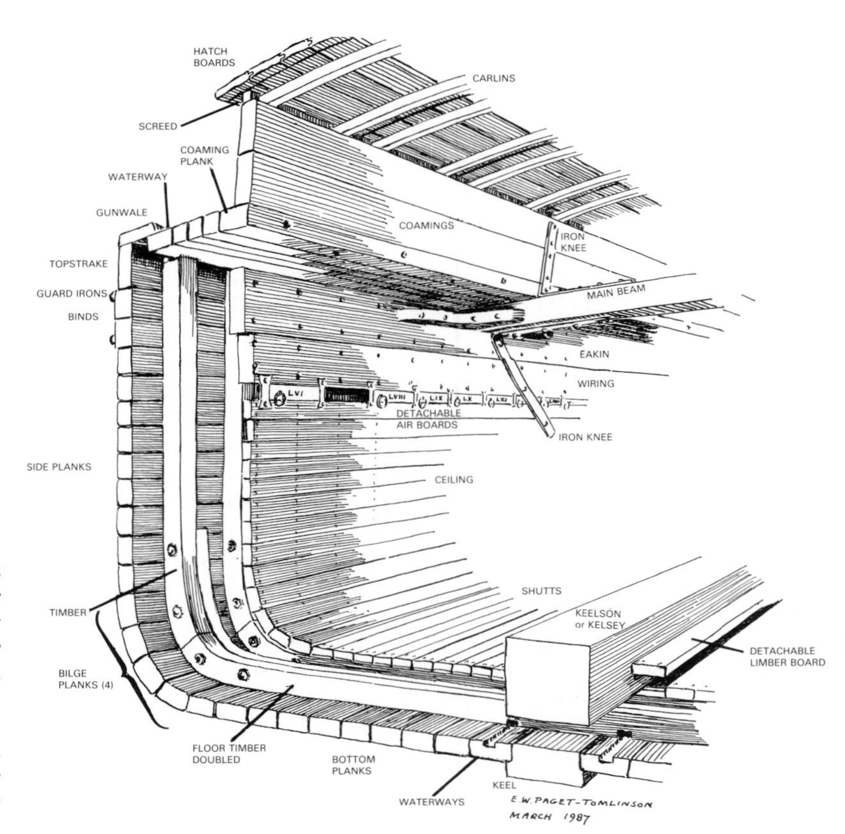

The midships section of a wooden keel showing the side planking, two inches by six, thickening to three inches at the bilge and on the bottom. The mast beam, part of which is shown, and the fixed middle beam and fore and aft headledge beams were secured by wooden and iron knees.

side was a run of removable air boards to ventilate the timbers.

The hold coamings were one foot ten inches deep amidships, slightly canted inboard, the headledges cambered to take account of the curvature of canal bridges, a tight one being Pottery Bridge at Swinton, near Mexborough. This camber was called the "crop", allowing passage under, or "giving briggage". The hold was spanned by twenty-nine hatches, five of these being divided into half hatches in way of the mastway board, so there were in reality a total of twenty-nine plus five, as well as the trap hatches at each corner of the hold and the fixed hatches at the fore and aft headledges. The hatches, each just under two feet wide, were made up of two beams or carlins and some twenty-two hatchboards, carlin hatches they were called, running from coaming to coaming following the camber of the headledges. Handholds were provided at the right-hand corner of each hatch, and each hatch was numbered, the number being cut in Roman numerals, for they were not interchangeable. Weather protection was ensured by canvas cloths secured by battens and wedges and by rope lashings which passed round hooks in the coamings. Lashings were also used to secure the stowers and boathooks resting on the stower clogs, and to secure the swape, sounding rod and footing plank.

Iron and steel keel hulls followed the same shape, the after deck only being laid with timber planks on the plates, while the hold was rarely lined with wooden ceilings unless needed to protect the cargo from condensation but had wooden shutts; there were wooden dennings for the cabin floor, although some of the later "flour packets" had steel shutts. Metal keels were all long stemmed, the stem top coming level with the top of the hawse plates. Wooden keels could be either short or long stemmed, a short stem coming only to the gunwale. Iron and steel keels needed fewer frames and beams, spaced at eighteen-inch centres. There were five strakes of plating, overlapped or "joggled" in and out, riveted along each seam and butted flush with double riveted butt straps behind. The binds were two bars of bulb iron; there were two on each bow, the upper one reaching right round the bows and the other not so long; there was one right round the stern. Sometimes the timber heads were iron, as was the stern rail, although the mainsheet horse would remain wood.

The mast of a keel was stepped in a lutchet which in turn was stepped on the keelson just aft of the main beam, with a wood or iron knee at each side to stop sideways movement. On the foreside of the lutchet was a short length of chain to the underside of the beam so the lutchet could move up or down independent of the beam as the ship took on or discharged cargo; it also allowed for any movement that might take place when she took the ground or in a heavy sea. In the early keels the lutchet was made in one piece

The lutchet, which rose the full height of the hold, clearing the hatches by some eighteen inches in older keels, much less in the later, larger ones. Although the lutchet bore against the main beam it was not held to it except by a chain from the beam to its foreside; knees prevented lateral movement but it was free to ride up or down as the ship flexed.

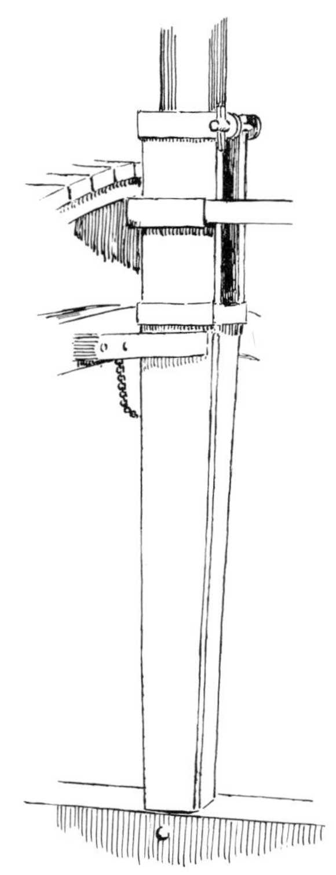

out of a baulk of oak about twenty inches square and long enough to reach from the keelson to at least fifteen inches above the hatches. The mast step was cut in the baulk to leave the after side open and was deep enough for the heel of the mast to be on a level with the beam when lowered and about to trip; an iron hoop was put round the lutchet at step level and an iron plate on the step and on its inside wall forward to take the chafe of the mast as it was lowered. Later the lutchet was made by riveting steel plates together.

Many people seem to think that the main beam of a keel was amidships, so I will put this straight now. The main beam of a keel was one third of the vessel's length from the stem, and that was the position for the mast. This was made from one pole that was as free of knots as was possible. To find this quality the pole had to have been grown in Norway or Sweden, where trees are grown closer together than they are in this country. Depending on the size of the keel and the size of the sails the captain or owner wished to set, the pole would have to be anywhere from forty-eight feet to fifty-five feet long and not less than nine inches diameter at four feet from the butt. Two more poles would be required to make the mainsail and topsail yards: one about thirty or thirty-one feet long and one about twenty-seven feet long. The main yard would have to be seven inches in diameter at the centre and three inches in diameter

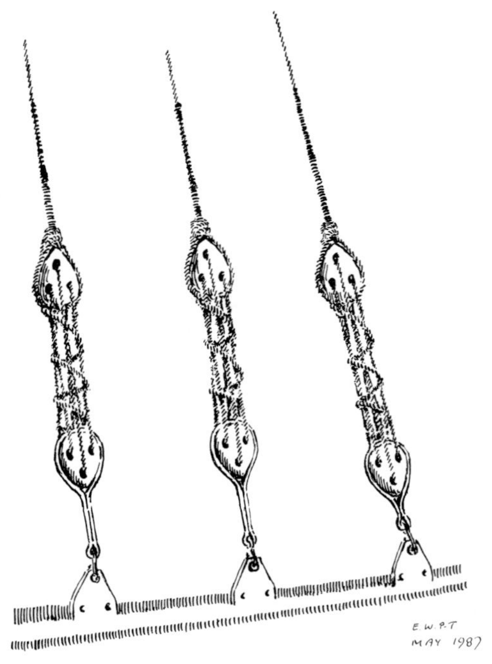

Made up in inch-and-three-quarter wire, the keel's shrouds were secured by pear-shaped deadeyes set up with two-and-a-quarter-inch lanyards. There were two main shrouds and a topsail shroud each side.

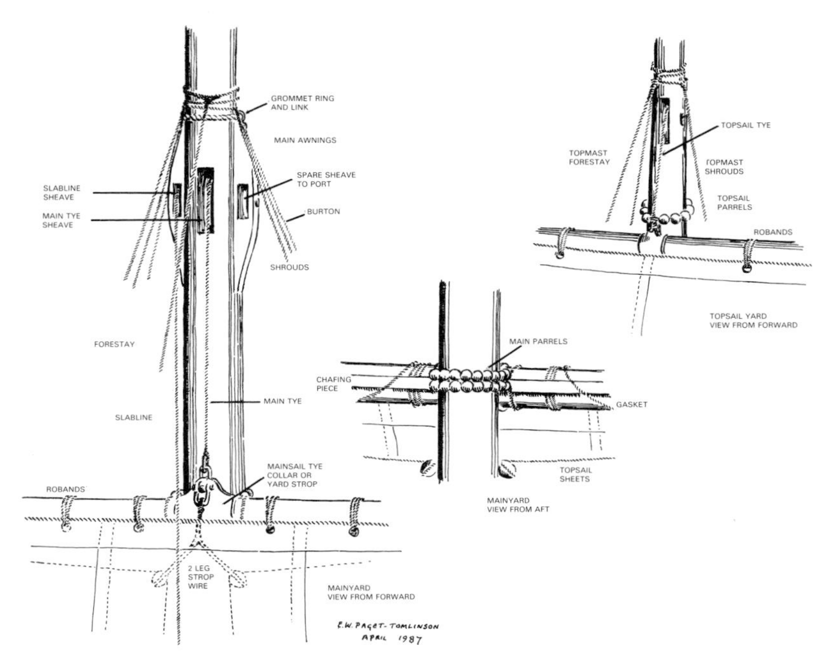

Nerve centre of a keel's rig were the main hoynings or awnings, or as deep-sea sailors would say, the hounds. Here were three sheaves, one six and a half inches in diameter for the mainsail tye, a smaller sheave to starboard for the slabline and a spare sheave to port.

at each end. A few inches from each end a slot was cut to take a two and three-quarter inch by three-quarter inch sheave for the topsail sheets. The topsail yard was four and a half inches diameter at the centre and two inches at each end. Some keels engaged mainly in the coal trade from the West Riding to York and above, using the Selby Canal for the passage between the Rivers Aire and Ouse, used a shorter mainmast with a fidded topmast which was removed for the passage of the canal.

In my time all the standing and running rigging was made of wire. The shrouds and backstay were set up by tarred hemp lanyards through pear-shaped deadeyes that had been used by keels probably for centuries; most other sailing vessels had changed to round deadeyes long ago. A mainsail and topsail was the usual suit of sails for a keel. Only a few of the York keels were known to set a topgallant, and then only in light winds. I have a photograph of Robert Wood of Beverley using one on his keel, the *Mary Jane*.

As I said, the running rigging was of wire, replacing the chain of earlier days, and was led to the many winches or "rollers" which I will describe in detail soon. Starting from the bow there were the mainsail tacks, of tapered chain and wire, led to the tack rollers forward. The mainsail sheets led aft to the sheet rollers, the sheets

The Mary Jane *sailing up the River Hull under mainsail, topsail and topgallant. Owned by Captain Bob Wood, she was built in 1882.* Author's collection

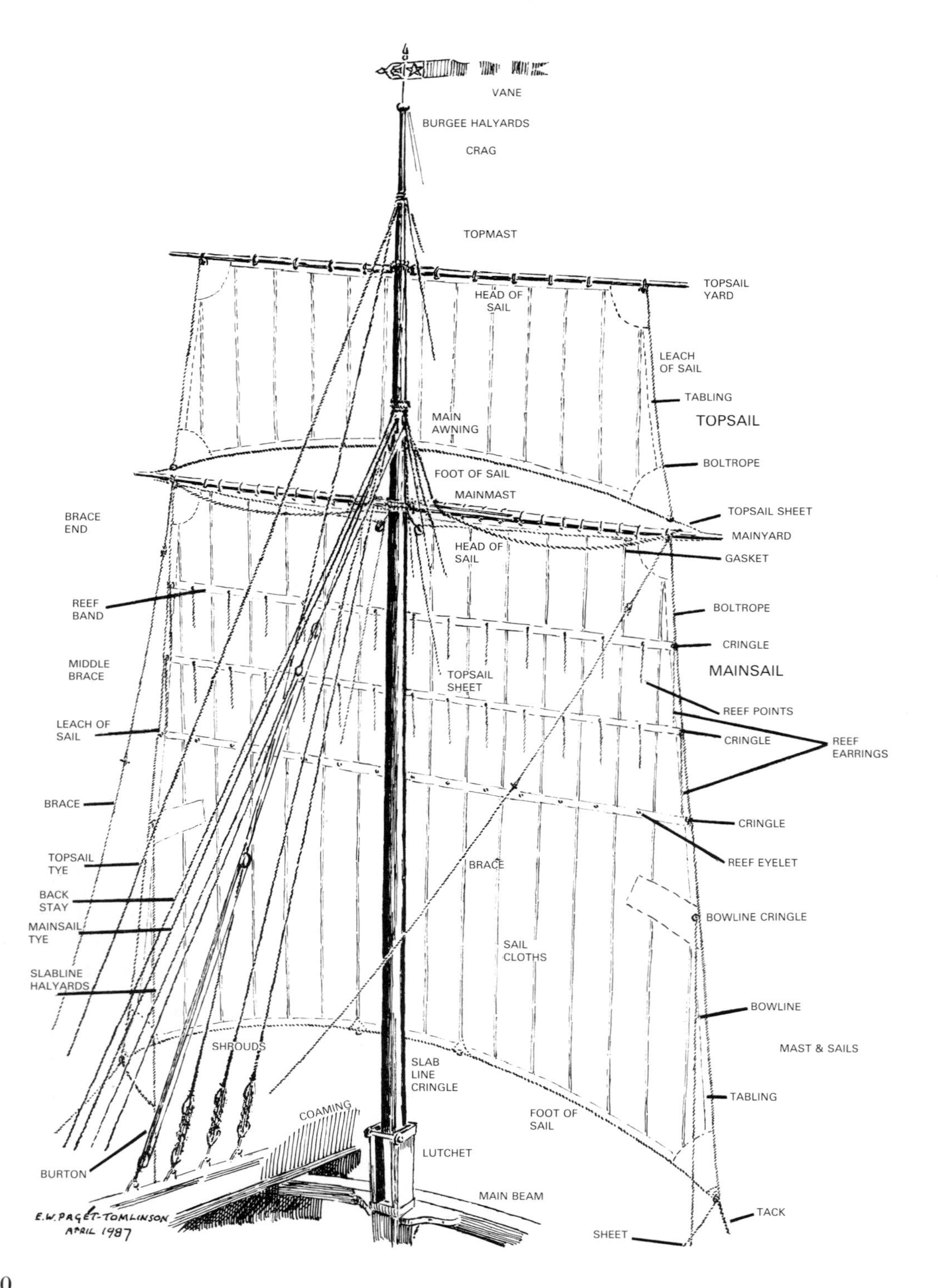
VANE
BURGEE HALYARDS
CRAG
TOPMAST
TOPSAIL YARD
HEAD OF SAIL
LEACH OF SAIL
TABLING
TOPSAIL
MAIN AWNING
BOLTROPE
FOOT OF SAIL
MAINMAST
TOPSAIL SHEET
BRACE END
MAINYARD
HEAD OF SAIL
GASKET
REEF BAND
BOLTROPE
CRINGLE
MIDDLE BRACE
MAINSAIL
TOPSAIL SHEET
REEF POINTS
LEACH OF SAIL
CRINGLE
REEF EARRINGS
BRACE
CRINGLE
REEF EYELET
TOPSAIL TYE
BRACE
BACK STAY
BOWLINE CRINGLE
MAINSAIL TYE
SAIL CLOTHS
SLABLINE HALYARDS
BOWLINE
SHROUDS
MAST & SAILS
SLAB LINE CRINGLE
TABLING
COAMING
FOOT OF SAIL
LUTCHET
BURTON
MAIN BEAM
E.W. PAGET-TOMLINSON
APRIL 1987
TACK
SHEET

crossing so that the starboard roller worked the port sheet and vice versa. The hemp topsail sheets led down, via blocks secured to the mainyard strop, to cleats on the coamings, while the braces of manilla led aft to cleats on the halyard roller posts on the after headledge. The halyard roller assembly, within reach of the steersman, handled the bulk of the running rigging. To this came the topsail tye and halyard, the mainsail tye and halyard, the manilla braces for the yards and the slabline with its halyard, also of manilla. This slabline lifted the foot of the mainsail to spill wind or clear obstructions on river, canal or quayside. Not to be forgotten were the bowlines on the mainsail, port and starboard, led forward to cleats on the windlass bitts, needed to put the ship about.

I am going to give only approximate dimensions of sails because they were always ordered for a particular vessel, and the sailmaker would take his own measurement. They were made of hemp or cotton or flax canvas, usually twenty-four inches wide cloth. The approximate dimensions of keel sails were:

Topsail	Width on head	23 feet
	Width on foot	26 feet 6 inches
	Depth in centre	10 or 11 feet
	Depth in leech	11 feet 6 inches or 12 feet 6 inches
Mainsail	Width on head	26 feet
	Width on foot	32 or 34 feet
	Depth in centre	25 or 27 feet
	Depth on leech	30 or 31 feet

The boltropes were of tarred hemp. Two sets of reef points were provided on the mainsail, with provision for a third reef by a lace line. It was rarely that the third reef had to be used in open water; its main purpose was to control the speed of the keel when on a canal or in a narrow river. The sails were rarely dressed but nearly always left white, and sail covers were used to cover them up and keep them dry when not in use.

Leeboards on the keels, sloops and billyboys were used to check sideways drift when working to windward, the leeward one being lowered to increase the effective draught and so reduce the leeway. The leeboard was not just a plain wooden board but of aerofoil section to ensure a firmer grip on the water. When navigating the Sheffield and South Yorkshire Navigation above Doncaster the leeboards would be put on shore at Thorne or Stainforth, where there were cranes provided for that purpose. The cogboat also had to be left at Thorne or Bramwith until the keel returned down the canal.

For handling all this gear the keel was fitted with eight winches as well as the anchor windlass; "rollers" was the keelmen's name for the winches. Starting for'ard, the anchor windlass was of the barrel

Opposite page: *The keel's mast and sails, showing the standing and running rigging, most of which was of wire. Out of sight on the fore side of the sail is the slabline, used to pull up the foot of the mainsail to clear obstructions or to spill the wind.*

Below: *Stayfall blocks and tackle. The chain was secured by a link not unlike a link in a bicycle chain to the wire rope passing round the mast roller.*

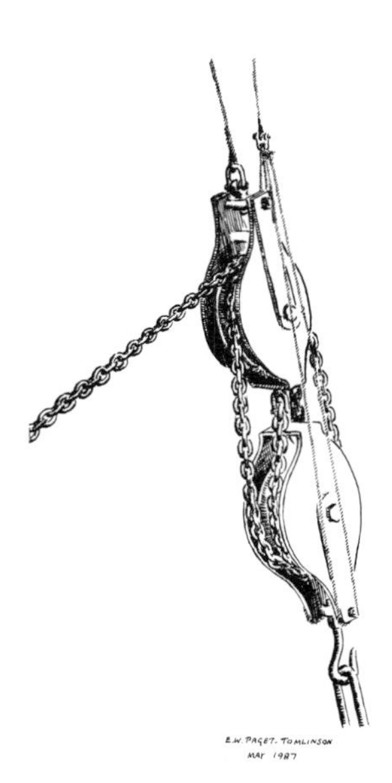

type set between the bitt heads, with the usual pawls on the samson post and the pump-action rocker arm on top of the samson post for working the two anchors.

On the fore headledge (the headledges are the thwartship coamings at the fore and after ends of the hold) were two oak winch posts with the steel tube roller between for heaving up the mast and for warping the ship about the docks or into and out of a creek or haven on the estuary. It was also used for heaving the cargo out of the hold by means of a derrick when a crane was not available. The roller was fitted with a pawl to hold it from running back if left unattended and with a slow purchase gear on the port side. With this winch and the stayfall, passed through two eight-inch two-sheave blocks hooked on the stem head, it was possible for one man to heave up or lower the mast by himself.

Underneath this roller and at right angles to the headledge were two short wooden rollers supported on an iron frame. These were the tack rollers for heaving down the tack of the mainsail. Pawls were fitted at the fore end so that the tack could be held in

The windlass was some eight feet across and was operated by a pump-action rocker arm with two connecting rods operating pawls which engaged teeth on the rings flanking the central pawl ring. Inset is a flitter, a stop on the cable to prevent it running out.

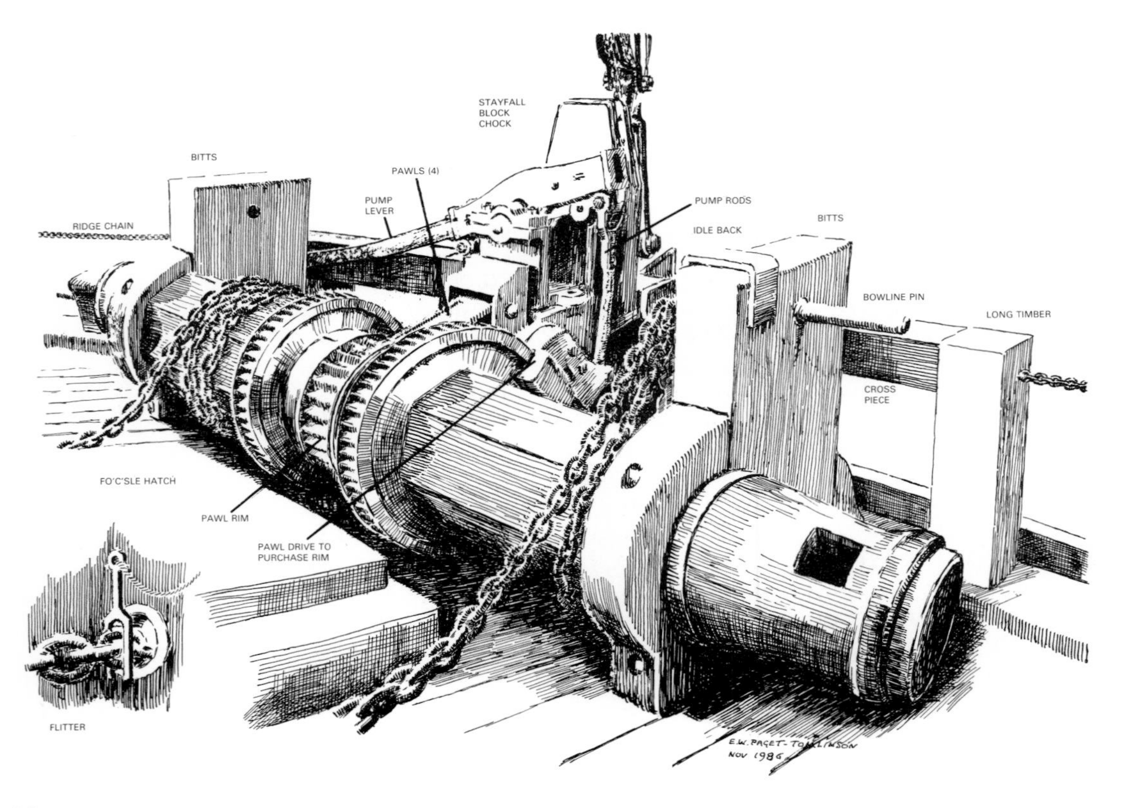

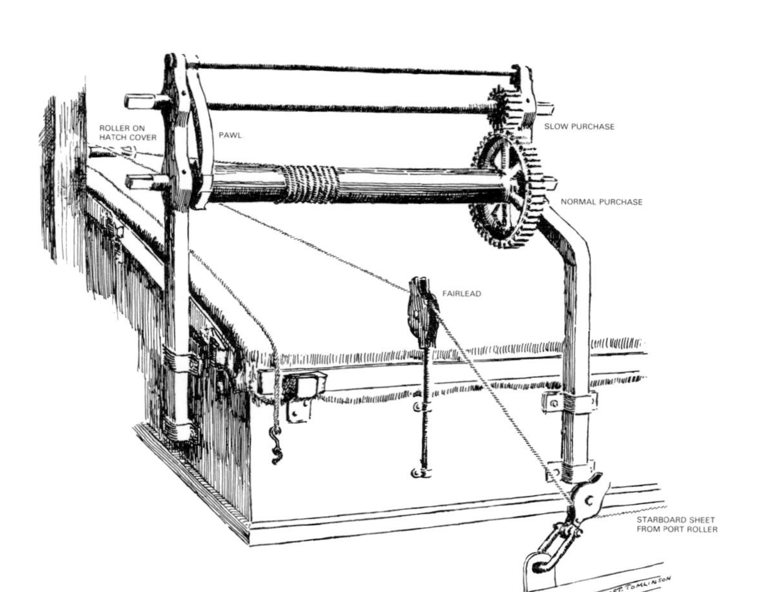

The starboard sheet roller which worked the port sheet. Such mechanical equipment enabled a keel to be worked by two men.

the position required. On the after headledge was another set of winch posts with two wooden rollers, the top one for the topsail halyards and the bottom one for the mainsail halyards. On the after side of the winch posts were two large cleats for making fast the braces from the main yard, and on the side of the starboard winch post was a smaller cleat and an eyebolt to take the slabline halyard.

Winches to control the sail sheets were made by the yard blacksmith and fitted on the after end of each coaming. They had a slow purchase for heavy weather and were fitted with pawls. The leeboard winches were fixed vertically at the fore end of each side rail aft.

The middle part of the after rail was a large piece of oak with a carved panel each side. On the outside of this was painted the keel's name and port of registry, and on the inside the name of the owner or master or both. This part of the rail was always known as the mainsheet horse. On to each side stanchion supporting the mainsheet horse was bolted a small timberhead known as the taffrail timber, used for making fast the cogboat painter.

The rudder, made of oak, was hung on the sternpost by four gudgeons, with the pintle made in one piece of round bar passed down from the top through all four gudgeons. This arrangement left a certain amount of free movement of the rudder when the keel had to take the ground, such as when she had to be laid on a tidal berth to load or discharge cargo. The underwater section of the rudder was built slightly concave on each side to make it more effective when the keel was sailing in narrow, shallow waterways. The tiller, made from a naturally grown crook of oak or ash, was fitted into the rudder head under the mainsheet horse. Many were elaborately carved with panels for the ship's name; part of the tiller might be carved to represent rope, and a dog's head was usually carved on the inboard end. For horse haulage on the canals it was usual to change from the wooden tiller to an iron one designed to fit over the rail so that the rudder could have a greater working arc. The iron tiller was in two parts so that the end could be taken off and the main piece left in the rudder head to push the rudder hard over clear of the lock gates and sills; the short part of the tiller left in the rudder head would not then foul the lock walls.

This introduces the subject of keel handling. The square-sail, antique in appearance, was versatile; by means of tack rollers, bowlines and braces the mainsail could be trimmed right round to a fore and aft setting for beating and close-hauled work; for a following wind or a wind on the quarter nothing can beat square rig. Sailing on the Humber depended on the tide as much as the wind; indeed it was essential to work with the tide, "driving" being normal practice, using flood or ebb to make progress, trailing the anchor on the bottom to give steerage way.

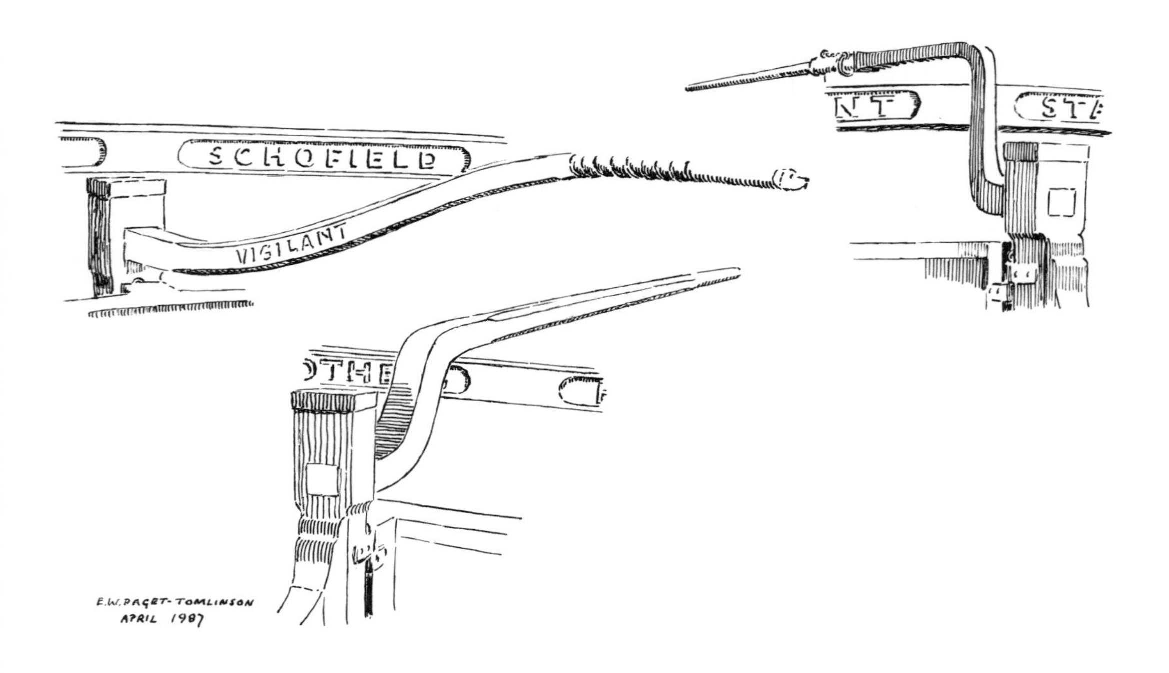

Tillers came in three shapes. There was the standard elegantly carved wooden tiller used by both keels and sloops; the iron canal tiller with a four-foot detachable handle; and the wooden tiller used by Trent catches, which was cranked sufficiently to pass over the mainsheet horse.

Now to ship handling, "heaving up the sail", "staying" or tacking, wearing ship, and lowering. I cannot do better than quote an article I wrote in *Slabline*, the Journal of the Humber Keel and Sloop Preservation Society, in issue No 9 of June, 1978.

A keel was normally manned by a captain and mate. If the captain had a reasonably experienced mate, shouted commands were often not necessary except in a few important instances.

Central on the aft headledge were the halyard rollers. The upper roller controlled the topsail tye, the lower roller worked the mainsail tye.

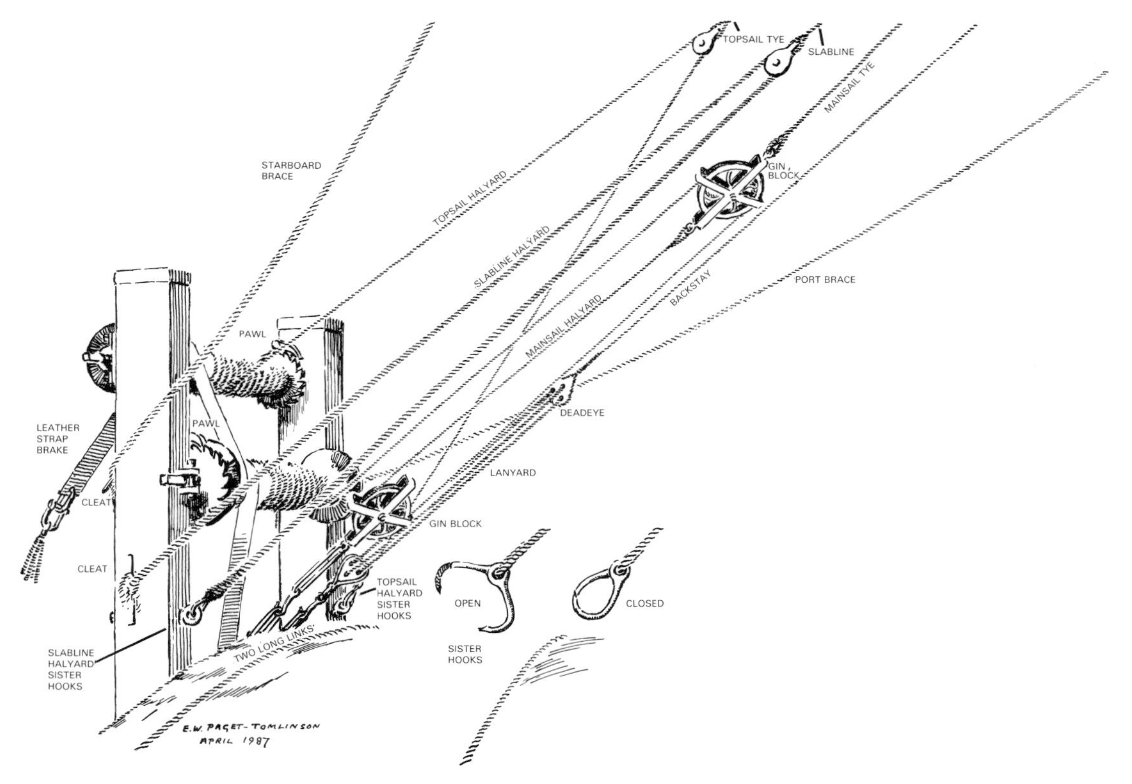

Heaving up the sail

Since the captain himself would be handling halyard rollers, slabline and brace, no orders would be needed in connection with them. If the topsail was to be set as well as the mainsail, and the wind was not of the lightest, both sails would be furled on the yard and made fast with rope yarns, strong enough to keep the sail furled until required to break.

The captain would first "heave up the slabline" so that the mainsail would not fill and break out before the main yard was in position. He would then "start up the topsail yard" with the topsail

Opposite page: *A keel staying or going about: 1 On the starboard tack, the captain puts the helm down, lets go the lee sheet; the mate releases, or "rises", the starboard tack. 2 As the ship passes through the eye of the wind the mate is ordered "let go the bowline"; the captain hauls the mainyard with the brace and the mate heaves in, or "gets down", the port tack. The captain heaves up the weather leeboard. 3 On the new tack the captain heaves in the starboard sheet and the mate passes the weather bowline over the forestay. The captain lets go the lee-side leeboard.*

halyard roller. The mate would first pass the fore end of the topsail yard between forestay and fore topmast stay when the yard was high enough, and shortly after "top the yard out" by heaving down the after end of the yard, using the topsail sheet*. The yard would then be sent up just above the "main hoynings" (sometimes called "hounds" or "crosstrees" in other ships).

The captain would then "start up the main yard". When it had reached fifteen or more feet up the mast the mate would "top out the yard" by heaving down the after end with the brace* and passing the yard end inboard of the shrouds. After the yard had continued up the mast to a point the captain judged high enough, he would "slack away the slabline" and break out the mainsail (breaking the rope yarns) by heaving in the lee sheet. Meanwhile, the mate would "get down" the weather tack; in earlier times the clew of the sail would have been hove down as far as the tack block. He would then "pass the bowline over the stay" ready to "make fast" as the ship gathered way. The mate would then "brail in the weather topsail sheet" and make it fast to the cleat, then do likewise for the lee topsail sheet. The captain would then "break out" the topsail by heaving up the topsail yard with the topsail halyard roller.

All this assumes that the ship was first sailing to windward. If sailing with a fair wind the sequence of events in hoisting the sail would be the same but setting sheets and tacks would be different.

Staying
(changing from one tack to the other, head to wind, when sailing to windward)

The captain would first shout to the mate to "stand by" and would put his tiller "hard down" to bring the ship up into the wind. When the sail started to flutter, he would let go of the lee sheet (say, the port sheet, assuming the ship had been on the starboard tack). The mate would then need to "rise the tack" (that is, release the pawl on the starboard tack roller and let the tack run out). He would then take up some of the slack in the port tack, bringing the port clew of the sail up to the shrouds. When the ship had passed through the eye of the wind, the captain would order the mate to "*let go the bowline*". This is one order which would always be given by the captain, and no mate, however experienced, would ever anticipate it. The reason is that the captain would have to haul the yard using the brace, and proper timing was vital. As soon as he had let go the bowline the mate would need to "get the tack down" (that is, the

* Sails could be topped in or out either to windward or to leeward. Given a choice, topping out to leeward and topping in to windward were preferable.

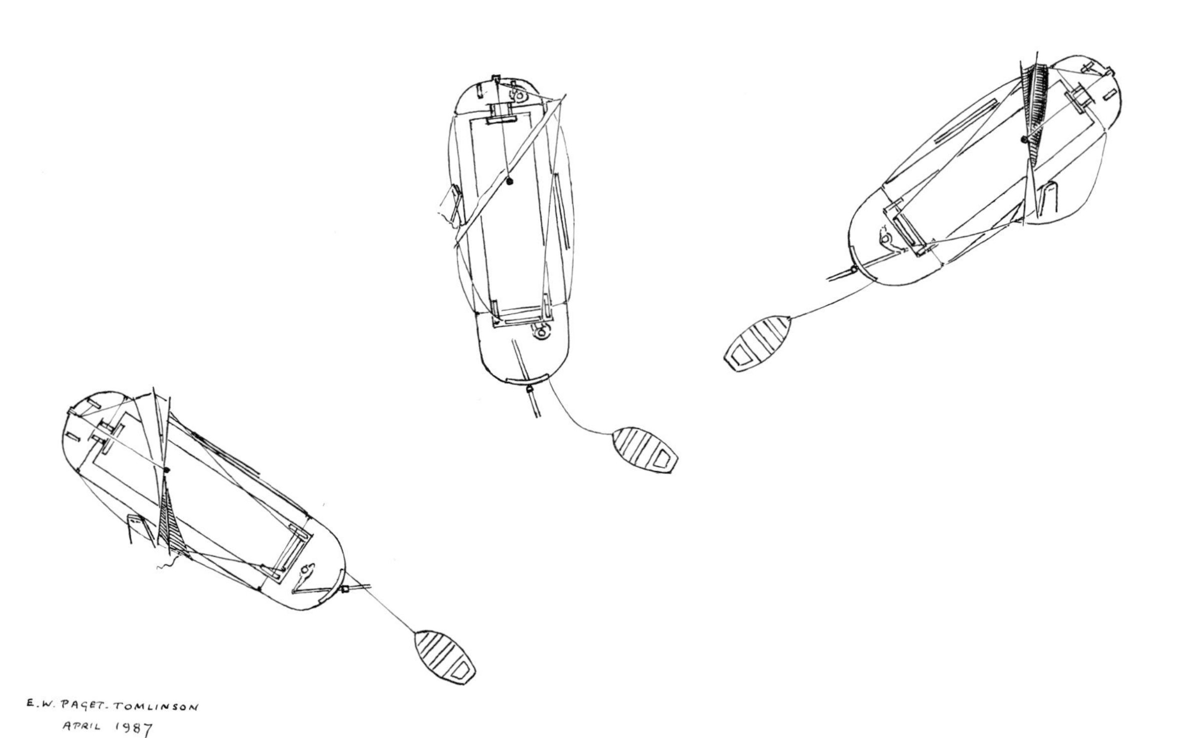

port tack) sharp and the captain would heave in the lee (starboard) sheet, "sailing her full" for a short time to allow the ship to gather way again. The mate would "pass the bowline over the forestay"* and, when the ship had gathered way again, he would "haul the bowline and make it fast". When turning to windward two-handed in a strong wind the mate would, after getting down the tack, go aft to assist the captain to heave in the sheet. If the leeboards were in use he would also heave the weather board up until it came alongside (the captain would have let go the board on the lee side as the vessel came round). When she was sailing close-hauled the mate would haul the weather bowline and clear the lee one ready for going about on the next board.

* The bowline was passed over the forestay and under the fore topmast stay when one was used.

To wear ship

Sometimes in heavy weather, and for other reasons, a vessel had to be put about on to the other tack with the sails full. This requires much more sea room than staying and is known as wearing ship. It is a straightforward manoeuvre with a square sail and perfectly safe given sea room, but can be very dangerous with the fore and aft rig, if the correct procedure is not carried out.

Lowering

If the vessel had been running with a fair wind, or rolling heavily with the swell, sails would be half lowered and yards would be topped in, then lowered on to the hatches. However, if the vessel had been sailing to windward and there was no great amount of swell, the following procedure was commonly used. After being told to "stand by for lowering" the mate would first "let go the lee shrouds, leaving the fore shroud as a steady". He would work from aft, removing topmast shroud, burton and after main shroud in turn. Each would be taken round the after side of the mast and laid forward of it on the windward side of the hatches. Just prior to lowering the fore main shroud would be treated in the same fashion. The mate would also see to it that the lee tack and weather sheet were brought inboard of the manrope to avoid them fouling anything.

The captain would first "lower the topsail" so that the wind was spilled from it. The two yards would then be close together and the topsail would be in the lee of the mainsail. The captain would then "heave up the slabline" to spill wind from the mainsail and help to prevent it billowing over the side when the yard was lowered. Finally, the captain would take the weight of the yards on the leather strap which forms a brake on the halyard rollers and when ready, let yards and sails come down with a run, stopping them short of the hatches with the brake. The mate, meanwhile, would have brought the yards on to the hatches by hauling on the lee brace. He would then quickly bundle the sails on to the hatches under the yards to stop them billowing over the side. The yards would then be lowered the short distance on to the sails, pinning them to the hatches. As soon as time allowed, the mate would "set up the fore main shroud as a steady".

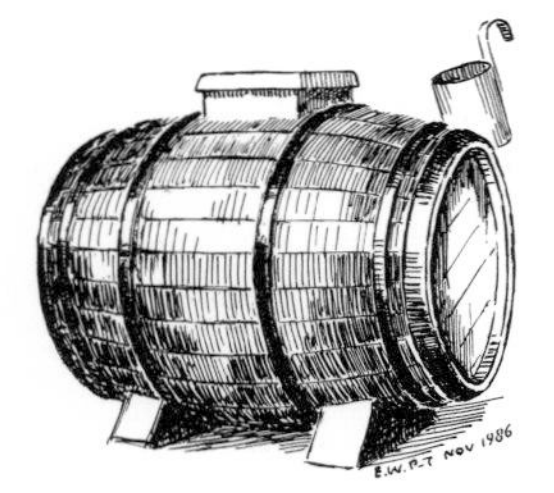

Water was carried on the stern deck in thirty-gallon casks.

If the vessel was going into a lock or alongside a jetty, the slabline would be pulled up first to bring inboard the tacks and sheets, then the topsail would be lowered behind the mainsail. If the wind was abeam or before the beam, the yards would or could be hauled round until the sails came aback, taking the way off the ship before lowering.

* * *

Until the twentieth century the fresh water was stored in two thirty-gallon oak casks placed on cradles, one on each quarter near the side rails. When the water was required it was ladled out with a one-pint copper dipper. Later when galvanized steel plate became available the water was stored in a tank holding one hundred gallons which was made to fit on the fore side of the after headledge; the water could then be piped down into the cabin.

The cabin of the keel was under the after deck, entered down a companion which was just big enough for a large person to pass through. The companion was always on the port side between the cabin chimney and the after end of the sheet roller, and within a few inches of the after headledge, which it never exceeded in height. It could be closed in bad weather by a sliding hatch over the

Looking aft in the stern cabin of the Comrade. *The drawing has been done from an impossible position above the stove, as this is the only way to show the complete layout of bedside (left), buffet and table, lockers and spareside (right).*

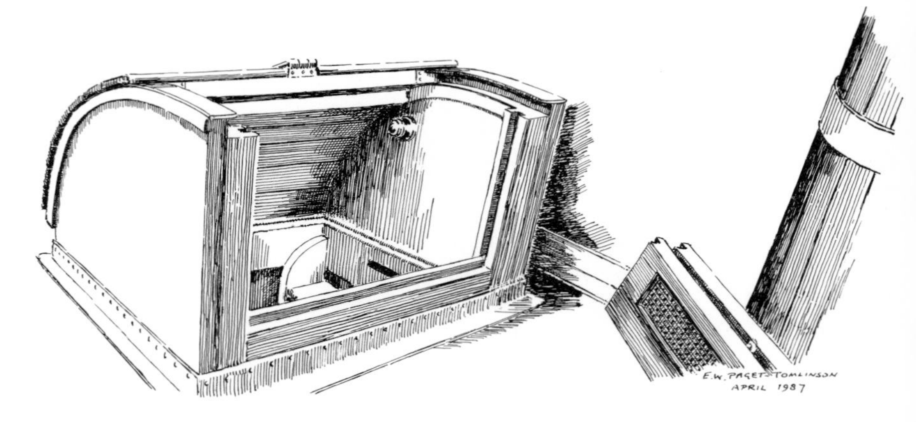

top and two portable slides on its open starboard side. To enter the cabin one had to descend by means of a near-vertical ladder held in place by two brass hooks. In some keels the bottom of the ladder would be on the locker; in others it would go down to the dennings, the name for the floor of the cabin. There was usually full standing headroom under the deck carlins in any keel's cabin, except in the very shallow-draught keels built for use on the River Trent.

On first entering the cabin it might seem to be panelled, in varnished oak or pine with some mahogany for decoration. On closer inspection one would see that the panelling was almost all cupboard doors. In one cabin that I am thinking of there were fourteen cupboard doors, five drawers and one door in the bulkhead that could be opened for ventilation and access to the hold when it was empty of cargo. This was really two doors; the first one opened into the cabin and the other, which was in two parts like a stable door, swung into the hold. The top part could be opened when the vessel was loaded if the cargo did not completely fill the hold.

Between the bulkhead door and the ladder was the fireplace for an open coal stove, which was built up of iron castings from the Doncaster foundry of Bashforth and Company. The front was cast with plenty of iron ornamentation and looked quite smart when polished with black lead. When the stove was installed it was set upon a thick iron plate, and stone flags were put at the back and on each side; it was then enclosed by the cabin panelling and a chimney piece was put on the front with a brass rail set on brass or wood stanchions to keep the ornaments in place. At the bottom of the stove in front of the ash place there would be a brass ash guard (known as the "tidy" by the keelmen). In front of the tidy was a brass fender complete with fire irons, and a cast-iron hob would be on the top bar of the fireplace for the kettle or pan to stand on.

Above: *The companion which gave entry to the stern cabin, with curved sliding roof and two detachable boards fitted in grooves at the head of the cabin ladder. The fo'c'sle companion was a simple lid.*

From the bulkhead near the foot of the ladder, and round the after end of the cabin, there was a locker with the front made of tongued and grooved boards with a polished mahogany top for sitting on. Under the locker on the port side was the storage space for coal, which was usually put into the locker when the hold was empty through a sliding door in the bulkhead; part of the locker top was loose for taking out the coal. That part of the locker across the after end of the cabin had a door on the front and was used to store the beef kettle, the frying pan, and saucepans; this locker was always called the pan locker. With the coal locker this was the main seating for the cabin; there would usually be a stool or a small chair for use on the starboard side.

Above the pan locker and the width of the seat further aft was another locker, known as the transom locker, running athwart the cabin from the bedside to the spareside, the top of this locker being of mahogany about six or seven inches wide; on the fore side were three doors. In front of the middle door there was a small dropleaf table with the legs on the pan locker, held in place by two brass hooks on to the transom locker. From the top of the transom locker to the deckhead the space was filled by three drawers about six inches deep, and above the drawers were three cupboards with two shelves in each. The middle drawer and cupboard were made of mahogany, with two doors and a glass mirror in each door. The other two cupboards would have single doors with frosted glass panels. Above the centre cupboard there was a place to fix the ship's clock. This cupboard assembly was always called the buffet; it was decorated on each side of the centre cupboard and in the corners of the transom locker with turned fancy mahogany pillars, and pillars of like pattern were used each side of the fireplace from the dennings to the chimney piece and from the chimney piece to the deckhead.

On the starboard side of the cabin were two drawers; above them and behind two folding doors was the double bed with a shelf at the bed foot which could be reached by a smaller door. At the port side was the spareside, which was about the same size as the bedside, with a middle shelf and a large food store at the after end, on a level with the shelf; this cupboard had its own door. A bed could be made up on the bottom on the spareside, but it was usually only occupied when a younger member of the family might be on board.

The fourteenth door was over the chimney piece, so that the deck pipe for carrying off the smoke from the fire could be replaced without disturbing the wood panelling of the cabin. The lighting of the cabin at night was by a swinging paraffin lamp, hung on a brass rail suspended by two brass stanchions from the deckhead; it could be moved over a limited range as required. In

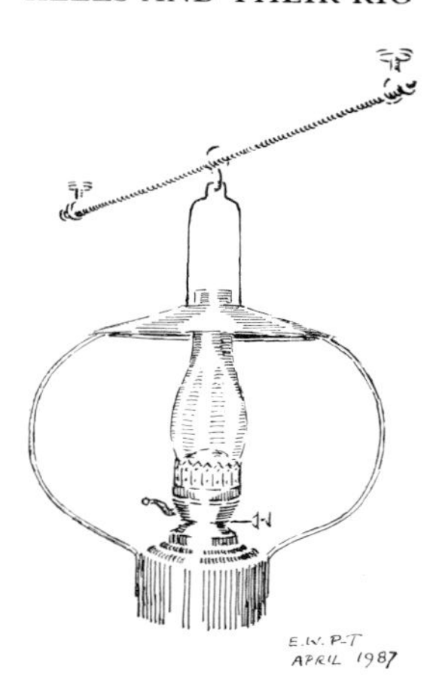

Above: *Cabin oil lamps hung from a three-foot rod secured to the deckhead, allowing them to be slid fore and aft. There were bulkhead lamps, too, with reflectors.*

the daytime the natural light came through two clear glass bull's-eyes set into a brass frame which screwed into another round frame fixed in the deck. The theory was that they could be removed for ventilation in warm weather, but fresh air was never any problem; in fair weather the companion hatch was never closed. Daylight over the bed was obtained by a nine inches by three inches glass prism let into the deck. On one or two of the steel keels the coal locker and spareside were made shorter and the bulkhead was a few inches further forward; it was then possible to arrange a small walk-in cupboard between the bulkhead and the locker on the port side which could be used as a washplace.

The fore cabin was known in all ships as the fo'c'sle, from the forecastle of the early warships. The entrance was down a hatchway set in the middle of the fore deck, down a near-vertical iron ladder set in front of the fireplace. Like the cabin stove, this one was made of cast-iron and polished by black lead; it was the

A wooden keel's fo'c'sle, viewed from forward, with the stove against the hold bulkhead flanked by the anchor chain lockers. The stove with its side oven was generally made by T. Bashforth and Company, of Doncaster. Further to the left is the boatswain's store, full of lines, paint, the dog leg anchor and the navigation lamps.

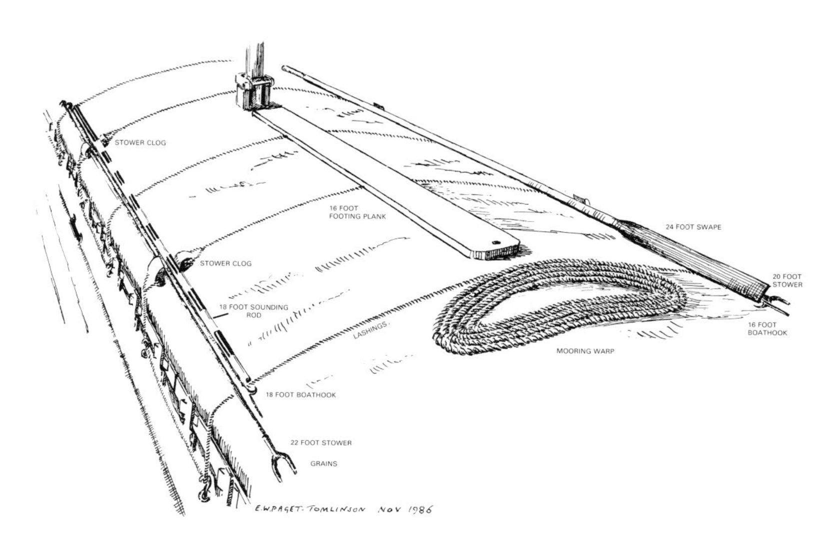

On the hatchcloths lie the boathooks and stowers, the latter used for "launching" the ship. One stower was twenty-two feet long, the other two feet shorter, the boathooks being eighteen feet and sixteen feet long; these measurements exclude the grains or tines. The sixteen-foot footing or gangplank lies amidships, the eighteen-foot sounding rod to port and the twenty-four-foot swape to starboard.

main cooking stove, with a side oven for baking and roasting. On the bulkhead each side of the stove were the chain lockers, each large enough to hold thirty fathoms of three-quarter-inch anchor cable. On the foreside right in the bows between the bitt heads were two large cupboards, and below them was the coal locker, which also served as a seat. On the starboard side was what might seem to be a walk-in cupboard; this was the bo'sun's store. Inside was the lamp locker for the navigation lights and two shelves for storing horse lines and warping line, also stocks of paint, linseed oil, and tar, kedge anchor and dogleg anchor. In the fo'c'sle the bed was on the port side, enclosed when not in use by one door. Underneath there was one large drawer. The forecabin was made much plainer than the after cabin; often tongued and grooved board was used until plywood became plentiful. It was always varnished when new, and as the years passed by it was painted with light oak graining paint. Underneath the fo'c'sle was the forepeak, which could be reached by lifting the dennings, which were always loose so that they could be taken up if the ship should overrun her anchor or damage herself in any other way.

The two main anchors were carried on the fo'c'sle deck. They would weigh about 250 pounds each. The working anchor would have a fast stock and the spare one a loose stock for easy stowage. On the hatches there would be a twenty-four feet long swape made of fir; this was for helping to manoeuvre the keel on the estuary when there was not enough wind to give steerage way. There would also be one sixteen feet long footing plank for getting on board or ashore while laid alongside of the river or canal bank, at least two stowers twenty-two feet or twenty-four feet each, two

Opposite page: *Keels were workaday craft, but they were often colourful in their paintwork and decoration, as this watercolour drawing by Edward Paget-Tomlinson shows.*

boathooks of sixteen or eighteen feet each, and one eighteen-feet sounding rod.

Two timber heads on each side of the fore deck had a socket for a metal crutch to take the swape, with which the vessel could be put round on to a fresh course when sailing in light airs. The swape could be worked from either bow.

The hull below the loaded waterline was always painted with coal tar once each summer. If the vessel was likely to be laid empty for any length of time in hot weather after the tar had been put on, it was followed twenty-four hours later by a coat of black lead made by mixing graphite and flour with water. This set as a dark grey paint; it stopped the planking from drying out and prevented dust and dirt from sticking to the tar. The top strakes, stem head, bitt heads, windlass barrel ends, rudder head, tiller, rails and main-sheet horse, winch posts and cabin companion way were all scraped and given three or more coats of varnish. The fore and after headledges were grained to represent oak panels while the coamings, following pieces, timberheads and hawse timbers might be painted light blue.

Furley's, who had been keel owners since 1774, had their keels' coamings and timberheads painted canary yellow and marked off with red and black. They had started as a wharfage business in Gainsborough and did well as merchants in the Russian hemp and tar trade, with an office in Hull. Their inland waterway interests revived in the later nineteenth century and they expanded both wharfage and warehousing. Their fleet of wooden and later steel keels was replaced between the wars by powered river craft, the first in 1931 being the *Gainsborough Trader*, built of steel at Thorne. Road vehicles were acquired and the company continued in operation up to 1975, after which they were absorbed by other interests.

The River Dun Navigation at Stainforth, looking east towards Keadby and the start of the Stainforth and Keadby Canal. In the middle distance is the crane used for lifting off keel's leeboards, with Stainforth Landing opposite. Miss E. A. Shirtliff collection

Life Aboard 2

BEFORE the 1914–18 War most keel families spent part of each year afloat, some more than others. When the family was on board a mate would not always be employed, often because the available accommodation would be required for the family.

Until the children were able to do the work round the ship the wife would act as mate, and casual labour would be engaged as required for loading and discharging cargo. When sailing on the tideway a purchase-man would be employed, usually a keelman too old for regular work; at that time the old age pension was only ten shillings (50p) per week, not payable until the age of seventy. When a purchase-man was on board he took over all the duties of mate, and the captain's wife would be responsible for cooking and catering for all hands. A purchase-man's remuneration or purchase, as it was usually called, was a fixed sum of money for the job, irrespective of time but inclusive of food.

It was usual with our family for Mother and us children to join or leave the ship at our home at Stainforth near Doncaster, usually on the downward part of the voyage. Before the Great War life on board could be very pleasant when all the family were together. If we had planned to join Father for any length of time, Mother would be busy a day or two before the ship was expected, making ready for closing the house, and getting all the washing out of the way. She also tried to have a good baking day. She would know to a few hours when to expect the ship to arrive.

Father always came home at the weekend if it was at all possible, for the loading rate of each pit was known. When passing down the Stainforth and Keadby Canal Father would always tie up for the remainder of the day on arrival at Stainforth. If conditions were favourable the next morning, after an early breakfast, the sails would be hove up, and with the mainsail trussed up with the slabline, to keep the clews from fouling Stainforth High Bridge, we would move under the crane on the East Bank, where the leeboards had been left. While the ship was in the upper reaches of the Sheffield and South Yorkshire Navigation we had to leave them ashore, because some of the locks above Doncaster were not wide enough to allow the passage of the lock with leeboards hung alongside. The crane, provided by the navigation company for this purpose, was attended to by the bridge keeper. The keelmen

Opposite page: *The restored keel* Comrade *sailing to windward on the lower Humber in 1986. When I sold her for preservation in 1974 she had been in the Schofield family for 45 years.* David Hartley

E.W. PAGET-TOMLINSON
JUNE 1987.

usually paid him one shilling (5p) for his trouble, or one shilling and sixpence (7½p) if the working anchor was left as well.

As we came within fifty yards or so of the crane, the topsail if set would be lowered behind the mainsail and with the mainsail still trussed up the yards would be hauled aback if possible, or if the wind was from directly astern it would be necessary to lower the yards and scandalize them the best way one could. After bringing up with a stern rope the starboard hand leeboard would be hove up and the crane tailed round by the rope fastened on the jib for this purpose. If the vessel was in the right position the crane jib, with the leeboard suspended from it, would pass to the afterside of the mast and under the backstay and mainsail halyards. When in the right position the leeboard would be lowered slightly so that the head could be manoeuvred outside the starboard shrouds; then it would be guided outside the gunwale and dropped until the head chain could be shackled to the traveller.

The tail chain would be rove through the leeboard clamp (the block on the leeboard stanchion) and shackled on to the fall. Then the board was lowered until the head and tail chains took the weight. Finally the vessel was moved ahead a few feet for the port leeboard to be put alongside: this was a straightforward job as there was no rigging in the way to complicate the operation. The ropes would be cast off, the slabline let go, and the sails trimmed. If the wind was a moderate westerly we could expect to be at Keadby in about six hours or so. A nice moderate breeze in which it was possible to set all the canvas often enabled one to make the fastest passage and to have more control over the ship. It was not prudent to try to drive her down or up a narrow and shallow canal or river, as if she was near the bottom she could become difficult to manage if driven too fast. Under gale force conditions with westerly winds there is a tendency for the wind to drive the water away from the Thorne end of the canal and over the lockgates at Keadby.

After being under way for about an hour we could expect to be near the top fixed railway bridge at Thorne, where the Hull–Doncaster line crosses the canal. As we approached this bridge the lee shrouds were let go and passed to windward on the after side of the mast. The slabline would be pulled up, and at the right moment Father would lower the yards while Mother took the tiller and hauled the yards fore and aft with the braces. When the yards were about two foot off the hatches the pawls on the halyard rollers were put down and the slabline let go. The parrel strop was then let go from round the mast and the yards pulled aft about three feet and made fast to the sheet roller before being lowered down on to the hatches. This was necessary to bring the yards clear of the fore roller. Father would then go forward and lower the mast while Mother steered.

Opposite page:
Replacing the leeboards which the keels had to leave ashore when going up the Sheffield and South Yorkshire Navigation. Here the starboard leeboard is being handed round the shrouds so that it can be lowered into position by the crane. The head and tail chains hang down ready to be shackled on, as I describe on this page.

Below: *A two-hundredweight coal basket and two coal shovels, the one with a square mouth being for shovelling coal off the shutts in the bottom of the hold and the round mouth for digging into a heap of coal and scooping it up.*

The westerly wind would enable the ship to carry her way through the bridge. As soon as the masthead was past the bridge Father would start to heave up the mast. He was able to do this by himself because the fore roller had a slow purchase, which he would use until the mast was at an angle of about 45 degrees; then he would change on to the main or fast purchase. When the mast was in position, Mother would heave up the mainsail yard a little so that Father could make fast the parrel strop on his way aft. He would then heave up the mainsail, while Mother looked after the tiller and sheets.

As we approached Thorne Lock the mainsail would be trussed up with the slabline, and as the vessel entered the lock the yards would be hauled fore and aft on the weather side, thus helping to take off the way. To make sure that no damage was done to ship or lock a four-inch manilla rope was put on the centre bollard on the lock side and a turn taken round the after timberhead on the port bow; with this the vessel could be held in just the right position in the lock. The lock keeper would already have drawn up two or three rounds of clough on the low gate, and this would hold the keel from going astern, and the stop rope would hold her from going ahead. The stop rope, ten fathoms long, was kept for this purpose, being renewed as soon as its condition became doubtful. At Thorne Lock or the Toll Bar bridge there were usually one or two purchase-men hanging around, and if one was required arrangements would be made.

If wanted the purchase-man would go home to fetch his gear and would rejoin us at the Low railway bridge, where the Grimsby–Doncaster line crossed the canal. This being also a fixed bridge, we again had to lower the sails and mast. We were not always able to sail Thorne "rack". When the wind was southerly the mast and sails had to be left down and the mate had to go on shore to haul by hand until the sails could again be set.

On the way down between Thorne and Keadby the ship would be made ready for the passage down the Trent and Humber. The working anchor would be bent on to the cable, the mastway board would be placed in position and covered up with the tarpaulins, the bag of wedges would be brought out of the fo'c'sle and the hatches would be battened down. Wind and tide being favourable, most keelmen liked to get away from Keadby on the afternoon tide and go down to Burton Stather or Cliff End or, if conditions were very favourable, out of the Trent into Walker Dykes, there bringing up for a few hours to go down the Upper Humber on the next high water.

Most of our coal cargoes in my childhood were for bunkering the steam trawlers in Hull Fish Dock. When arriving off the dock on the ebb, if the weather was fine, we would moor in the lock tail;

Keels under tow approaching Thorne Lock. Richard Dunston's yard can be seen at left, with a keel in frame.

if the wind was fresh southerly we would have to let go the anchor just below the dock while (until) the flood. We also had to do this at spring tides while the cloughs were drawn to sluice the silt out of the lock. As soon as we were alongside and the sails were made up the purchase-man would go to look for a job to work his way back home.

Depending on the number of trawlers arriving, we might have to wait up to a week or more before getting discharged, this being done entirely by hand with derrick and basket. The trawler owners employed several gangs of men for coaling, usually six or seven to a gang, and supplied the gear, which was transferred from keel to keel. When our turn came round the keel that had just finished came alongside and the derrick pole (which was just a ricker with the bark off and about thirty feet long, possibly about six inches diameter at the butt) was transferred on board with the strops, while the baskets and shovels and duck lamps were being put in the fore hold.

One man would bend on to the topsail tye a bo'sun's chair; on

E.W. PAGET-TOMLINSON
DECEMBER 1986

this he would sit with the heel strop on the chair and the head strop and head rope on his shoulders, and two of his mates would heave him up the mast with the topsail halyards. After putting the head strop round the topmast and reeving the head rope through the block, he was lowered down the mast until about fifteen feet from the deck. The derrick heel was then hoisted by the slabline to be placed in the heel strop, which he had now put round the mast. He was then lowered to the deck, and after putting on the guys and the gin with runner rove all hands would pull up the derrick head and make it fast to one of the after timberheads. Afterwards the large handles were fastened on to the fore roller. We were then ready for the next trawler.

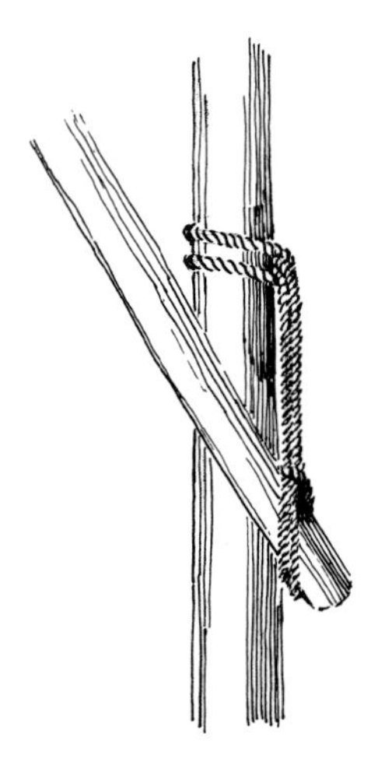

Shopping was no problem while in the Fish Dock. A Mr Samman who had a shop in West Dock Avenue would make his rounds of the dock each morning for orders, and deliver them the same day. He went round William Wright and Albert Docks as well. These two docks were collectively known as West Dock. While we were lying in Hull during this pre-1914 period we used to visit the old Theatre De Luxe, where they were showing the new moving pictures, I remember.

When discharging coal, the crew of the keel was expected to find one man or to pay for one to make the team up. He usually worked in the hold filling the baskets along with one man from the gang. There could be twenty or thirty keels loaded with coal in the dock at any one time.

When the coal was discharged the freight could be collected from the trawler company's office in cash, often on the same day. To people in the trade discharging cargo was known as livering. When the operation was completed, keelmen would say they had livered, a lazy way of saying delivering and delivered. A day or two before we were likely to liver our coal cargo, Father would pay a visit to the High Street to meet freight brokers and try to find out the state of the market. If the return cargo was iron in any form, it would most likely be arriving in West Dock; if wheat or seed, in Alexandra Dock; King George Dock was not opened until July, 1914; Victoria Dock was mainly timber, although sometimes the ships would have a small amount of iron under the timber.

Iron came in several forms to Sheffield before the 1914–18 War: there was pig iron, dish metal, ingots, bar iron and billets. Pig iron and dish metal were bad cargoes for both men and ship. There was only a small quantity in the bottom of the hold, and being low down it had a pendulum effect, in bad weather making the ship roll with an uncomfortable motion. When livering at Sheffield or Tinsley every piece had to be picked up by hand and put into a pan before being hoisted out by steam crane. Bar iron, ingots and billets were not too bad; they could and should be

Opposite page: *Coaling a trawler in the Fish Dock, Hull. A keel belonging to Robinson Brothers, the Rotherham flour millers, lies alongside the trawler* Amber, *owned by the Kingston Steam Trawling Company, one of the last trawler owners to use keels for coaling their vessels. Above is the heel of the derrick in the heel strop on the keel's mast.*

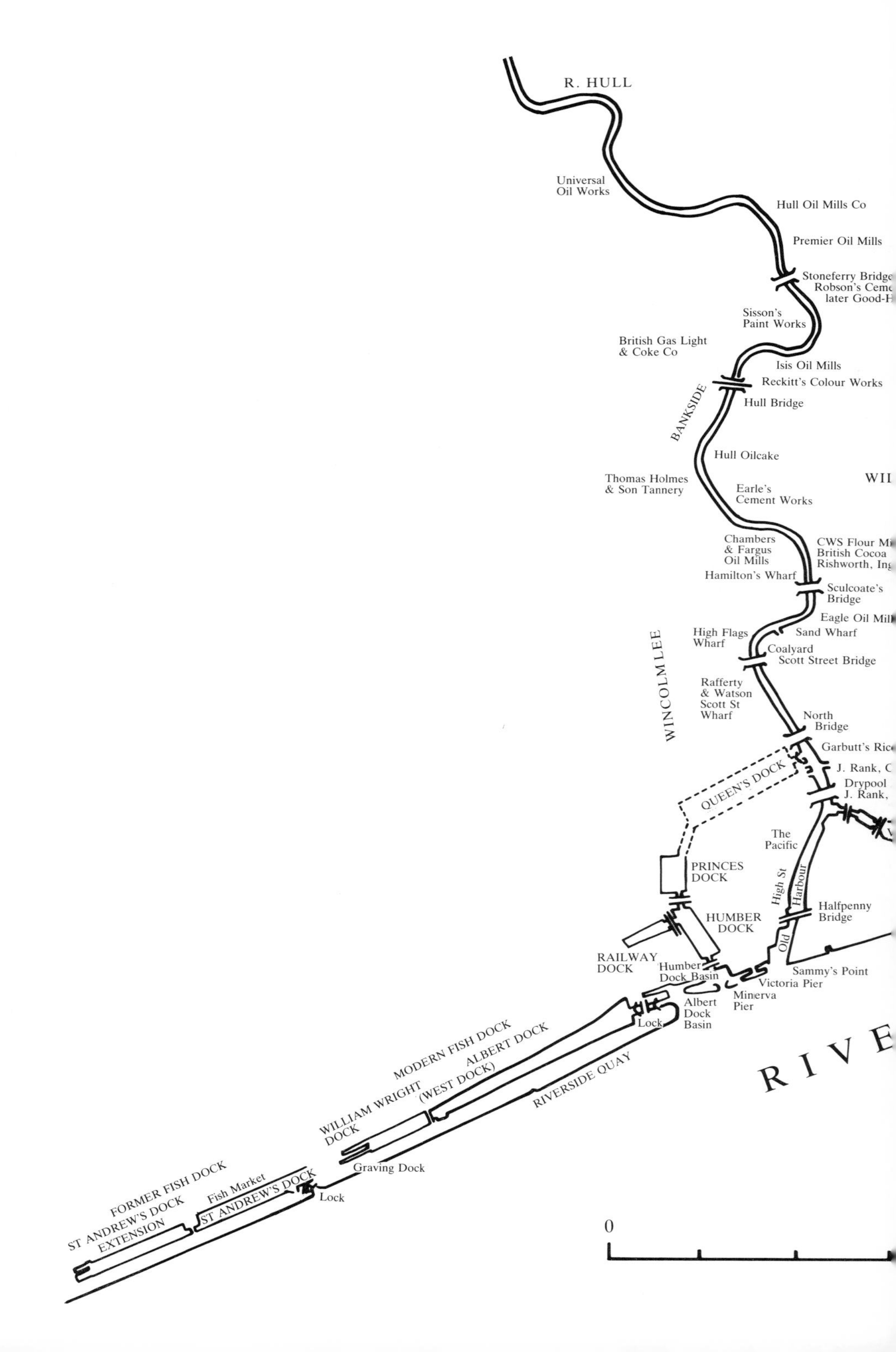

R. HULL
Universal
Oil Works
Hull Oil Mills Co
Premier Oil Mills
Sisson's
Paint Works
British Gas Light
& Coke Co
Isis Oil Mills
Reckitt's Colour Works
Hull Bridge
BANKSIDE
Hull Oilcake
Thomas Holmes
& Son Tannery
Earle's
Cement Works
Chambers
& Fargus
Oil Mills
British Cocoa
Hamilton's Wharf
Sculcoate's
Bridge
High Flags
Wharf
Sand Wharf
Coalyard
Scott Street Bridge
WINCOLMLEE
Rafferty
& Watson
Scott St
Wharf
North
Bridge
QUEEN'S DOCK
Drypool
The
Pacific
PRINCES
DOCK
High St
Old Harbour
Halfpenny
Bridge
HUMBER
DOCK
RAILWAY
DOCK
Humber
Dock Basin
Sammy's Point
Victoria Pier
Minerva
Pier
Albert
Dock
Basin
Lock
MODERN FISH DOCK
ALBERT DOCK
(WEST DOCK)
RIVERSIDE QUAY
WILLIAM WRIGHT
DOCK
Graving Dock
FORMER FISH DOCK
ST ANDREW'S DOCK
EXTENSION
Fish Market
ST ANDREW'S DOCK
Lock
0

TONEFERRY

wan Flour Mill
later Spillers Ltd)

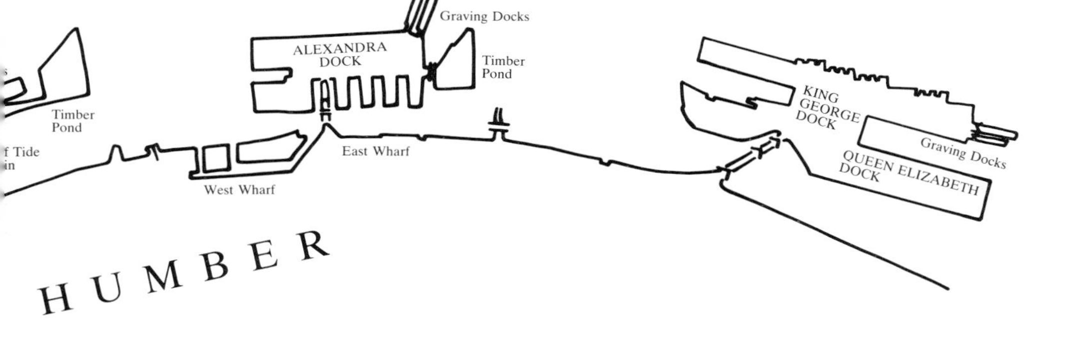

HULL DOCKS
&
RIVER HULL

2 3

MILES

E.W. PAGET-TOMLINSON
JUNE 1987

stowed fore and aft and athwartships in alternate tiers, giving an easy motion in bad weather and making them easy for slinging when they have to be got out.

In Alexandra Dock the ship with cargo for overside discharge lay stern on to the quay with both anchors down. Lighters and keels could then lie on both sides of the ship to receive cargo direct, this being handled by the ship's own derricks and steam winches. Most grain cargoes were carried in the steamers in bulk, but the grain was weighed in sacks on the ship's deck. When preparing for overside discharge, the riggers would make a stage next to the bulwarks and level with the bulwark top. This stage would be large enough to carry two weighing machines capable of weighing up to seven hundredweights, also two large baskets, and six men. If the wheat was to be loaded into the receiving craft in bulk, there would be fastened over the side two wooden spouts with wide hopper mouths.

When all was ready the dockers in the steamer's hold would pair off. One man of each pair would take a large canvas sack with two thimbles in the top hem for attaching the derrick runner; his mate would fill the sack with a scoop, which was rather like a large metal dish with wooden handles, putting in about four bushels. The first sack was emptied into a basket so that the weigher had a quantity at hand for making up the weight if necessary. As the sacks came out of the hold they were placed on the scales and the weigher would make up the weight or take a little out as required. After being weighed they were then tipped into the hopper and so the grain poured into the craft.

If, as was so often the case, the receiving mill was not equipped with elevators or other machines for dealing with bulk cargoes, the wheat had to be weighed up into four-bushel sacks. To get these into the keel a framework of upright poles was erected on the steamer's bulwarks with a pole across the top about seven feet above the stage. Around this crosspiece was passed two turns of manilla rope with a strop spliced into the end for placing round the sack. From the keel's coaming on to the ship's side were placed two nine-inch boards about five foot long, fastened together with battens. When the sack had been weighed and tied up, the strop was placed over it about two thirds of the way down. The sack was then pushed over the side and lowered down to the keel, the boards guiding it into the keel's hold. The first ten sacks or so were used to make a stage at a suitable height for a man to get them on his back well up on his shoulders. A boy would be already stood on the stage ready to remove the strop. Then the keelman carried the sacks on his back and stowed them in position, taking care to fill up under the deck first.

All the dealing in the grain trade was done in bushels and

Opposite page: *Loading bulk grain overside from a steamer in Alexandra Dock, Hull. The stage between the steamer's hatch and the bulwarks supported two weighing scales, two baskets, two hoppers and spouts and six men.*

quarters. These are really bulk measures, but to meet the needs of present-day methods of handling a standard agreed weight was used for each kind of grain, taking note of the difference in bulk for a given weight. The equivalent weights of grain per quarter as used when transshipping from deep-sea vessels to river and coastal craft are as follows:

Wheat 504 pounds per quarter
Barley 448 pounds per quarter
Maize 480 pounds per quarter
Rye 480 pounds per quarter
Oats 336 pounds per quarter

Freights were often charged at so much per last, which is ten quarters.

If any provisions were required while in Alexandra Dock or the Old Harbour (the lower part of the River Hull) an order would be placed with Bristow's, a large provision store in the Market Place to which I remember going many times with Mother. The floor was covered each day with fresh sawdust. The assistants were all male and they all wore white aprons.

When the vessel was loaded she would be washed down and the hatches would be battened down before making a visit to the office to sign the bills of lading, and if bound on to the Sheffield and South Yorkshire Navigation or the Aire and Calder a declaration note would have to be obtained; this would be exchanged at Keadby or Goole for a pass note which would allow the vessel to pass to her destination and the dues to be charged to account.

The state of the tides and direction of wind would be taken into consideration before deciding whether to tow or to sail up the Humber. Spring tides on the Humber and its tributaries will run in some parts of the rivers at up to five knots, so even with a fair wind a strong breeze is needed to keep command of any vessel dependent solely on sail. If the wind was light it could mean a lot of anchor work and it would take two tides to reach Keadby. If leaving Hull on the evening tide this would be acceptable as no time would be lost, since navigation on the canals officially ceased at 10 pm until 5 am next day. If leaving on the early morning tide it might well be better to tow to Keadby, which would take about four hours. Then with easterly winds it would be possible to sail up the canal to Doncaster or Mexborough.

The towage service between Hull, Keadby, and all places on the Trent to Nottingham was provided by Thomas Gray and Sons of Hull. All their tugs except two had names ending with -man: *Bowman*, *Yorkshireman*, *Frenchman*, etc. The exceptions were the paddle tugs *Stephen Gray* and *Robin Hood*. In 1921 Gray's combined

The keel Energy *on tow from Keadby to Hull passing through the Redcliffe Channel on the Humber, with her master-owner Jim Wilson of Stainforth standing by the leeboard. I took this picture from on board the* Guidance.
Author's collection

with other Hull tug companies to form the United Towing Company, which is today the largest British tug company, with tugs all over the world on salvage and oil rig duties. Most of the tug crews were Hull men, and they liked to leave Hull for upriver on the morning or midday tides and to return on the ebb. As the tides are progressively later, 15.00 hours (3 pm) was the latest sailing time for the day; they then went back to the early morning sailing, the keelman bearing this in mind when deciding whether to tow or sail. The tug company had brokers going the rounds of the docks, and if the decision was to tow arrangements would be made with the broker.

About two hours after high water when all penning was finished for the tide before the one on which the tug would sail, the keel would have to be warped to the lock head. To do this the cotton warping line, ninety fathoms long and an inch and a half circumference, was coiled into the cogboat; then the boat was sculled across the dock, paying out the line as she went ahead. When at its full extent the line was made fast to any convenient point and the vessel could be hove ahead with the line attached to the fore roller. This was necessary to make sure of a place in the four-hour pen on the following tide. At Hull the flood tide flows for about five hours, so at five hours before high water the lock head staff opened the inner lock gates to allow craft for upriver to take their place in the lock. The tug broker would be there and would instruct the captains of vessels booked with him how to place their vessels for towing. At four hours to high water the gates would be closed and craft penned down, and the tug would back into the lock to take up her tow.

The Humber Conservancy Board's Humber and Lower Trent Navigation Byelaws (No 23 paragraphs (g) and (h)) limited the

length of tow to not more than eight keels or other craft to be towed on two ropes, that is four on each rope. If it was found necessary to tow nine keels or other craft they had to be towed on three ropes, that is three on each rope; the tug and the craft being towed were thus in vee formation until reaching Keadby. Then for towing up the Trent they had to be singled out on to one rope. But not more than six craft were allowed to be towed in a single tow between Keadby Bridge and Gainsborough Bridge, and at no time was the length of tow to exceed eight hundred feet. This limitation was necessary on account of the strong tides. Similar regulations were in force on the Ouse. To keep vessels clear of each other when the tug had two or more lines of craft in tow, the outside lines had to arrange their towropes so that if the first craft had her rope from her starboard bow on to the tug the next in line would also have her rope from her starboard bow, but connected to the first craft's port quarter, and so on.

By whatever means they arrived at Keadby, keels would try to

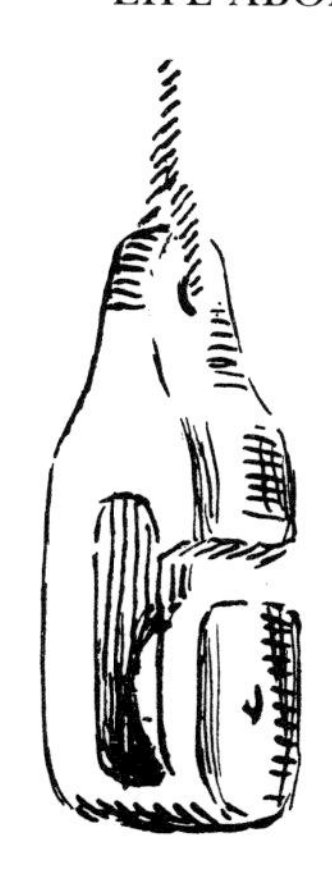

Twelve-foot cogboats were not only the keel's lifeboats but were of value for laying out anchors and handling the ninety-fathom warping line, paid out by the fore roller. When warping, the line was passed through a snatchblock (above) on the forestay to achieve a more direct pull and to clear the keel's deck fittings. The cogboat had but one oar and was normally sculled over the stern.

Some companies and individual owners had their own liveries which they applied to top strake, hawse timber or hawseplate, feathering, gunwale, long timber, cross piece and timberheads. Distinctive colours were also applied to coamings and headledges. On the opposite page are typical liveries of wooden keels and sloops.

sail to Doncaster. If the wind was southerly, a horse would have to be arranged at Stainforth. Should the wind be westerly, a horse if available at Keadby would be engaged straight away. At that time the steam tug *Clara Marian* was plying between Keadby and Doncaster, with a trip to Mexborough when necessary, mainly in "fresh" time. Darwin Oglesby was her captain.

The first bridge on the canal after Keadby Lock bridge was a railway bridge; it was not always possible for the keeper to open it straight away if a train was due. If we had to wait a few minutes, we would put the working anchor and the thirty-fathom nine-inch coir towrope into the cogboat, the anchor stowed athwartships. The warping line would be pulled off the roller and loosely coiled down to dry, the stayfall tackle put on the roller and connected to the chain tackle, so we would be able to lower the mast when required. If we were favoured with a fair wind this would not have to be done until we arrived at Thorne Low railway bridge, the first fixed bridge on the Navigation. There was here a crane worked by hand, provided by the railway company, so that any vessel not able to lower her mast could unstep it and leave it ashore until they came down. Leeboards could be left at the railway bridge: we usually left ours at Stainforth. I remember one voyage while taking off our leeboards the crane jib collapsed, causing us to be delayed. Next morning the canal manager, George Welch*, came from Sheffield on the first train to Stainforth station. This was over a mile from the canal, so he brought his bicycle with him. Motor cars were very scarce in those days; I think I would have been about six years old before I had a ride in one. I remember it quite well. Some friends had come on a visit by car and took Father to the *Fox Inn*, so my brother and myself went along for the ride.

We did not usually stop at Stainforth on the way up for more than a few hours, for overnight or for the weekend, if it should fall that way; but Mother liked to have two or three days at home on the way down. It was rarely possible for us to sail above Doncaster on the way up; it is mainly a river navigation from Doncaster to Tinsley, and the section from Doncaster to Conisbrough is blanketed by hills, while the fixed bridges are more numerous. If we had been lucky enough to sail as far as Doncaster, the time had come for us to engage a horse. If the river was at normal level one would do, but if there should be any storm water or "fresh", as the keelmen would call it, we would need an extra horse for each extra foot of fresh until we got to the Mexborough Low Lock. Then one horse would do until Kilnhurst Flood Lock, where we would be back on the river again, and the same conditions would apply to Eastwood Low Lock. Here, depending on the state of the river, we

* George Welch was manager of the Sheffield and South Yorkshire Navigation from 1895 to 1921.

FRED SCHOFIELD, STAINFORTH

GEORGE ROBERT SCAIFE, BEVERLEY

ALBERT WOOD, SOWERBY BRIDGE

THOMAS CLAXTON, CASTLEFORD

AIRE & CALDER NAVIGATION CO., LEEDS

ROCHDALE CANAL COMPANY

TRENT NAVIGATION

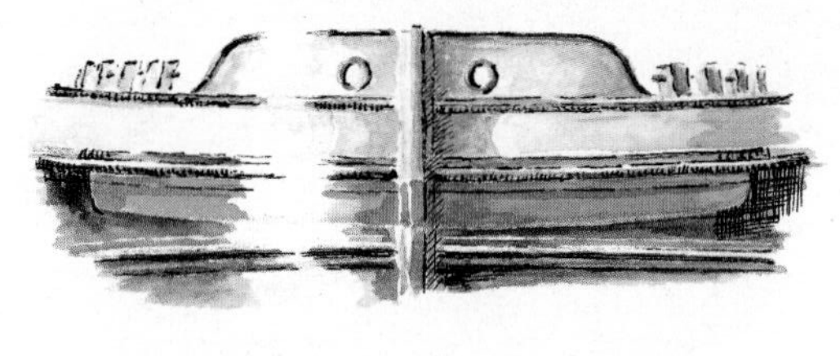

JAMES BARRACLOUGH, HULL

W. BLEASDALE & CO.

JOHN HUNT, LEEDS

FURLEY & CO.

RISHWORTH, INGLEBY & LOFTHOUSE

More owners' liveries, as applied to steel vessels.

would either pay off the extra horse or retain it until we got to Tinsley Low Lock.

The drivers of horses used for hauling craft on the Yorkshire canals were known as horse marines. Often referred to simply as the marines, they were a tough breed, as hard as nails, tramping the banks with the horse in all weathers, often walking twenty or more miles in a day. At night they slept on the fo'c'sle locker with the corn bag for a bed and the fire for a blanket. Many were known only by a nickname. Some owned their own horse, others worked on a share system. The remuneration or purchase, as it was called by the marines and keelmen, was at so many shillings per stage, and the marines got their food while the job lasted. I cannot remember what the rate was before 1914, but in the period 1920 to 1930 the rate was fifteen shillings (75p) per stage for a loaded craft and ten shillings (50p) for a light craft (that is, a vessel that is empty). The last or top stage from Rotherham to Sheffield was one pound. The first stage going up the canal was Keadby to Thorne; second stage Thorne to Doncaster; third stage Doncaster to Mexborough; fourth stage Mexborough to Rotherham and the fifth stage Rotherham to Sheffield. From Doncaster to Sheffield the cost was two pounds ten (£2.50) plus the cost of the marine's food. By starting at some time between 2 am and 4 am the haul could be completed in one long day if necessary. More than often a break would be made at the House Lock or the Top Lock at Tinsley; then an early start the next morning would get the vessel into the basin at Sheffield in time for work at 8 am.

All meals were taken while under way if possible. When the marine came on board for his meals Mother would steer while Father drove the horse. The changeover would be arranged at a lock or bridge. Some horses could be trusted to look after themselves and would obey the marine's instructions shouted from on board. George Eastwood of Rotherham would control his horses by whistle signals like those of a shepherd to his dogs. The horse also had to have his meals under way. A specially made nose tin was carried for this purpose, and the fodder, usually oats, bran and sharps mixed together in equal parts, was carried in a calico bag. The tin would only be about one third filled and then damped down with canal water before being fastened on with a leather strap. The marines would not allow their horses to drink water drawn straight from a tap; they said it was too cold and would give them colic.

Horse marines were to be found at many places along the canal, but Doncaster and Mexborough had more than any other. Some of the names coming to mind are Bernard James of Sheffield, George Eastwood of Rotherham, Jack Smith and Jim Smith of Kilnhurst, Albert Ramsden, Bill Golden and Bill Wilson

If the mast had been left on the bank the horse would haul a loaded keel from a pit prop or the spare anchor stock stepped in the lutchet; keels which worked only in non-tidal waters had a special post, the neddy, for this purpose. To aid the horse round bends a fore rope or bridle was run from the hauling line to the bitts; this could be hove in for the straight lengths or slacked off as the navigation twisted and turned. The handspike was stuck in the windlass barrel to help the helmsman. Light keels were towed from the after timber forward, because bridge clearances were too tight for the lutchet to be used.

of Swinton, Jack Rawnsley, Jim Rawnsley and Conor Rawnsley, George Bisby and Cherry Roper of Mexborough. At Doncaster there were Frank Fawley, John Arthur James, Tom Hanks, Bill Skinner and several others. One known as Webby used to tell of the time when he challenged my father to a hand of dominoes, to which Father agreed providing the stake was to be a pig. Webby was allowed to win, whereupon he asked to be shown the pig that he had won. Father told him it was on board, and away he went to collect the pig. When he got on board Father removed a hatch and told Webby to take his pick. On looking into the hold he saw that the cargo was pig iron; he had a good laugh.

The line used for horse haulage was a cotton one of one and three-quarter inch circumference and forty-five fathoms long, always known as the horse line. When the mast was lowered the line was made fast to the forestay in a position over the lutchet, the bight being taken down to the leeboard traveller on the opposite side to the hauling bank so that the line would be over the lutchet when the horse stood tight. As an aid to steering, the handspike was put in the windlass barrel and a line was made fast from the horse line to the bitt head; this was called the fore rope. On arrival at Doncaster the sails and mast would be made ready for putting ashore at Mexborough. At that time there were three privately owned yards at Mexborough, two below the lock and one between Mexborough Mill and the top boatyard, and each had a hand operated crane. The topsail was made up and stowed in the fo'c'sle, but the mainsail was left bent to the mainyard and was put on to a gantry with sail covers in place. The mast was also put ashore on to a gantry at the other side of the yard. The shrouds, back stay, fore stay, mainsail and topsail tyes were left on ready for a quick fit out when we came back down. To keep them on the mast the slabline halyards were passed round the lot as they were laid on the mast. The charge for this service was one shilling and sixpence (7½p).

When the mast was ashore a pit prop or the spare anchor stock

was put into the lutchet to make the horse line fast for hauling. Canal boats not fitted with a mast had a special timber for this purpose, made to fit the lutchet and rounded off at the top with a hoop and a pin through. This piece of timber, called a neddy, was left in place except when passing under bridges. The handspike in the windlass barrel end and the fore rope were still used to aid the steering; passing through the cuts the fore rope or bridle would be pulled tight, and it would be slackened off again in the rivers. The hauling bank was not on one side all the way; there were several changeover points, and the horse had to be ferried over the river twice, once at Kilnhurst Ferry and again at Eastwood Low Lock. On arrival at Tinsley Low Lock we would find one or two men hanging about hoping to get a job helping vessels up the Tinsley locks, twelve altogether. For this work they expected only two shillings (10p). Some of them were also on the lookout for the job of livering us when we came to our turn. On our way up the canal we would already have passed through nineteen locks, each with a full-time lock keeper living on the job. In the next two miles we would have to pass through another twelve, with only three lock keepers, one at the Tinsley Low Lock, one at Plumber's Lock, and one at House Lock. When we reached the top level we would have passed through thirty-one locks and risen about two hundred feet above sea level. Before I retired three of these locks were to be removed

If the mast was still aboard the horse line was secured to the forestay but taken round the offside leeboard traveller so that it would pass over the lutchet when the horse pulled.

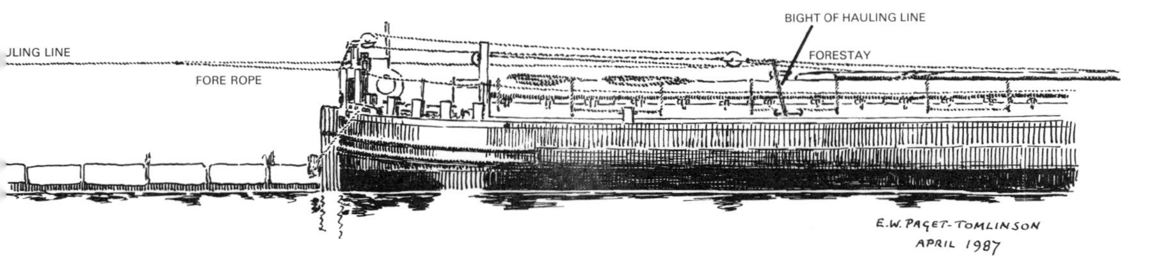

Jack Hinchcliffe, master and owner of the keel Unique, *sitting on the water cask of his keel in St Andrew's Dock at Hull. He used to live at Stainforth but by the time this photograph was taken in 1930 he had moved to Thorne.* Author's collection

as improvements were made to the navigation. From the Top Lock to Sheffield Basin is about two miles. It was the shallowest pound on the navigation, and in that length there were eleven bridges, two stopways and one aqueduct. The marine, with his five shillings (25p) extra purchase for the top stage, was not overpaid.

For work on board the keelman would usually be wearing brown corduroy trousers, and a blue worsted gansey with a white or grey gingham neckerchief just showing above the gansey neck. In cold weather he might wear over his gansey a waistcoat which could be either single or double breasted. Headgear was mainly a flat cap but could be a trilby or bowler hat; just a few would wear a seaman's peaked cap. Seaboots in my early days were heavy leather ones to just below the knee. Oilskin coats, sou'westers and leggings were made from calico, with many dressings of a mixture of boiled linseed oil and lamp black. I well remember being measured for my first pair of trousers at Waistills in Scott Street, Hull; the cost just after the First World War (1919) was fourteen shillings (70p).

The ganseys were usually knitted by the keelmen's wives. After my father was demobbed out of the Navy he had some ganseys knitted for himself and for me by a Mrs Welbourn of Thorne, a keelman's widow. After that I do not remember my mother knitting another gansey, but she did knit new necks and sleeves. Mrs Clark, the wife of Charlie Clark, a Thorne keelman, was always ready to accept an order for a gansey. The last person to knit me a gansey was Mrs Phoebe Carr, wife of Alfred Carr, also a keelman of Thorne. That was in 1946, when she knitted me six ganseys at £6 each. In the early 1920s they were costing £3 each. Now in 1983 I still wear one of Mrs Carr's ganseys. Each knitter had her own patterns handed down to her without any written instructions, and they were all different combinations of stars, diamonds, cables, ladder patterns, zigzags and lines.

Now about myself and my family.

Jack Williamson of Thorne, seen here with his cogboat on the Dart stone heap in the East Trent, was my regular purchaseman until he was eighty. He had been born on board a Lincoln catch while it was laid in Brayford Pool, and worked on the rivers and canals all his life.
Author's collection

The Schofields 3

I HAVE been told that I came into this world on the 11th day of July, 1906, in the reign of Edward VII when the world was enjoying a short period of peace. My father, Arthur Schofield, a keelman of Stainforth, was married to Alice Kershaw, a daughter of George Kershaw, farmer, of Plum Tree Hill Farm, Bramwith Woodhouse, the place of my birth. I was their first child.

Father was the owner and master of the keel *Fanny*. I made my first voyage in her at three weeks old. She had been bought in January, 1877, by my grandfather, John Christopher Schofield. He sold one half share in 1892 to his eldest son William Henry Schofield and the other half share in 1900. My father bought her from William Henry in 1904, and I joined her in August, 1906, and for the next few years she was my second home. A house was maintained at Stainforth, but until the impending arrival of my elder sister nearly five years later more time was spent on board than at home.

I think one of my earliest recollections in life was one morning in February, 1909, while the ship was berthed in Alexandra Dock at Hull. I was taken on board another keel where there were some young people who kept me amused and entertained all day. At nightfall I remember being collected by Father and taken back on board to find his youngest sister Ginny in charge of the cabin, and Mother in bed with a new addition to the crew, who had arrived sooner than expected. In later years I heard Mother refer to him as a seven months baby. He was later named James after Father's uncle, James Schofield of Grimsby.

The Schofields are a large family. The Grimsby branch, to which Uncle James belonged, had left keels in the early days of steam. The same James Schofield had at one time been captain of one of the early passenger steamers on the Humber and Trent. Later he changed to the towing business with which the family were still connected. His son John Henry Schofield was manager for a Grimsby tug company, and his grandson Harry Schofield went into the trawlers and later became marine superintendent for a trawler company at Grimsby. All Father's uncles, cousins and brothers, except one, were in keels or other shipping. The one exception was his youngest but one brother, who trained as an engineer; after a time with Yates, agricultural engineers of Doncaster, and a period

Opposite page: *The* Annie Maud *riding at anchor at Cliff End in the River Trent. If we found the water on the ebb was getting too low to go down the upper Humber in safety we would anchor here until the next high water. I took this photo from the cogboat.* Author's collection

The launching of the Guidance *from Worfolk's yard at Stainforth in July, 1905. She was built for my uncle, William Henry Schofield, and on his death in 1931 I bought her from the estate.*
Author's collection

at Bristol he started in business on his own account at Henley-on-Thames. Later he went into the Methodist ministry.

Grandfather, in addition to owning and sailing keels, always kept some horses for hauling the keels on the Sheffield and South Yorkshire Navigation. As well as hauling his own keels they were hired out to others. After the *Fanny* he had a keel called the *Fleming*, which was larger than Sheffield size; I think she was iron or steel, but I have not much information about her. A later one was the *City of Sheffield*, a Sheffield-size carvel-built wooden keel a little in advance of her time. She was built with an aperture for a propeller, though power was never installed; I suppose they could not accept the idea of giving up cargo space for a steam boiler and engine.

My Uncle William Henry's next ship after the *Fanny* was a carvel-built wooden keel called the *Integrity*, which became the *Greta* when she was sold to "Ginger" Joe Barraclough of Grimsby. She was lost on the Hessle Sand in the early nineteen-twenties. In 1905 William Henry had built at Worfolk and Company's yard, Stainforth, the wooden carvel-built keel *Guidance*, a ship for which I was to have a great affection; she was the first vessel that I was to own. From the same yard about twenty-three years later he ordered the *Rupert C*, another wooden carvel-built keel, the last from Worfolk's. These three vessels were all built to the standard size for the Sheffield and South Yorkshire Navigation, 61 feet 6 inches by 15 feet 6 inches and from 7 feet to 7 feet 6 inches depth of hold. William Henry had married Mary Ann Parish, daughter of John Parish, who was also a keel owner of Stainforth. Because he lived just over the river from Stainforth and was in the parish of Fishlake, Uncle William Henry always had Fishlake shown as the hailing port on all his vessels.

Grandfather's second son was also called John Christopher. He owned and sailed a steel Sheffield-size keel called the *Sophia* and later another steel one called the *Whim*, built to suit the Barnsley Canal, 70 feet by 14 feet 4 inches. Walter, sometimes called Rick, was the third son and then came Father. After a time in keels and sloops Walter went into the coal business at Long Eaton on the Upper Trent. Next was Albert, the brother who went into engineering and the Methodist Church. The youngest, Harry, went from keels to be mate in billyboys, and was for a time in both the *Mavis* and the *Halcyon*. These were both ketch rigged, trading on the East Coast and down Channel, with sometimes a continental voyage. The *Mavis* had been built of iron at Beverley in 1896 and was 71.8 feet long by 17.8 feet beam, with a depth of 7.2 feet, while the *Halcyon* was built of steel by Henry Scarr at Hessle in 1903 and

My uncle William Henry Schofield and his wife. He owned several keels and was in partnership with J.J. Tomlinson, of Thorne, sharing a considerable fleet of keels and sloops. Author's collection

My uncle Harry Schofield, youngest of my father's brothers, with a model keel. Author's collection

had dimensions of 84.3 feet by 20.0 feet by 7.8 feet. When he married Edith Peck, daughter of Walter Peck, another Stainforth keel owner, he came back to keels until the 1914–18 War when he went into the Royal Navy.

As well as six sons, Grandfather had three daughters. The eldest, Jemimah, married Sidney Woodall, a keelman of Stainforth. Clara, the second daughter, married William Jolliffe, a Mexborough keel owner, and the youngest, Ginny, married Luther Dishman, the son of Charles Dishman of Stainforth, owner of two Sheffield-size cutter-rigged billyboys. One was the *Immanuel*, built at Stainforth in 1888 and sailed by a man called Tate, and the other was the *Rescue*, built at Boston in 1895; Charles Dishman sailed her himself. Both were in the East Coast trade with coal from the West Riding collieries to various places round the Lincolnshire, Norfolk and Suffolk coasts and the Thames. Luther was a schoolmaster at the time and later he had some official post with the education authority in the Wolverhampton area.

At Thorne there were five of father's cousins, William Schofield, Bob Schofield and John Schofield and their two sisters, who also married keelmen. William and Bob had very poor eyesight and so were not able to fully follow their trade or take command of a keel, but they were very good as crew in spite of their great handicap. John owned at that time one of the earliest iron keels, the *Progress*, built of iron boiler plates riveted with cup-head rivets; when she became too old to trade on the estuary she was sold to Tinsley Rolling Mills and finished her days as an open boat carrying coal from Roundwood staithe to Tinsley. John also owned the wooden carvel-built keel *John*, later called the *Regent*, and in 1923 he bought from Staniland and Co. Ltd of Thorne the last wooden keel they were to build, carvel, which he named the *Vigilant*; seventeen years later I was to become her owner. At Stainforth lived another of father's cousins, Edwin Schofield, with a large family of five sons, three of whom became keelmen, and three daughters. Edwin was master of the keel *Endcliffe*, one of Bleasdale's fleet, founded in the late nineteenth century by William Bleasdale, a clerk in a Goole shipping office. With expansion of the firm offices were opened in Hull and Sheffield, the fleet operating as the Hull, Goole and Sheffield Transport Company. Bleasdale's, for whom Edwin later became ship's husband, owned wooden and steel keels but no sloops, going over to motor craft in 1933/34 with 21-horse-power Lister diesels. The Sheffield and South Yorkshire Navigation had a major stake in the company, so it passed on nationalization to the Docks and Inland Waterways Executive, later British Waterways. Vessels were named with a "cliffe" suffix and the colour scheme was preponderantly blue. Edwin's father was Matthew Schofield, who is on record as having sailed the keel *Ancholme* in the 1874 Hull Keel Regatta and the keel *Mog* in the 1875 regatta. Matthew Schofield also had three daughters, two of whom married keelmen; one married Jack Blacknell and the other Charlie Barley.

My father's first command was the keel *Vine*, owned by Thomas Wilson, Sons and Company, the Hull shipping line who then owned a large fleet of keels. After the *Vine* he took charge of a small sloop called the *Karma*, owned by Watson's, the Gainsborough shipyard. His brother Rick was mate with him in this vessel. She would carry only about ninety tons and was used for carrying steel plates for shipbuilding to the yard at Gainsborough, loading from the weekly Continental vessels at Hull. She was built on finer lines than was usual for Humber craft, as Watson's had hoped that she might attract some interest from the Norfolk Broads area as a steel wherry, but not finding any customer they rigged her as a sloop for their own use. After being in the *Karma* Father bought the keel *Fanny* and married in 1904. For a time the couple made their home on grandfather Kershaw's farm at Bramwith Woodhouse, a small hamlet of two farms and one cottage about a mile north of Stainforth. There, as I said, I was born.

Our usual cargoes in the *Fanny* were coal from Elsecar, Cortonwood, Wombwell, and Manvers Main collieries to Hull,

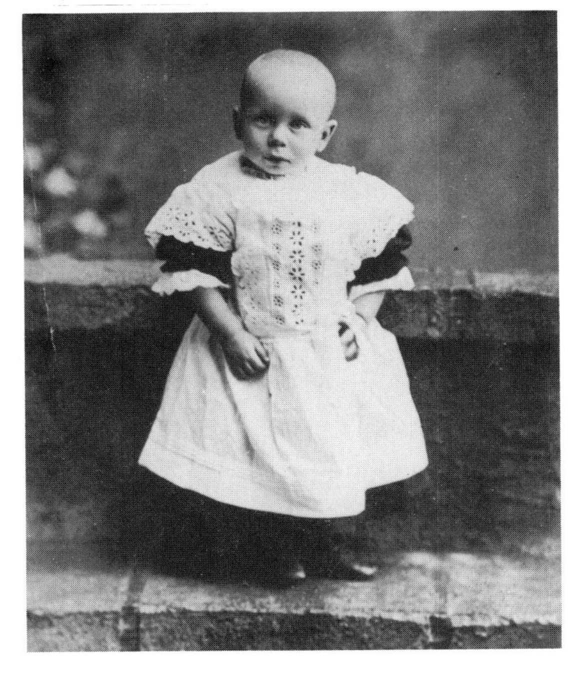

Myself aged three. By this time I had already had quite a lot of experience of living afloat in the Fanny. Author's collection

My father, Arthur Schofield, points out a detail in the Reuben Chappell painting of his keel the Fanny. *Chappell used to paint a lot of the keels when he lived at Goole, before his move to Cornwall.* Yorkshire Post

sometimes to the mills in the Old Harbour and sometimes to the Fish Dock to bunker the steam trawlers. After discharging it was usual to pick up a return cargo for the Sheffield and South Yorkshire Navigation, either Swedish bar iron, pig iron or dish metal, or ingots for Tinsley or Sheffield or wheat for the flour mills at Doncaster, Mexborough, Rotherham or Sheffield; if the wheat was for Doncaster or Rotherham it would be loaded in bulk, but for Mexborough and Sheffield it had to be in sacks of eighteen stones each. At that time Grimsby was busy with the "near" Continental trade, and sometimes it was more profitable to sail light from Hull to Grimsby to pick up a cargo, usually bar iron, pig iron or ingots, sometimes sugar or timber.

Soon after the birth of the second son, James, on board at Hull the *Fanny* was sold to Ellis Naylor of Thorne. Father then went as master of the Sheffield-size keel *Confidence*, owned by Herbert Fox of Keadby, who besides owning three keels was toll collector and harbour master at Keadby for the Sheffield and South Yorkshire Navigation Company. He also did a bit of shipbroking for the schooners and spritsail barges which loaded coal at Keadby for the Thames and South Coast. While in the *Confidence* we made some voyages up the Trent as well as on the Sheffield and South Yorkshire. Our upgate cargoes on the Trent were sometimes oil seed for the mills at Gainsborough and sometimes wheat in sacks for transshipment at West Stockwith into narrow boats on the Chesterfield Canal.

After discharging we would often go higher up the Trent

above Laneham to load a cargo of Trent sand or gravel for Hull or Grimsby, where it was sold for building. At this time it was dredged by hand from the bed of the river. When going up to the sand and gravel beds a telegram would be sent to a Mr Cook Williamson at Laneham telling him that we were on our way. He was the labour contractor and supplied for hire the special gear that we would need for loading. If he had no work he would keep watch for us coming up the river and as we passed would come off to us with his boat loaded with the dredging gear which we would tow behind. He would then tell us where he thought we would be likely to find the best sand or gravel, whichever it was that we wanted. When we arrived at what he thought a most likely spot, he would get in our cogboat with a stower and go prodding about on the bottom. If he was satisfied that he had found a good bed, the ship would be moored fore and aft with the anchor and kedge.

Then the derrick was prepared and the two-man handles were fastened on to the fore roller, so that four men could heave the sand spoon up with it. The dredging spoon was a blacksmith-made

A ketch-rigged billyboy and other craft, including a clinker-built paddle tug, in the Old Harbour at Hull a century or so ago. This part of the Old Harbour was known as Three Crane Wharf; just across the river was the Drypool entrance to the Victoria Dock. Hull Town Docks Museum

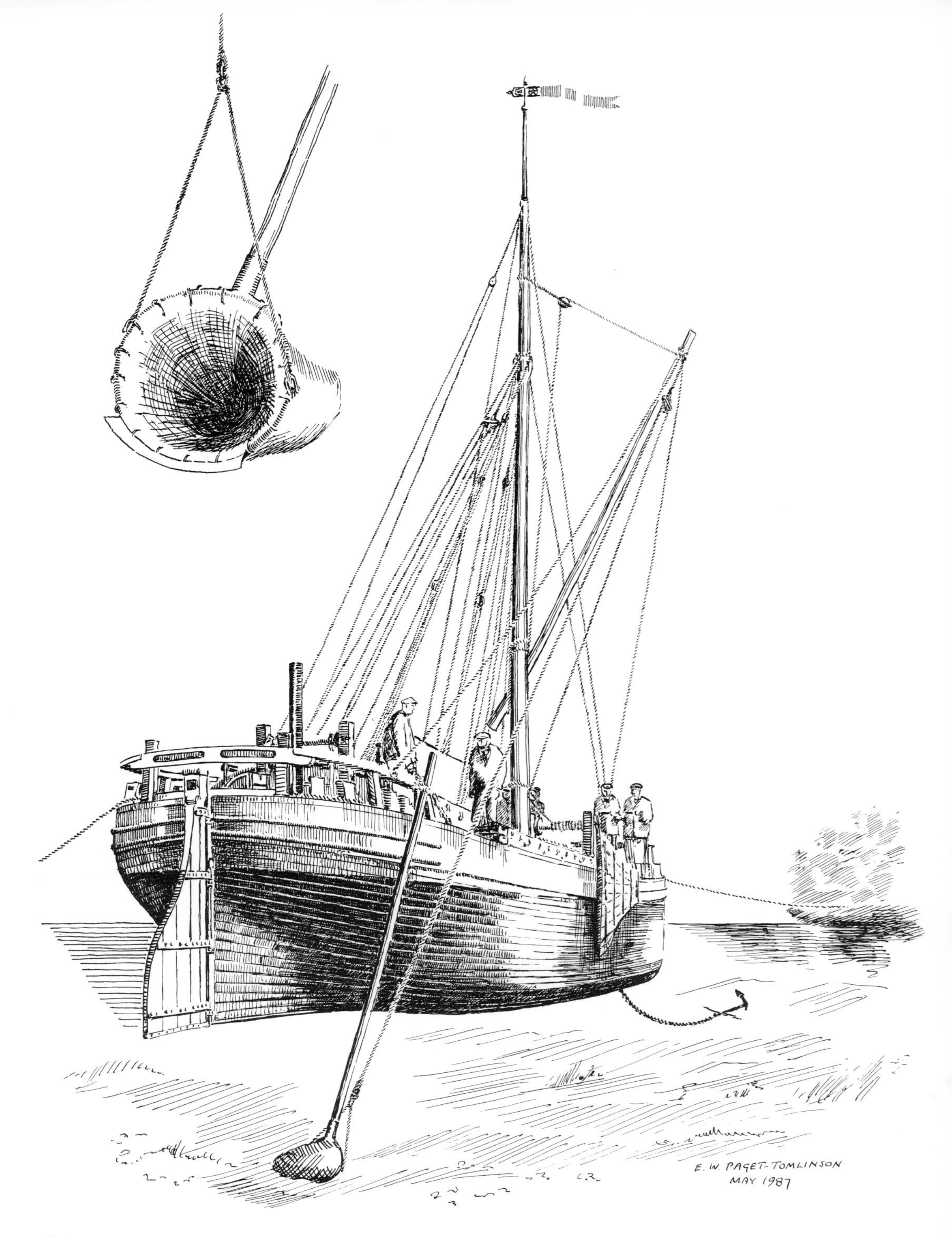
E. W. PAGET-TOMLINSON
MAY 1987

frame with a lip on one edge and a socket on the other side, like the socket on a boathook or stower grain. The spoon was secured to a ricker (a pole) about twenty feet long, and on the frame was a hessian bag with a piece of leather on the front to take the chafe; this was usually referred to as "the bag". The dredging procedure was that the bag was lowered over the side, and as it sank to the bottom was pulled aft towards the stern rail, helped by the flow of the river, the loading being done during the ebb. There was never much flood tide as high up the river as this; it was really only on the spring tides that the flood made any slack water. On pulling the bag as far aft as the rail end it was set with the ricker leaning slightly forward at the top, and two or three turns of cotton line were put round it to hold it in position. Then the four men for'ard would heave away on the fore roller. As the bag filled the line was let go, and the bag was brought high enough to clear the coamings. At the place where it would come on board a man would be standing on a stage ready to tip it over the coaming into the hold. It was the mate's job to keep this trimmed and to pump out the water.

When loading sand or gravel it depended on the state of the tides how deep the keel was loaded. The usual capacity would be 100 to 110 tons. The *Confidence*, incidentally, could load five hundred quarters of bulk wheat under the hatches (112 tons 5 cwt), but with this weight she would be too deep for the Sheffield and South Yorkshire Navigation; if loading for Doncaster we would take 480 quarters of wheat (108 tons) and for Mexborough 450 quarters in sacks (the wheat being 101 tons and the sacks two tons). For Rotherham mill we loaded 420 quarters (94 tons 10 cwt) of wheat in bulk and four hundred quarters (90 tons) in sacks for Sheffield. Ninety tons of any sort of cargo was usually plenty for most vessels on the Sheffield top level; for House Lock, Tinsley, they might risk a few tons more.

While we had the *Confidence* I made my first voyage from Hull to Leeds. I cannot give the date or remember what the cargo was, but I remember the complete contrast to the Sheffield trade; I also remember having my photograph taken in a studio along with my brother, and attending Sunday night service with my mother at the Seamen's and Boatmen's Mission Church just across the wharf from our berth at Warehouse Hill in Leeds.

I can also remember being waterbound at Stainforth while on a voyage to Sheffield. That was when the River Don, or Dun as it used to be called, was in flood and unnavigable. It had overspilled its banks on the Fishlake side and flooded all the country between the river and the New Junction Canal. Grandfather Kershaw's farm, being on high ground, was completely surrounded by water. Father fetched some help, took the cogboat over the river and launched it on the floodwater. We made several trips across the

Opposite page: *Dredging for sand in the Trent above Laneham. The dredging spoon was about eighteen inches in diameter with an iron lip and a hessian bag some thirty inches deep, all secured to a twenty-foot pole. Four men were needed to heave the spoon up because of the weight of the wet sand; another man made the pole fast to the stern rail, letting go when the bag filled, and a sixth man tipped the sand into the hold.*

One of the Aire and Calder Navigation tugs passing under Leeds Bridge with a keel in tow. The pound from Leeds Lock to River Lock, the entrance to the Leeds and Liverpool Canal, had no towpath; many of the vessels trading on this length were coal boats from the West Riding coal staithes bound for places on the Leeds and Liverpool Canal, and as these were usually horse drawn a steam tug was used to tow them from one lock to the other. Leeds City Museum

flooded fields and over the hedgetops to and from Grandfather's front door with food and other supplies.

Some time during 1912 Mother started to spend more time at home and I started to attend school. In February, 1913, my elder sister was born and after that we had only the odd trip on board during school holidays. About this time Father went as master of the keel *Aureola*, a Sheffield-size iron keel like the *Confidence* owned by Herbert Fox. I do not remember many voyages in this vessel, because it was only during the summer holidays that we could make a trip, with me trying to spend some time at school while Mother now had three of us to look after.

The next move of Father's was to the seventy-foot steel keel *Integrity*, built at Gainsborough in 1897 and owned by J. J. Tomlinson of Thorne, which was too long to get to Stainforth. I can only remember making one voyage in her, and that was in the summer of 1914 when I was just eight years old; it was holiday time but Mother decided she was not making a trip that year. Dad had just bought me my first bike, and he came home one weekend from West Stockwith, where the *Integrity* was in the basin of the Chesterfield Canal, loaded with wheat for transshipment into narrow boats; there was also some cargo for Gainsborough. I asked to go back with him on the Monday morning, and he agreed. Then brother Jim wanted to come as well; he was just over five years old. This was before the days of motor buses running all over the countryside, so Father put Jim on his carrier and we set off on our bikes; it was the most convenient way. We lived a mile from the nearest railway and we would have had as far to walk from Misterton station to West Stockwith, with the inconvenience of having to change at Doncaster and wait for a suitable train. This was my first long bike ride, about twelve or fourteen miles, the first of many Monday-morning rides to all parts of Yorkshire and Lincolnshire over the years to come.

We set off very early and arrived at Stockwith by work time. The cargo was in eighteen-stone sacks and was to be transshipped using our own gear. The topsail yard was already rigged for a derrick, and soon after arriving on board we started to discharge, with two men on the fore roller. The bags were secured to the wire runner by a chain snotter, then the men on the winch hove away until the bags cleared the coaming. The guys were set so that as the bags came over the coaming they swung out over the narrow boat and were then lowered into her. By late afternoon all the Stockwith cargo was out, about thirty tons being left on board for Furley's wharf, Gainsborough.

On the Tuesday morning we went stern first into the lock to wait for the afternoon tide. At flood we penned out into the River Trent, and as there was little or no wind and a good tide running we "drove" to Gainsborough long before high water. Father was for'ard, working the anchor, and I stood by the tiller to carry out his orders. Wednesday was a day of rest waiting for a turn at the wharf. On Thursday morning the cargo was out in good time. Again the weather was calm and warm, and as soon as the hatches and covers were on we cast off and "drove" down the Trent with the ebb. After passing Owston Ferry the anchor was hove up to the hawse pipe and the tiller removed from the rudder head, the vessel being allowed to drive down until we reached Keadby Bridge, when she was again brought under control with the anchor. This was long before the banks were protected with stones as they are today; in those days the banks were all soft mud, and willows were growing in most places between the foreshore and low water mark. After passing through the bridge, we went alongside the canal jetty at Keadby to wait for the next flood so that we could go into the canal to load gas coal for Hull.

At Keadby the coal was loaded from the railway, where there was always a good stock in the sidings which had come from the inland pits with no direct access to water transport. There were two staithes in the canal and one on the Trent side for schooners and other craft that were too big to pass through the lock or too deep for the canal. Having two or three days to wait for a turn, we got on our bikes after breakfast on Friday and had another twelve-mile ride home to Stainforth. This was the last trip I was to have for a while; a few days later, while we were on holiday at Cleethorpes,

Germany invaded Belgium, Great Britain declared war on Germany, and the world was thrown into turmoil.

A news item on the local radio recently mentioning a shipment of six hundred tons of potatoes from a Trent-side wharf for export reminded me of trips in the keels *Confidence* and *Aureola*. Before the 1914–18 War this was a regular feature of the Trent trade; we often loaded potatoes direct from the farms in North Lincolnshire, mostly from Amcotts, Burringham, Meredyke and Luddington. Before the keel could be berthed for loading, the farm hands had to go on to the Trent foreshore at low water and prepare a berth by levelling an area of the bank foot large enough for the vessel to lay on. This was called digging a dock. At high water the vessel was warped alongside; the anchor was left off in deep water so that she could be hove off after loading. Kedge anchors and "dog legs" were put over to the bank to hold the vessel alongside, and when she was firmly aground a gantry was placed from ship to shore. The farm wagons then backed up to the flood bank and the sacks of potatoes were wheeled on board and lowered over the coaming by hand. This could not be done today at many of the farms because the banks have since been pitched with stone to give protection from the wash of the powered vessels which ply the river.

With two reefs in her mainsail to keep her speed down in the narrow waterway, a Beverley keel approaches Brigham Bridge on the Driffield Navigation.
Hull Town Docks Museum

Stainforth 4

STAINFORTH today would be described as a mining village on the Sheffield and South Yorkshire Navigation, but long before the pit shafts were sunk in 1911 it had been populated by generations of keelmen and farmers. Stainforth was home to keelmen even before the River Dun Navigation was opened, making it the entry port to this from the River Don and the Dutch River before the cutting of the Stainforth and Keadby Canal, opened about 1802. Until the early years of the twentieth century it had two shipyards and two dry docks, one boatbuilder, a sailmaker and a ship's chandler's shop, but the sinking of the shafts for Hatfield Main Colliery was to change the character of the place.

The Don or Dun originally had two mouths, one to the Aire at Rawcliffe, the other via Thorne, Crowle and Eastoft to the Trent at what is now Island House Ness, this being the main channel in the Middle Ages. Improvement was considered as early as 1343, and with the draining of Hatfield Chase by the Dutchman Cornelius Vermuyden came the need to cut a relief channel from Newbridge to the Ouse, completed in 1633 at a cost of £30,000. Sluices were fitted but they were carried away in a flood in 1688, causing the river to widen. This new channel, appropriately called the Dutch River, became the main one, allowing thirty-ton vessels up to Wilsick House at Thorpe in Balne, about half way between Stainforth and Doncaster; on spring tides vessels could reach Doncaster.

Moves to promote further improvement were made in 1698 and again in 1721, and in 1726 an Act was secured to make the Don navigable to Tinsley, near Sheffield. Locks were built upwards and improvements made downstream; the river was deepened from Wilsick House to Bramwith, a cut was made to Stainforth and locks were built at Bramwith and Stainforth. As the head of the tidal river and the entry to the improved River Dun Navigation, Stainforth took on a new importance which was enhanced when the Stainforth and Keadby Canal was cut to the Trent.

Coal came down for Gainsborough and Hull and corn for Hull, and general goods were carried in both directions, so Stainforth became a convenient place for keelmen to settle. I know that at least three generations, possibly more, of the Schofield family had been born there before me. When my great-grandmother was left a widow she used her keel as a houseboat, moored in Stainforth Ings, and was able to supplement her income with the money she received for looking after the keels' boats and other gear which they had to leave while making the voyage up the navigation and back. Her son, my grandfather, as well as being a keel owner and having one or two horses for hire, kept a few dairy cows as well. At that time he lived in a house near the entrance to the lock, and that was where most of the family were brought up. Later he bought a house with some land on the west bank of the navigation opposite the top carpenter's yard, and on the spare land he built a house for his second son John Christopher when he married.

The first house that I can remember living in was on the south bank opposite the crane where the keels lifted off their leeboards before going up the navigation. Later, by the time I started school, we had moved into a house in Finkle Street, then just before the 1914–18 War we moved back on to the waterside, this time on to the west bank into a larger house which I later found out used to be the local pub. Just before the same war, Uncle William Henry Schofield had two new houses built on some land which his wife had inherited from her father, John Parish, also a keel owner. This land was just over the river bridge on Fishlake Nab. Uncle John

My grandfather John Christopher Schofield's house on the west bank at Stainforth. Author's collection

Christopher lived on the east bank but later moved to Hull; when the time came to move he took his keel into the river and loaded up his furniture and other belongings over the backyard wall, then he took the old way to Hull down the Dutch River, thus avoiding having to pay dues on the Stainforth and Keadby Canal.

I have already mentioned that father's eldest sister married Sidney Woodall. They lived on the south bank and Uncle Sidney was at that time in his mother's keel. Clara, the second sister, lived in the house on the west bank which used to be my grandfather's, and her husband William Jolliffe owned and sailed the keel *Garland*, a wooden carvel-built vessel 57 feet 6 inches by 14 feet 8 inches by 6 feet 6 inches depth of hold, suitable for the Dearne and Dove and Wath Canal.

My father's cousin Edwin Schofield, the son of Matthew, lived in the house near the lock where my grandfather used to live. He was at this time master of the *Endcliffe*, one of Bleasdale's Sheffield-size keels. The related Parish family had three or four generations living in the village at any one time and all seemed to be keelmen or keel owners. There was John Tommy Parish on the east bank, very old and frail; then there was Joe Parish and his two sisters, all three over sixty and unmarried. They were, I think, cousins to Aunt Mary Ann, my Uncle William Henry's wife. Joe was willing to make himself available as purchase-man to one or two keelmen trading between Hull and Sheffield. Another of the clan was William Parish, usually known as Old Billy or Whisker Parish, who was retired and lived in the part of the village known as West End. For his second wife he had married a Miss Cockerton, who had a shop where she sold haberdashery. My father, who was mate with him for a time, would tell how particular he was about the appearance of his vessel, insisting on the dust being washed out of the coal for the cabin fire before putting it in the locker.

William's eldest son Frank had the steel keel *Sobriety*, which was built to Sheffield dimensions at Joseph Scarr's yard, Grovehill, Beverley, I think about 1910. Ernest, his second son, went deep sea and until about 1920 was master of a steamer in the foreign trade. When he left the sea he founded a bus company which ran one of the first local services between Goole, Thorne, Stainforth and Doncaster.

Another John Thomas Parish, also retired, lived in East Lane and had four sons. Tommy, the eldest, had a Sheffield-size wooden keel, Walter was with Bleasdale's and Ralph went into oil tankers, first with the Medway Tanker and Oil Storage Company and then with Shell, while the other son took a shore job with contractors who had the job of preparing the new Hatfield Main colliery. Another member of the Parish clan, Alf Parish, was the owner of the keel *United*, a wooden carvel-built vessel 57 feet 6 inches by

Bridgefoot, Stainforth, or as it was offically named, Water Lane, with the navigation swing bridge at the top of the rise, by the white house. Miss E. A. Shirtliff collection

14 feet 8 inches by 7 feet depth of hold, built I believe at Parkgate near Rotherham, while his brother Walter, a confirmed bachelor, owned the *Edith Anne*, a keel about the same length and beam but a few inches lower. When he retired, the people who bought his ship did not require her sailing gear so I was able to buy the mast, main yard and cotton mainsail (eight yards two feet in depth)* and her green cotton sail covers for ten pounds; the mast was resold for eight pounds. Alf Parish's second son Raymond became master of the keel *Invincible* and later of the *Honour*, both owned by Robinson Brothers, of Town Mills, Rotherham.

Also related to us was William Walter Peckson Peck, owner of the Sheffield-size carvel-built wooden keel *Faith*, a member of a Beverley family who had made Stainforth his home after marrying a Stainforth girl. In his youth he had been a pupil at Hull Trinity House Navigation School. He was very deaf and quite a character. A keen Jehovah's Witness, he would if he could get a lead steer the conversation round to the Armageddon and start telling how millions now living would never die with the second coming of the Lord. One got to know his ways and took avoiding action. He died at the age of eighty-four, leaving four sons and four daughters.

Those daughters married keelmen and the sons followed their father as keel owners. The eldest was Walter, who at first owned a keel named the *Alice*; then after marrying Edith Holmes he went to Goole to join G. D. Holmes, Holmes being his wife's uncle. Ernest and Sam, the second and third sons, went as masters of the *Lapwing* and the *Jupiter*, two small keels owned by Jonas Braithwaite of Hull, who had the contract for the carriage of coal from Manvers Main Colliery to Reckitts of Hull. In 1924 Braithwaite ordered two steel keels named *Charles William* and *Brasso* for the trade, 57 feet

*The keelman measured a sail by the depth in the middle of the hoist, and rendered it in yards and feet; this sail was 26 feet deep.

6 inches long, and Ernest and Sam took charge of them, the older two being sold. Sam later moved to Braithwaite's Sheffield-size keel *Eleanor B*, while Ernest went ashore to be cargo superintendent for Reckitts. When Jonas Braithwaite died, Reckitts took the ships over. The youngest son, Stephen, had a try with the keel *Forward*, but soon gave up and went to Goole to join his brother Walter with G. D. Holmes. Uncle Harry, Dad's youngest brother, married Edith Peck, the eldest daughter, and they went to live at Hull, later moving to Newhaven, Sussex.

James Dyson Wilson, who lived on the east bank, was probably younger than he looked; his white beard down to his chest and his stoutness gave him an appearance of great age. He had been retired all the time that I knew him and so had James Snowdon

Jonas Braithwaite's Brasso *and other keels at Keadby. The* Brasso, *built at Howden in 1924, took her name from one of the products made by Reckitts of Hull, for whom Braithwaite carried coal from Manvers Main Colliery.* E. W. Carter collection, Gainsborough Public Library

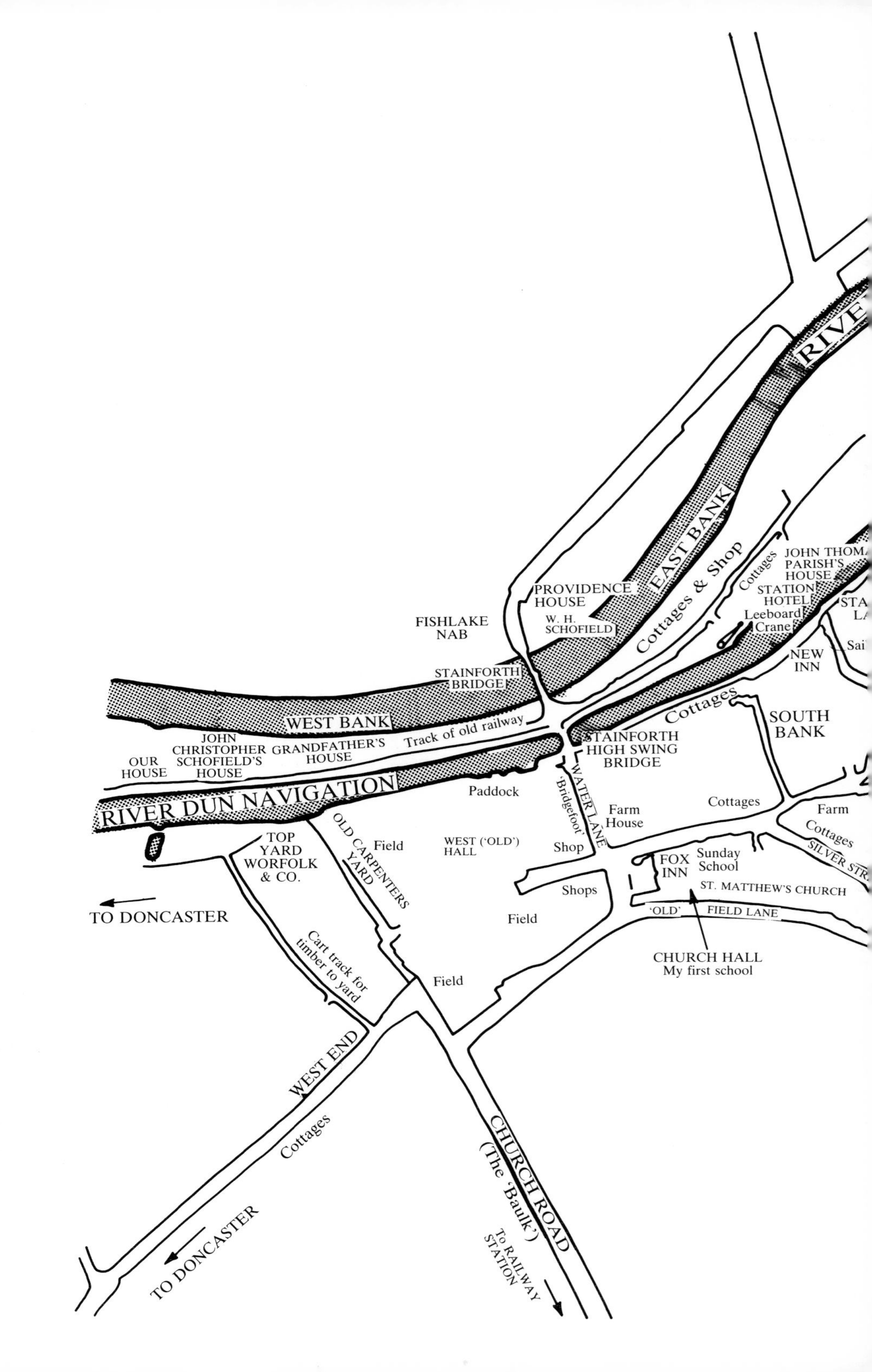
RIVE
EAST BANK
Cottages & Shop
Cottages
JOHN THOMA
PARISH'S
HOUSE
STATION
HOTEL
STA
LA
Leeboard
Crane
Sai
PROVIDENCE
HOUSE
W. H.
SCHOFIELD
FISHLAKE
NAB
STAINFORTH
BRIDGE
NEW
INN
WEST BANK
Track of old railway
Cottages
SOUTH
BANK
JOHN
CHRISTOPHER
SCHOFIELD'S
HOUSE
GRANDFATHER'S
HOUSE
OUR
HOUSE
STAINFORTH
HIGH SWING
BRIDGE
RIVER DUN NAVIGATION
Paddock
'Bridgefoot'
WATER LANE
Farm
House
Cottages
Farm
Cottages
SILVER STR
TOP
YARD
WORFOLK
& CO.
OLD CARPENTERS
YARD
Field
WEST ('OLD')
HALL
Shop
FOX
INN
Sunday
School
Shops
ST. MATTHEW'S CHURCH
'OLD' FIELD LANE
TO DONCASTER
Field
Cart track for
timber to yard
CHURCH HALL
My first school
Field
WEST END
Cottages
CHURCH ROAD
(The 'Baulk')
TO DONCASTER
To RAILWAY
STATION

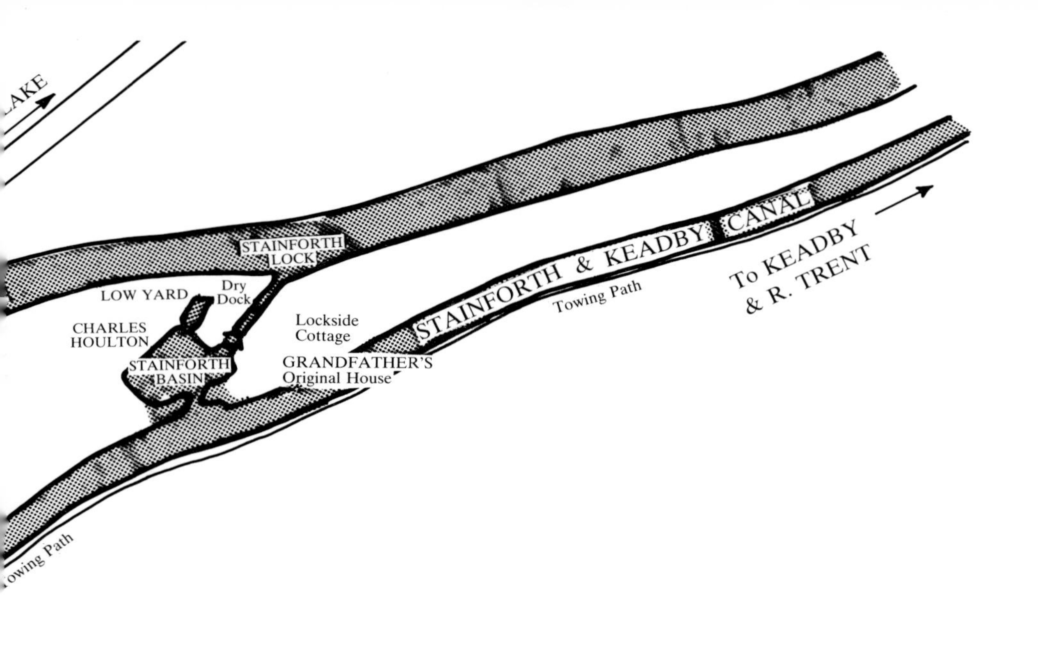
LAKE
STAINFORTH LOCK
LOW YARD
Dry Dock
CHARLES HOULTON
STAINFORTH BASIN
Lockside Cottage
GRANDFATHER'S Original House
STAINFORTH & KEADBY CANAL
Towing Path
To KEADBY & R. TRENT
Towing Path

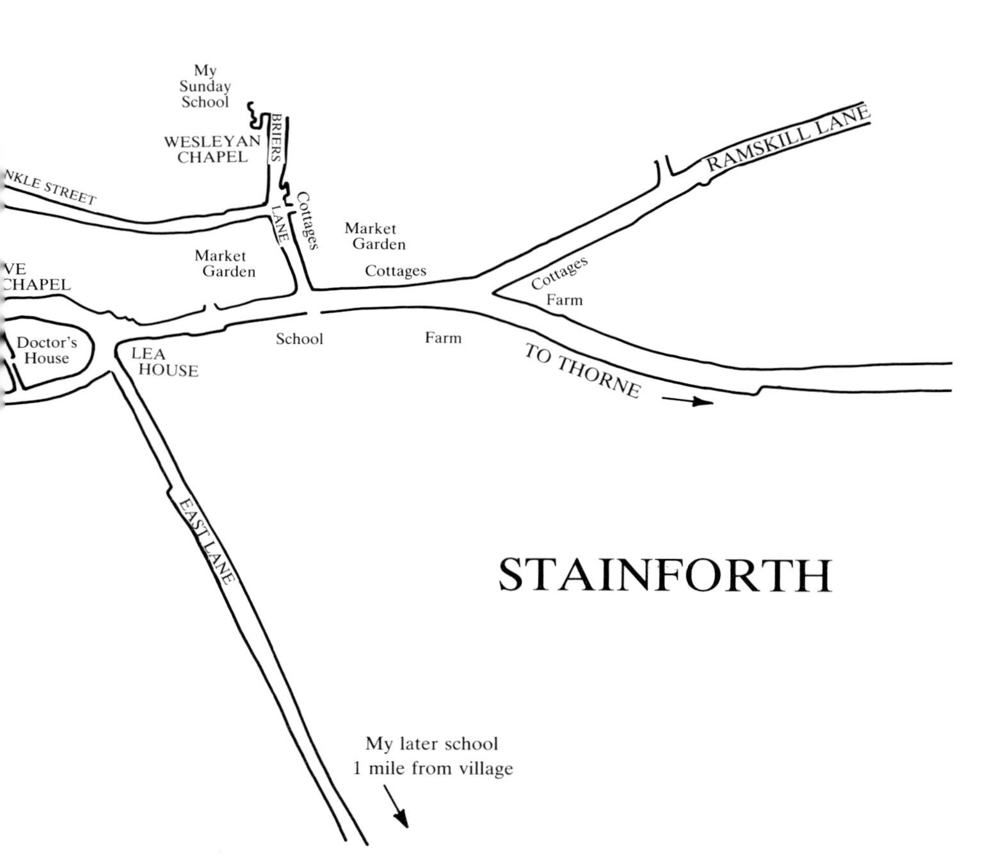
My Sunday School
WESLEYAN CHAPEL
BRIERS LANE
NKLE STREET
Cottages
Market Garden
RAMSKILL LANE
VE CHAPEL
Market Garden
Cottages
Cottages
Farm
Doctor's House
LEA HOUSE
School
Farm
TO THORNE
EAST LANE
My later school
1 mile from village

STAINFORTH

Wilson, father of Jim Wilson, owner and master of the keel *Energy*, a wood built Sheffield keel. Jim married Kitty Parish, daughter of old Billy. James Snowdon and Jim lived in Silver Street next door to each other. William Wilson owned the wooden keel *Lily*, Sheffield size and carvel built, his son being master of her until she was sold to Teddy Walker of Thorne. William Wilson then bought the steel keel *Medina* from William (Billy) Patrick of Thorne; she was Sheffield size. The younger son Charlie, who had the wooden keel *Carrie*, married Amy Peck, the second daughter of Walter Peck (Senior).

They all lived on the east bank, as did George William Wilson and Leonard and Alan Wilson. George William was retired. Leonard Wilson owned the last clinker keel to be owned at Stainforth, the *Marvel*, which like most of the clinker-built keels was 57 feet 6 inches by 14 feet 8 inches and 6 feet 6 inches deep in the hold. When she was no longer fit for work she was sunk for bank protection near Denaby coal staithe and he then bought the *Emily*, a wooden Sheffield-size keel built by E. V. Waddington at Swinton. Leonard Wilson's brother Alan, who also owned his own keel at one time, followed me in 1932 as master of the *Annie Maud*, a keel belonging to Robinson Brothers, owners of the Town flour mills at Rotherham. Other keels owned by them were the *Invincible*, *Amity*, *Expedient* and *Honour*, all wood carvel keels and all Sheffield size except the *Invincible*, which was Dearne and Dove size, 57 feet 6 inches by 14 feet 8 inches. Also living on the east bank was Edwin Appleton, owner and master of the keel *Sylvia W*, Sheffield size and wood carvel built, who married a Wilson; they had two daughters, one of whom married Sam Peck and the other a collier.

Sam Whitehead, who also lived on the east bank, owned the keel *Blanche* but sold her to Albert Beckitt of Thorne when they started to sink the pit and he went to work for the contractors. Next door to him lived Tom Shirtcliffe, who had the keel *Primrose*; later he sold her to Jim Major of Thorne and went to live in Hull, where he started in business as a lighter owner. On the south bank lived Bill Shirtcliffe; I am not certain of his relationship with Tom, but I think he was a cousin. He was a sloop man when I first knew him, though I think the family had owned billyboys, and later he became one of the first Trent pilots. He had three sons, Clarence, Victor and Jess; Clarence was master of a sloop owned by G. D. Holmes of Goole, Victor was in keels and Jess was master of the steam seagoing tug *Scindia*, owned I believe by T. W. Thomson of Hull.

Also on the south bank lived Ernest "Fiddler" Downing, who owned and sailed the keel *Samaritan*. A local preacher, he played the fiddle for any chapel event, accompanying the carol party round the village at Christmas and New Year. He had a brother living on the east bank named Robert, also known as "Whistling

Stainforth High Bridge, where the towpath changes sides. This view is looking towards Doncaster.
Miss E. A. Shirtliff collection

Bob" or just "Whistler"; his keel was named *Welfare*. He had two sons, Ernest and Donald, both of whom followed their father's trade, and I believe two daughters. Ernest died early and Donald is now a shopkeeper at Beverley.

The bridge keeper at Stainforth High Bridge was an old retired keelman named John Hasting. If he saw a keel coming with not much wind and in calms with the mate ashore hauling by hand (or bow hauling) he would go with his seal and bend it on to the man'sline and help until near the bridge. Then after opening the bridge and closing it after the vessel had passed through he would again assist with the hauling for about half a mile before returning to the bridge.

George Dyson Holmes was a Stainforth man who moved to Goole before I knew him and founded the firm of G. D. Holmes Ltd. Starting with one keel, he became a large owner of sloops and lighters, a director of several companies, a ship broker and a forwarding agent. His brother Billy, who still lived on the east bank in my schooldays, owned a sloop, the *Shamrock*, a wood carvel-built Sheffield-sized vessel. After the war in the early twenties he had built at Howden Dyke a steel keel about seventy-five feet long and won a contract for carrying bulk wheat from Hull to Leeds for Leeds Co-operative Society. There was a good cheap steam towage service between Hull and Leeds, so the *Valour*, as she was called, was never fitted out for sailing. Billy Holmes had two sons and two daughters, Edith marrying Walter Peck Junior and Florrie marrying a Goole sloop man called Tate. The eldest son George went as master of one of his Uncle George's lighters for a few years, then married into the Seven family who were newcomers to the village; they owned a fleet of buses by the mid-twenties and George went into the business. The other son Billy went into his uncle's firm and became manager after his uncle's death. Charlie Barley and his family, who were brought up in Stainforth as sloop men, followed the Holmes family to Goole. Charlie and his two eldest sons were with G. D. Holmes for most of their lives.

Albert Chester, who also lived on the east bank, had a wooden keel called the *British Oak*, built at Thorne in 1889, on a regular trade from Rank's flour mills at Hull to Brigg. In the early thirties he sold the *British Oak* and bought the steel Sheffield keel *Voluta*, in which he soon installed a diesel engine of Swedish make; it was at first intended as an auxiliary, but before long it became the main means of propulsion. His brother George, also living on the east bank, had been master of the keel *Parade T* of Thorne, built at Thorne in 1926 and owned by J. J. Tomlinson, but finished his working days with G. D. Holmes.

Another family living on the east bank were the Moxons, who were retired all the time that I knew them. Then there were Herbert Hinchcliffe and his father. Herbert had a little old keel called the *Tibby*, then he went as master of the keel *Annie Maud* of Rotherham, into which I followed him in 1929 when he took a shore job at Hull with a trawler company. The old man, also called Herbert, had owned the keel *Fairy*, but retired about 1930. There was also Jack Hinchcliffe, known to everyone as "Bacca Jack"; he was owner and master of a wooden 57 feet 6 inches carvel-built keel named the *Unique*. He later exchanged houses with his brother William, who lived at Thorne and owned the keel *Industry*, carvel built of wood at Mexborough in 1895 and also 57 feet 6 inches long. These 57 feet 6 inches vessels were usually called canal boats because they were built to navigate on the Dearne and Dove and Wath Canal.

One little old man I remember well was Darwin Oglesby, who had some connection with a steam towing company that had been formed in the late nineteenth century for towing vessels from Goole to Stainforth up the Dutch River before the New Junction Canal was cut. I believe the first tug was named *Don*. After the New Junction Canal was opened in 1905 the service was switched on to the Stainforth and Keadby Canal and by the time I can remember the *Don* had been replaced by the *Clara Marian*; she continued until some time during the 1914–18 War, when I lost sight of her.

Captain William Pattrick with his wife Maria and young son George aboard their clinker-built keel Hannah & Harriet *about 1894. Sam Fowler's* Alpha *was a very similar vessel.* Mrs E. Holt

Oglesby was also ship's husband for Bleasdale's, the keel owners of Hull.

When we first went to live on the west bank, our next door neighbour was old Sam Fowler, who had the keel *Alpha*. She, too, must have been very old, for all the blocks were large wooden ones and the sail tyes were chain. He had four sons and three daughters; at that time only two of the sons were keelmen, Arthur being with Bleasdale's and at that time having the *Brightside*. Clarence, the eldest son, kept the village fish shop and lived at the old sail loft on Stainforth landing, while young Sam had left keels and was working for the pit sinking contractors. Another son Harry had a small Dearne and Dove keel (57 feet 6 inches by 14 feet 8 inches) named the *Eclipse*, a handy little vessel with a nice entrance, a long forefoot and a sweet run; she sailed like a little yacht. Her end came one winter's day when towing down the Humber loaded with coal for Hull Fish Dock. I am not sure of the cause but she was towed foul of Hessle Sand light float and stove her side in. Harry's wife was on board with him and had the presence of mind to grab her

Silver Street, Stainforth, where boatbuilder George Houlton had a boatyard in which he built cogboats and where Mrs Smith had her shop in which you could buy almost anything.
Miss E. A. Shirtliff collection

handbag with their ready cash and jump on to the light float. After he lost the *Eclipse*, he did a bit of purchasing until the bridge keeper's job at Stainforth became vacant. Harry Fowler had one daughter and a son called Edward, who went as master of Bleasdale's *Bringcliffe*, a wooden carvel-built Sheffield keel, when she was new. Old Sam Fowler's youngest daughter married Ernest Oglesby, the youngest son of Darwin Oglesby.

Another character living in the last house on the west bank was Aaron Barras, an old sloop man now working for the pit sinking contractors; he was the local preacher. Fred Barras, another retired keelman, lived on the west bank and had a horse with which he did a bit of hauling when he felt like it; he did not like to go beyond Doncaster upgate. William Wadsworth, usually called "Billy Waddy", was another retired keelman; his last ship was the steel keel *Energetic*. John Woodward was master of Bleasdale's *Thorncliffe*, a wooden carvel-built Sheffield keel built at Stainforth by Worfolk and Company. Jack Chapman lived on Fishlake Nab and owned the *Coalite*, a steel Sheffield-size vessel that was in turn both keel and sloop rigged. He later sold her to Whitakers of Hull and went to live at Immingham. In 1979 *Coalite* was in use as a pump vessel. Round about 1925 or a little later Hewitson Ward, a Mexborough keelman, came to Stainforth to be the bridge keeper, and Albert Philpson came from Mexborough to live at Stainforth; he was a younger member of a family that had originally been Stainforth people but had moved to Mexborough. His brother Edgar had left keels and was master of one of the steamships out of Goole; later he had command of the Humber Conservancy Board's buoy tender the *Queen*, an iron steamer built at Hull in 1892. About the same time the Emerson family also moved from Mexborough to Stainforth and Bill Lister brought his family to Stainforth, I believe from Hull.

The last sailmaker at Stainforth was named Barras, but he went out of business before I was born, and the sail loft was turned into a private house. George Houlton and his son Charlie had a boatbuilding business in Silver Street, where they built cogboats and ships' lifeboats and also rowing skiffs. After the 1914–18 War the old man retired and Charlie moved to the low carpenter's yard by the side of the basin where the old lock gave passage between the river and canal. At the top yard the Worfolk family were repairing keels and building them, when they could get an order. The staff consisted of old Isaac and his two sons Philip and Percy; his brother Benny, Arthur Wilson and Sammy Wilson were carpenters and John Franklin was the blacksmith. Old Benny Worfolk made me my first wheelbarrow when I was quite young, and the first time I moored at the yard after being made captain he came to the ship's side and presented me with a stool for the cabin; I still use the same stool today on board the *Comrade*.

Before the sinking of Hatfield Main Colliery the only activity in the village other than activities connected with the water was farming. There were six farms in or near the village and two at Bramwith Woodhouse. Old Canny Smith and his son-in-law Joss Lee, an ex-keelman, farmed Thorne Road, and Old William Green and his son Billy had two large houses in the village and a farm on the east side known as Ramskill Park. There was another family named Green consisting of a brother and two sisters, none of whom had ever married. They had a dairy farm in the west end of the village. Ben Butterfield also farmed at the west end, while Bootham Farm was managed by a family named Broderick.

There were three pubs in the village. Jack Whitely, landlord of the *Fox Inn*, combined the duties of landlord with a bit of cattle dealing, and later when his son Jack grew up he opened a butcher's shop for him. Harry Bowling also combined farming with butchering. The other two pubs were on the waterside, the *New Inn* on the south bank and the *Station Hotel* on the east bank. Now over a mile away from the nearest railway, the *Station Hotel* was built hard by Stainforth station on the Manchester, Sheffield and Lincolnshire line between Doncaster and Grimsby.

Compared to some of the nearby villages Stainforth was well off for shops; we had four general stores, Fishlake had only one. On the east bank was a little shop kept by a widow called Mrs Storr. At the Bridgefoot was a new shop, very modern, with a newness that did not fit in with the character of the village. Mrs Smith's shop in Silver Street was much more what you would have expected in a village store; here you could find almost everything. On one side was a row of bins in which were stored flour, bran, sharps and middlings, also oats, so she could supply food for yourself or fodder for your animals. Paraffin was on sale from the back of the shop. Mrs Smith had been a widow for many years, and when Ernest Barras, the village joiner and undertaker, lost his wife it was not long before the name over the shop was changed to Mrs Barras. At the east end of Silver Street opposite the Primitive Methodist Chapel was Mrs Mawson's shop, another general store, if anything more crowded than the others. She sold boots and other footwear, her son Charlie being the village cobbler; he worked from an outbuilding behind the shop. She had been brought up on a keel; her maiden name was Rusling, and her brother, John Thomas Rusling, was in business in Hull as a keel owner, broker and forwarding agent; at that time he lived in Waverley Street.

The Wesleyan Chapel where I had to attend Sunday School whenever possible was in Briers Lane. On alternate Sundays the superintendent was George Houlton the boatbuilder and Uncle William Henry, who would ride many miles on his bicycle on Saturday afternoons so that he could take his Sunday School; then he would ride back to the ship early Monday morning. The Church

My first school was St Matthew's Church Hall in Stainforth, seen in this view behind the church. Miss E. A. Shirtliff collection

of St Matthew was in "Old" Field Lane; the vicar and his wife, who lived in a vicarage far too large for them, appeared to be very old and rode about on tricycles.

At my first school, in the church hall of St Matthew's, there were only three rooms, two small and one large. My first teacher was Annie Cockerton. The head was a Welshman called Hughes, "Taffy Hughes" to everyone. We also had a teacher called Schmidt, but on the outbreak of war he changed his name to Smith.

This was the Stainforth that I knew before the 1914–18 War, before the pit was sunk. Now it is full of Irish, Welsh, Geordies and Durhamites, and where we used to be able to walk on Monday morning through green fields to catch the early train for Hull, it is one big sprawl of bricks right through Hatfield.

Three miles east of Stainforth is Thorne, at that time a small country town with a grammar school and a market place, and a larger number of resident keelmen and keel-owners even than Stainforth. From what I can remember, there were more keelmen in the Stainforth and Thorne area than in any other place. Before the cutting of the Stainforth and Keadby Canal in the early eighteen-hundreds the keelmen of Thorne lived in the small hamlet of Thorne Waterside, about a mile to the north-west of the town.

Thorne Waterside was a busy port in the early days; in 1737 a wharf and warehouse was built for the transshipment of goods from boats to keels and keels to boats, for when the River Dun Navigation was first in operation the traffic in the upper part of the river seems to have been carried in boats. Before 1762, when the first towpath was made for horse haulage, they would have been hauled by manpower. In 1763 there was a good traffic in coal, charcoal, lead, corn, stone, lime, timber, bark, Sheffield goods, groceries and all kinds of merchandise, and by 1771 there was a regular service of keels between Rotherham and York, and in 1789 a regular service to London. The Act of Parliament authorizing the cutting of the Stainforth and Keadby Canal was obtained in 1793 and subsequently Thorne Waterside lost its importance.

By the end of the 1914–18 War there were only two keel families at Thorne Waterside, William (Billy) Patrick and John Tom Chester, but in Thorne itself there were many more. Some of the names that come readily to mind, in addition to the Schofields, cousins of Father's, are Bisby, Clark, Holt, Dean, Sutton, Hinchcliffe, Chester, Watson, Foster, Ramsden, Barley, Walker, Taylor, White, Tomlinson, Moverley, Beckitt, Williamson, Fletcher, Robinson, Gillyon, Ward, Lawrence, Hunt, Schooley, Raper, Stead, Swash, Naylor, Raywood, Hodgson, Brackenbury, Guest, Youl, Carr, Barras and Rhodes. Many of these names will be met with frequently in this book.

Hull to Sheffield before 1914 5

SAIL had not quite given way to steam at the time of the voyage I am about to describe, and there was still the occasional barque to be seen in Hull's Victoria Dock, where the Baltic timber trade was handled. Granite chippings and china clay arrived from the Channel Islands and Cornwall in topsail schooners, which would load coal as a return cargo, and the ketch-rigged billyboys, along with spritsail barges, were carrying coal and other supplies to all the creeks and havens between the Humber and the Thames. The ubiquitous Dutch motor coaster of later days was quite unknown; when we did see a Dutch vessel it was usually a galliot.

Before 1914 the largest of the Hull docks was the Alexandra Dock, which had been built by the Hull and Barnsley Railway Company and opened in July, 1885. The layout and design of this dock, in which ships lay stern on to the quay, was favourable for overside discharge to lighters and other vessels, and this was the method adopted by most ships using the dock. Construction of the King George Dock was started while we had the *Confidence*, and we took several cargoes of Trent gravel to Hull for the contractors. One Sunday while the ship was laid in the Alexandra Dock I remember walking around the construction site and seeing the cranes and tramways on the dock bottom.

On the banks of the River Hull there were several oil and cake mills, two flour mills and many accommodation wharves. They created work for some hundreds of lighters which, as well as transporting cargo from ship to mill, were sometimes used to store cargo for several weeks. Large quantities of linseed, wheat, maize, pollards and bran came into the dock from the River Plate, barley and wheat came from California and Chile, and in the open water season wheat and maize came from the St Lawrence. Then there was cotton seed from Egypt and the Sudan. Not surprisingly there were times when Alexandra Dock became congested, and it would then be necessary to make two pens for small craft bound upriver on the flood tide; the rule was for keels and sloops to go in the first pen at four hours to high water, lighters bound for the Old Harbour (River Hull) leaving in the second pen, which would be made as soon as the lock could be turned round.

On this March day we loaded wheat in bags from a ship in

Opposite page: *Keels and a three-masted barque in Albert Dock, Hull.*
Hull Daily Mail

Alexandra Dock for the Sheffield and South Yorkshire warehouse in Sheffield Basin. After penning out, some keels sailed independently, but Father decided to take advantage of the towage service up the Humber, which operated every day except Sunday. Most weekdays at least three tugs, each towing six vessels, would leave Hull; often there were more.

Sometimes when towing up the tug would have to round up between Victoria Dock and the Old Harbour to pick up a spritsail barge riding at anchor and wanting a tow up to Keadby to load coal for somewhere on the East Coast between the Wash and London River, but today there is no barge there.

By the time we reach Old Warp (Read's Island) a number of steamships bound for Goole and the Trent are overtaking us, and then as we round Whitton Ness, opposite Brough, we meet several ships that had spent the ebb at Blacktoft Jetty steaming down the Ouse; deep-draughted vessels took two tides to come down from Goole, waiting at Blacktoft Jetty until there was sufficient depth for them to proceed downriver.

We take the west channel into the Trent; by this time there is plenty of water. It was usual to take the channel through the West Trent when bound up on the flood, but vessels coming down would take the east side because the ebb sets through that channel. At Keadby we find several spritsail barges riding at anchor in Keadby Roads waiting for a turn to load coal at the railway staithe below the lock.

The tug lays us alongside the canal jetty and we get ourselves through Keadby Lock by using the boathook. The lock takes one Sheffield-size keel at a time; it was made 80 feet long by 22 feet 6 inches wide so that seagoing craft could load coal in the canal, where the railway had two more spouts. There are a good few craft here waiting to load not only coal but also other cargoes, including some sloops and keels alongside the railway sidings to load foundry sand direct out of railway trucks by basket and barrow. A gantry is placed over the coamings, and another one thence to the truck; after filling the basket in the truck it is wheeled on board and tipped into the hold. Basic slag in one-hundredweight bags was loaded by the same method.

Penning through into the Stainforth and Keadby Canal, we launch with boathooks and stowers a few hundred yards to a mooring on the south bank. Vessels bound up the canal always lay on the south bank, while vessels bound out of the canal into the river lay on the north bank between the coal staithe and the lock while waiting for the tide.

On the south bank directly opposite the Keadby loading berths there was a mast and blockmaker's shed and house, and near the lock was a sail loft and ship chandler's shop. The main road crossed

Victoria Dock Basin, Hull, in the days of sail with a veteran clinker-built sloop, a steel sloop and a billyboy. The clinker-built sloop's mast is stepped well forward.
Hull Daily Mail

the canal at Keadby Lock by a wooden swingbridge designed to carry only local traffic. At the west end of the basin was a railway bridge, operated by a steam engine; when the time came for us to go through it was swung into a recess on the north bank. Today that bridge has been replaced by a drawbridge worked by electricity on the south bank. Above the railway was another wooden swing bridge giving access via Chapel Lane to the farms on the south side of the canal. The next bridge, more than two miles up the canal, carried the Isle of Axholme Light Railway, and was swung by means of a hot bulb engine. The length of canal below this bridge was known to us as Bonny-ale.

As soon as we were moored in the canal Father went to telegraph to George Eastwood at Rotherham. As we had to wait for the horse marine and we had got a slant of wind we sailed up to meet him.

All the bridges to Doncaster except the railway bridges were wooden swing bridges for local traffic; they had the sort of names that roll off the tongue, Crowle wharf, Godnow, Medge Hall, Mauds, Moors, Wike Well, Toll Bar, Dunston Hill, Stainforth High, Bramwith, North Field, Kirk Sandall, Long Sandall. In 1844 the Navigation Company had ordered all bridges below Doncaster to be made opening bridges, and in April of that year the first vessel with a fixed mast reached Doncaster by canal, but with the

The keel Progress *of Stainforth, Tom Parish, owner and master, passing through Keadby Lock into the Stainforth and Keadby Canal. The lock has four pairs of gates so that it is workable at all states of the tide; the Trent at low water can be ten feet below the canal level, and at high water springs it can be eight or ten feet higher than the canal.*
E. W. Carter collection, Gainsborough Public Library

coming of the railways fixed bridges appeared again. At the time of this trip there were four fixed railway bridges and two opening ones below Doncaster Lock. The first fixed bridge was a railway bridge below Thorne carrying the Doncaster–Grimsby line, and the railway company had to maintain a crane here to lift off the mast of any vessel with a fixed one. Some sails and leeboards were also left here to be looked after by Titch Hinchcliffe, the bridge keeper at Wike Well Bridge, the first swing bridge below Thorne; when he was at the crane his wife or daughter attended to the opening of the bridge. He would also look after the cogboat of any vessel that cared to leave it at the bridge, but Father, like most captains, liked to take his boat to Bramwith Lock where it would be looked after by the lock keeper, who kept it bailed dry until we came down again; for this service he received sixpence (2½p). Thorne Lock would take a Sheffield keel and her boat, but not Bramwith Lock, which was one of the shortest on the navigation until it was lengthened in 1930–32 to enable compartment boats from Goole to reach Hatfield Main Colliery. Doncaster Lock had been lengthened in 1910 so that the compartment boats could load at Denaby, but the trade did not develop as expected.

Half a mile above Crowle Wharf Bridge there is a keel lying at a small jetty on the north bank of the canal; the jetty is so small that, unless there is a vessel lying there, you would hardly notice it if you were not looking for it. Midway along the jetty there is a small tunnel under the railway, which is within six feet of the canal at this point, with tram rails running through it so that keels and sloops can load bricks from the nearby brickyard. Because the railway is so close to the canal there is a notice board on the bank warning craft with a bowsprit to swing head to the hauling bank on the other side to avoid fouling the railway line.

In Thorne rack there are, as on most days, five or six keels below the Toll Bar Bridge waiting for a wind, or perhaps just having a few days at home. In summer they lay there for two or three weeks at a time to get their fettling done. Fettling to a keelman means cleaning and painting; waterproofing tarpaulins or hatch covers would be referred to as fettling covers. To be in good fettle is a common saying meaning to be in good condition.

Above the Toll Bar Bridge is the Navigation Company's maintenance yard where they made and repaired all the lock gates and bridges; they also had a slip for the repair of flats and workboats. Between the company yard and the lock is the yard of Richard Dunston Ltd, one of the two shipyards at Thorne; in local terms they were known as carpenter's yards, though Dunston's were building and repairing both wood and steel vessels. At that time Dunston's would build you a ship and fit her out in every

Crowle Wharf on the Sheffield and South Yorkshire Navigation with a keel passing upgate and two others on their way down. Author's collection

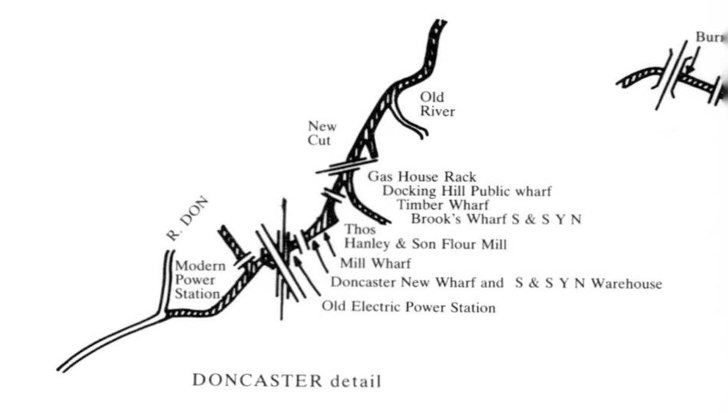
Old
River
New
Cut
Gas House Rack
Docking Hill Public wharf
Timber Wharf
Brook's Wharf S & S Y N
R. DON
Thos
Hanley & Son Flour Mill
Mill Wharf
Modern
Power
Station
Doncaster New Wharf and S & S Y N Warehouse
Old Electric Power Station
DONCASTER detail

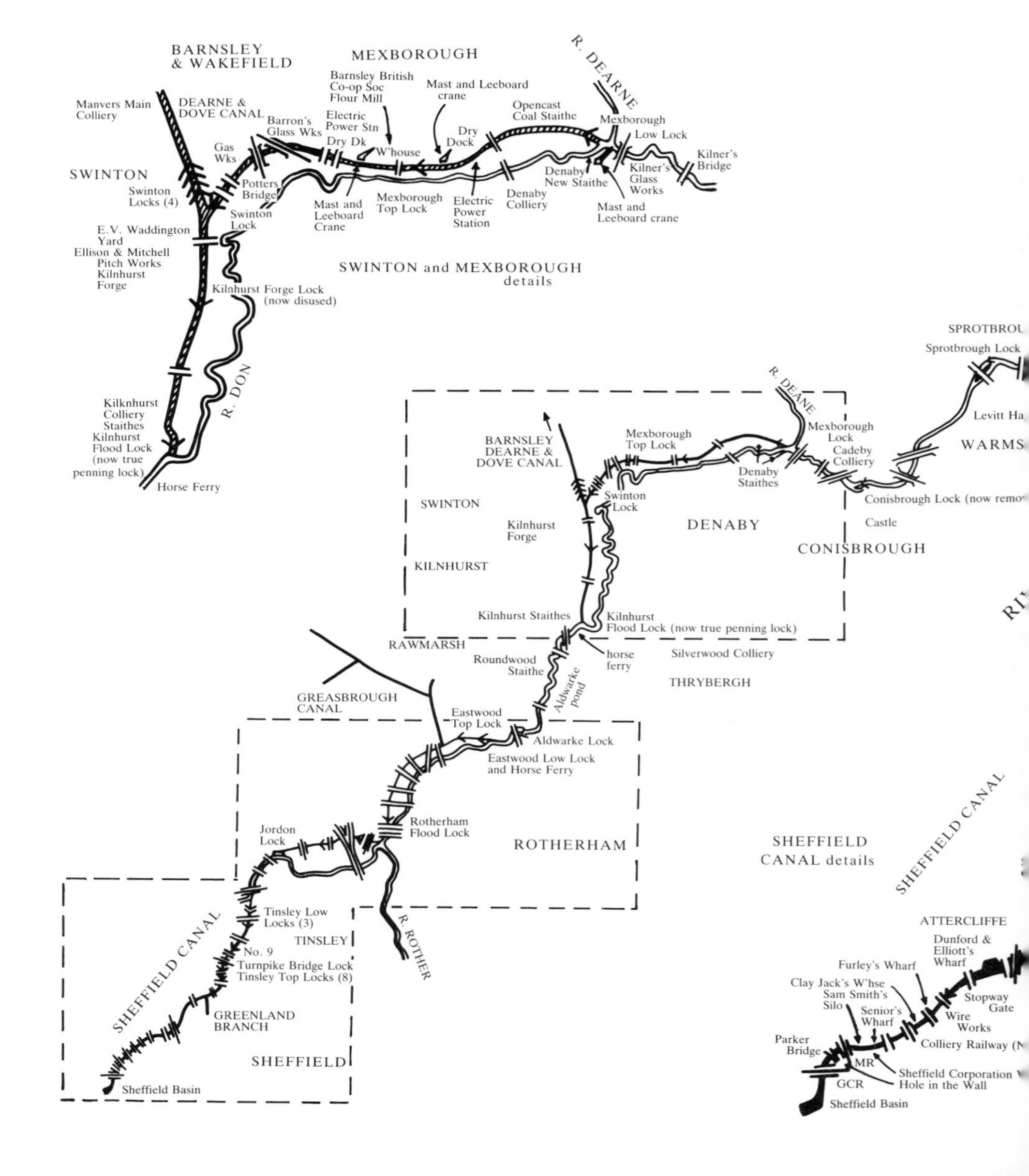
BARNSLEY
& WAKEFIELD
MEXBOROUGH
R. DEARNE
Manvers Main
Colliery
DEARNE &
DOVE CANAL
Barnsley British
Co-op Soc
Flour Mill
Mast and Leeboard
crane
Opencast
Coal Staithe
Mexborough
Low Lock
Barron's
Glass Wks
Electric
Power Stn
Dry Dk
W'house
Dry
Dock
Gas
Wks
Kilner's
Bridge
SWINTON
Potters
Bridge
Denaby
New Staithe
Kilner's
Glass
Works
Swinton
Locks (4)
Swinton
Lock
Mast and
Leeboard
Crane
Mexborough
Top Lock
Electric
Power
Station
Denaby
Colliery
Mast and
Leeboard crane
E.V. Waddington
Yard
Ellison & Mitchell
Pitch Works
Kilnhurst
Forge
SWINTON and MEXBOROUGH
details
Kilnhurst Forge Lock
(now disused)
R. DON
Kilknhurst
Colliery
Staithes
Kilnhurst
Flood Lock
(now true
penning lock)
Horse Ferry
SPROTBROU
Sprotbrough Lock
R. DEANE
Levitt Ha
BARNSLEY
DEARNE &
DOVE CANAL
Mexborough
Top Lock
Mexborough
Lock
Cadeby
Colliery
WARMS
Denaby
Staithes
SWINTON
Swinton
Lock
Conisbrough Lock (now remo
Castle
Kilnhurst
Forge
DENABY
CONISBROUGH
KILNHURST
Kilnhurst Staithes
Kilnhurst
Flood Lock (now true penning lock)
RAWMARSH
Roundwood
Staithe
horse
ferry
Silverwood Colliery
Aldwarke
pond
THRYBERGH
GREASBROUGH
CANAL
Eastwood
Top Lock
Aldwarke Lock
Eastwood Low Lock
and Horse Ferry
SHEFFIELD CANAL
SHEFFIELD
CANAL details
Jordon
Lock
Rotherham
Flood Lock
ROTHERHAM
Tinsley Low
Locks (3)
TINSLEY
R. ROTHER
SHEFFIELD CANAL
No. 9
Turnpike Bridge Lock
Tinsley Top Locks (8)
GREENLAND
BRANCH
SHEFFIELD
Sheffield Basin
ATTERCLIFFE
Dunford &
Elliott's
Wharf
Furley's Wharf
Clay Jack's W'hse
Sam Smith's
Silo
Senior's
Wharf
Stopway
Gate
Wire
Works
Parker
Bridge
Colliery Railway (N
MR
GCR
Sheffield Corporation
Hole in the Wall
Sheffield Basin

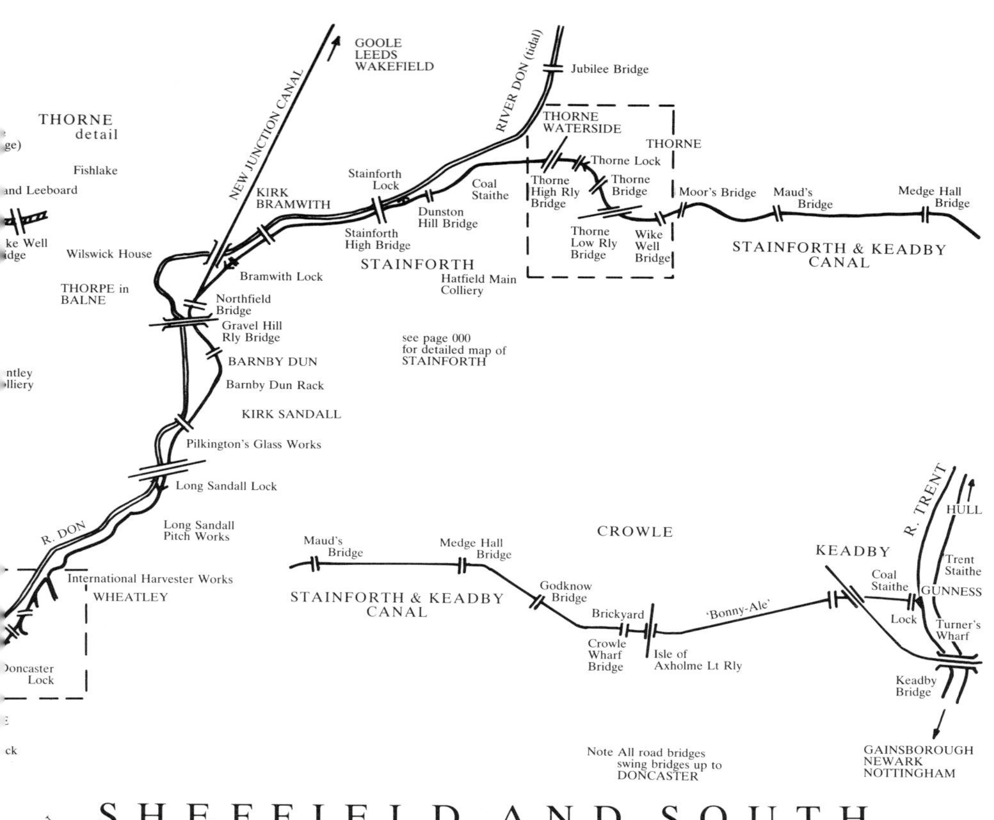

SHEFFIELD AND SOUTH YORKSHIRE NAVIGATION

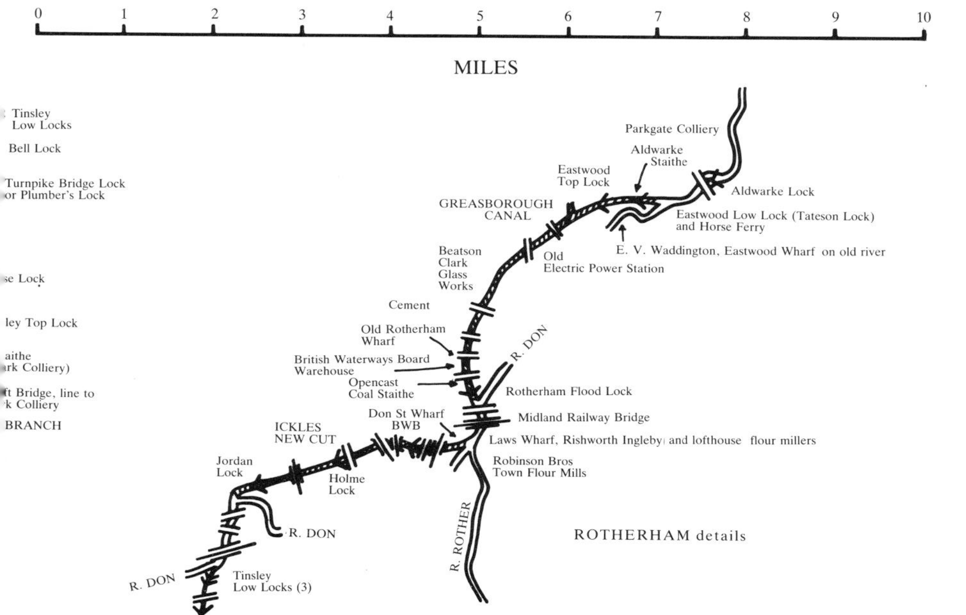

detail; they had their own ropewalk across the road from the yard, their own sailmaker, and their own mast and blockmaker. For repairs they had one slipway and a dry dock. Charlie Houlton, the boatbuilder at Stainforth, supplied boats to them. The second yard, that of Staniland and Co Ltd, was above Thorne Lock; it had two dry docks and built and repaired wooden keels and lighters.

Lying alongside Burr's pitch works, next door to Staniland's, where one could obtain supplies of tar, black varnish, creosote and naphtha, is a small wooden keel, flush decked and with a house on deck, the *Don,* which Burr's use as a tanker to transport the tar from Doncaster gasworks; a Thorne man named Barley was her captain. She has a small stump mast and a six yards high mainsail for use with a fair wind.

Stainforth Lock, connecting with the River Don, is still workable and Stainforth High Bridge is a swing bridge, the first changeover point for the hauling bank since leaving Keadby; the horse is unhitched so that he can walk over the bridge. The carpenter's yard and dry dock in Stainforth basin is closed, but Worfolk and Company are still building and repairing wooden keels; they have a dry dock. We put our leeboards on shore at Stainforth.

At Bramwith Lock, the first short lock and the second changeover point for the hauling bank, we get a fair idea of the

A keel with mainsail and topsail set under the crane at Stainforth lifting off leeboards. In this view south bank is on the right and east bank on the left; the Stainforth and Keadby Canal starts at the basin in the distance. Miss E. A. Shirtliff collection

A nineteenth-century engraving of keels in the River Don at Doncaster. The nearest keel has two rollers forward, one for raising the mast and the other for warping; this has not been in my lifetime, but I have talked to old people who remembered it.
Robert Malster collection

amount of traffic on the navigation by the number of cogboats left in the care of the lock keeper. About four hundred yards above the lock the New Junction Canal joins the Sheffield and South Yorkshire. A little further on is Gravel Hill railway bridge, still operated by hand.

At Long Sandall there is another pitch works, and at Sandall Lock the horse again crosses to the other bank by means of a swing bridge as he had done at Bramwith Lock. After penning through the lock, we enter a section of the navigation which is along the original bed of the River Don. In the early days of the River Dun Navigation Company this section was still tidal to Doncaster. Later the river was diverted at Doncaster into a new and straighter channel, the old course was canalized, and at various times it was improved by straightening; the old and the new now run parallel for most of the way. Near Doncaster there is one long bend left, with the gasworks wharf along most of its length, known to keelmen and horse marines as Gas House rack.

Beyond that we come to Docking Hill, the public town wharf and mooring place; keels for down the navigation often tie up here for a day or two to wait for a slant of wind. Next to Docking Hill is a timber yard, and Brook's wharf, owned by the Navigation

Company; then comes the flour mill of Thomas Hanley and Sons, who own keels and receive all their supplies of foreign wheat by canal. Below the lock is an electricity power station receiving coal from the local pits by canal.

The two pounds from Doncaster to Conisbrough are the most attractive part of the navigation, passing between well-wooded hills. Sprotbrough is particularly beautiful in early spring, and there are masses of snowdrops in the woods; we can see a carpet of white in places. Rowing boats and skiffs can be hired at Hexthorpe Flats, and they are in great demand in the evenings and at weekends in the summer; but in March they are not much in evidence.

In Sprotbrough Cut the water mill is grinding corn by water power, and there is another mill built into the dam at Conisbrough using water power to drive machinery for making cotton bobbins out of birch logs, which they receive by water. As we approach Conisbrough Lock on our way up, the village and the castle on the hill make a pretty picture. On the top pound we come to the first signs of industry; we shall be among industrial surroundings most of the way to Sheffield. Cadeby pit is right alongside the river and Denaby pit lies on the other side, about a mile above the coal staithe that has been built over the river in anticipation of coal being shipped by Tom Puddings, as compartment boats are often called.

A keel laden with pit props bound upgate to the collieries passing under Rainbow Bridge, Conisbrough. With her clinker sides she must have been an old craft when this photograph was taken about 1910. Rainbow Bridge, opened in 1849, carried the South Yorkshire Railway, which from 1864 formed part of the Manchester, Sheffield and Lincolnshire, over the River Don. Humber Keel and Sloop Preservation Society

When keels and sloops load at that staithe they have to put their masts and sails on shore by the hand-operated crane provided by the colliery company. The Denaby and Cadeby Colliery has a subsidiary shipping company which manages the sales side of the business and also owns some keels trading to Hull with coal, as well as some seagoing ships that load at Goole from the railway. As the coal was mined there has been considerable subsidence, and over the next fifty years I shall see the land between Hexthorpe and Denaby subside many feet.

In the same pound as the coal staithe is Kilner's glassworks, which owns three or four open boats for carrying supplies of coal from the local pits and also two schooners for bringing supplies of white sand from the Continent to Goole, at which place it is transshipped into keels and open boats for carriage to Conisbrough and to Mexborough, where Barron's have a glassworks.

At Mexborough we put the mast and sails on shore at one of the three private storage yards. The cranes at these yards are all hand operated, but they work easily and the whole operation takes only a few minutes. It is very much a matter of practice makes perfect; when the mast was lifted out for the first time care was taken to find the centre of balance for a single strop, and Father marked the mast so that the strop would always be put in just the right spot.

The keel Ino *approaching Sprotbrough Lock on the Sheffield and South Yorkshire Navigation.*
John Wain collection

The keels Welfare *and* Annie Maud *at Roundwood staithe in flood time in August of either 1930 or 1931. On board the* Welfare *is Bob Downing, of Stainforth; Charlie Wilson of Swinton can be seen on board the keel* Cedar, *moored astern of the* Welfare. Author's collection

Mexborough did at one time have two carpenter's yards with dry docks, but only the top yard remains in business. A keel lies alongside the Barnsley British Co-operative Society's flour mill unloading wheat in eighteen-stone sacks; they will not have facilities for handling grain in bulk for some years yet. At Barron's glassworks there are several open boats loaded with coal or white sand.

Hardly have we passed through Mexborough than we are at Swinton and passing the junction with the Dearne and Dove Canal. The canal is open and carrying a good trade of coal, sand and wood pulp, and Waddington's are building wooden vessels at their yard above the second lock, while Swinton gasworks receives its coal by water from the local pits.

Back on the navigation at Kilnhurst, Ellison and Mitchell's pitch works are receiving tar by water and shipping pitch in their own vessels for transshipment at Goole for the Continent. The aroma of pitch is mixed with other smells emanating from Kilnhurst Forge, which obtains its coal by water. At least a dozen vessels are waiting to load at Kilnhurst pit, which has two staithes, one for loading open boats for the local trade and one for keels; it is usual to find ten or fifteen vessels waiting here, for between them the two staithes can load five or six hundred tons per shift.

Kilnhurst Lock is a flood lock. Extra care has to be taken on the length of the river from Kilnhurst Lock to Aldwarke Lock, known as Aldwarke Pond, because it is liable to heavy silting during fresh time and can be a difficult length to navigate; as on most river sections, it is essential to know the channel and to keep to it. In some parts the channel is only a few feet wider than a loaded vessel, and there is no room for error. About three hundred yards above Kilnhurst Lock we have to pause while the horses are taken across the river by a ferry, a wooden carvel-built, decked craft about thirty-five feet long by fifteen feet wide, operated by a winch and submerged chain. We have to have two horses on the part of the navigation above Kilnhurst because of the fresh in the river; the way things are, we shall probably keep the second horse on all the way to Tinsley Low Lock.

In a bight further up the pound we come upon Roundwood coal staithe, where vessels load coal from Silverwood Colliery. We have a bit of difficulty getting the keel into Aldwarke Lock; it is a deep lock only just wide enough to accept a Sheffield-size keel, and it always takes several minutes to get in and out of this lock because it is so narrow, only taking the bare draught of the vessel on the low sill. We have problems, too, at the next lock, Eastwood Low Lock, also known as Tateson Lock; there is a good deal of mining subsidence in this area and the lock has already subsided so much that the handrails are under water in flood time. Here the horses are ferried back over the river on a boat like the one at Kilnhurst. As we set off again, the horses splashing through the pools of water on the hauling path, we pass Aldwarke coal staithe, which is just above the lock; the coal shipped here is mainly gas coal from Parkgate pit, brought down from the collieries by rail.

Smoke and fumes from the steelworks and other industrial premises clog the air as we make our way into Rotherham with the railway line close on our starboard hand. Just below Rotherham wharf and across the railway line is the glassworks of Beatson Clark, who have a gantry built out from the works over the railway and the hauling bank, with a small crane on the end for discharging cargoes of white sand. At the wharf itself there is a warehouse where keels discharge cargoes of flour and cement; there is also a hand-operated crane used for loading keels with wagon wheels and axles for export. After passing through Rotherham Lock we rejoin the River Don for a short distance. Ahead of us we can see the two spans of the Midland Railway bridge, one which presents us with a difficulty. The deep water is on the opposite side to the hauling bank, so the horse line has to be passed round the centre pier of the bridge and brought back on board. To enable this to be done fender piles have been driven into the river bed and a catwalk has been constructed on top; at the right moment the mate, with the line coiled on his shoulder, springs on to the catwalk, walks round the bridge pier, jumps back on board and makes the line fast to the neddy; the vessel does not stop.

On this pound is Laws wharf, where Rishworth, Ingleby and Lofthouse, owners of the Swan Flour Mill at Hull, have a flour warehouse. They send flour by water to Rotherham and Leeds for local distribution and own some steam keels which they employ in the Leeds trade and the small steam keels *Swiftsure* and *Ril* in the Rotherham trade. The *Swiftsure* was built as a motor craft with a paraffin engine but has been converted to steam. On our left we can see the River Rother; on the Rother is Robinson Brothers' flour mill, which receives its supplies of foreign wheat by water, the firm running some keels themselves and also employing several bye traders.

The sound of steam hammers and the stench of hot metal leaves us in no doubt that we are in one of the great steelmaking

The wooden keel Watchful *at Rishworth, Ingleby and Lofthouse's warehouse on the River Don at Rotherham in August, 1930. Inside the* Watchful *can be seen the white funnel of the steam keel* RIL. *I took this photograph on a Sunday after a flood; that is why the anchor cable has been used to moor the keel.* Author's collection

centres of the world as we approach Tinsley Flight, a series of twelve locks which will lift us many feet; by the time we get into Sheffield we shall be some 250 feet above sea level. The bottom lock has a lock keeper who is responsible for the first three locks going up. A couple of men are dodging about hoping to get a job helping craft up the locks, and Father takes one of them on; the charge is two shillings (10p). With our cargo of wheat we do not need somebody to help liver, but if we had had a cargo of deals, dish metal or bar iron Father would have been glad of an extra man to help with that, and would have kept the man on.

There is a rolling mill opposite the second lock; that is a very noisy lock. The first three locks have just a hundred or two hundred yards between them, then we come to a pound about half a mile long which brings us to Plumpers Lock, which has a lock keeper who is responsible for the next two locks up to House Lock. Tinsley wharf, in the two pounds below the present lock house, is known to keelmen as House Lock wharf. It has two steam cranes which always seem to be fully employed, and there are several vessels there waiting to liver their cargoes of pig iron, dish metal, ingots and billets.

On the top canal level about four hundred yards from Tinsley Top Lock is a coal staithe at which coal is loaded from Tinsley Park Colliery; keelmen always call it Peacock staithe. Laying at the staithe is a short decked vessel with tram lines on the deck; the coal is brought down from the colliery in wheeled tubs which are run on to the deck and taken into Sheffield for the house coal trade. All along the banks of the canal one gets glimpses of white-hot metal being sent through the rollers; the noise of the rolling mills is shattering.

The railway was on the same level as the canal at Plumpers Lock, but as we come out of the top lock it is many feet below us, but climbing all the time. After passing Broughton Lane station we can see it running between the canal and the steelworks, still climbing, and as we draw near to Attercliffe station it is only about fifteen feet from the canal. I notice the canal narrowing to no more than twenty feet or so, and look up on the starboard side at Attercliffe station several feet above us. Another hundred yards or so ahead I can see where the railway, still climbing, passes over the canal at Attercliffe Bridge.

Without thinking much about it I direct my gaze to the port side—and am amazed to see a street a good twenty feet below us. We are in fact passing over an aqueduct.

Between the railway bridge and Sherman Lane Bridge we pass the private wharf belonging to Dunford and Elliott's steelworks. Then on emerging from Sherman Lane Bridge we find ourselves in a deep cutting for four or five hundred yards, a place that makes you hope the world is not going to crash in on you or swallow you up. This part of the canal, from the aqueduct to Staniforth Road Bridge, is already subject to subsidence caused by the colliery workings underneath.

Above Staniforth Road bridge there is a wireworks on both sides of the canal with a connecting gangway over the water; a craft is lying under the gangway and coils of wire are being lowered into its hold from a trapdoor. Three or four craft are waiting their turn at Furley's wharf, where two steam cranes are busily unloading cargo which is being put straight on to horse-drawn rullies or carts to be delivered to the nearby steelworks; there is not much storage space here. Just above Furley's wharf is Clay Jack's, a warehouse built up to the canal for the storage of china clay, which is being livered by hand with derrick and basket and wheeled through a doorway opening directly on to the canal. Further along is Senior's steelworks and wharf, taking iron and steel ingots by water.

Next door to Senior's is the grain silo of Sammy Smith's, one of the four flour mills in Sheffield, the mill itself being some distance from the canal. They are the first of the Sheffield mills to have their grain carried in bulk; it is transferred from silo to mill in horse-drawn box vans. The other flour millers in Sheffield, Price's, Ibbotson's and Hazelwood's, have their wheat carried in eighteen-stone sacks; their mills are all some way from the canal. Price's have their wheat landed straight on to a horse rully by derrick, while Hazelwood's and Ibbotson's have theirs handled through the Navigation Company's warehouse.

Between the Midland Railway bridge and Parker Bridge bar iron is being handed out of a keel one bar at a time, carried over the hauling bank and pushed through a hole in the wall of a factory. To make the work easier a roller is clamped on to the keel's coaming top; this same method is used in Sheffield Basin when the bars are to be stored on the wharf.

Sheffield Basin is our destination on this trip. What a busy place it is! Keels are continually arriving with cargoes of wheat in eighteen-stone sacks, flour in ten-stone bags, granulated sugar in hundred-pound bags, cube sugar in wooden cases, rolls of newsprint, bundles of strawboard, cement in one-hundredweight bags, nickel in barrels, chrome and ferro-silicon in barrels and boxes, sulphur in bulk, pig iron, dish metal, iron and steel billets, bar iron, bog ore in bulk and dried fruit in boxes. Among the outward cargoes being loaded are bright steel, empty sacks, copperas (green vitriol), and ganister, the last used for furnace linings.

Sheffield Basin is a dark, dreary place to lay in. On the south side a canopy extends out over the basin for the length of four berths, and beyond this is the old warehouse with a waterway right

Effingham Road wharf, Sheffield, was Furley and Company's depot on the Sheffield and South Yorkshire Navigation. Most of the cargoes handled here were for the local steelworks.
Furley and Company, Hull and Gainsborough

inside; it is impossible to see anything in the cabin without having the lamp burning all the time. On the north side it is more open, but with two coal-burning steam cranes and the steelworks belching out their smoke and soot it is not much brighter.

Never mind, Sunday morning is fine and Mother takes us along to the service held on the wharf side by the chaplain of the Seamen's Mission. Later in the day we all attend the evening service at the meeting room in Exchange Street near the wharf gates.

After livering at Sheffield we make our way down to Roundwood coal staithe to load coal for our return to Hull. We have to wait several days for a turn, the loading rate being about five craft per shift, the loading gang working one shift a day from 6 am to 2 pm. While we are waiting Father gives a helping hand to the crews of the vessels that are loading, assisting them to open out and cover up; this is the usual practice. When our turn comes I find it fascinating to watch the method of running down the ten-ton railway wagons and tipping them. The staithe has a steam engine for pulling the wagons on and off and also for tipping them. At Kilnhurst staithe instead of the ordinary ten-ton railway wagons they have only five-ton wagons, used for the job of loading only. The tracks are so arranged that the wagons, once started, run on and off by gravity. Before attempting to move a wagon the staithe man takes a stick with a few rags tied on the end and dips it in a bucket of water, then wipes the rails before using a crowbar under the wheels to start them rolling; the wet rag removes the coal dust from the rails.

Roundwood coal staithe is in an isolated position about a mile above Kilnhurst Flood Lock. Apart from the colliery and the staithe the only buildings are the foreman's house and a lobby provided by the colliery company for the use of keel crews; inside is a large coal-fired cooking range with a side oven and a boiler for hot water which is taken full advantage of by the keelmen's wives to do their laundry and baking. At night the lobby is the meeting place for the crews.

Mother has her own washing gear on board which she uses whenever she has the opportunity. The peggy tub and wash tub when not in use are stowed on the shelf across the after headledge in the hold; the folding wringer and peggy legs are stowed in the fo'c'sle. A coal staithe is a dusty place, but all the same such an opportunity as this must not be wasted; wash day has to be when we are tied up somewhere for the day, and here we are waiting for a turn. So the beef kettle goes on the fire to heat up the water; it will remain there, refilled from time to time, until the washing is all hanging from the man'sline stretched from the backstay to the mast. The footing plank is lashed across the after rails and the wringer is screwed to it, and soon all is hustle and bustle as Mother gets to work on our dirty clothes.

Another day Mother decides to do some baking. The cooking range in the lobby ashore proves useful on this occasion; normally Mother would bake her own bread in the side oven of the fo'c'sle stove on which the main cooking was done. In the cabin breakfast was cooked in a cast-iron frying pan on the open coal fire; it was also used for other quick meals when under way. But the main method of cooking while under way was the beef kettle, a cast-iron pan holding about two and a half gallons, used for boiling joints of meat and game together with suet dumplings and potatoes, all put in to time them to be ready together. Our appetite was usually healthy.

After loading at Roundwood we had a horse to haul us to Doncaster, then with a favourable wind we set our sails for Hull.

The unrigged West Country boat Thomas Sugden *on the Calder and Hebble Navigation between Wakefield and Brighouse. She traded regularly with bulk grain between Hull and Brighouse, being towed by steam tug as far as Wakefield, where a horse took over. The horse marine is "Manny Waddy" Wadsworth of Wakefield.* T. E. Claxton collection

Working as Mate 6

I REMEMBER being on holiday at Cleethorpes in 1914 when Germany invaded Belgium. Soon after, a call went out for volunteers for the Armed Forces; I can see the famous poster now, with Kitchener's eyes and pointing finger, and the words "Your Country Needs You".

Father offered himself for service with the Navy. He had not long to wait before he was asked to report to Hull, where he was drafted to the minesweepers, his first ship being one of the old steam trawlers from Hull which had to be taken to Leith for conversion to a minesweeper. From Leith he went to the depot ship at Liverpool, HMS *Eagle*, and after a while he was drafted to a steam trawler working out of Fleetwood for minesweeping in the Irish Sea. A few months later he was transferred to the Scottish auxiliary lugger *Jeanie Campbell* which was to be delivered to Stornoway; they did the trip in easy stages, moving in daylight only. He stayed in her for the remainder of the war, ferrying service personnel and mails between Stornoway, Kyle of Lochalsh, Mallaig and Oban, and once or twice through the Caledonian Canal to Inverness.

Early in the war Father's two younger brothers and sister got married. Ginny married Luther Dishman, a schoolteacher at Doncaster and the son of Charles Dishman, billyboy owner of Stainforth. Albert married Carrie Brown of Thorne, the daughter of Captain Brown, a schooner master, and owner of the schooner *Clarita*, then joined the Royal Engineers and went to France. Harry married Edith Peck and joined the Navy, towards the end of the war going to live at Newhaven, Sussex. Uncle Chris Schofield's son Harry joined up for minesweeping, and his second daughter Annie went on board with her father and worked as mate until the end of the war.

During the war years I was able to attend school, which I enjoyed. In the autumn we had organized parties to gather brambles for jam making and later, when gas warfare came, we collected nut shells to make charcoal for use in gasmasks. On my way home from school I would often linger at the open door of the blacksmith's forge next door to the *Fox Inn*.

The sinking of the pit between Thorne Road and the railway was already causing the village to grow, with new houses on

The Barnsley-size steel keel Whim, *owned by my uncle John Christopher Schofield, which my father took over in 1919 so that his brother could have a holiday.*
Author's collection

Thorne Road and in East Lane. The old village school was too small, and the school rooms of the church and the Wesleyan chapel were used for the older pupils. I attended both in due course, and moved on to the new school in East Lane when it was built. During the war I can remember two particularly severe winters, when the canal froze over and stopped the traffic completely for several days; when they did break the ice they had to have five horses for the ice boat. While the canal was frozen over I crossed it several times with my wheelbarrow to fetch firewood from the carpenter's yard. I was staying at Caister in Lincolnshire with some of Mother's relations when the first Zeppelin raid was made on Hull.

The ice boats on the Sheffield and South Yorkshire Navigation were built of wood, about 15 feet long and 7 feet wide, and sheathed with light sheets of galvanized iron. There were rails each side so that a team of eight men could make the boat roll by throwing their weight first one side and then the other; this helped to break the ice as the horses towed the boat forward.

The newly opened port of Immingham provided a convenient base for the Royal Navy's operations in the North Sea, and the War Department soon chartered several keels to transport stores from the dock to naval vessels riding at anchor in the estuary. Later when the Inland Water Transport Division of the Royal Engineers was formed they bought keels and sloops for use on the inland navigations of the Continent and for service out of Immingham to warships in the estuary. Several keelmen and lightermen volunteered for service with the Royal Engineers, and after the war I talked with them about their experiences. Sadly many men and vessels did not return.

Father was demobilized from the Navy in the late spring of 1919 and went to take charge of the keel *Whim* while his brother Christopher took a holiday. I had a few days with him during the summer holidays on a voyage to Gainsborough loaded with white cotton seed for Pearson's Ashcroft Mill. While we were laid at Gainsborough there was a public holiday for the Peace celebrations; parties were held in the streets, and a programme of athletic events was arranged. After the trip it was back to school for a few more months.

After the war there was a rush of imports of various kinds, particularly of feeding stuffs and oil seeds, and the warehouses were soon full up, creating a demand for lighters and keels for storage. This made it difficult for Father to obtain a suitable vessel, though after a time he did manage to find two small vessels which he used as storage lighters, taking advantage of the good demurrage rates on offer at the time. One was the *James and Mary*, which he bought from someone at York; she had been used in the coal trade to York from the West Riding via the Selby Canal. The other one which he bought from Henry Mason of Hull was a West Country keel, the *Amity*. His brother-in-law, Uncle Billy Jolliffe, owned a 57 feet 6 inches keel called the *Garland*, and they worked the three keels together as lighters, on demurrage most of the time. Early in 1920 the lighterage trade began to ease off and Father sold the *James and Mary*.

In late March, 1920, he loaded a cargo of cement in the *Amity* from G. and T. Earle's Ltd, Wilmington cement works, for Lincoln, and not having a mate he sent a telegram to my mother asking her to put me on the train for Hull. I was then thirteen years and eight months, and should have continued at school until July, but the education authorities were not so strict in those days, so no fuss was made. Father was waiting when the train arrived at Paragon Station. The *Amity* was laid at Hamilton's wharf near Chapman Street bridge over the River Hull, and as the wharf was a good distance from the station Father engaged a hansom cab, the commonest form of transport at that time in Hull. The hansom was entered from the front, and had two half doors for protection; the upper half was open to the weather, and the driver sat at the back in the open, communication with the driver being by means of a trapdoor in the roof. Away we went with a good view of the backside of the horse bobbing up and down, and arrived on board in time for tea. That was the start of a career that was to last for fifty-five years.

At high water on the afternoon tide we went by hand, Father using a stower and me steering, into the lower part of the River Hull, known as the Old Harbour. The following tide we towed up the Trent to Torksey with one of the tugs owned by Thomas Gray and Company, who ran, as I said, a daily service from Hull to Keadby, West Stockwith, Gainsborough, Torksey and Newark. There was a lot of fresh in the Trent and progress was slow above Gainsborough. We had been under way all day, and it was dark before we penned up into the Fossdyke at Torksey. Next morning the wind was fair for Lincoln, and there was enough fresh in the Dyke to make lightening the cargo unnecessary, so we stepped the mast, bent the sail to the yard and got under way. Like many other West Country keels, the *Amity* had only a small rig; when not in use the sail was unbent and put away in the fo'c'sle and the mast unstepped and lashed on the gunwale. We did have sheet rollers, but no tack rollers or leeboards. There was only five foot draught in the Dyke under normal conditions, and if there had not been the extra fresh water we would have had to transship about thirty tons of our cargo into an open lighter, which we would have hired from Jack Kendall of Lincoln; he had a small tug for towing vessels on the Dyke, and a carpenter's yard at Lincoln for building and repairing wooden craft.

The wind was only light but we made Lincoln in the late afternoon, helped by the draw towards Lincoln when we passed Saxilby. The cement was in one-hundredweight jute bags which had to be put ashore and on to the builders' drays by our derrick. Casual labour had to be hired to help with the discharge. When livered we restowed our mast and derrick and towed back to Torksey with Jack Kendall's tug, then up the Trent to Girton with the paddle tug *Robin Hood* to load Trent gravel. The demand for Trent gravel and sand was growing, and to help meet it Tim Tomlinson had placed on station in the Trent near Girton a narrow boat fitted with mast and derrick and a motor winch to heave up the pan from the river bed. Keels could moor alongside and be loaded without the trouble of rigging gear themselves. Frank Thornhill, known to all on the river as Rusty, was in charge of the boat and lived on board the narrow boat, which was later replaced by an old wooden Trent catch, fitted with an upright steam boiler and winch. Tim Tomlinson was the owner and master of the steel keel *Lady Ellen*, built at Watson's Gainsborough shipyard in 1910 for the Trent trade. She was 74 feet long by 15 feet 4 inches by 7 feet 3 inches.

After loading we towed down with the paddle tug *Robin Hood* as far as Torksey, where we transferred to one of the screw tugs to tow to Hull. The *Robin Hood*, a shallow draught tug built of iron on the Thames at Cubitt Town in 1881, was kept on the Torksey to

Newark run. When we arrived at Hull a ready market for the gravel was found with Earle's cement works for twelve shillings (60p) per ton, and we again loaded cement for Lincoln at eleven shillings (55p) per ton. We continued in this trade for about a year. Sometimes our upriver cargo was wheat in eighteen-stone sacks, which we put on to horse-drawn drays with our derrick, and in the winter months we had one or two cargoes of phosphate from Immingham which we loaded overside for the fertilizer works at Lincoln.

Gravelling in the Trent. A steel keel is laying alongside the narrow boat which Tim Tomlinson placed on station near Girton. Humber Keel and Sloop Preservation Society

During May, 1920, we put the *Amity* on Jack Kendall's slip for bottom caulking and were up on the slip when a cloudburst occurred over Louth on the 29th, a Saturday. The town of Louth was badly flooded and the Louth Navigation so badly damaged that it became unusable. I remember this because one or two trips before we had been in company at the gravel beds with the keel *Albatross*, whose master and owner was George Wright of Louth; she was the only keel I had seen hailing from there. My father told me that she usually made about six voyages a year from the Sheffield and South Yorkshire Navigation to the Louth Navigation. Later at Beverley I was to see the billyboy *Swallow* hailing from Louth; she had a cutter rig and was 56 feet by 14 feet 8 inches; her owner and master John Day had his wife aboard with him. Shortly after this he sold her to Albert Leggett of Owston Ferry and retired. Albert used her for a time as a market boat between Hull and Owston Ferry and also as a diver's boat engaged on lifting or blowing up wrecks, and while engaged on salvage operations off Clee Ness, Grimsby, she was run down and sunk by a steam trawler.

Another vessel worth a mention that we used to see on the Trent was the iron sloop *Sarah*, owner and master Dick Cook of

The sloop Sarah, *built at Gainsborough in 1889, at Owston Ferry on the Trent. Her tiny mizzen can be seen; she had also sailed as a keel.* Author's collection

Tetney Haven below Grimsby was the entrance to the Louth Navigation, opened in 1770 and closed by the disastrous floods of May, 1920. The keel by the lock is an old clinker-built one; the only Louth keel I remember was the Albatross.
W. E. R. Hallgarth collection

Owston Ferry, who had both his son and grandson with him as crew. She was 61 feet 6 inches long by 14 feet 4 inches beam. They traded on the rivers in winter and in summer to the Wash ports, often bringing back a cargo of shingle off the beach at Snettisham, near Hunstanton, for Grimsby. When on the Trent she was steered with a tiller, but when in the estuary or on the coast with a wheel. A mizzen mast was stepped on the mainsheet horse stanchion, the sail being sheeted to a bumkin which made her into a yawl, the only vessel I know of to have had this rig.

Snettisham gravel was also brought into Grimsby until about 1926 by the motor vessel *A Triumph* and the steamer *Girton*. The *A Triumph* was built at Thorne in 1925 for the east coast trade with a hull on the lines of the typical Humber keel, 81 feet long, 16 feet beam and 8 feet deep. Her first engine was a diesel of about 100 hp and one of the Barracloughs of Barton her first captain; after him a man named Brown. For the first years of her life she would load cattle food from the mills on the River Hull to Wells and the Wash ports, returning with a load of Snettisham gravel. The *Girton* had been built at Saltney on the Dee in 1915 for the War Department and had been employed taking stores across to France by the Inland Water Transport Division of the Royal Engineers. After the war she was bought by a Hull owner and shortened to suit the Fenland rivers.

During this period in the Trent trade we were able to go home

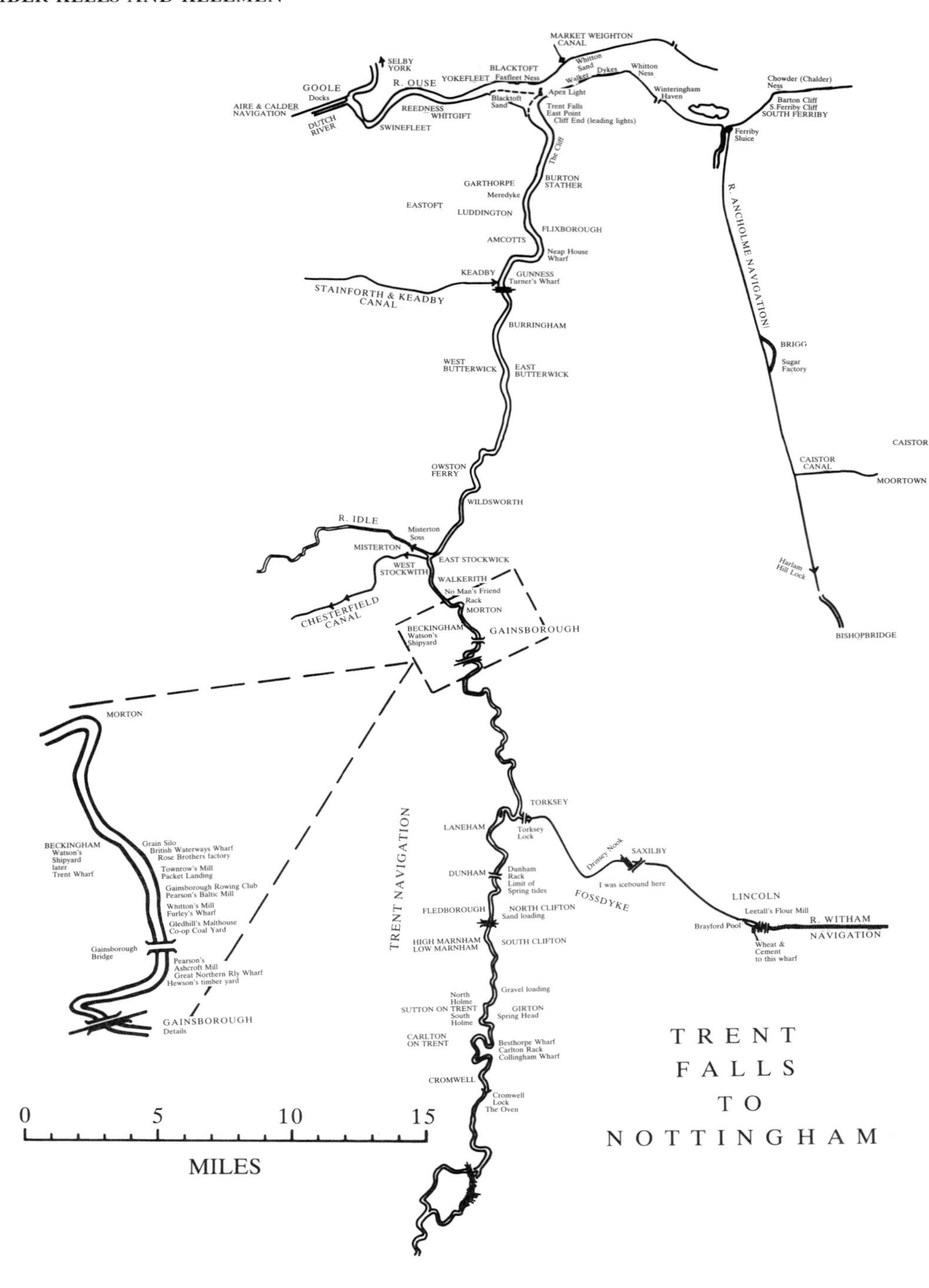
MARKET WEIGHTON CANAL
SELBY
YORK
BLACKTOFT
Whitton Sand
Walker Dykes
Whitton Ness
GOOLE
Docks
R. OUSE
YOKEFLEET
Faxfleet Ness
Apex Light
Blacktoft Sand
Winteringham Haven
Chowder (Chalder) Ness
Barton Cliff
S.Ferriby Cliff
SOUTH FERRIBY
AIRE & CALDER NAVIGATION
REEDNESS
WHITGIFT
Trent Falls
East Point
Cliff End (leading lights)
DUTCH RIVER
SWINEFLEET
Ferriby Sluice
The Cliff
GARTHORPE
BURTON STATHER
Meredyke
EASTOFT
LUDDINGTON
FLIXBOROUGH
AMCOTTS
Neap House Wharf
KEADBY
GUNNESS
Turner's Wharf
STAINFORTH & KEADBY CANAL
R. ANCHOLME NAVIGATION
BURRINGHAM
BRIGG
Sugar Factory
WEST BUTTERWICK
EAST BUTTERWICK
CAISTOR
CAISTOR CANAL
MOORTOWN
OWSTON FERRY
WILDSWORTH
R. IDLE
Misterton Soss
MISTERTON
EAST STOCKWICK
WEST STOCKWITH
WALKERITH
Harlam Hill Lock
No Man's Friend
Rack
MORTON
CHESTERFIELD CANAL
BECKINGHAM
Watson's Shipyard
GAINSBOROUGH
BISHOPBRIDGE
MORTON
TORKSEY
LANEHAM
Torksey Lock
TRENT NAVIGATION
BECKINGHAM
Watson's Shipyard later Trent Wharf
Grain Silo
British Waterways Wharf
Rose Brothers factory
Townrow's Mill
Packet Landing
Gainsborough Rowing Club
Pearson's Baltic Mill
Whitton's Mill
Furley's Wharf
Gledhill's Malthouse
Co-op Coal Yard
Gainsborough Bridge
Pearson's
Ashcroft Mill
Great Northern Rly Wharf
Hewson's timber yard
GAINSBOROUGH
Details
Drinsey Nook
SAXILBY
DUNHAM
Dunham Rack
Limit of Spring tides
I was icebound here
FOSSDYKE
LINCOLN
FLEDBOROUGH
NORTH CLIFTON
Sand loading
Leetall's Flour Mill
Brayford Pool
R. WITHAM NAVIGATION
HIGH MARNHAM
LOW MARNHAM
SOUTH CLIFTON
Wheat & Cement to this wharf
Gravel loading
North Holme
SUTTON ON TRENT
South Holme
GIRTON
Spring Head
CARLTON ON TRENT
Besthorpe Wharf
Carlton Rack
Collingham Wharf
CROMWELL
Cromwell Lock
The Oven
0
5
10
15
MILES
TRENT FALLS TO NOTTINGHAM

only at the weekends. This was easy from Hull because most trains between Hull and Doncaster stopped at Stainforth, though this did mean a one-mile walk from the station to our house, and on Monday morning I had to be up very early to catch the six o'clock train to go on board for work time. When laid at Girton Lane End waiting for a turn to load gravel we had to walk across Sutton Holme, then to Crow Park Station on the main King's Cross to Doncaster line. Often we would arrive at Doncaster to find there was no train to Stainforth for about two hours. This was before the bus service had started to run, so rather than hang about waiting for the train we would set off to walk the seven miles to Stainforth. After walking out of town we went across Wheatley Park to Long Sandall Lock, then down the canal bank to Stainforth. After doing this a few times I bought myself a bike, and during the next seven years I must have ridden hundreds of miles at weekends.

During a period of frost early in 1921 the market for Trent gravel was a bit slow, and one trip we laid in Queen's Dock, Hull, for over a week before we found a sale. When we did secure a customer it was a firm of builders at Beverley. On the afternoon

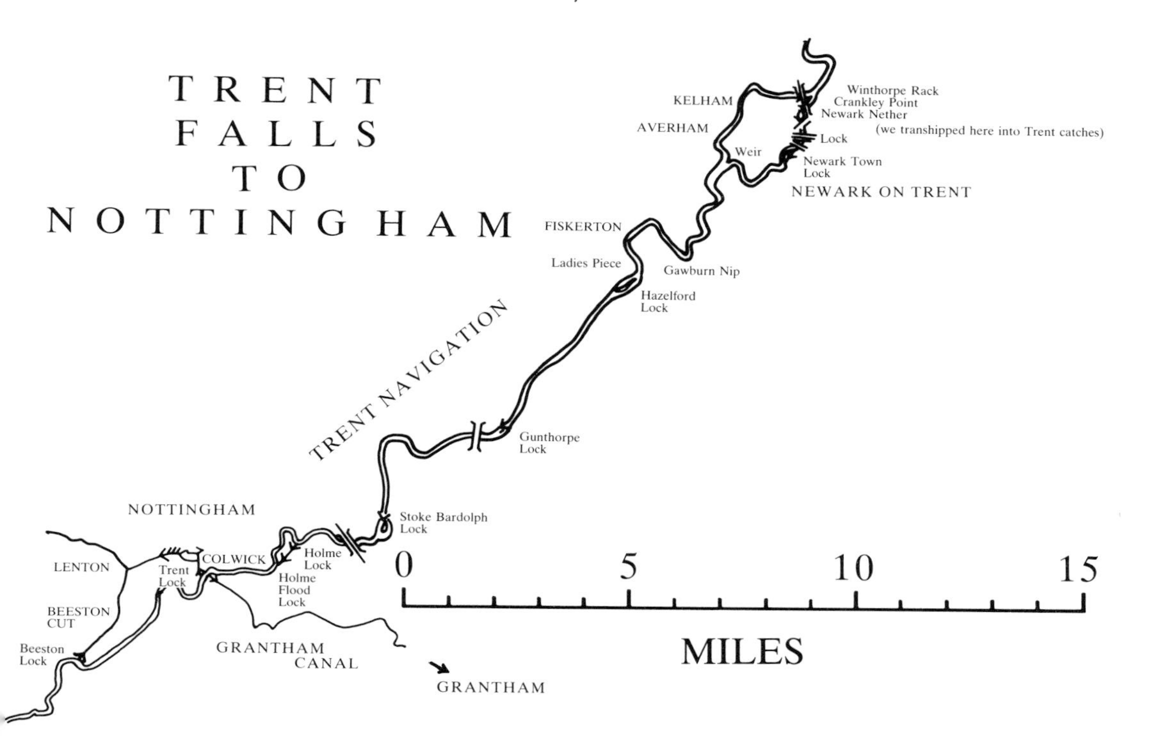

The Sheffield-size steel keel Loxley, *built by Dunston's at Thorne in 1925 for Furley and Company, at Morton Bight on the River Trent just below Gainsborough. She probably left Gainsborough on the flood tide, and by the time she got to Morton Bight it could have been high water slack, so the captain has decided to help her along with the stower. As he gets round the bight he will come into No Man's Friend, where the wind will be against him; he will have to lower the mainsail and, as there will not at this stage be an ebb strong enough to drive, he will have to keep close to the bank and make some headway with the stower.* Humber Keel and Sloop Preservation Society

tide we penned out into the River Hull and dropped up to Stoneferry, where we swung ready for the next tide. At Beverley the gravel had to be filled into baskets, which were then hove out with our derrick, placed on a running barrow and wheeled along a gantry to the waiting horse-drawn carts. That was my first voyage to Beverley.

Soon after that the *Amity* was sold to Ella Pettinger, a tug broker with Thomas Gray and Company, so we had a spell at home looking for another vessel. After a week or two Ellis Naylor put the *Fanny* up for sale, as he had taken a shore job; Father went to see him and bought her back from him. She was laid at Thorne, and it was arranged that we would go to fetch her home to Stainforth, so next morning we got on our bikes and went to Thorne to find Billy Caldicott waiting for us; he had come from Butterwick to buy the *Fanny* from Ellis Naylor and found her already sold.

I went on board to make her ready for the trip to Stainforth while Father and Billy Caldicott adjourned to the *Canal Tavern* to talk things over. After about three hours Father came out to tell me that he had sold her to Caldicott for a good profit, so I went home while Caldicott and Father went back into the pub to complete the deal. When Father arrived home he told me that Caldicott was

changing the *Fanny's* rig from keel to sloop to run a weekly market trip between Hull, Burringham, Keadby, and Crowle wharf and would offer me the mate's berth when she was ready. The wages would be a pound a week all found; most people at that time would pay only ten shillings to fifteen shillings (50p–75p) and all found.

The Galatea *at York about 1910 when she was sloop rigged and owned by her skipper, George Brackenbury, who is seen on board with his wife. Father bought her in 1921 and soon afterwards changed her to keel rig.* Humber Keel and Sloop Preservation Society

But before she was ready Father bought the wooden Sheffield-sized sloop *Galatea* from George Brackenbury of Thorne, who was going to retire, with the result that I did not after all take up my job with Caldicott. The *Galatea* was laid at Docking Hill, Doncaster, with a cargo of wheat for Thomas Hanley and Sons, and when it was her turn to discharge I went over to give a hand, then helped to haul her by hand to Thorne so that George Brackenbury and his wife could take off their personal gear. George had already disposed of the sloop gear before Father bought her, so after a few voyages we decided to re-rig her as a keel. We went to Worfolk's yard at Stainforth to have the main beam moved aft a few feet and have the winch posts and rollers fitted; these were all made at the yard by the carpenters and yard blacksmiths. A mast was ordered from Charles Pearson, mast- and blockmaker of Hull, and a mainsail was made for us at Keadby sail loft.

The *Galatea* was iron fastened, so while we were at the yard we put her in dry dock to have a look at her bottom. Some shutts were taken up and a few seam spikes were drifted out for examination. They were found to be badly corroded; next we took all the shutts up so that we could drift out all the old spikes and replace them. The new ones were hand made by the yard blacksmith out of square rod iron, a size larger than the old ones so that they would fit tight in the old holes. If the *Galatea* had been fastened in the old way with trenails the fastenings would have lasted the whole life of the ship.

Now that we had a larger ship we were in a better way to accept almost any cargo on offer, and over the next seven years while I remained mate in the *Galatea* we traded to most places on the Humber and connecting waterways. Once when we were engaged to load phosphate overside at Immingham for Lincoln the stevedore made us wait until he had put a quantity on the railway, because the factory at Lincoln was in danger of becoming short. The broker asked us to make the best of our way to Lincoln once we had finished loading, and we arrived at Lincoln for work time on a Saturday morning. When Father went into the office to report our arrival, the works foreman would not believe we were there until he came out to see for himself; the rail wagons which had loaded before us had not arrived, and he was so desperate for the phosphate that he arranged for us to start livering on Sunday morning, something rarely thought of in those days. We had about five tons left to get out on the Monday morning when the railway wagons that had had a two-day start of us arrived in the works siding.

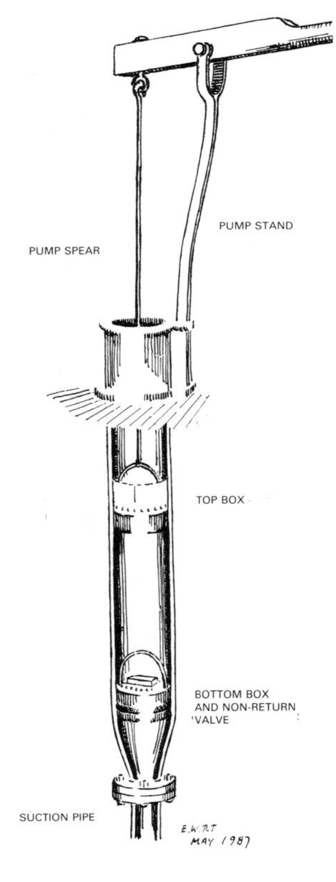

One of my favourite voyages was to load bulk wheat direct from the ships at Hull for Hudson Ward's flour mill at Goole, where we would load from a ship a cargo of strawboard or newsprint for transshipment at Newark into open Trent catches for Nottingham; wide vessels could not at that time go further than Newark Nether Lock. Transshipment was made by a crane barge coming alongside, with the catch laying alongside the crane barge. After the Nether Lock was built in 1926 we could go up Newark Dyke and through the Town Lock by taking one leeboard on deck; the tugs only went to Nether Lock, so we had to have a horse to pull us up the Dyke. After livering at Newark we usually returned to Hull or Grimsby with Trent sand or gravel. Once only we loaded at Newark some kind of mineral for Sissons' paint works at Stoneferry, Hull. At Grimsby we livered the gravel at the river head by our own derrick. Sometimes we would see the *A Triumph* or the *Girton* livering Snettisham gravel; they did not work as hard as we did, as the *Girton* was able to use her steam winch and the *A Triumph* had a small motor winch.

There was always plenty of water to pump out when loading

Trent sand or gravel direct from the river bed, all by hand. The pumping had to be done at least once every twenty-four hours as the water drained from the cargo and through the shutts into the ship's bottom. To help the drainage we lifted some of the limber boards at each end of the hold and raised them by placing a piece of wood on the floor timber top; then after putting the board down on to the wood, we would cover the whole limber with at least two hessian sacks. This arrangement helped the drainage of water and prevented any sand getting into the ship's bottom. One time at Grimsby we seemed to be pumping more water out than usual, and as it continued to flow to the pump after the cargo was out, it became apparent that we had a leaky ship. We lifted all the limber boards and found the place where the water was running, from the starboard bilge to the limber channel; it was only slight, and a bucket of ashes emptied under the bilge soon stopped the flow. Our next cargo was to be a cargo of bulk wheat ex ship King George Dock, Hull, for Doncaster mills. On arrival at Hull we found we had two or three days to wait for a turn, so as the tides

Several keels can be seen in this view of King George Dock, Hull, in the nineteen-thirties. We loaded many cargoes of bulk grain from steamers in this dock for mills at Doncaster and elsewhere. Hull Town Docks Museum

were taking off we decided to beach the *Galatea* near No 7 quay in King George Dock; the south-west corner of the dock was at that time unfinished and at neap tides dried out as the dock water level became lower when ships were penning in and out; it filled again when the tides began to make.

There was a hard canch about sixty feet off No 7 quay with deep water alongside. We put her on this and spent some time looking for the leak, but could not find anything that needed attention. When we loaded we had to stop the leak each day by a bucket of ashes or sawdust. After we livered at Doncaster we went down to Thorne, where Staniland's had a dry dock empty. After docking we spent two days looking for the cause of the leak, but it could not be found until the timber began to dry out on the third day, when we discovered the cause, a dead knot in one of the bilge planks. We had to bore this out and plug up the hole; then to make it safe a graving piece was fitted over the end of the plug so that it could not come out. Small graving pieces like this were referred to as dominoes by both carpenters and keelmen.

Before we had left Hull arrangements had been made to load coal at Kilnhurst after our Doncaster cargo, so the first priority after seeing the *Galatea* settled on the blocks in dry dock was to send our laying on note off to the colliery; this was a letter from the yard manager certifying that we were in dry dock at their yard which would claim us a ready turn on arrival at the pit staithe under a long-standing arrangement between the keel owners and

The West Country keel Getrude *at York about 1910 with her owner-skipper Alf Mullett and his wife on board. Built at Mirfield, she was rather high for a West Country boat. She had loaded 460 quarters of wheat ex-ship at Hull for Leatham's mills.* Humber Keel and Sloop Preservation Society

colliery owners, designed to help anyone who had to lay up for repairs.

When we came out of dry dock the wind was westerly, so a horse was hired to haul us to Kilnhurst. While on passage up the canal the sailing gear was made ready for putting on shore at Harry Scarborough's crane at Mexborough, the lowest of the three privately owned cranes here for storing masts and sails; our mast and sail had to be put ashore to allow us to go under the staithe at Kilnhurst. We also had to take down the winch posts and sheet rollers to pass under Pasture Bridge at Mexborough and Pottery Bridge at Swinton; they had subsided through coal being mined from under them. Work for the day had finished when we arrived at the pit, which made us first turn next day. The staithe men only worked the morning shift 6 am to 2 pm, the loading rate being three keels per day. When we finished loading, it was my job to go to the pit office for the loading note. With the note I received half a crown (12½p) allowance; this was customary at all the pits in this area. I think it must have been intended to buy beer to slake the dust; it was usually given to the staithe men. On our loading note the coal was described as Best Steam Hards; we were provided with two copies, one for ourselves and one for the toll office at Swinton, the canal dues being charged to the account of the coal factor.

BOTTOM BOAT Dec 20th 1806
Deliverd to William Batty for & on Acct. of Himself Nineteen & Half wagg. of Messrs. Smithson & Co. Haigh Moor Coals by me
19½ Waggons James Hodgshon

A loading note recording that nineteen and a half waggons of coal had been loaded into William Batty's boat on 20th December, 1806.
Hull Town Docks Museum

Our sailing gear was picked up at Mexborough and the horse marine paid off. On the top pound between Mexborough Low Lock and Conisbrough Lock there were three railway bridges and one footbridge, so when we sailed down from Mexborough the mast was usually lowered at Mexborough Low Lock and left down until we got to Conisbrough railway bridge. The mate would haul from the bank with a canvas seal bent on to a cotton line three-quarters of an inch in circumference and thirty fathoms long, made fast to a handspike placed in the socket of the windlass barrel. The captain would assist with a stower as well as steering.

The wind being west, we had to lower the sail at Hexthorpe rack and launch through with the stowers. We moored below

Doncaster Lock for the night, and were under way early the next morning to pass through Gas House rack before the wind freshened. We also had to lower sails and mast at Barmby Dun rack and haul through by hand. The cogboat was picked up at Bramwith Lock. We moored at Stainforth top yard in the early afternoon and had the rest of the day at home. Next morning after an early breakfast we moored under the crane to ship our leeboards, then sailed down to Keadby in about seven hours and went out into the Trent shortly before high water on the afternoon tide. After about two hours' sailing we brought up in Cliff End Roads, in a good position for sailing down the Humber on the next high water.

All the time that I was mate in the *Galatea* Father sailed if the wind was fair; in strong head winds it was better to tow rather than risk damage to sails and gear. Sometimes we would be unlucky, and after starting with a fair wind would have the wind change. One time we left Alexandra Dock, Hull, on a hot summer day with a light wind from the north-east, but by the time we reached the top end of Hull Roads we had a thunderstorm and the wind flew round to south, then west, and freshened. Before high water the middle seam of the mainsail had split up to the reef band; we only fetched Winteringham Haven that tide, and spent half of the ebb repairing the mainsail. The towage service was cheap and was used frequently by both keels and sloops, this being encouraged by most of the keel owning firms, who would pay the captain one-third of all towing on the tideway; often when a cargo was wanted urgently they would pay the full cost of towing.

As I said, trade picked up after the war and there was a shortage of craft and men; better money could be earned on lighterage than on the upriver trade, which only made the shortage worse. The Ashcroft and Baltic Oil and Cake Mills at Gainsborough owned by Pearsons were busy and we had a few cargoes of cotton seed and linseed for them. I did not care for this trade, because cotton seed was loaded in bulk, a dirty job, and with it being so light it was necessary to load above the coamings to get a cargo big enough to make a profit, making much extra work; boards had to be fixed on the coamings to hold the bulk in place. At the Ashcroft Mill discharging was by elevator. This was easy with linseed, but hard work with cotton seed as the fluffy lint on the seed prevented it from running and every bit of seed had to be trimmed to the elevator. At the Baltic Mill it was worse, there being no elevator; discharging was by hoist, and the seed had first to be filled by hand with a scuttle into two bushel canvas sacks with brass eyelets for attaching to the hoist hook. The empty sacks were returned into the hold down a canvas sleeve.

Once after livering at the Baltic we towed up to Girton with the

Bill Dean and his wife bow-hauling the steel keel Danum, *owned by Thomas Hanley, the Doncaster flour millers. Both wear the canvas "seal" or harness round the shoulders to which the man'sline or hauling line is secured. So far as I know this is the only photograph of man-haulage of a keel.* Yorkshire Post

steam packet *Essex*, an old iron vessel built at Sunderland in 1879; she had a steam winch for working the derrick, and had her own gear for dredging the gravel. After loading the *Galatea* with gravel she loaded herself and we towed with her down to Hull. The *Essex* was about eighty feet long by about sixteen feet beam and six feet deep; she was registered at London and owned by Joe Tomlinson, who worked her with Harry Paling as mate and engineer. Known as "Hooky Joe" because he had lost one arm and wore a hook on his stump, he had been a captain with Gray's tugs; his last command with them was the steam tug *Dalesman*. His new venture did not last long and he went ashore to keep a pub at Gainsborough; I believe it was called the *Half Moon*. Later Watson's, the shipyard on the Beckingham side of the Trent opposite Gainsborough, built him a dumb craft for the Gainsborough trade named the *Demo*; Uncle Harry Schofield went to take charge of her from the yard and worked her on thirds for a time.

Later in 1921 we loaded our last cargo of Trent sand by hand after having been to Lincoln with wheat for Leetalls. When we finished discharging in Lincoln we dropped the derrick, set the mainsail and sailed to Torksey in time to tow up with the paddle tug *Robin Hood* on the Friday morning, picking up Cook Williamson and his gang as we went by Laneham. He told us that we should find some good clean sand below Fledborough railway bridge, so we towed to just below the bridge and prepared the gear while Cook Williamson went out in our boat with a stower and prodded around on the bottom until he was satisfied that he had found sand in sufficient quantity to load us. It was essential that the sand be clean and suitable for the building trade or we might find that we could not sell the cargo; or if we already had a buyer he might refuse to accept delivery. This cargo was for a builders' merchant at Rotherham. We made a start loading on the Saturday morning and by mid-afternoon had loaded about seventy-five tons. The men then went ashore to go to their homes at Laneham for the weekend and I went to North Clifton to do some shopping.

Sunday was spent cooking and pumping out the water that had drained out of the sand. On the Monday morning we finished

Horse marines were a tough breed, driving their horses twenty or more miles a day, starting at five o'clock in the morning. One such was Tom Rawnsley of Mexborough, seen here at Sprotbrough. Humber Keel and Sloop Preservation Society

Two keels at Furley's wharf, Gainsborough. The inside ship, with her main yard with mainsail furled on it topped up in the port shrouds out of the way of the steam crane, is discharging a cargo, possibly of bagged grain. The outer vessel is awaiting her turn.
Humber Keel and Sloop Preservation Society

by high water, Cook Williamson and his gang transferred their gear to the keel *Pioneer* and we got under way with a southerly wind. As we came in sight of Herman Chapman's bungalow on the Trent bank at Torksey we shortened sail to give him time to come off to us in his boat to collect the river dues and royalties that were due to the Trent Navigation Company for the dredged sand. We entered the canal at Keadby on the Tuesday morning ebb, having come from Butterwick on the high water. A telegram was sent to George Eastwood, the horse marine at Rotherham, to inform him that we were sailing up the canal and would require his services when available; if he was already engaged in a job his wife would telephone to one of the locks and ask the lock keeper to pass on the message. We managed to sail to Stainforth by nightfall and George Eastwood arrived soon after with his horse. After stabling and feeding the horse and himself, he and my father managed to find time to visit the *Fox Inn* for a pint and a hand or two of dominoes, yet by four o'clock the next morning George was on his way to the stable to give the horse a feed before starting work; he was taking the line by five o'clock. We then started breakfast so that George would be able to have his from Bramwith Lock to Northfield Bridge (Gravel Hill Bridge to keelmen). Good progress was made and we moored at Rotherham at about eight o'clock in the evening. The builders' merchant's yard was about half way between Rotherham road bridge and Greasbrough road bridge. Three lime kilns were burning; the limestone was brought up the navigation in an old open boat from Levitt Hagg Quarry near Warmsworth. There was no crane on the wharf; all materials had to be moved by hand. Our mast had to be put ashore as we came up, so we used the mast and other gear supplied by the builder; Father and myself filled the baskets, and casual labour was employed to heave and wheel.

When the sand was out we went down by hand haulage to Aldwarke coal staithe to load gas coal for Beverley Corporation gasworks. The staithe was in the pound between Eastwood Top and Eastwood Low Locks, which was convenient. Aldwarke Colliery was an old one, and years of mining had resulted in the surrounding land and buildings subsiding by several feet, so it was impossible for a vessel to put the staithe chute over the coaming until the water level had been lowered. The land continued to subside over the years until the staithe had to be abandoned; the coal was then sent by rail to Roundwood staithe for shipment. There was no machinery at Aldwarke staithe; as at Kilnhurst rail tracks were sited so that the wagons would run on and off by gravity after being started by levering a crowbar under the wheels. When the wagons were over the hopper on the staithe the bottom doors were opened; then the remainder of the coal was trimmed out by hand. The foreman's name was Wood; he lived within fifty yards of the staithe, and near his house was a brick building with cooking and washing facilities for the use of the keelmen.

On the day that we loaded George Eastwood arrived about half an hour before we finished, which allowed him to give the horse a nose-tin full of corn before he had to start work. When we had covered up and cleared the decks I went to the staithe foreman and he gave me the wagon tickets and a note of numbers to take to the weigh office at the pit, which was near Parkgate, while the check weighman gave me a consignment note and a copy for the dues office at Doncaster Lock. In the meantime the ship would be on the way down, and I set off to walk to Aldwarke Lock to meet her. We collected our traps (mast, mainsail and yard) at Mexborough. As the wind was not very favourable we kept the marine with us until we reached Doncaster, where we stopped for the night. Next day we sailed to Stainforth by about noon, having had to haul by hand through Gas House rack at Doncaster and Barmby Dun rack. As was usual on the way down, we tied up at Stainforth until breakfast the next morning, when we got under way to catch the afternoon high water at Keadby. We were fortunate to have spring tides and were able to enter the Beck straight away on arrival at Beverley; if they had been neap tides we might have had to wait several days. In dry summers it was sometimes not possible to navigate right up to Beverley on neaps until, as we say, the tides started to mend.

We tied up at the Crane Hill near the Gashouse steam crane, the only one there was at Beverley for discharging vessels. The Gashouse was on Hull Road about four hundred yards away and coal was conveyed between the two points in horse-drawn carts which would hold about twenty-seven to thirty hundredweights of gas coal. We reported our arrival and arrangements were made with the carting contractors to start livering the next morning at 7.30 am, starting time at Beverley for most day workers.

At 6 am we heard the crane man come to put a fire under the boiler to raise steam. By 7.30 two carts had arrived and another was on the way. The first of the two coal pans in use was lowered on to the coal in the forehold; these pans were circular with a flat bottom and a bow bar for lifting them, and they could be tipped when

A keel horse-hauling down the River Don past the lime kilns at Levitt Hagg, between Conisbrough and Sprotbrough. The horse line is slacked off for a vessel going upriver to pass over it. I cannot say what the cargo is, but it is lighter than coal; the hatches are raised in the after hold. Sheffield Library

hung over the cart. Gas coal is lighter and more bulky than steam hards, and before shipment it is cracked down at the pit into pieces of about two inches square. The *Galatea* was full to the hatches with about 103 tons and it would take about an hour of hard digging to get down to the shutts. With steam coal the skirt, the bottom part of the cargo, would have been only about three feet up the bulkhead with that weight, and unloading we would have been down on to the shutts sooner. Once on the bottom the work became easier; we could two-thirds fill the pan by scooping straight off the heap, then top up by picking up the coal from the shutts with the square-mouth shovel. A round-mouth shovel was used for digging and scooping.

After every third cart we would have a short break until the next one returned. At 9.30 am we had a twenty-minute break for lowance (it would be called a tea break today). No carts were loaded after about 11.30 in the forenoon to give the carter time to feed his horse and himself. Work started again at 1 pm and continued until 4.30 pm. There was no lowance break in the afternoon. About seventy tons was discharged on the first day and the remainder was out by noon on the second day.

Beverley Beck in the early nineteen-thirties looking towards the head, with Crane Hill and Baker's and Lee Smith's mill on the left. For this mill I unloaded coal and various oil-producing seeds for the making of cattle food. The steel keel Fido *was owned by a local partnership; at this time she was fully powered.* Author's collection

Beverley and Elsewhere 7

BEVERLEY BECK used to be a tidal creek off the River Hull running for three-quarters of a mile up to Beverley. It has been navigable since 1344 and has long been under the care of Beverley Corporation, who did some repair work in the early eighteenth century. The Beck joins the Hull at Grovehill, where a lock was built in 1802, and rebuilt in 1958. Traffic held up in spite of the opening of the Hull and Bridlington Railway in 1846 and the Beck was still busy in the early nineteen-twenties. At that time almost all the house coal on sale in the town was brought from the West Riding collieries by keels and sloops and there were five coal merchants with warehouses on the Beckside, able to take delivery straight from the vessels. On the north side were Alf Owen, Robert Clark, and George Welburn; on the south Ernest Wilson and the Hull and East Riding Co-operative Society. The coal was filled into baskets, then hove out by hand with the ship's derrick, placed on a running barrow and wheeled on a plank on trestles across the road into the warehouse. All the warehouses on the south side had an upper floor which could be used to store grain from the farms until this could be loaded into keels; there was a spout built into the wall, on to which could be fitted an extension to carry the grain over the roadway into the ship's hold.

Major coal users in the nineteen-twenties were the tanners Richard Hodgson and Sons Ltd, who received up to five cargoes of steam hards a week for use at the tanyard and factory in Flemingate; at that time it came from Manvers Main and Kilnhurst collieries. This, too, had to be discharged by hand with a derrick. A plank was placed from the hatches on to a trestle, so that the baskets could be wheeled on the barrow and tipped into horse-drawn carts; Richard Hodgson and Sons had their own horses and carts and also employed others. When large consignments of tanning materials were arriving they would have as many as five gangs working at once on the Beck discharging vessels. There were five carting contractors living near Beckside and making a living by carting cargoes to and from keels; they were George Lount, Alex Hamilton, George Oldfield, John Palmer and Harry Meadley.

Barker's and Lee Smith at the Beckside oil mill were receiving a cargo of coal about every five or six weeks by keel from Kilnhurst Colliery, and in the season all their oil seeds were brought up the

The steam trawler Ontario *was built at the Grovehill shipyard at Beverley in 1895 of iron for the Hull Steam Fishing and Ice Co. Ltd. She is seen here alongside the shipyard wharf in the later stages of construction.* Simpson, Beverley

river by keel after loading direct from the ships in Hull Docks. They had an elevator for discharging the seeds, but the coal had to be discharged by basket and barrow in the usual way. After the seed had been crushed the cake went direct to the farms, often by the farms' own horse-drawn wagons, and the oil from the seed was shipped out by keel in steel casks weighing, when full, about fifteen hundredweights. These were rolled out of the mill on to the wharf, then loaded in the keel by a hand-operated crane. One keel was constantly employed in this trade, returning with the empty casks.

The Queensgate whitening works received their coal by keel, discharged by hand with a derrick in the usual way into carts at the brick wharf, while the gasworks were taking about three cargoes of coal a fortnight. On most working days there would be one or more vessels loading or discharging at the Crane Hill on South Beckside, besides those at other berths. Hodgson's used the hand cranes for discharging wet hides brought from the Hull Town Docks by keel; they came to Hull in the weekly steamers from London, Yarmouth, Newcastle, Aberdeen and Dundee.

Tanning extract and tallow in barrels was loaded for transshipment in Hull Docks and the empty barrels were landed at the Crane Hill on return. We once loaded the *Galatea* there with cow hair for transshipment in Railway Dock, Hull. We had fifteen tons, full to the hatches! At Grovehill the Tyger manure works was

William Henry Harrison and employees of one of the Beverley carpenter's yards. The keel is the Jane & Maria. Humber Keel and Sloop Preservation Society

receiving phosphate and pyrites by keel, and after treatment the burnt ore was sent to West Stockwith chemical works by keel*. In the spring of 1922 we loaded at this factory a full cargo of fertilizer for farms near the Trent side at Garthorpe, Luddington, Amcotts, Owston Ferry and Wildsworth; this was discharged by our own derrick into farm wagons with the help of the farm hands.

At Grovehill there were two shipyards, one on each side of the river. That on the west bank, Cook, Welton and Gemmell, took their coal from an inland pit; it was carried on the railway to Keadby, then shipped into keels for onward carriage to Beverley, where it was delivered to the shipyard. Their main work was building trawlers, coasters, tugs, lightships and small tankers. On the east bank was the yard of Joseph Scarr, builder of steel keels and other small craft; he also had a slip to haul out vessels for repairs.

Just inside the Beck were two carpenter's yards, each with a dry dock. That near the lock, with a frontage to both Beck and river, was worked by Edwin Harrison and his two sons Teddy and Tom; they employed three or four carpenters and labourers. The one to the west of Barmston Drain was worked by three brothers,

Pinnock Tyger had used the building as a paint factory before it became a manure works.

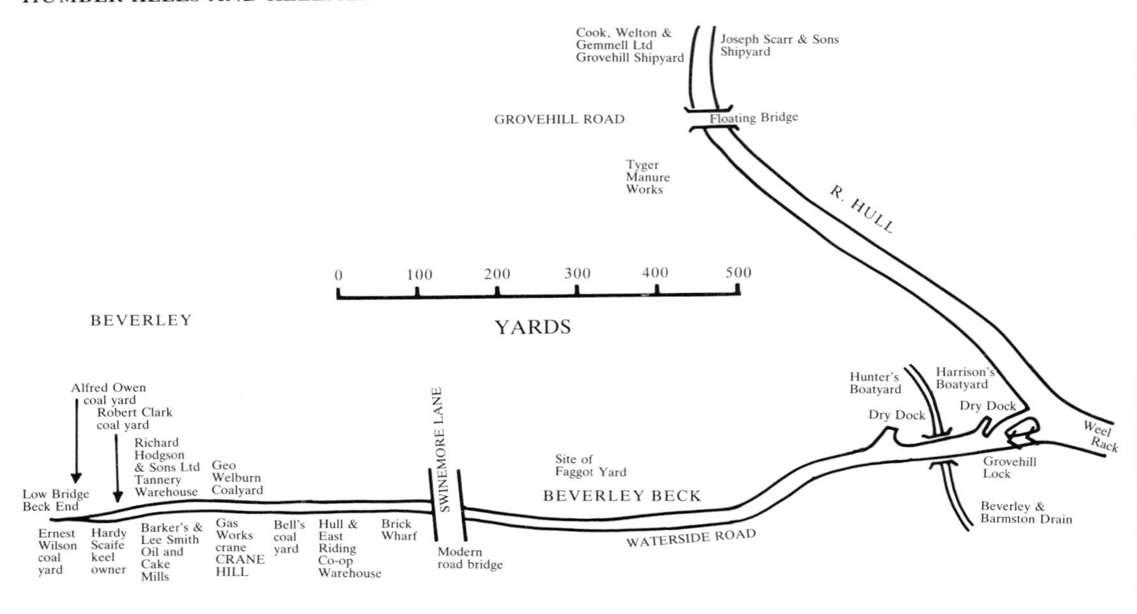

BEVERLEY BECK

William, Harry and Jack Hunter, who during the period 1920–1938 built two wooden keel hulls. The first was to the order of Fred Hall, a Hull lighter owner; named *Hall's Avance*, she was a little larger than Sheffield size and was fitted with one of the early diesel engines and a small fore-and-aft rig. She made a few voyages to Wells and the Wash ports, but the engine gave much trouble and she had to be towed in at least once. After a time her rig was taken out and she was put on the Hull to Leeds run, carrying timber and towing timber lighters. The other hull, after standing on the stocks part-built for several years, was finished for the London and North Eastern Railway and used as a dumb lighter in the Hull–New Holland cargo trade. When that service finished during the 1939–45 War she was bought by Albert Barrass of Thorne, who named her *Zelda* and fitted her with a 21 hp Lister diesel engine, using her for carrying coal from Denaby to Flixborough.

There were several keel owners and three sloop owners in Beverley, most of them living within easy walking distance of the Beck. Many Beverley keels were only fifty-seven feet in length, enabling them to use the Dearne and Dove Canal to fetch coal from pits in that area; they could also use the Calder and Hebble to take barley to Mirfield.

One Beverley owner was Jack Armstrong, who in the

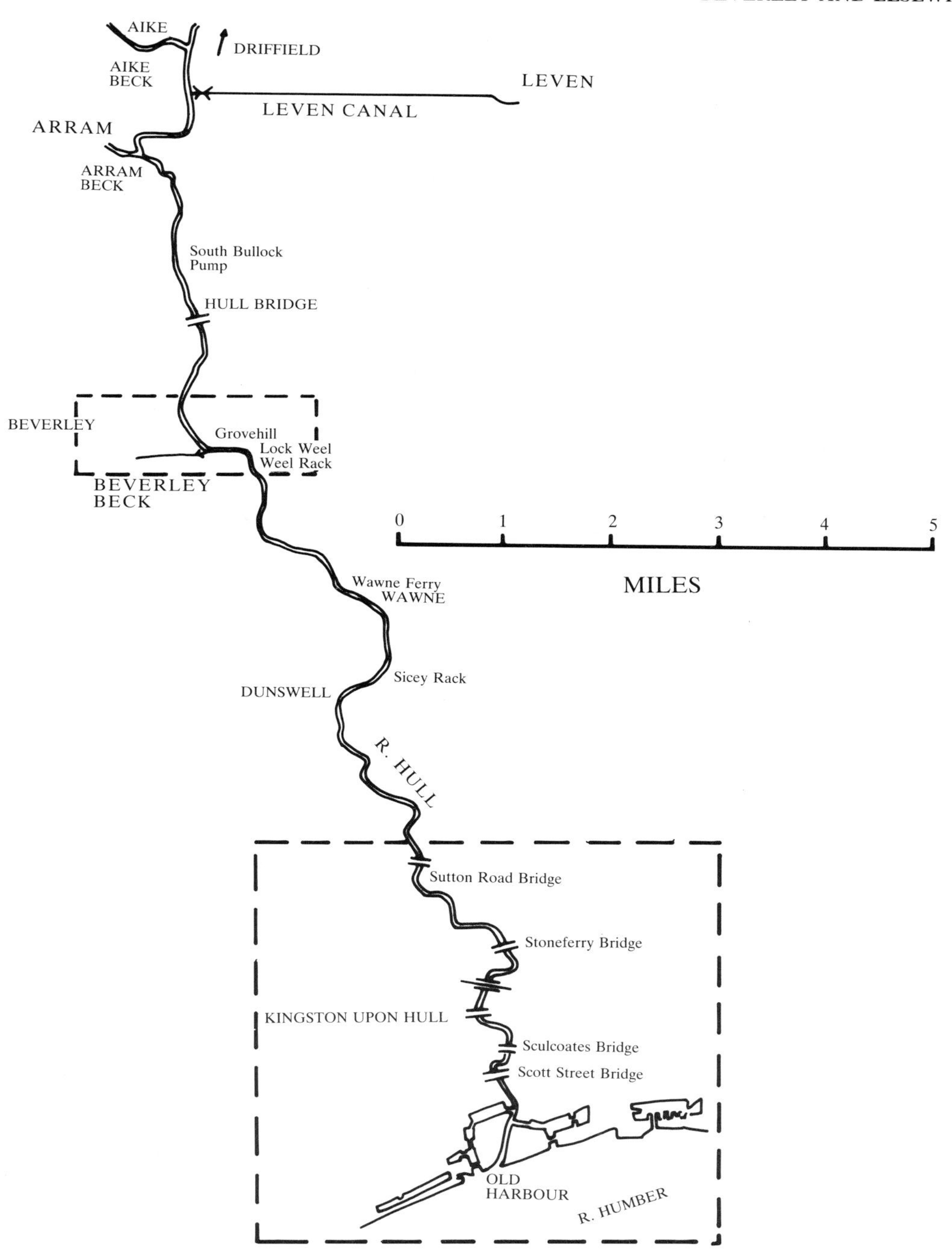
AIKE
DRIFFIELD
AIKE BECK
LEVEN
LEVEN CANAL
ARRAM
ARRAM BECK
South Bullock Pump
HULL BRIDGE
BEVERLEY
Grovehill
Lock Weel
Weel Rack
BEVERLEY BECK
0
1
2
3
4
5
MILES
Wawne Ferry
WAWNE
Sicey Rack
DUNSWELL
R. HULL
Sutton Road Bridge
Stoneferry Bridge
KINGSTON UPON HULL
Sculcoates Bridge
Scott Street Bridge
OLD HARBOUR
R. HUMBER

nineteen-twenties had three keels, the *Mayflower*, *Friends* and *Jessie*. Jack Armstrong himself worked the *Mayflower*, one of the early iron vessels and, like many other Beverley vessels, of suitable dimensions for using the Leven Canal and the Driffield Navigation; he employed her between Hull and Beverley to carry cotton seed and linseed to Barker's mill. The *Friends*, an iron Sheffield-size keel and a good carrier but not one of the best to sail, was also in the same trade. Stan Simpson tried her for a year or two after being demobilized from the Navy but then left to be a lighterman for the Olympia Cake and Oil Mills at Selby; later he became master of their steam tug, the *Robbie*, towing lighters between Hull and Selby. After Stan left "Yankee" Tom Gillyon took charge of her, stopping with her until his retirement. George Porter was master of the *Jessie*, a small wooden keel whose job was to take the casks of oil extracted from the seed down to Hull from Barker's mill and to bring back the empties.

Another Beverley keelman was George Armstrong, master of a small wooden keel named the *Mary Jane* in which he traded to Driffield more than to Beverley. Jack Porter's keel, the *Olive*, was Sheffield length, 61 feet 6 inches, and Driffield beam, 14 feet 6 inches, built of steel. He worked her with his wife as mate, and some casual labour when loading and livering, carrying coal from Keadby to Beverley for both the Co-op and the shipyard of Cook, Welton and Gemmell, and taking any other cargo on offer if time allowed. Jack was in charge of the runner crews when new vessels were being moved down river to Hull for fitting out. Ernest Porter had the steel keel *Resolute*, trading anywhere work was offered. She was later sold to someone in Hull, re-rigged as a sloop and put in the freshwater sand trade, dredging her own cargo from the bed of the Ouse at Hook or Clot Hall or from the Trent near Meredyke, and Ernest then went to take charge of the keel *Hope* for the SLD Market Boat Company of Flixborough*. They had bought her from a Thorne owner, and after a few months re-rigged her as a sloop. He stopped with her until he retired, trading between Hull and Neap House wharf on the Trent.

Charlie Peck was much overweight; round about twenty stone. By the nineteen-twenties he was retired, and his daughter Eva, who had been mate with him on the *George and Eva*, was Mrs Day; she later became a Beverley councillor. One of Charlie's six sons, Hardy, took over the *George and Eva*, a small wooden vessel nearing the end of her useful life, on being demobbed from the Navy, but was finding the going a bit rough. Before the 1914–18 War it had been possible to make a good living with her carrying imported pit props from Hull to the various collieries in the West Riding and

* I was told that SLD were the initials of the three partners' surnames, Sheffield, Lloyd and Didby.

returning with coal to Beverley, but in the nineteen-twenties the competition from the railway made it impossible for the keels to make a profit.

Another of Charlie Peck's sons, Jack, was master of the sloop *Mafeking*, a wooden vessel owned by the SLD Company and working as a market boat between Hull and Neap House wharf. A third, Ted, was owner and master of the *Ivanhoe*, a steel vessel at first under the keel rig; later he changed her to sloop rig and put her in the market boat trade with the same SLD company that owned the *Mafeking* and *Hope*. Tom, the youngest son, was making

This sloop lying at Hull Bridge on the River Hull between Hull and Beverley sets a tall, narrow squaresail. A derrick is rigged in a strop on the mast for unloading. Hull Town Docks Museum

a living on the Beckside, filling out cargoes of coal and purchasing vessels between Hull and Beverley. The other son, George, had early in life joined the customs service and was an officer on King George Dock at Hull.

"Commerce" Peck, a cousin of Charlie, was baptized John Thomas but his Christian names were rarely used; the family had once owned the keel *Commerce* and John was stuck with this name. He had had to take charge of his mother's keel the *Onward*, a Sheffield-size keel built of wood, when his father drowned in Hull Town Docks, and was trading to Leeds and Wakefield with malting barley and general cargo, returning with house coal from Parkhill Colliery, near Wakefield, for Robert Clark at Beverley. When "Commerce's" mother died there was some outstanding loan on her estate and the keel had to be sold, but he then found the keel *Warrior*, a Sheffield-size vessel built of wood by Richard Dunston for George Lawrence of Thorne; her name was changed to *Pride*. "Commerce" had only one in the family, a son named Fred, who was left with his grandmother to go to school; after leaving school he had three or four years with his father as mate, then joined Jack Peck as mate on the sloop *Mafeking*, becoming master when Jack retired.

Jim Owen had sold his keel and was working for Tom Fletcher and Sons of Hull, trading to Wakefield with wheat for the flour mill there, and loading gas coal at Whitwood basin for Hull gasworks as return cargo. At the time, none of Tom Fletcher's craft carried sailing gear as they relied on the towage service of the Goole and Hull Steam Towing Company and the daily service of

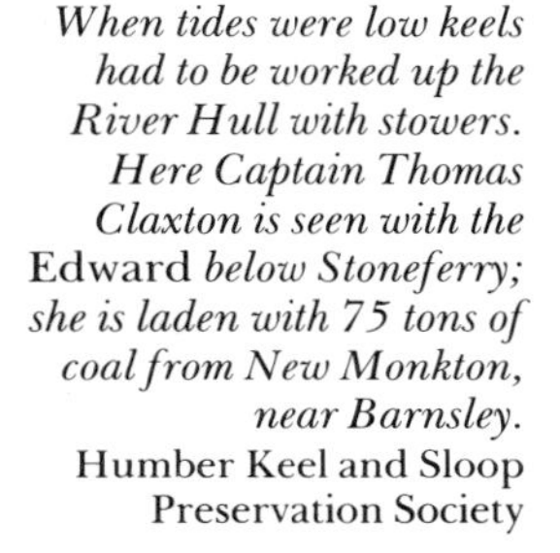

When tides were low keels had to be worked up the River Hull with stowers. Here Captain Thomas Claxton is seen with the Edward *below Stoneferry; she is laden with 75 tons of coal from New Monkton, near Barnsley.*
Humber Keel and Sloop Preservation Society

David Holgate in 1906 with the many trophies he had won at the various aquatic sports events.
Humber Keel and Sloop Preservation Society

the Aire and Calder Navigation tugs between Goole and Wakefield.

I first knew David Holgate (Senior) in the year that Salmon Trout won the St Leger. We had loaded bales of bark from a ship in Alexandra Dock, Hull, along with two other Stainforth-owned keels and with David's keel *Mizpah*, all for the Yorkshire dyeworks at Selby. The four captains clubbed together and chartered the steam tug *Seeker* from Humber Tugs to tow the four keels to Selby, towing up on the day that the St Leger was run; they arrived at Selby Lock in the early afternoon, helping each other to pen into the canal. There was a strong westerly wind blowing and the dyeworks was half a mile up the cut, so we all ganged up to haul one vessel at a time by hand to the works. Just as the last vessel was tying up the works foreman came to make arrangements for discharging and David asked him if he had heard the winner of the St Leger; he answered "Salmon Trout".

David, who was then over seventy, traded anywhere that profitable cargo was offered. A year or two later he had the misfortune to break a leg, and his ship was sold. When he was over eighty he would wander on to the Beckside and reminisce about his working life. One story he liked to tell was how he had frightened off two fishermen who were trying to persuade him that he would need help to take the keel *Thomas Scarr* into Bridlington Harbour. He was on passage from Ferriby Sluice up the coast with a cargo of bricks and tiles and when a few miles to the south of Bridlington he was hailed by two fishermen in a coble who, on finding that the keel

Keels on the Driffield Navigation, which was completed in 1770. Driffield, the capital of the Yorkshire Wolds, had a busy enough basin until 1914 and even had its own motor vessel, the Skelfleet, *built at Howden in 1924 as a sloop; she also took part in the Market Weighton brick trade. The locks limited width to 14 feet 6 inches, keels and sloops being specially built for this trade, mainly in coal and grain.* Humber Keel and Sloop Preservation Society

was bound for Bridlington, tried to persuade David to engage them to help him in. When David refused their help one jumped on board, making the coble fast astern, and endeavoured to convince David that he would not make Bridlington with such a small crew. As they approached the harbour David ordered the mate to make ready for lowering the sails, and following the usual practice when a keel is sailing with the wind on or before the beam he began to cast off the lee shrouds. The fisherman, convinced that the mast and gear would fall on top of him, made a dash for the coble as David steered for the harbour and, with the usual good timing gained from long experience, lowered the sails and berthed the keel while his mate set up the lee shrouds again.

David had three sons, David, Alfred and George Henry, and I

believe three daughters. Their keel, the *Mizpah*, was a steel vessel about seventy feet long. There were two vessels named *Thomas Scarr*, one a keel and the other a sloop, and old David sailed them both. He was always called "Old David"; his son, of course, was "Young David" even into his old age.

The sloop *Hope*, not the same as the SLD market boat, was a Sheffield-size steel vessel built on spec by Joseph (Joss) Scarr at his Grovehill yard in, I think, 1905. When she was completed, Joss Scarr invited David Holgate Junior to "take her away and see what he could do with her". These are Young David's own words; I have heard them more than once. In the nineteen-twenties he was trading to the West Riding as much as possible so that he could pick up a cargo of house coal about every four or five weeks for George Welburn of Beverley. His wife and eldest daughter usually accompanied him on his voyages, the second daughter being left at home to keep house and look after the rest of the family. After George Welburn retired and David's son Edgar had left school to work as mate, David hired the *Hope* to Furley and Company on time charter for a few years, trading from Hull to Gainsborough and from Hull to Sheffield. He then changed the *Hope* over to a keel rig, and after his contract with Furley's finished in about 1936 he installed an Elwe diesel engine, trading anywhere that cargoes were on offer. "Young David" worked on board until he was well over seventy, then his son Edgar took over and in 1979 was still working the *Hope* under power, though rarely was any cargo on offer for Beverley. David died quietly in his sleep in May, 1977, at the age of ninety-four.

David's brother George Henry Holgate had a wooden keel named the *Charlotte*, then bought from Billy Booth, of Hull, a new steel keel, the *Radio*, less than a year old; as she was 61 feet 6 inches long but only 14 feet 6 inches beam she was suitable for most canals, and George Henry would go anywhere if he could make a profit. He had a house near his father and brother David in Holme Church Lane, but it was always closed from the time the keel left Beverley until she arrived back; his wife worked as mate, there being only a daughter in the family, and casual labour was employed to help with cargo working. About 1935 he installed a Petter diesel engine in the *Radio*, which was sold to the British Waterways Board when he retired.

The third brother Alfred, who lived in Flemingate, had the *Jane*, a keel with Sheffield length and Barnsley beam so that she could fetch house coal from the Barnsley Canal for Ernest Wilson of Beverley. The *Jane* was built of wood, but about 1923 or 1924 he had a new steel keel built to the same dimensions by Joss Scarr at Grovehill, naming her the *Bessie* after the younger of his two daughters. Later he too installed an engine.

Old Mark Holgate, who lived on the side of the Beck and owned an old wooden keel named the *Williams*, was brother to "Old Dave". He was getting on in years and did not want much work, using the *Williams* only for transporting chalkstone from Beverley down to a mill at Stoneferry. John Darwin of Driffield bought the *Williams* when Mark retired. One day when in a talkative mood Mark Holgate told me that in his youth he had made a voyage or two in a three-masted full-rigged ship to Australia and had sailed in a steam screw auxiliary barque, where they had some means of lifting the screw propeller on board when it was not required. He spoke, too, of a spell with a sailing smack fishing from Scarborough and of sailing in a Burton Stather "clipper", producing a painting of a two-masted topsail schooner that had been built at Burton Stather.

Three Stainforth keels at Hunt's chemical works at Castleford during the celebrations of the jubilee of King George V in 1935. The Guidance *is on the inside berth,* Energy *in the middle and* Sobriety *in the outside berth.* Author's collection

The powered sloop Dekar, *built at Beverley in 1925, unloading coal at the head of Beverley Beck during the 1939-45 war. The horse worked the derrick, the baskets being placed on a wheelbarrow to be taken into the coalyard.*
Simpson, Beverley

When he married he lived for a few years at Castleford and was master of a small vessel owned by Hunt's chemical works there which was used to carry acid in carboys from the works to Sheffield via the Barnsley and the Dearne and Dove canals and the Sheffield and South Yorkshire Navigation. Mark had a family of two daughters and two sons.

The younger son Mark, who was called "Little Mark", owned a West Country keel and occasionally went up to Mirfield with cargoes of malting barley; he also traded to Driffield. The elder son, William Henry Holgate, owned the keel *Excel*, a wooden carvel vessel fifty-seven feet long. Like other members of the family he would trade anywhere that he could make a profit, returning from West Riding voyages with coal to Beverley for the tannery. He had three sons, the eldest of whom went to work for Tom Fletcher when he left his father; the middle son had a spell with Harker's tankers and with Hodgson's motor vessels, and the other took a shore job.

George Tattersall, who owned the small wooden keel *Empress*, married a daughter of old Mark Holgate and lived at Beckside. They had a large family of five sons and two daughters, and would trade anywhere that work could be found. Just before the 1939–45 War he sold the *Empress* and bought from a Leeds firm a vessel with a transom stern in which he installed a motor, during the war spending some time carrying flour from Rank's mill at Hull to Boston, via the Trent, Fossdyke and Witham, with, sometimes, English wheat as a return cargo.

All the house coal coming in keels to the coal merchants in Beverley at that time had to be discharged by hand, two men filling the baskets, with two on the winch and one wheeling the barrow. Sometimes if it was a long wheel there would be two men with

Two paintings by Goole ship portraitist Reuben Chappell, who was born at Hook, near Goole, in 1870 and began his career as a painter at a time when the Humber ports were at the height of their prosperity. Top is the keel Ada *of Hull, Captain Gardiner, seen off the Middle lightship in the Humber; Grimsby hydraulic tower is visible on the horizon at left. Below is the Trent catch* Brothers *of Hull, Captain J. Gardiner, also seen off the Middle lightship.* Hull Town Docks Museum

Overleaf: *A busy scene in Albert Dock, Hull, just before the outbreak of war in 1914 painted by Edward Paget-Tomlinson. On the right the Wilson liner* Calypso *of 1904, employed in the Hull-Christiania (Oslo)-Gothenburg service, is unloading her cargo of Swedish iron and possibly other goods into keels. On the opposite side of the dock another keel is receiving bulk grain or seed, while a sloop is warping down the dock. In the foreground are two keels with derricks rigged for ship bunkering.*

barrows; this was acceptable when labour was plentiful, and men were pleased to do this kind of work, as they could often make more money by casual work than by labouring jobs in factories. During the 1939–45 War labour became hard to find, so the merchants then began to use a horse to pull the full baskets out of the hold on to the barrow.

One vessel could not keep Ernest Wilson supplied with coal, for he not only took coal from the Barnsley Canal but found supplies from Whitwood and Allerton Main collieries on the Aire and Calder. Fred Burn helped with these latter with his sloop the *Spring*, a wooden vessel, Sheffield size. This was his second sloop, the first being a small one named the *Providence*. The carriage of coal did not occupy him full time, for he had a contract to supply a firm at York with Spurn gravel, loaded off the Binks by hand after the vessel had been grounded on the ebb, loading having to be completed before the flood tide covered the shoal. About 1925 he ordered from Joss Scarr a steel sloop with diesel auxiliary power, the *Dekar*. She was full Sheffield size, and to make the work of loading gravel easier she had round removable plates fitted in her gangway decks so that the gravel did not have to be thrown over the coamings. Her sailing gear was transferred from the *Spring*, which was sold to Tommy Claxton of Castleford and used to carry wheat from Hull to Allinson's Mill at Castleford.

Fred Burn, who lived on Grovehill Road, had three brothers, two of them living in Hull. The eldest, William Burn, had the smallest billyboy I ever saw, the *Liberty*, a carvel-built wooden vessel, cutter rigged, with two hatchways and steered with a tiller; she would only carry about seventy-five tons deadweight. He found most of his living from the Spurn gravel trade and also carried coal and other supplies for the lifeboatmen and the lighthouse at Spurn. Charlie Burn, the second brother, left his father's keel while still a young man and sailed in barques and full-rigged ships until he secured his square rig master's certificate; then he went into steam. During the worldwide recession in the early nineteen-thirties he found his ship laid up with no prospect of any profitable work, and rather than stay on as ship keeper in 1936 he ordered from Joss Scarr a steel vessel, Sheffield size with full diesel power, which he named the *Sequel*. He traded with her in general cargo until about 1941, when he sold her to the General Steam Navigation Company of London; she went to work in the Thames Estuary. The youngest brother, Sidney Burn, went into the Civil Service, spent most of his working life abroad, and retired to live in Harrogate with a knighthood as Sir Sidney Burn.

Living on Beckside near the low bridge was another keel character, George Robert Scaife, who for some unknown reason was called "Cuckoo" Scaife—but not to his face. He had at one time

ADA

BROTHERS

E.W. PAGET-TOMLINSO
MAY 1987

The Kiero *winning the first race organized by the Hull Keel Regatta Club in 1874, from an oil painting by W. R. Nixon in the Hull Town Docks Museum. The* Kiero *is shown abreast of the Trent packet* Isle of Axholme, *which had been hired as the committee boat and was filled with members and spectators. An announcement of the formation of the Regatta Club in the* Hull and Eastern Counties Herald *of 23rd July, 1874, refers to the "old club having retired from the field some years past"; there were certainly races for keels in the Hull Grand Regatta of 20th-21st July, 1864, organized under the patronage of the Royal Yorkshire Yacht Club and various local worthies.* Hull Town Docks Museum

Right: *A poster advertising the second Keel Regatta to be held on 4th and 5th August, 1875. It included keel races on both days as well as rowing and sculling matches, a punt hunt and climbing the greasy pole. "The Keels to be anchored in a line off the Albert Dock Engine-house at Nine o'Clock each day; sails close down until the firing of the second gun. All Keels to sail with mainsail and topsail only; mainsail not to exceed eight yards in hoist, thirteen breadths in the head, and eighteen in the foot; topsail not to exceed twelve breadths in the head, fourteen in the foot, and eleven feet hoist; to be made of twenty-four inch canvas."* Hull Town Docks Museum

a small wooden keel, the *Florence*, but he never kept a vessel long. Just before the 1914–18 War he had a steel keel built at Grovehill by Joss Scarr, which he named the *Sophia* after his wife; both he and his wife pronounced it as "Sofire". She was converted to sloop rig in 1916 and renamed the *I Know* in 1920, passing in 1922 to W. H. Barraclough, who renamed her again as the *Amy Howson*. Now she has been re-rigged by the Humber Keel and Sloop Preservation Society as a sloop, the partner of our family's *Comrade*.

Before the *Sophia* George Scaife had a steel keel named the *Comrade*, which he had verbally agreed to sell to my father. However, when Ambrose Holt of Thorne bid a higher figure he let her go without asking if Father would care to increase his bid. He was having another keel built by Henry Scarr at Hessle; he named her *George A1*, but she was sold within two years to John Joe Tomlinson of Thorne, who renamed her the *Pelican* and employed her in the cement trade from Earle's Melton works to Sheffield, returning with coal for the factories at Hull. Later John Joe renamed her the *Junior T*. As soon as the *George A1* had been sold, George Robert ordered another at Joss Scarr's which was to be his last; when ready she was named the *Powerful*. He worked her for only a few months before selling her to James Barraclough, who put a sloop rig in her and changed her name to the *Fleetgate*. George Robert and his wife did not have any family.

I am not sure what the relationship might have been between George Robert and Hardy Scaife, who was younger and had inherited a keel-owning business from his father of the same name. He was the main contractor in Beverley for the carriage of goods by water for the tannery, the Queensgate Whitening Company and the Tyger Manure Works at Beverley and for the Yorkshire Dye Works at Selby. With the business were two steel fifty-seven-foot keels and two or three wooden ones. The two steel keels, named after his sisters *Bertha* and *Olive*, were mainly used between Beverley and the docks in Hull. The smallest of the wooden keels, the *May*, was used only for carrying wet hides from the weekly coastal steamers that berthed in the Town Docks in Hull. Hardy Scaife employed several keelmen who were moved about from one vessel to another as required, so the craft were not given the usual care and attention that they would have had if each man had been responsible for one particular craft. Some of the keelmen that come to mind were Billy Bugg, Jack Jenkinson, Frank Holgate, better known as "Old Buzzard", and Tommy Gillyon and his son; the old man was usually called "Bellyache Tommy" and always had the hide boat. Within a few years the keels and business were sold to Benjamin Ackerby and Sons Ltd, a firm of ship brokers at Hull, who carried on the business until the tannery decided to go into carrying themselves; but more about that later.

Aboard in the Twenties 8

THE aquatic sports, which had been an annual event for the keelmen at Thorne, Stainforth, and Beverley before the 1914–18 War, were revived soon after it ended. At Thorne, where they were one of the attractions of the June Fair, the sports were held in the canal near the Toll Bar bridge and were well supported by the public. At Stainforth the sports were held on the Saturday of the Village Feast, in the third week of September. It is possible that the Feast has been held annually since the middle of the fourteenth century, when King Edward III in 1348 granted, at the request of Edmund, Duke of York, a charter to Stainforth to hold a market on a Friday and a ten-day fair in September.

When I was young the Feast was one of the highlights of the social year. For several days before the Feast keels on passage would tie up at Stainforth, and on one of the loaded ones they would set up over the bows a fifty-foot pole marked off in feet to be used as a greasy pole. The pole would have a flag fixed on the end and would be liberally smeared with soft soap, ready for all comers to try their luck for the flag; after most of the soap was off pillow fights would be held on the pole.

On the day of the sports keels would hoist their burgees, and an empty keel would be made available as a changing room. There were swimming races, but the sculling races with the keels' cogboats were the events most popular with the keelmen. The cogboats were twelve feet long, and sculled by one oar over the stern. The width of the channel would allow only four boats to enter each heat, so there were usually several heats and semi-finals to be sculled before the champion could be found. Hand paddling races with teams of four men to a boat, tub races and sea horse races were also favoured. A tub was half a barrel, paddled by hand, while a sea horse was also made from a barrel with a horse's head attached. The rider sat astride it and paddled it like a canoe.

The prizes were provided by donations from the spectators and tradesmen, and at Thorne and Stainforth the aquatic sports were managed by committees set up for that purpose. At Beverley, the Beverley Mariners' Society were the organisers, the sports being held on August Bank Holiday in the river just below the lock, with a marquee in Figham Pasture to provide refreshment. In winter the Society held dances and whist drives, and had at least one excursion by rail each summer.

Opposite page: *The Beverley keelmen's aquatic sports in Edwardian times, when they were held in the Beck. When the Beck became too polluted they moved into the River Hull just below the lock, continuing as an annual event until the outbreak of war in 1939. A competitor in the sea horse race is fending himself off from the clinker-built keel* George and Eva, *owned by Charlie Peck of Beverley, which is serving as a grandstand.*
Humber Keel and Sloop Preservation Society

In 1946, the Stainforth Sports were revived for the second time. A new committee was formed with the title Stainforth Mariners' Society, and my father presented the Arthur Schofield Challenge Cup for boat sculling by men over forty years of age. Wilf Barley of Goole won the cup in 1946, '47 and '48, and the last winner was Mick Hunt of Thorne in 1953. After that year there were no further entries, and the cup remained in the possession of my family until presented to the Humber Keel and Sloop Preservation Society. It remains for safe keeping in the Town Docks Museum, Hull.

The Arthur Schofield Challenge Cup. Hull Town Docks Museum

During the time that I was mate in the *Galatea* I gained a wide experience with many different trades and various types of cargo, knowledge that was to serve me well in later years. In the early nineteen-twenties there were still a few well-paid lighterage cargoes about, and we would load these if they were readily available rather than a cargo for up the canals, where the freights were being kept rather low by railway competition. The lighterage cargoes were mainly meal, pollards or sharps in bags, loaded from ships laid stern on to the quay in Alexandra Dock, Hull. They were often for delivery to the railway in the same dock, or they might be for storage in one of the warehouses in the Old Harbour.

We had just finished loading one of these cargoes in August, 1921, when we heard the drone of engines, and looking to the westward I could see the airship R.38 passing over Hull heading south. I had seen her before from off the river bank at Stainforth when she was brought out of the building shed at Howden to go on trials. She had now been sold to America and renumbered ZR–2; I believe she was on a trial flight before crossing the Atlantic. I stood on deck admiring her as she passed over; then to my amazement the fore end began to fall off. Luckily she cleared the city and fell on to the Middle Sand. It was low water at the time, so the tugs and pilot launch that went to try to help the survivors could not get near the wreck, and only five men were brought ashore. Forty-four lives were lost, possibly in the two explosions that were heard as the airship was falling. When we passed by a few days afterwards the wreckage reminded me of seeing Wilson's *Bayardo* on the same sand with her back broken in 1912.

One lighterage cargo that we had was black cotton seed, which we loaded from a small steamer in Albert Dock. After loading we went out of Albert Dock into Humber Dock by hand, using the warping line and boathooks, then through Prince's Dock into Queen's Dock, where we laid for two or three weeks on demurrage. On receiving orders to deliver the cargo to King's Mill at Stoneferry, we penned out into the River Hull and drove up with the tide. About this time we also loaded cotton seed from a steamer in Alexandra Dock for the Olympia Cake and Oil Mills at Selby.

Opposite above: *The committee of the Stainforth aquatic sports, mainly keel captains and owners, pose for their photographs in 1914.* Author's collection

Opposite below: *Competitors line up for the cogboat race at Beverley sports in the early years of the century. David Holgate is third from the right.* Humber Keel and Sloop Preservation Society

R. HULL
KINGSTON
UPON HULL
Victoria Dock
Town Docks
West Dock
Piers
Fish Dock
Riverside
Quay
Hull Middle
Sand
HESSLE
BROUGH
Hessle Haven
Shipyard
H. Scarr
R. Dunston
North Ferriby
Capper
Pass
Works
Melton
Cement
Works
Redcliffe Sand
Jetty
Oyster Ness
Humber
Bridge
Pier
Warren's Shipyard
NEW HOLLAND
Barton Haven
Barton Clay
Hole
Chowder
(Chalder)
Ness
W. Stamp
& Son
Clapson's
Yard
Gilstrap
Heap & Co maltings
BARTON ON HUMBER
Redcliffe
Middle Sand
Winteringham
Haven
WINTERINGHAM
READ'S
ISLAND
Barton Cliff
South Ferriby
Cliff
FERRIBY
SLUICE
SOUTH FERRIBY
R. ANCHOLME
NAVIGATION
RIVER
HUMBE
MARKET WEIGHTON
CANAL
BROUGH
Weighton
Lock
Whitton
Sand
Capper
Pass
Works
Melton
Cement
Works
North Ferriby
Redcliffe Sa
Jetty
Oyster Ness
Whitton
Ness
Pudding Pie
Sand
YOKEFLEET
BLACKTOFT
Jetties
Faxfleet Ness
Blacktoft Sand
Apex
Lt.
Walker Dykes
R. OUSE
OUSEFLEET
WHITGIFT
Trent Falls
East Point
R. TRENT
Cliff End
Leading Lights
Winteringham
Haven
WINTERINGHAM
Redcliffe
Middle Sand
READ'S
ISLAND
Barton Cliff
FERRIBY
SLUICE
SOUTH FER
R. ANCHOLME
NAVIGATION

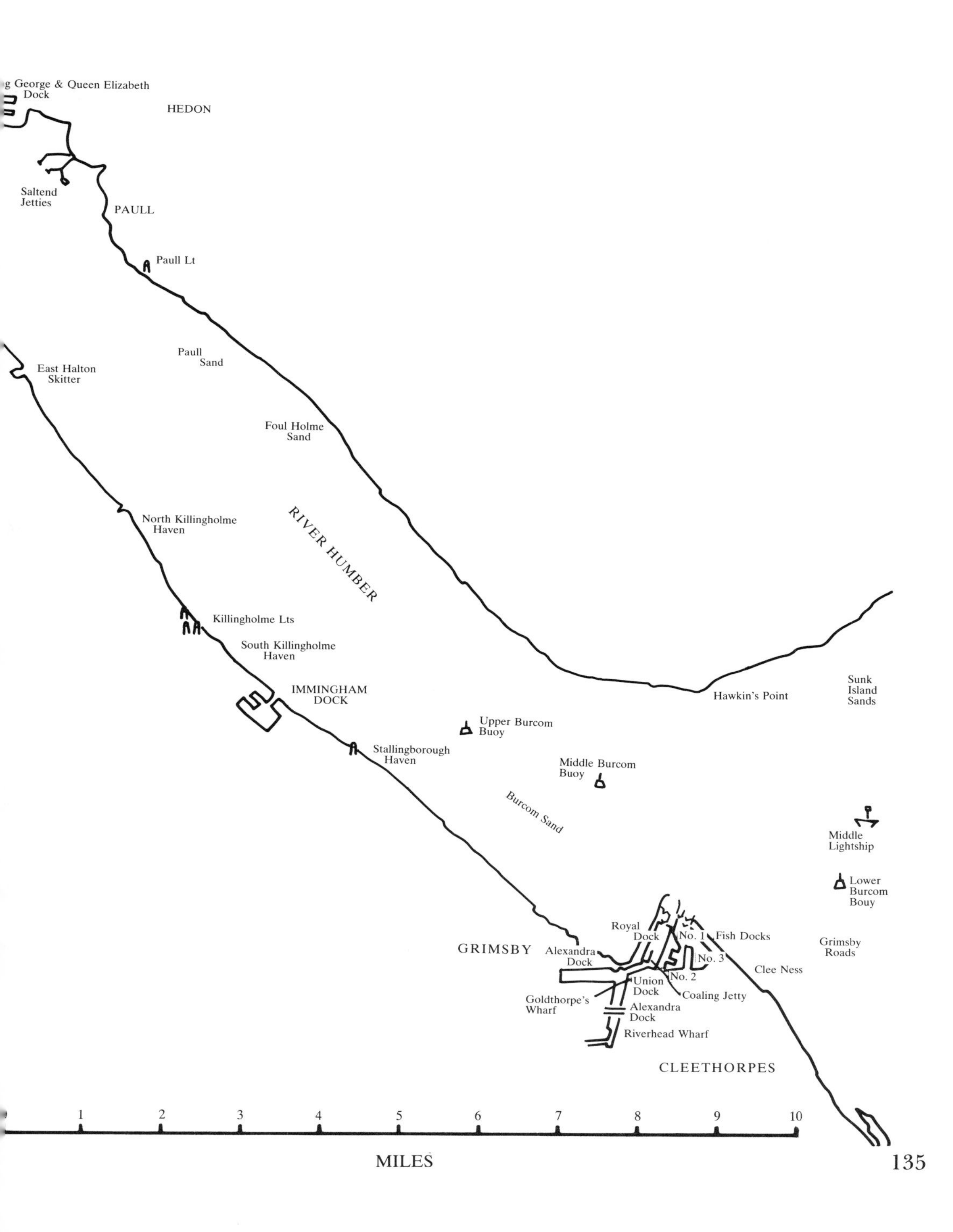
g George & Queen Elizabeth Dock
HEDON
Saltend Jetties
PAULL
Paull Lt
Paull Sand
East Halton Skitter
Foul Holme Sand
North Killingholme Haven
RIVER HUMBER
Killingholme Lts
South Killingholme Haven
IMMINGHAM DOCK
Hawkin's Point
Sunk Island Sands
Upper Burcom Buoy
Stallingborough Haven
Middle Burcom Buoy
Burcom Sand
Middle Lightship
Lower Burcom Bouy
Royal Dock
No. 1
Fish Docks
Grimsby Roads
GRIMSBY
Alexandra Dock
No. 3
Clee Ness
No. 2
Union Dock
Coaling Jetty
Goldthorpe's Wharf
Alexandra Dock
Riverhead Wharf
CLEETHORPES
1
2
3
4
5
6
7
8
9
10
MILES

Craft waiting to load at Denaby staithe, all of them old vessels owned by E. V. Waddington of Swinton used in the local coal trade. I think the one in the outside berth is the Claxby, *built at Beverley as a sloop.* Sheffield Public Library

After loading we towed to Selby with the steam tug *Robbie*, owned by the Selby Warehousing and Lighterage Company, a subsidiary of the mills. We laid at Selby for a few days, then received orders to lay on the berth ready for discharging the following day. At 6 am we opened out and two elevators were moved along the jetty, one being put in the fore hold and one in the after hold; by 9 am they had emptied the *Galatea* completely.

After breakfast we cleared away the dust and fluff, then after replacing the hatches and covers we dropped through the bridges and sailed and drove down to Goole on our way to Denaby for another cargo of gas coal for Beverley. We missed the afternoon high water at Goole as the wind was westerly and would not do us any good up the Knottingley and New Junction Canal, so Father decided to go up the Dutch River to Stainforth and then take a horse from there to Denaby. We brought up to our anchor just below the mouth of the river ready for the next flood, which would be early morning. At the first of the flood the anchor was weighed and with the stowers we started to launch ahead, managing to pass through the bridge at Goole before the tide became too strong for us to keep control. We then had to let the anchor knock on the bottom to turn the ship round head to tide so we could drive stern first with the anchor giving steerage way. We did not manage to save briggage at Rawcliffe Bridge, so we had to bring up while high water. On the high water slack we hove up and moored in the bridgeway head up river, ready for the next flood. On the late afternoon tide we started to launch ahead with the stowers as soon as we could against the last of the ebb, and just managed to save briggage at Jubilee Bridge, Thorne Waterside.

After that we took it easy, just keeping her end on with the stowers, the tide carrying us along. By the time Stainforth Lock came in sight the tide was about spent. We laid in the lock tail until the next morning, then John Rawson, who combined the duties of lock keeper and rent and toll collector, came and penned us into the basin. We had a day at home. The following morning at 4.30 am Fred Barras put our horse line on the cobble stick of his horse and hauled us to Denaby; then he tramped back home.

The coal staithe at Denaby had been rebuilt for the hoped-for Tom Pudding traffic via the New Junction Canal at about the same time that Doncaster Lock had been lengthened, about 1910. But it had been rebuilt in such a way that it was not possible for a keel to load with the mast stepped, so our first job on arriving was to put the mast and mainsail ashore, using the crane provided. The last time Father had navigated the Dutch River was when he had the keel *Aureola* with a cargo of locust beans for the small oil and cake mill at Thorne Waterside; this mill was at the time of which I am writing used as a store, and the only vessel using the Dutch River on a regular trade was the keel *Medina*, owned by Billy Pattrick of Thorne Waterside. This voyage was the first time I had been on the Dutch River, and I only passed through Stainforth Lock once more before it closed in 1939.

That "once more" came about because of a miners' strike. We had been to Doncaster mill with a cargo of wheat, and after discharging brought the ship back to Stainforth to lay until the strike was settled or we could find another cargo. After a few days at home, we were offered a cargo of foreign coal to be imported into Goole for Pilkington's glassworks at Kirk Sandall, so after tea one summer evening we penned out of Stainforth Lock and set the mainsail to a westerly wind, passing through Jubilee Bridge before we met the flood. Then we sailed on until we reached Rawcliffe Bridge, where we lowered the anchor on the bottom and had two hours' sleep until we could go under the bridge; then we drove down into the Ouse ready for entering the docks at Goole on the morning tide.

Goole was primarily a coal-exporting port, and it was strange to see vessels coming in with coal. To load we laid between the ship and the quay, then the grab cranes got to work and we were soon loaded. At Kirk Sandall we discharged by steam crane and grab into railway wagons. From Sandall we went down light into Victoria Dock at Hull for another cargo of foreign coal, this time for the Rotherham glassworks of Beatson Clark. When loaded we went out of the dock at level on the afternoon tide and fetched Walker Dykes. The next tide was early morning, when the weather was calm and not very clear, what a keelman would describe as "moosey". We hove short at flood and after a time began to drive up. As we were trying to sheer across the tide into the East Trent we struck the lower end of the Trent Middle Sand with enough force to douse our sidelights and shift the cargo; when we floated clear we had a list of several inches to starboard which had to be trimmed off before going up the canal. At Rotherham the railway ran between the glassworks and the water, and an overhead gantry with a small electric crane on the end gave access to the wharf. The coal had to be filled into barrows, which were then hoisted up and wheeled into the works. Some time later we loaded at Goole a cargo of white sand for Beatson Clark, and the method of discharge was just the same.

Just before Hull Fair in October we again loaded for the Olympia Cake and Oil Mills at Selby, this time a cargo of palm kernels from a ship in King George Dock, Hull. Before loading we

Perhaps bound for York, a keel negotiates Cawood swing bridge on the River Ouse six miles below Naburn Lock. She is driving up on the flood tide, using her anchor to give her steerage way. The bridge carries the Selby to Tadcaster road over the river. Author's collection

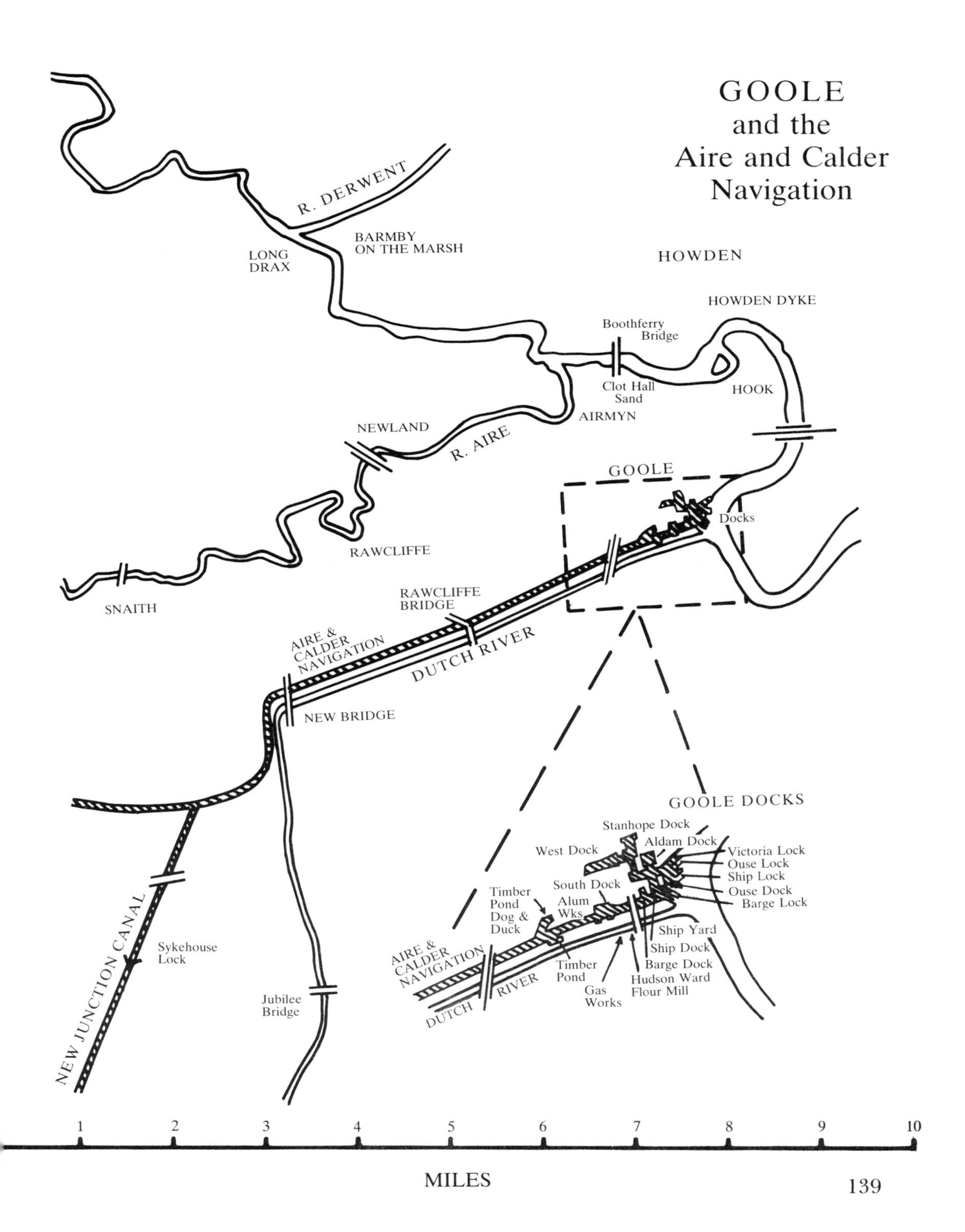
GOOLE
and the
Aire and Calder
Navigation
R. DERWENT
BARMBY
ON THE MARSH
LONG
DRAX
HOWDEN
HOWDEN DYKE
Boothferry
Bridge
Clot Hall
Sand
HOOK
AIRMYN
NEWLAND
R. AIRE
GOOLE
Docks
RAWCLIFFE
SNAITH
RAWCLIFFE
BRIDGE
AIRE &
CALDER
NAVIGATION
DUTCH RIVER
NEW BRIDGE
NEW JUNCTION CANAL
Sykehouse
Lock
Jubilee
Bridge
GOOLE DOCKS
Stanhope Dock
Aldam Dock
West Dock
Victoria Lock
Ouse Lock
Ship Lock
Ouse Dock
Barge Lock
South Dock
Timber
Pond
Dog &
Duck
Alum
Wks
Ship Yard
Ship Dock
Barge Dock
Hudson Ward
Flour Mill
Timber
Pond
Gas
Works
AIRE &
CALDER
NAVIGATION
DUTCH
RIVER
1
2
3
4
5
6
7
8
9
10
MILES

Boats laden with coal, timber and other cargoes waiting to discharge at Leeds in the nineteen-thirties. Humber Keel and Sloop Preservation Society

were told we might be on demurrage for some time, so we found a berth on Number 1 quay, then using the mainsail halyards we hauled the cogboat out of the water and put her on the hatches to prevent her getting damaged by lighters and other craft. A lighterage job at the back end of the year and during the winter months was always attractive; while laid up there was less wear and tear on the gear, and one could have more time at home, thus missing some of the bad weather. We laid at Hull about a month, then received orders to move up to Selby; then we laid another fortnight in the rack before the mill could take our cargo. When the cargo was out we moved down to the overhead crane and the night shift loaded us with slabs of linseed cake for the Wincolmlee mill of Chambers and Fargus at Hull. Twelve years were to pass before I loaded for the Selby mill again; that was while I had the keel *Guidance*, the cargo this second time being bulk linseed. We did not lay long enough to be paid any demurrage, but were lucky enough to find a return cargo of soya meal in bags to Immingham for export.

The following February, 1923, during a period of frost we loaded bulk wheat at Hull for Hudson Ward's flour mill at Goole. By the time we had discharged, the New Junction Canal and the Stainforth and Keadby Canal were frozen fast, so we could not load coal at any of the pits on the Sheffield and South Yorkshire Navigation. There were also ice floes drifting up and down the

Keels at Leeds in the early nineteenth century, from a steel engraving published in 1829. The size of the warehouse reflects the considerable amount of trade on the Aire and Calder Navigation after the improvements made in the last quarter of the eighteenth century.
John Hainsworth

Ouse which would make navigation hazardous for wooden craft. We decided to wait for better conditions, but we were offered a cargo of sootcake from Whitley Bridge on the Knottingley Canal to Alexandra Dock at Hull for export. We had not loaded this before, but the canal was ice free, so we decided to give it a try and booked a tow with the daily tugs which left Goole each morning for Leeds and Wakefield. That night we had a blizzard, and when the tug captain called the crews of his tow the next morning at four there was a thick layer of snow. Because the *Galatea* was light and all the other vessels in the tow were loaded we had to tow tight up to the tug, moored in cross ropes so that the tug could keep us under control when speed had been slacked for any reason. Being tight up relieved us of the necessity of having to steer; we had to keep a look out, but we could do that from the shelter of the cabin companionway. This sootcake was a kind of fertilizer which we loaded from horse drays backed up to the vessel's side, the bags being tipped over the coamings and lowered down into the hold by hand. The first bags were used to make a stage so that we could take the others on our shoulders and stow them in tiers as required. This was a one-off job; I had not heard of it before and have not heard of it since 1922 or 1923.

Up to that time I had not seen much of the Aire and Calder Navigation; indeed, I can only remember making three voyages to Leeds while we had the *Galatea*, once with a cargo of maize in sacks

The Waterside at Barton-on-Humber, with two sloops laying at Clapson's yard. Gillstrap Heap's maltings are on the right of the picture. Hull Town Docks Museum

for Hudson Ward from Hull to their warehouse and twice with bulk wheat from Hull to the grain silo just above Leeds Bridge for the Leeds Industrial Co-operative Society. We went to Wakefield more often with barley for Sutcliffe's, who were maltsters, with kilns at Wakefield and Mirfield. The barley was imported through Hull, from California and Australia in bags and from the Black Sea in bulk. The bags, which were often sun scorched and rotten, had to be weighed on the ship's deck before we loaded them, and the bulk barley had to be filled into four-bushel sacks and weighed off at 224 pounds nett. Samples of barley had to be taken at intervals during loading and placed into marked linen bags, then sealed with wax; should there be any dispute about the condition of the cargo between merchant and carrier these would show the condition as received at the time of loading. Sutcliffe's had three berths at Wakefield, one at Doncaster Road, one at Belle Isle, and the other at Thornes Lane wharf, where the barley was discharged by our derrick on to horse-drawn drays. The power for hoisting was supplied by a horse who knew just how many yards to walk for the sacks to clear the coamings and swing on to the dray.

Malthouse wharf, on the Calder at Wakefield, handled open cast coal, which would be tipped down the chute into the holds of craft like the Hegaro. Author's collection

When we first started in the Leeds and Wakefield trade we had to make a light voyage into the Sheffield and South Yorkshire Navigation via the New Junction Canal to pick up a cargo of coal. Then the tannery at Beverley changed over from steam hards to washed singles for their boilers and took part of their coal from the Castleford area, which made the Wakefield trade more attractive as we could load a return cargo from the pits nearby. The towage rates charged by the steam tugs owned by the Aire and Calder Navigation were so low that it was not worth while attempting to sail on the Aire and Calder except when bound to or from the New Junction Canal. All the road and railway bridges were fixed, so on arrival at Goole the anchor was brought inboard and unbent and the leeboards hove on deck with the mainsail tye and halyards used as a burton, to keep them safe from damage while passing through locks and bridgeways. Then the mast had to be lowered and the mastway covered against the weather. To comply with the by-laws of the navigation all the cogboats had to be left at the *Dog and Duck* while the keels were up the canal. This was nearly a mile away from the picking-up point for the tugs in the Barge Dock, so if you arrived on a late-night tide at Goole it was all go to have this done and snatch a few hours' sleep before the Leeds tug got under way at 4 am and the Wakefield tug an hour later. Depending on the number of vessels in tow and their draft, it could be from twelve to eighteen hours to Wakefield; the downgate trip when most of the vessels were empty would take much less time.

Occasionally we also took barley for malting to Barton Haven

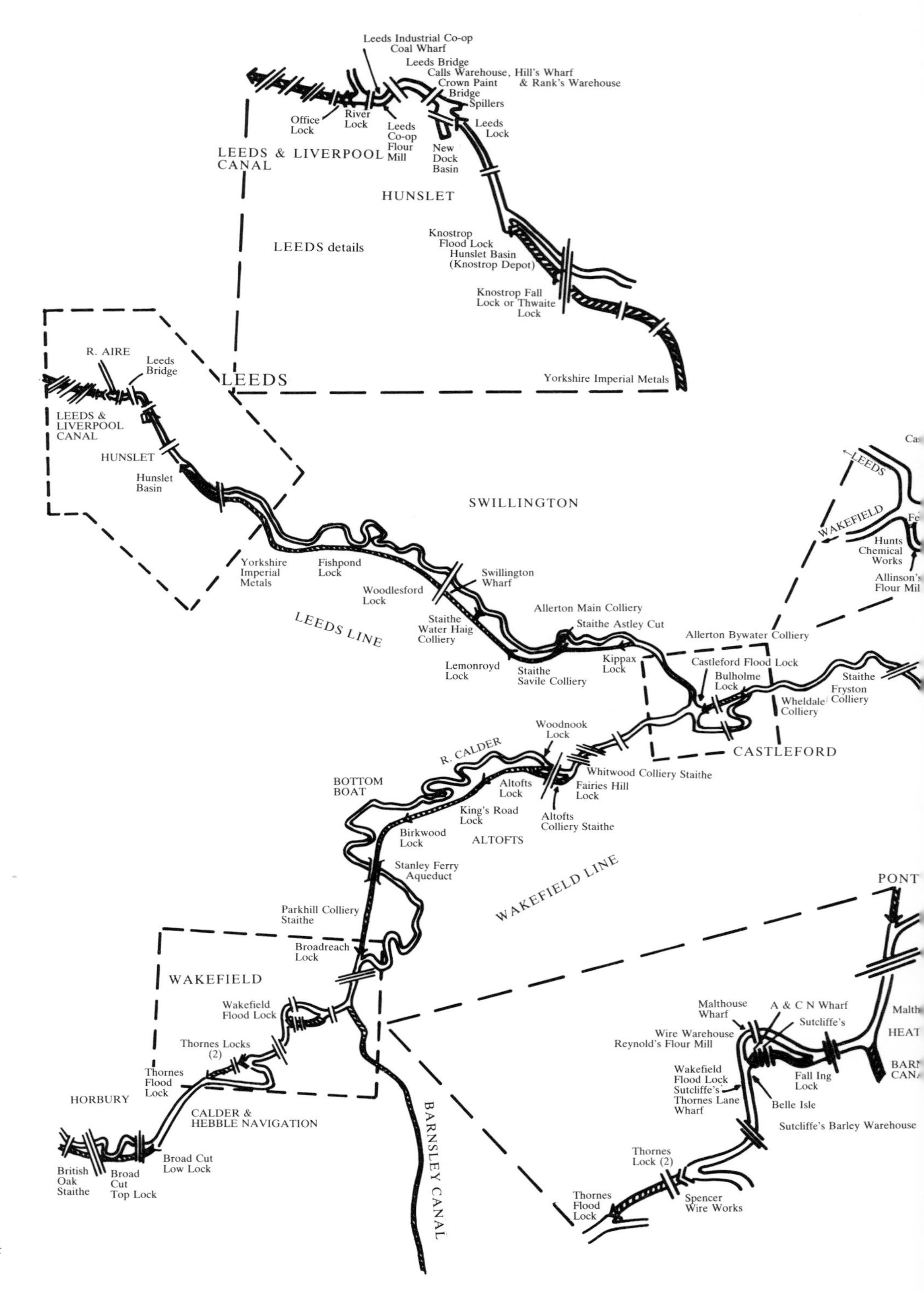
Leeds Industrial Co-op Coal Wharf
Leeds Bridge
Calls Warehouse, Hill's Wharf & Rank's Warehouse
Crown Paint Bridge
Spillers
Office Lock
River Lock
Leeds Co-op Flour Mill
Leeds Lock
New Dock Basin
LEEDS & LIVERPOOL CANAL
HUNSLET
LEEDS details
Knostrop Flood Lock
Hunslet Basin (Knostrop Depot)
Knostrop Fall Lock or Thwaite Lock
Yorkshire Imperial Metals
R. AIRE
Leeds Bridge
LEEDS
LEEDS & LIVERPOOL CANAL
HUNSLET
Hunslet Basin
SWILLINGTON
LEEDS
WAKEFIELD
Hunts Chemical Works
Yorkshire Imperial Metals
Fishpond Lock
Swillington Wharf
Woodlesford Lock
Allerton Main Colliery
Staithe Water Haig Colliery
Staithe Astley Cut
LEEDS LINE
Allerton Bywater Colliery
Lemonroyd Lock
Staithe Savile Colliery
Kippax Lock
Castleford Flood Lock
Bulholme Lock
Staithe
Fryston Colliery
Wheldale Colliery
Woodnook Lock
CASTLEFORD
R. CALDER
Whitwood Colliery Staithe
BOTTOM BOAT
Altofts Lock
Fairies Hill Lock
King's Road Lock
Altofts Colliery Staithe
Birkwood Lock
ALTOFTS
Stanley Ferry Aqueduct
WAKEFIELD LINE
Parkhill Colliery Staithe
Broadreach Lock
WAKEFIELD
Wakefield Flood Lock
Thornes Locks (2)
Thornes Flood Lock
HORBURY
CALDER & HEBBLE NAVIGATION
BARNSLEY CANAL
British Oak Staithe
Broad Cut Top Lock
Broad Cut Low Lock
Malthouse Wharf
A & C N Wharf
Sutcliffe's
Wire Warehouse
Reynold's Flour Mill
Wakefield Flood Lock
Sutcliffe's Thornes Lane Wharf
Fall Ing Lock
Belle Isle
Sutcliffe's Barley Warehouse
Thornes Lock (2)
Spencer Wire Works
Thornes Flood Lock

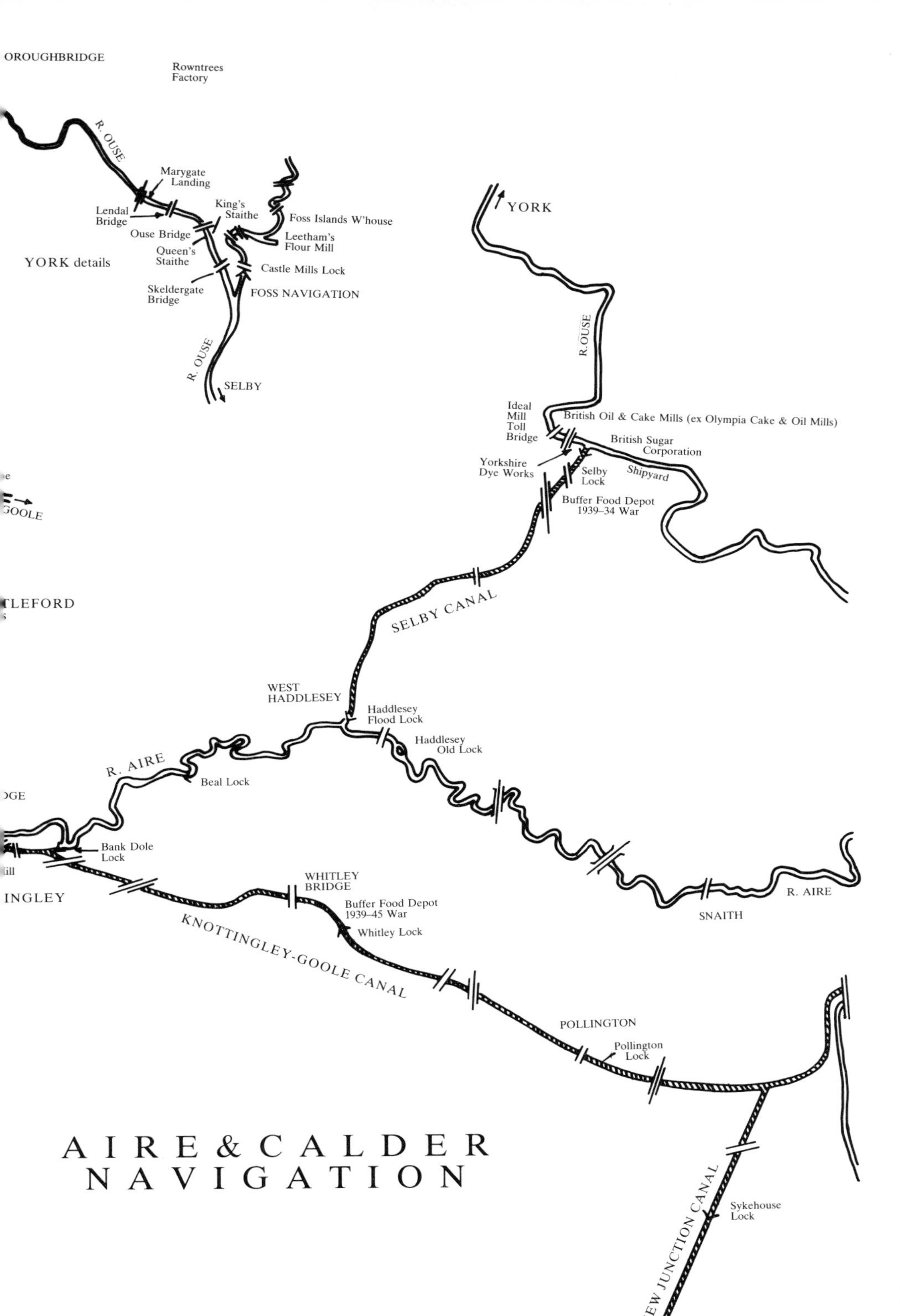
OROUGHBRIDGE
Rowntrees Factory
R. OUSE
Marygate Landing
Lendal Bridge
King's Staithe
Foss Islands W'house
Ouse Bridge
Leetham's Flour Mill
Queen's Staithe
YORK details
Castle Mills Lock
Skeldergate Bridge
FOSS NAVIGATION
R. OUSE
SELBY
YORK
R. OUSE
Ideal Mill
Toll Bridge
British Oil & Cake Mills (ex Olympia Cake & Oil Mills)
British Sugar Corporation
Yorkshire Dye Works
Selby Lock
Shipyard
Buffer Food Depot 1939–34 War
GOOLE
TLEFORD
SELBY CANAL
WEST HADDLESEY
Haddlesey Flood Lock
Haddlesey Old Lock
R. AIRE
Beal Lock
DGE
Bank Dole Lock
INGLEY
WHITLEY BRIDGE
Buffer Food Depot 1939–45 War
Whitley Lock
KNOTTINGLEY-GOOLE CANAL
R. AIRE
SNAITH
POLLINGTON
Pollington Lock
NEW JUNCTION CANAL
Sykehouse Lock
AIRE & CALDER NAVIGATION

for Gillstrap Heap and Co. Ltd. Their warehouse and malt kiln were on the east bank of the haven just inside and opposite the wharf of William Stamp, who operated a market boat service between Barton and Hull with the sloop-rigged billyboys *Rosalie Stamp* (built Barton, 1911), *Rising Hope* (built Thorne, 1898), and *Ever Ready* (built Barton, 1908). A full cargo could only be carried to Barton on spring tides; should the tides be missed by only one we could be neaped anywhere from five to eight days before we could go on to the berth.

Charles Sheffield was the forwarding agent and ship broker for the two maltsters Sutcliffe's and Gillstrap Heap. He lived at No 3 Weighton Grove, Hull, and had an office in High Street near the *Pacific*. The *Pacific*, a club, was where the merchants and businessmen of Hull would meet daily to transact business, particularly the merchants and buyers in the grain trade. Many hundreds of tons of wheat, barley, maize and oil seeds would be bought and sold each day. Charles Sheffield had inherited the business from his father, and often fixed other freights for us as well as the barley. When he received notification from clients that they wished him to look after their interests in any consignment of cargo, they would usually indicate what means of transport they wished him to use. At the time of receiving instructions the cargo might be on the dock side in a foreign port or it might be on the high seas; it might be part of a bulk cargo or a parcel in the hold of a liner among other general cargo. First he would find out from the ship's agent the expected date of arrival, and as that date drew near he would ask the shipping clerk to find from the stowage plan the position of the consignment in the ship's hold. If it should be in the tween deck and near the hatchway, the receiving craft would have to be in the dock ready to load when the ship docked. If it should be in the lower hold she would have more time.

Arrangements would have to be made with the stevedore for the labour to work the cargo. It was the custom for the keel to supply two men for loading and the consignee to supply any further number that might be needed. Sworn weighers would have to be engaged to weigh and sample the cargo. The samples would be taken at intervals as loading proceeded; they were then placed in marked linen bags, as already explained. When loading was completed, the broker would sign one bill of lading on behalf of the shipowners and captain. This was the keel's receipt for cargo received on board, showing the number of quarters loaded and the equivalent weight in pounds per quarter; any damaged or stained bags would be noted and the port or place of delivery would be stated; at the bottom in small print were the conditions of carriage. One copy would be posted to the consignee and another copy delivered on board with a declaration note for the dues office when

For clarity this scene at the Horsewash, by Victoria Pier, Hull, could hardly be beaten. The Rosalie Stamp, *owned by W. Stamp and Son of Barton-on-Humber, was a market sloop bringing vegetables to Hull from the Lincolnshire side; built at Barton-on-Humber in 1911, she lasted into the nineteen-fifties.* Hull Town Docks Museum

Pullan & Ward
WHOLESALE GROCERS
CONFECTIONERS &
YEAST MERCHANTS
43 & 44 WITHAM
ROSALIE STAMP HULL

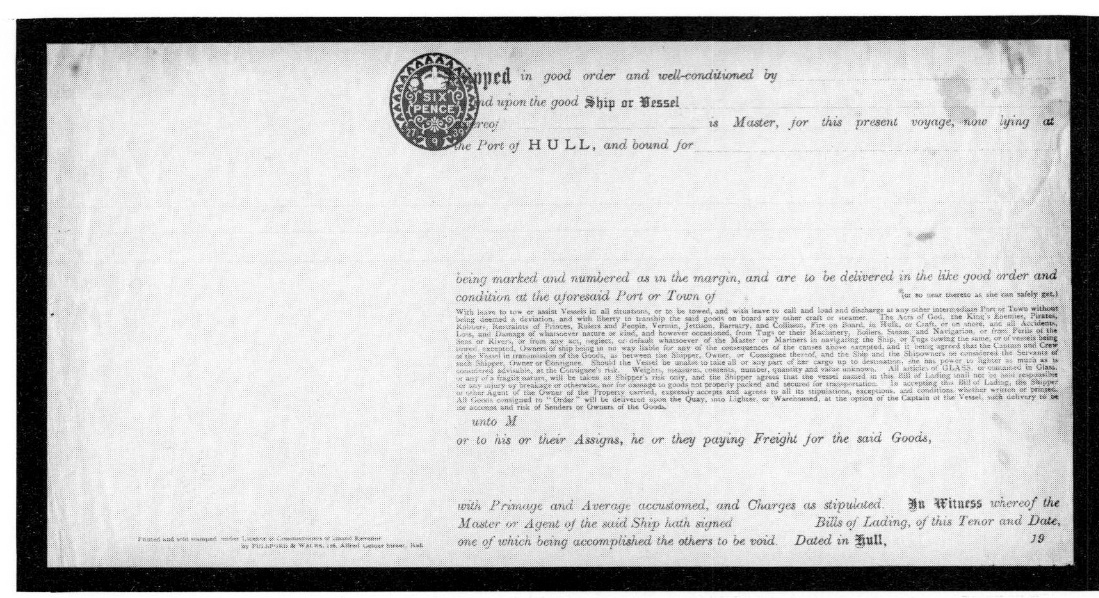

SIX PENCE

hipped *in good order and well-conditioned by*

d upon the good **Ship or Vessel**

ereof *is Master, for this present voyage, now lying at*

he Port of HULL, *and bound for*

being marked and numbered as in the margin, and are to be delivered in the like good order and condition at the aforesaid Port or Town of (or so near thereto as she can safely get.)

With leave to tow or assist Vessels in all situations, or to be towed, and with leave to call and load and discharge at any other intermediate Port or Town without being deemed a deviation, and with liberty to tranship the said goods on board any other craft or steamer. The Acts of God, the King's Enemies, Pirates, Robbers, Restraints of Princes, Rulers and People, Vermin, Jettison, Barratry, and Collision, Fire on Board, in Hulk, or Craft, or on shore, and all Accidents, Loss, and Damage of whatsoever nature or kind, and however occasioned, from Tugs or their Machinery, Boilers, Steam, and Navigation, or from Perils of the Seas or Rivers, or from any act, neglect, or default whatsoever of the Master or Mariners in navigating the Ship, or Tugs towing the same, or of vessels being towed, excepted, Owners of ship being in no way liable for any of the consequences of the causes above excepted, and it being agreed that the Captain and Crew of the Vessel in transmission of the Goods, as between the Shipper, Owner, or Consignee thereof, and the Ship and the Shipowners be considered the Servants of such Shipper, Owner or Consignee. Should the Vessel be unable to take all or any part of her cargo up to destination, she has power to lighter as much as is considered advisable, at the Consignee's risk. Weights, measures, contents, number, quantity and value unknown. All articles of GLASS, or contained in Glass, or any of a fragile nature, will be taken at Shipper's risk only, and the Shipper agrees that the vessel named in this Bill of Lading shall not be held responsible for any injury by breakage or otherwise, nor for damage to goods not properly packed and secured for transportation. In accepting this Bill of Lading, the Shipper or other Agent of the Owner of the Property carried, expressly accepts and agrees to all its stipulations, exceptions, and conditions, whether written or printed. All Goods consigned to "Order" will be delivered upon the Quay, into Lighter, or Warehoused, at the option of the Captain of the Vessel, such delivery to be for account and risk of Senders or Owners of the Goods.

unto M

or to his or their Assigns, he or they paying Freight for the said Goods,

with Primage and Average accustomed, and Charges as stipulated. **In Witness** *whereof the Master or Agent of the said Ship hath signed* *Bills of Lading, of this Tenor and Date, one of which being accomplished the others to be void.* *Dated in* **Hull,** *19*

A stamped bill of lading, the master's receipt for cargo received on board. Bills of lading were usually made out in triplicate, one having an embossed sixpenny stamp; one of the unstamped copies would travel with the vessel and the other would be sent by post to the consignee. Humber Keel and Sloop Preservation Society

bound for any place on the canals. The broker would, if required, arrange for ready cash to be supplied to the captain for the expenses of the voyage.

By custom one third of the freight was considered earned and due when the ship was loaded and a further third when she arrived at her port or place of discharge; the final third was due after delivery. However, in practice the total amount was generally paid over at one time. When overtime was worked during loading the broker would debit the ship's agents for their part of the cost and collect the amount due on behalf of the keel captain. For his services the broker would receive five per cent of the net freight from the owner or captain after payment of dock and canal dues.

Many of the lighterage cargoes that we loaded at Hull were passed on to us by Charlie Wilkinson, who was dock superintendent for Spear and Thorpe, grain merchants with offices in Bishop Lane, Hull. Wilkinson owned two or three lighters which he used for any lighterage that came his way while carrying out his duties for Spear and Thorpe, and if he found that he had more work than he could cope with he would pass on the surplus to any keel captain or owner who might be waiting for a cargo. Later, in about 1930, he looked after the wheat trade to the flour mill at Mexborough owned by the Barnsley British Co-operative Society Ltd.

Somebody named Drury was the broker in the Lincoln trade, but that was later taken over by Furley's, who had been keel owners and wharfingers at Gainsborough since 1774. Their office at Hull, where they were dock labour contractors, was on Prince's Dock side. To Gainsborough they carried general cargo to their wharf, oil seeds to the Ashcroft and Baltic mills, and wheat in sacks to West Stockwith for transshipment to Worksop by narrow boat. They carried general cargo to Sheffield Basin, and to their own wharf at Atterclife, on the Sheffield top level, iron billets, ingots, pig iron, bar iron and dish metal; from Sheffield bright steel was loaded for export from Hull; from Rotherham, wagon wheels and axles were loaded for export to railways all over the world, and at Aldwarke coal staithe Furley's loaded gas coal for the gasworks of the British Gas Light and Coke Company at Bank Side, Hull. The Sheffield office was in Exchange Street, at the entrance to Sheffield Basin. Any work obtained through Furley's office was subject to a deduction of five per cent brokerage charge.

Many owners and captains of keels would charter their vessels to Furley's for a year at a time, Furley's paying to the owner a fixed fee for the use of the vessel for that period. The master would take orders from Furley's as if the vessel were owned by them and he would receive the same rate of freight that Furley's paid their own captains. At the settling, the cost of towing on the tideway was

"Copy"

An Agreement made this 14th day of May 1891, BETWEEN John Christopher Schofield of Stainforth Owner of the good Keel or Vessel called the "Fanny" of Doncaster. whereof John Christopher Schofield is Master at the present time (hereinafter called the Owner), of the one part, and FURLEY & CO., of the Borough of Kingston-upon-Hull, River and Canal Carriers and Forwarding Agents (hereinafter called the Hirers), of the other part, WHEREBY the said parties mutually agree with each other as follows :—

1. The Owner shall place the said Vessel (which is now in good and seaworthy order and condition and repair, tight, strong, well equipped, and in every respect fitted for the contemplated service) at the disposal and under the control of the Hirers for the term of one year from the 14th day of May 1891, for which the Hirers shall pay hire at the rate of Sixty pounds (£60) per annum, payable quarterly on the 14th days of August, November, February ~~respectively.~~ and May respectively

2. The said Vessel shall carry cargoes to and from Hull, and/or Grimsby, and/or Goole, and/or any places on the Humber, Ouse, or Trent, or the Canals connected therewith, as ordered by the Hirers. The Captain of the Vessel shall work her on the "thirds" system usual and customary in the trade of similar vessels; but the Owner's "third" shall be paid to the Hirers, and not to the Owner, whose sole remuneration shall be the hire aforesaid.

3. The said Vessel shall be loaded and discharged in regular turn with other vessels owned by the Hirers, or worked by them under agreements similar to this, and the rate of freight shall be the usual and current rate of freight at the present time paid by the Hirers on similar cargoes carried to or from the place or places of trading in vessels owned by them. The Captain shall obey all the lawful orders of the Hirers or their Agents, and shall use his utmost diligence in furthering their interests. If any Captain should be or become drunk, incapable, or his conduct become in any way prejudicial or unsatisfactory to the Hirers, he shall be forthwith discharged by the Owner on receipt of a written notice to that effect given to the Owner by the Hirers, and a fresh Captain shall be appointed, approved by the Hirers.

4. The Owner shall keep the said Vessel in good repair, and he shall have the option of withdrawing the Vessel from hire for the space of six days during the con-

A hire agreement made by my grandfather with Furley and Company in 1891. For the period of the agreement grandfather worked the vessel on thirds, the owner's thirds going to Furley and Company; he received £60 for the year for the hire of his keel, the Fanny. Humber Keel and Sloop Preservation Society

deducted from the gross freight, then Furley's took one third of the net freight as owner's share, and the captain received the other two-thirds, from which he had to pay his mate and any casual labour. This is the system of earning by thirds to which I refer in chapter nine. In my grandfather's time the going rate of hire seems to have been one hundred pounds per year for each vessel.

We only rarely loaded with W. Bleasdale and Co. Ltd, who were keel owners and inland waterway carriers trading mainly to Sheffield from Hull, Goole and Grimsby. Their Hull office on Prince's Dock side was managed by Sidney Rycroft, and Harry Simms was the cargo supervisor. At the Sheffield office in Exchange Street Tom Thornton was in charge. Bleasdale's had a large fleet of keels, but they often needed to engage other craft to help out. Their main trade was with the steel industry: pig iron, dish metal, bar iron, billets, ingots, ferro-silicon and chrome. A small amount of general cargo was carried such as sugar, imported through Goole from the Continent, and canned goods. Wheat was carried in bulk for Sammy Smith's Victoria flour mill in Sheffield

• BLEASDALE •

CANAL CARRIERS AND FORWARDING AGENTS
Regular Service from HULL and GOOLE
TO DONCASTER, MEXBRO', ROTHERHAM, SHEFFIELD, etc., and VICE VERSA
Through Rates Quoted to and from all parts.
W. BLEASDALE & CO. LTD., PRINCES DOCK SIDE, HULL
Telephone No. 16653 Central.
Telegrams: "Barges, Hull."

Bleasdale's advertisement from the Aire and Calder Navigation handbook issued in 1937. Two of their steel keels, both built by Dunston's at Thorne in 1923, are shown in the advertisement.
Humber Keel and Sloop Preservation Society

and discharged into his own silo. Occasionally Bleasdale's had one or two cargoes of bog ore for Sheffield gasworks. When engaged by Bleasdale's, the freight was paid clear of dues, wharfage, and brokerage. On certain classes of cargo the charge for canal dues and wharfage would be more than fifty per cent of the total cost of transport.

The greater part of the wheat cargoes that we carried came to us from John Thomas Rusling, also known as John Tommy, or "Baggy", who lived in Waverley Street, Hull, where he carried on the business of keelowner and forwarding agent and managed the keels owned by Robinson Brothers, flour millers on the Rother at the Town Mills, Rotherham. He was also agent for Thomas Hanley and Sons, flour millers at Doncaster, Hudson Ward, flour millers at Dock Mills, Goole, the Barnsley British Co-operative Society's flour mill at Mexborough, and the three small mills at Sheffield, Price's, Ibbetson's and Hazlewood's. These three were receiving their supplies of wheat in sacks until 1925 when they combined to lease from the Navigation Company a warehouse for conversion to a silo to hold two thousand tons of grain; this silo had a bucket elevator. John Tommy had spent his youth on his father's keel.

Sheffield Basin was well supplied with cranes and warehouse space, but up to the new silo being ready Price's mill was using a jury-mast and derrick to heave the sacks out of the keel's hold by hand, and carting them away by horse and dray. It is possible that the *Galatea* might have been the last to discharge by this method; we were there with a cargo early in 1925 when the contractors were ready to test the new elevators. After agreeing a price for the job, we finished discharging the sacks of wheat and moved down the covered wharf, where a large amount of Karachi wheat was stored in twelve-stone bags. A stage was made over the hold by placing planks across the coamings, the jigger crane lifting the bags of wheat on to the stage where one man cut the sewing while another emptied the wheat into the hold. We loaded about two hundred quarters. It was blowing and raining all the time we were on this job and I can remember thinking how lucky we were not having to navigate down the Tinsley locks in that weather. There was a canopy over both the loading berth and the elevator; the snag was the dust, Karachi wheat was the dirtiest there was and the damp weather made it stick.

About this time we found ourselves caught in a dock strike. We were left part loaded, wanting about 120 quarters of bulk wheat to finish our order of 420 quarters for Rotherham mill. After waiting a few days with no sign of a resumption of work we trimmed about a hundred quarters of wheat from the middle to the fore hold, then went to Rotherham and returned to Beverley with a cargo of coal before we could load the remainder of the wheat.

We fared better in the General Strike of 1926, when we were due to load flour and offal at Rank's mill, Hull, for Doncaster, Rotherham and Sheffield. It was usual in this trade to load a full cargo. About twenty tons or so of flour and offal would be landed at Brook's wharf, Doncaster; a further twenty tons or so of flour would be landed at Rotherham wharf, leaving about sixty tons for Sheffield. This made for easy working as the depth of the navigation became less in the higher reaches. After a delay of about a day we were given a dispensation to load ninety tons of flour only for Sheffield. Two pickets and two policemen were on the quay while we loaded; an inspector came down to see us leave and told us that there would be a policeman to meet us at Keadby, he would travel to Thorne with us and be relieved by a Doncaster man, other reliefs to be provided at Mexborough and Rotherham.

All the time that I was mate with Father we tried to avoid any ship movement on a Sunday, and always tried to arrange our work so that we would be able to tie up in a safe berth by noon on Saturday, so we could go home for Saturday evening and Sunday. The only exception was if we were on a voyage that would take us by home and it would be possible to arrive on the Sunday before noon.

One Saturday in February, 1924, on our way down with a cargo of coal, we passed through Doncaster Lock at about 6 pm; we decided to stop there overnight and to continue down to Stainforth on the Sunday morning, or if the wind was not suitable to go home on our bikes. On the Sunday morning the wind was a fresh westerly and the prospect of being at Stainforth by noon was good. We hauled two reefs in the mainsail before we got under way, not because there was too much wind for the gear but to keep the speed down to a level that would allow us to keep control. We would have a head wind through the Gas House rack at Doncaster and through Barnby Dun rack, so we made an early start. We sailed as far as possible into Gas House rack, then lowered the mainsail and launched through with the stowers.

It was only a short distance and we soon had the mainsail at work again, making good time into Barnby Dun rack where we again had to lower and launch with the stowers until I could get ashore with the man'sline at the bridge. I hauled to the railway bridge, then re-boarded to help with the gear, the mast having been lowered as well as the sail to reduce the windage. The wind had now increased and veered to the north of west, making it a close reach to the New Junction Canal about half a mile away, before we would be able to bear away. We also had to pass through the Northfield swing bridge which was within about three hundred yards of getting under way. The *Galatea* laid aground about fifteen feet from the lee bank while we hove up the mast and set the reefed mainsail. I helped her off the bank by setting with a stower as she got under way. Sailing fast, she heeled and luffed into the middle of the canal. We immediately slacked off the sheet and trussed up the mainsail with the slabline, at the same time checking the weather brace so as to slow the ship down for passing through the bridge. As we entered the bridgeway the pressure of the water on the lee bow forced the vessel over to windward and the weather bow struck the bridge abutment. Because she was heeling, the force of the blow was taken low down about the turn of the bilge.

Isaac Worfolk.

A quick check showed that she was making water fast, and the fore pump gear was got out and shipped ready for use. When clear of the New Canal end we lowered the mainsail and let her lay to the lee bank. The time was then about 10 am and we could see my brother Jim coming up the bank to meet us. We took him on board and set him to work with the pump, while we pulled out a soft tarpaulin and foddered the ship by pulling it under her bottom, which eased the flow immediately. Jim was then sent to Stainforth to fetch a carpenter to help shore down the damage. Meanwhile I manned the pump while Father removed the gear from the forecastle and took up the dennings so that we could attack the damage from the inside; we found it was all in the forepeak. Jim arrived back at about 1 pm with Isaac Worfolk, who had brought with him a carpenter's bag of tools and was soon at work shoring down the damage with timber that we had on board. He was not long before he made a tight job and we got under way again, pumping out the water as we went along. We tied up at Worfolk's yard by 4 pm and went home to do justice to the meal that Mother had waiting for us.

No water was made during the night, but to make the shored-down damage absolutely safe it was decided that a concrete box should be built in the forepeak over the damage. Worfolk's put this in hand right away. When it was in place and hardened off, old William Smurthwaite, the insurance surveyor, came from Hull and passed the ship seaworthy and fit to proceed on her voyage. After the cargo was discharged at Beverley the contract for the repairs was awarded to Hunter's yard at Beverley. I waited until she was in dry dock, then went to Hull and shipped as purchase-man with Herbert Rhodes for a voyage to Gainsborough with the keel *Britannia*. We loaded linseed from a steamship in Alexandra Dock and towed to Gainsborough, because the Trent was full of fresh. I made a bit of extra money for myself and was back on board the *Galatea* in time to clean up after the repairs were completed.

The keel *Britannia* was owned by a man named Christie who worked in the Sheffield office of the Sheffield and South Yorkshire Navigation; I believe that he was the engineer or surveyor. He also owned the keel *Viola*; her captain was Harlington Clark. Both were

The Annie Maud *delivering wheat at Robinson Brothers' Town Mills at Rotherham during the time I was in charge of her.* Author's collection

Sheffield size and built of wood. Their captains were Thorne men with long family connections with keels. I know of only one other keel owned at Sheffield; her name was the *Industry* and she was owned and captained by Alfred Hall, who lived at Walkley, a suburb, making part of his living by carrying coal from the Sheffield and South Yorkshire to the seed mills at Gainsborough.

In my time no sloops were owned at any place above Stainforth on the Sheffield and South Yorkshire, and not many keels, if we discount the open boats, which were old vessels no longer fit for use on the estuary. After removal of coamings and side decks, these were used as day boats on the shorthaul jobs such as carrying coal from the pits to the factories on the canal. Tinsley Rolling Mills had three working between Tinsley and the coal staithe at Roundwood. To discharge the coal a stage was made across the hold and coal was thrown into a wheelbarrow, which was wheeled direct to the boilers. Sam Slater was their boatman for many years; he worked each boat in turn. The boats were hauled between the pit and the mill by the firm's own horse, which was used for carting work when not required for boat hauling.

Robinson Brothers, the Rotherham flour millers, owned four well-found Sheffield-size wooden keels named the *Amity* (not our

Amity, see chapter six), *Annie Maud*, *Expedient* and *Honour*. They also had a half share in the keel *Invincible* with her captain George Tyler; she was only 57 feet 6 inches long and built of wood. These, along with others owned by master-owners, were employed to bring wheat from Hull to the mill, usually loading coal at Roundwood or Kilnhurst staithes as return cargo, either for the factories on the River Hull or for the bunkers of steam trawlers. No keelman lived at Rotherham in my time; the Rotherham keels were all manned by keelmen from Thorne, Stainforth or Hull. The captain of the *Amity* was a Hull man named James Horton, his usual crew being his wife and two daughters. After he retired his son Harold took over for a few years. Herbert Hinchcliffe, another Stainforth man, was captain of the *Annie Maud*, and his son was mate with him. Later, in the Spring of 1929, I was to take her over as captain after she had gone aground on the Pudding Pie Sand and filled. The captain of the *Expedient* was Joshua Matthews of Thorne. On his retirement his son Joshua took her over, and his stepson Herbert Moxon was mate with him; after a few years Herbert became captain of the *Amity* and married. George Tyler, master and half-owner of the *Invincible*, also lived at Thorne. Sam Chester lived at Thorne and was captain of the *Honour*, fourth of the Robinson fleet, for many years until his retirement; then she was taken over by his son George, who lived at Stainforth, having married into the Moxon family.

There was one open boat owned at Rotherham, used by a builders' merchant to carry limestone from Levitt Hagg to his yard on the waterside at Rotherham. He had four kilns in the yard in which the stone was burnt to make lime.

At Kilnhurst there lived three keel families. There was Dick Allen and his son Leonard, who were captain and mate of the keel *Ainsty* (built York, 1913), owned by Furley and Company of Hull. Then there were the Swales, old Charlie and his son young Charlie, who were owners and crew of the wooden keel *Glance*, and another son William, who had an old open boat which he used for carrying coal from Kilnhurst staithe to the Sheaf steelworks at Sheffield. There was also old Charlie Ridgeway, known to many keel people as "Old Bent Legs", who was captain of the iron keel *Martha*, owned by Ellison and Mitchell, tar distillers and pitch makers at Kilnhurst. They owned in addition the wooden keel *Emily*, her captain being Albert Phillipson, at that time living at Stainforth. The *Martha* and the *Emily* were used for taking the pitch to Goole for export, and when not required for this they accepted any other work they could find. Ellison and Mitchell also owned two iron tank boats for carrying tar from Doncaster gasworks to their Kilnhurst works.

Charlie Wilson's *Cedar* was the only keel owned at Swinton. She was a wooden carvel-built vessel a little less than Sheffield size, but too big for trading on the Dearne and Dove. Charlie worked her himself, employing casual labour to handle cargo, and a purchase-man when necessary. His only son worked in light engineering and in the early nineteen-thirties persuaded his father to install auxiliary power, using an old bus engine coupled to an outboard drive which he designed himself. The engine was fixed on a shelf just forward of the after headledge on the starboard side and drove the propeller, on the starboard quarter, through a system of bevel gear wheels.

E. V. Waddington had a carpenter's yard with a dry dock on the Dearne and Dove Canal at Swinton, but in the early nineteen-twenties did not own any keels, building up a fleet soon after. His son, also E. V., continued to expand the business after his father's death.

There were several open boats owned at Mexborough and employed in the local coal trade from the three coal staithes at Roundwood, Kilnhurst and Manvers to Swinton gasworks, Barron's glassworks and the power station at Mexborough. Only two keels were owned there, the *Pioneer* and *Progress*, both steel built to Dearne and Dove Canal dimensions and owned by George Bisby, who worked the *Progress* himself with his grandson as mate; the *Pioneer* was worked for him by a keelman on the usual thirds system, the keelman finding his own crew. George Bisby had a contract to carry coal from Manvers coal staithe to Gainsborough for the Gainsborough Co-operative Society; after discharging at Gainsborough he would either sail to Hull to pick up a cargo for Sheffield or go up the Trent to load sand or gravel. Kilner's glassworks at Conisbrough owned three or four open boats which they used for transporting coal from Kilnhurst staithe to the glassworks; occasionally they would go to Goole to load white sand from the railway steamers which had brought it from the Continent.

Thomas Hanley and Sons, the flour millers, were the only keel owners at Doncaster. In the nineteen-twenties they owned five Sheffield-size keels built of wood, *Daystar*, *Dayspring*, *Daybreak*, *Mayday* and *Triumph*, all well found with good sailing gear and full keel rigs. Later they were replaced by two new steel keels named *Danum* and *Daybreak*, built at Thorne with full rigs in 1932 and 1934 respectively, which were joined a few years later by a fully powered motor vessel named *Hanley's Pride*; she had a 100 hp diesel engine and could tow two keels and carry ninety tons of wheat. The two steel keels were unrigged and given diesel engines in the nineteen-forties.

All the Doncaster mill keels were manned by Thorne keelmen. Freddy Watson was captain of the *Dayspring* until he retired; for relaxation on Sundays he would take the service at one of the local

Thorne Waterside, with a tug, believed to be the Don, *towing two keels on the River Don. This tug was owned by Peter Foster of Hull, who later had the* Clara Marion. *Before the opening in 1905 of the New Junction Canal the* Don *operated between Gode and Stainforth on the River Don and the Dutch River.*
Humber Keel and Sloop Preservation Society

Methodist Chapels. His son, Billy Watson, had many years with the *Triumph* until the *Hanley's Pride* was built; he took charge of her straight from the yard and remained with her until his retirement. Jim Holt then took over and stayed with her until she was sold to be scrapped. Bill Dean transferred from one of the wooden keels to the new steel keel *Danum* when she was ready, and Bill Foster to the new steel keel *Daybreak*. Frank Moverley and Tom Dean also spent some time with Hanley's as keel captains. Isaac Walker had charge of the *Mayday* into the thirties, when he left to join the Goole firm of G. D. Holmes, being given command of the 250 tons deadweight motor vessel *De Brakeleer*; he was her captain when she was destroyed with all hands by an enemy mine while approaching Alexandra Dock in the 1939–45 War.

John Good, a house coal merchant at Doncaster, owned three or four open boats which he used to fetch his supplies of coal from Manvers Main Colliery to Doncaster. He discharged them at Brookes wharf by steam crane before the navigation was straightened in 1934, afterwards at the new wharf. An old keelman known as "Snab" Jackson worked the boats in turn, with a horseman to look after the horse. The gas and electricity works at Doncaster made use of a number of open boats to bring coal from the local collieries, and the electricity works continued to do so until 1981. In the old days they were all horse hauled; I never knew of any open boats having sailing gear. Now they have diesel engines.

LINCOLN
CAKE MILL

Captain 9

STAINFORTH was transformed after the opening in 1916 of Hatfield Main Colliery, about half a mile away. By the mid-twenties the colliery needed a larger workforce and new houses were being built in Stainforth and along the Thorne road, bringing a demand for better transport. A bus service was started between Stainforth and Doncaster, then extended to Fishlake and Sykehouse, and Fritz Freeman Bowling reopened the Friday market on land owned by his mother. By now our family had increased to five. My sister Winifred had been born in October, 1918, and my brother John in December, 1924; my brother Jim had left school and started work with Fritz Bowling in the butcher's shop and my elder sister Rhoda was helping my mother at home.

After the post-war rush, when the demurrage had gone sky high, trade settled back into the normal seasonal pattern, when in spring and early summer we would often find ourselves with a long wait between freights. This time was not wasted; it was the opportunity to do the fettling and painting. A start would be made by washing and scrubbing the tarpaulins, then dressing them with double-boiled linseed oil and tar. The brightwork on the winch posts, bittheads, cabin companionway and top strakes would be scraped and sanded down before being treated, over a period, with at least three coats of copal varnish. If we could come alongside a low bank or wall, we would scrub the hull between the light water mark and the top strakes, giving the planks a coat of coal tar, and if we expected to be laid light for more than a few days this would be followed by a coat of flour and graphite. All the blocks and windlass pawls were unshipped, cleaned and inspected before being hung on a line stretched from the backstay to the mast ready to be painted. The headledges were cleaned and primed, then allowed to harden a few days before being grained light oak. The cross pieces and featherings were taken off to be cleaned and gilded with gold leaf. Our coamings, hawse timbers and following pieces, with the timberheads, were always painted light blue. We mixed this ourselves to find the shade we wanted, using white lead as a base and ultramarine blue for colour, mixing with linseed oil and turpentine as required. The gunwale, coaming planks, and the fo'c'sle hatch were painted middle green. Some keelmen preferred sage green for the coamings, following pieces, timberheads and

Opposite page: *Keels waiting to load at the Lincoln cake mill about 1910. The picture was taken from Magpie Bridge, now known as Thorn Bridge.*
W. E. R. Hallgarth collection

hawse timbers. The steel keels had their top strakes painted a light grey and many had the coamings and timberheads painted red.

Midsummer of 1927 found me still mate with my father. I had had several offers to ship mate with other people, at more money than Father could have paid, but that was not what I was looking for. At that time I had my mind on some job ashore, but connected with shipping if possible, the reason being that trade in general was on the decline; there were many unemployed and this had an effect on our trade. The freight that can be charged on inland waterways is that which is competitive with the railways; and they were bringing their freights down in the grain and mineral trades to the point at which they were barely profitable to themselves, let alone the waterways. The grain and coal trades have always been bread and butter to the keelmen since the sinking of the first pits in the West Riding. Now, too, came the first signs of competition from road transport.

In the autumn I was tipped off that the Humber Conservancy Board were looking for a mate on one of their vessels and would give preference to a keelman. I applied for the job, and found that I was the third applicant. The first applicant was five years older than me, and he was given the job on six months' trial; he became master and remained with the vessel until he retired at sixty-five.

There were not many keelmen with regular mates; at that time casual labour was easy to find, and I could usually find a job helping some friend to load or liver when we had nothing to do on

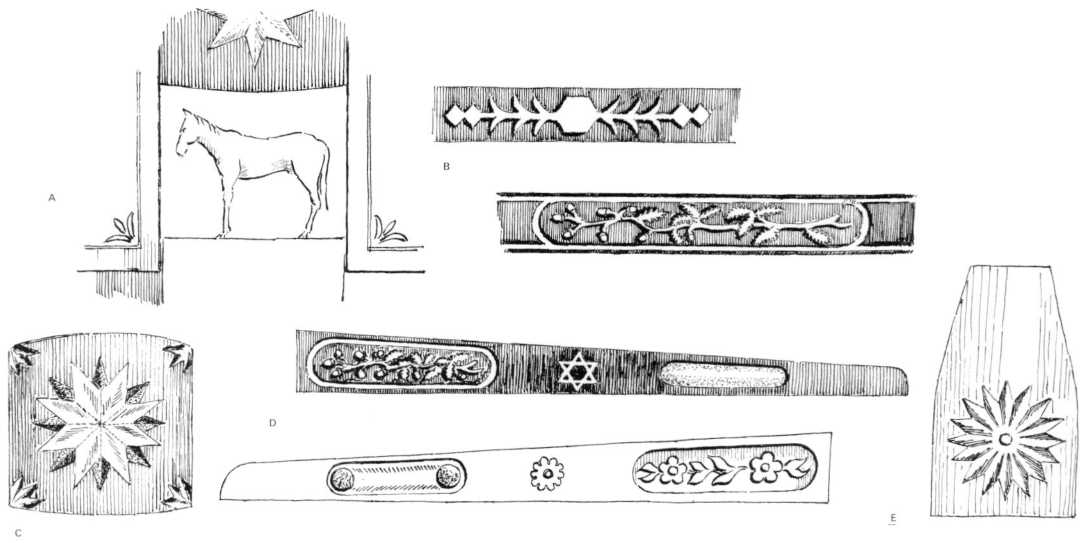

Wooden keel decoration: **A** *One keel I remember had a freestanding metal statuette of a horse at the stemhead.* **B** *Two examples of decoration, in carved and gilded low relief, of the cross timbers between the hawse and long timbers. The upper one is from one of Albert Wood's boats, the lower from my own keel* Guidance. **C** *Stem chock from the collection in the Hull Town Docks Museum.* **D** *Two featherings flanking the hawse timbers. The upper one is from the* Guidance, *the lower one from the Hull Town Docks Museum.* **E** *Stayfall block chock, also from the Town Docks Museum.*

J · J · TOMLINSON
SLOOP & KEEL OWNER · SAND & GRAVEL MERCHANT · FORWARDING AGENT
TRENT CHAMBERS · NELSON STREET · HULL

TRANSIT OF GOODS BY INLAND WATERWAYS BETWEEN
HULL · GRIMSBY
IMMINGHAM
●
KEADBY · THORNE
DONCASTER · MEXBORO'
ROTHERHAM · SHEFFIELD
●
GOOLE · CASTLEFORD
LEEDS · WAKEFIELD
●
SELBY · YORK
GAINSBORO' · NEWARK
NOTTINGHAM · LINCOLN
BARTON · BRIGG
BEVERLEY · CUNNESS

TELEPHONE: HULL 16214
CONTRACTOR FOR INLAND WATER TRANSPORT
●
RELIABILITY ALLIED WITH SPEED AND EFFICIENCY ASSURES THE BEST POSSIBLE SERVICE
●
BETWEEN NOV. 1st, 1935 AND OCT. 31st, 1936, MY TOTAL TONNAGE WAS 76,156

"Reliability allied with speed and efficiency" is promised by J. J. Tomlinson in his advertisement in the 1937 Aire and Calder Navigation publication. Humber Keel and Sloop Preservation Society

our vessel, so I could wait for some opening somewhere. With the onset of winter Arthur Walker, a Thorne keelman who was captain of the keel *Guidance*, decided to retire. The *Guidance* was owned by Uncle William Henry, Father's eldest brother; she was built in 1905 at Worfolk's Stainforth yard and was Sheffield size, carvel built of wood. Until about 1923 Uncle had worked her himself in the Sheffield trade, having a contract with Rank's to carry flour and offal from their mill at Hull to Doncaster, Rotherham and Sheffield; for return cargo he loaded steam coal for the trawlers at Hull. The flour trade was regular and provided work for four or five keels most of the time; Uncle owned two himself and engaged others as required.

About 1923 or 1924 Uncle William Henry went into partnership with John Joe Tomlinson, "Make a Penny" as he was nicknamed. Tomlinson lived on South Parade, Thorne, and owned two steel sloops and one steel keel, all Sheffield size, his main trade being the carriage of cement from Melton and Hull cement works to Sheffield. His keel was the *Parade T*, captain Fred Rhodes of Hull; the sloops were the *Humber T*, captain Freddy Walker of Barton-on-Humber, and the *Noble*, captain George (Buck) Harness of Barrow-on-Humber. J. J. Tomlinson and Uncle had three more sloops built, the *Clarence T* and the *Spider T* at Warren's of New Holland in 1925 and 1926 and the *Earl T* at Dunston's of Thorne in 1926. Additionally they had a keel built in 1924 at Dunston's named the *Leslie*; later, when the partnership was broken up after the death of William Henry, her name was changed to the *Nita*.

My keel the Guidance *in dry dock at Stainforth in 1934.* Author's collection

Jack Raper of Thorne was her captain, and Joe Holt of Hull was captain of the *Spider T* for several years. The *Guidance* was still owned entirely by William Henry, and later he bought the last wooden keel to be built at Stainforth, the *Rupert C.* Worfolk's had started her on spec in about 1915, then she was left on the stocks until Uncle William Henry had her finished in 1928.

By this time he was only going to the office in Hull about one day a week, and John Barlow, who was a ship broker on his own account, joined the partnership to look after the clerical side. About this time they bought from George Scaife, of Beverley, a new steel keel which he had named the *George A1*; she was renamed the *Junior T*, the T standing for Tomlinson. It was general on the Humber to add an initial as suffix to the ship's name to signify ownership, allowing common names to be used several times without confusion.

When Arthur Walker left the *Guidance* she was put in dry dock for survey and overhaul at Stainforth, and remained there for the winter while all the main timbers between the bulkheads were renewed. In February, 1928, Uncle told me that she would be ready by the end of the month and he would be wanting a captain; would I care to take her? I decided there and then that I would accept his offer. Like most other masters of keels I would be on thirds and expected to keep in touch with the office, but I would have a free hand to fix any cargo myself and collect the freight; and to engage the mate and any casual labour.

Thirds worked as follows (see also chapter eight):
Out of the gross freight the master would deduct and pay direct the cost of any brokerage or commission, usually five per cent of the gross; any dock and canal dues, and the cost of any towing that might be necessary on the estuary. The net sum would then be divided by three, one third going to the owner and two-thirds to the master. The owner would, out of his share, pay for the maintenance of the ship and gear, also any marine insurance. The master, out of his two-thirds, would pay the mate, casual labour needed to work ship or cargo, and horse haulage on the canals; he was responsible for feeding the marine in charge of the horse.

As I write this it is over fifty-three years since I made my last voyage as mate of the *Galatea* and my first as master of the *Guidance*, but the details are still clear in my mind. February of that year (1928) was wet and the rivers were full of fresh; my last cargo with the *Galatea* had been coal from Roundwood staithe to Beverley, and the river was so high the coal would not run freely from the spout, most had to be trimmed into the hold with round mouth shovels. When we loaded and swung to get under way, the horse had to go at a fast pace to keep the line tight; even then we

The Annie Maud, *bound for Hull Fish Dock with steam coal, in Conisbrough Lock about 1930—my own photo. The horse marine is Tom Rawnsley of Mexborough, and the man standing by the lock gate is the lock keeper. This lock has since been removed, the level of the lower pound being raised to the level of the top pound.* Humber Keel and Sloop Preservation Society

barely had steerage way. At Kilnhurst ferry we rounded up and dropped down to the lock while the horse crossed over and came to pull us into the chamber. When we stopped at the top crane at Mexborough to pick up our traps (mast and the mainyard with mainsail bent on) we did not step the mast in the lutchet as we normally do; instead we had it lowered on to the starboard side of the hatchway, so that it was completely inboard and safe from breakage by fouling.

Because of the fresh the horse would not be able to give us steerage way from Mexborough Low Lock to Doncaster, so we had to drop down stern first between each lock with the anchor, minus stock, trailing on the bottom to keep control. The horse pulled us into the locks and through the cuts. Between Conisbrough and Sprotbrough the hauling bank was under water and the horse had to use a bridleway on higher ground. Below Doncaster Lock we paid the marine his purchase, stepped the mast and continued under sail. When we entered the River Hull it, too, was full of fresh. We had a brisk fair wind, but with the mainsail and topsail set I had to go ashore with the man'sline and seal to help pull her through the narrows on Figham side below Beverley.

Next morning I went back to Stainforth by train to have the *Guidance* ready for work. As I was preparing to go, Father asked me how I was fixed for money, and thinking he might give me a few pounds to help me start, I told him about the few pounds that I had saved and asked if he thought I could manage until I could draw my first freight. He said I was better off than he had been, for when he took charge of his first ship he had to ask for a sub. I had made many friends at Beverley and enjoyed trading there, so before leaving I arranged with Hardy Scaife that my first cargo with the *Guidance* would be coal from Dalton Main Colliery, which I would load at Roundwood staithe, for the Beverley tannery of Richard Hodgson and Sons Ltd.

One of the first jobs I did when I went into the carpenter's yard at Stainforth was to ask Isaac Worfolk, the yard manager, to send a note to the colliery office at Roundwood certifying that the keel *Guidance* had been under repair at their yard, ensuring a ready turn at the staithe when I was ready to load; we called this a "laying on" note. Being in charge was not a new experience; for some time Father had been taking long weekends and leaving me to discharge cargo at Beverley and Rotherham.

From an early age Father had given me the tiller and left me by myself. I remember one time, just before Christmas, 1925, when we were laid in Sicey rack in the River Hull on passage to Beverley. The river was full of fresh and the tides in the neaps. It had been dead calm for several days, with no hope of a move until we had some wind from a southerly direction, and at breakfast on the morning of Christmas Eve Father suggested that we toss a coin to decide which of us would go home for Christmas. I told him not to bother, I would stop on board to keep watch and if possible take the ship to Beverley, so he gave me some money and put me ashore to go to either Beverley or Hull and buy some food to last over Christmas. I walked down the lane to Dunswell, and the first bus to come along was for Beverley, so that was where I did my shopping. While waiting for the bus back, John Holgate came up and I told him the situation; he volunteered to go back with me to help if there was any chance of moving on the next two tides. We were back by noon and put Father ashore to go home.

Just before dark I thought I could see a change coming, so I had the mainsail ready and rove the topsail sheets, then bent the topsail to the yard ready for use. About 8 pm there was enough wind from the south for us to get under way. By the time we reached Wawne ferry we had as much wind as we wanted, and at Figham Bottom we had to lower the topsail behind the mainsail.

Wawne Ferry on the River Hull as it was before 1939. Simpson, Beverley

The night was black with the wind freshening all the time; in Weel rack I slacked off the sheets and trussed up the mainsail with the slabline to slow her down as much as I could. As I neared the lock at Grovehill I could see, by the oil lamp on the lock side, that the low gates were open and as we entered Jack Hoggard, the lock keeper, came out and told us that the top gates were also open, so we sailed straight through and up the Beck into our berth under the gashouse crane. Next morning I woke to find everything under a foot of snow. After breakfast John arrived with an invitation to Christmas dinner.

When the *Guidance* was ready to leave Worfolk's yard, the *Galatea* was laid at Roundwood waiting a turn to load, so Father came to give me a hand to the pit. The mast and mainsail were ashore at Mexborough, but there was on board a short jury mast; so after breakfast we both bent on the topsail and set it to a light easterly wind. It was so light that I spent most of the day ashore hauling with the man'sline, while Father was steering and helping by launching with a stower. The next day we helped each other to load, and horse hauled back to Mexborough, there taking on board the mast and mainsail that had been ashore all winter.

The following morning the marine was on the bank and

The masts and yards and the leeboards of keels bound upgate lie beside the crane at Stainforth. Humber Keel and Sloop Preservation Society

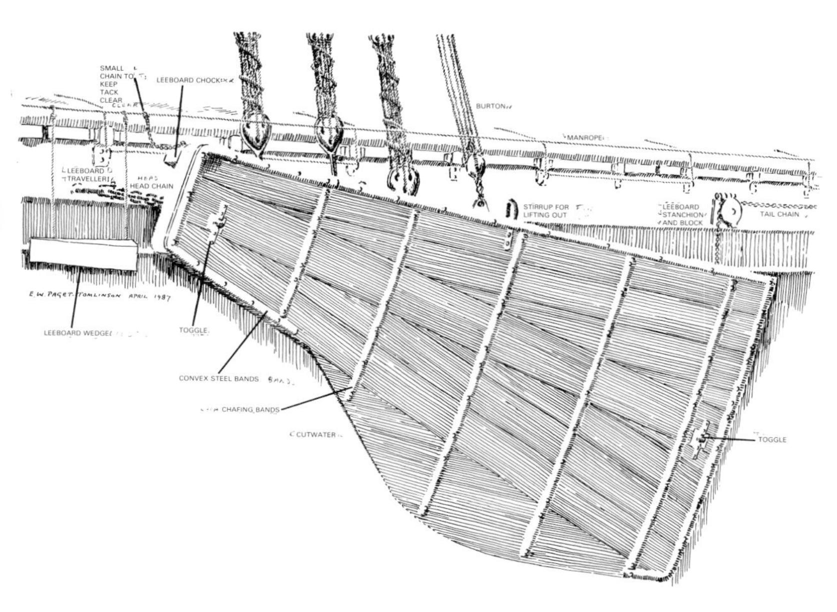

Measuring fourteen feet long by nine feet across the tail end, leeboards were built up of oak boards springing from a central member, with the edges of the boards bevelled and shaped so that the outer surface was cambered to give a better grip on the water. At the same time the boards were tapered from forward to a finer point aft, and stiffened on the inside with battens which also stopped chafe, the whole assembly being locked together by iron strapping.

waiting for the line by 5 am. He hauled us to Doncaster and we then sailed to Stainforth and picked up the leeboards from the crane near the *Station Inn*. Father arrived soon after with the *Galatea* and tied up in his usual berth at the top yard; he only had to scull the cogboat across the canal and then he could step ashore near his own front door. The keel *Eclipse* was also moored there, loaded with steam coal from Manvers Main on the Dearne and Dove Canal for bunkering the trawlers at Hull. She was owned and sailed by Harry Fowler, who lived across the field on Doncaster Road. After making everything ready for the morning I went home for the night; Mother had a meal waiting for us. She had had a busy day; there were now two ships to bake for. When she was expecting either Father or myself passing up or down she always had a cooked joint of meat and a basket of home-baked bread and pies ready for us to pick up. We all had breakfast at home the next morning, then got under way with a fresh westerly wind to catch the afternoon high water at Keadby. The *Eclipse* went first; being narrower in the beam and a few inches less draft than either the *Guidance* or the *Galatea*, she was faster in the canal. She would have about ninety-five tons of coal, while our cargo would be about 105 tons. I got under way after helping Father with his leeboards. At Thorne Lock I found Joe Holt waiting for a job and set him on straight away as purchase-man until we reached Beverley. Joe Holt was one of the large family of that name at Thorne, all keelmen

A busy scene in the Old Harbour at Hull with keels and a variety of other craft lying at the wharves.
Humber Keel and Sloop Preservation Society

and keel owners; his wife was also from a keel family, being one of "Baggy" Rusling's daughters. Joe had now reached retiring age and did a bit of purchasing to help out. Nothing ever worried him, either gale or calm, so long as there was food for the table and coal for the fire. While I penned down, Joe went home for his gear and then joined me at the Toll Bar bridge. Jack Williamson was at the bridge looking for a job and I sent him to the lock to meet the *Galatea*.

We were at Keadby in the early afternoon and high water was not while about 7 pm, so we had time to have a meal before we went out. We only intended to go to Cliff End on the first ebb, so there was no hurry. About one hour to high water the *Eclipse* went out and I followed. Two hours afterwards we were all brought up to our anchors at Cliff End ready for a good start on the next high water. I was just finishing breakfast the next morning, when I heard the clatter of windlass pawls, and looking up I could see the *Galatea* weighing anchor. There was a strong tide flowing, but we only had a few hundred yards to go, then we would get the benefit of the eddy tide (or outwent as it was called by keelmen), which would take us down the East Trent until we made East Point, when we would again have to stem the flood, which by then would be losing strength.

The sound of the pawls brought the crew of the *Eclipse* on deck, so we all got under way at the same time. She was in the lower berth and soon had the benefit of the outwent, leaving us standing still in the full strength of the tide until she again had to stem the tide at Trent Falls. The main channel at that time was south of Read's Island ("Old Warp" to a keelman), and by timing ourselves to be at Whitton Ness by about high water we could make a straight course to Oyster Ness, then down the Redcliff channel. When the wind was southerly this saved time and much hard work. As we opened out the Ness I had the pleasure of seeing the *Guidance* gain on the *Galatea* and pass her, beating her into Hull Old Harbour by about twenty minutes. It was about two hours after high water, just in time to have the Half Penny Bridge opened so that we could sail up to Victoria Dock Basin. (Half Penny Bridge, a toll bridge, was to the south of the present Myton Bridge.)

After livering at Beverley, my next freight was ninety tons of cement in paper sacks from Melton cement works for Sheffield. For this voyage my purchase-man was an out-of-work lighterman, Jack Carter, a young man about my own age. He was engaged to go with me from Hull to Melton, then help me to load and sail the keel to either Keadby or Goole for a fixed sum of money, plus his food on board. The sum, as far as I can remember, would be about three pounds. We had to be on the loading berth at Melton jetty for a 7.30 am start on the Monday morning, so we went up from Hull on the afternoon tide on Sunday.

The loading berth at Melton above North Ferriby was in a drain head which had tide doors and a sluice to hold back a head of water. Then, at low tide, the water could be let out to scour the berth and prevent silting. We had to go in stern first ready for coming out on the tide. There was a buoy moored about half a cable (one hundred yards) off shore, so that a warping line could be used to move vessels in or out in calm weather; there was also a wire attached to the buoy, the other end being on the jetty ready to sheer a vessel off into deep water when leaving with a strong tide running. The cement came down to the jetty from the factory on a ropeway, ten sacks at a time on pallets, the sacks being lowered into the hold by a crane. Each sack contained a hundredweight and was hot to the touch. The loading was done while the vessel was aground and ninety tons were on board by 4 pm, so we had time to cover up and batten down before we floated again. The wind was north-east, so both sails were set while on the berth, and the wire from the buoy was made fast to the after timber on the port bow. When I was sure that she had water to go out of the creek without touching the bottom on the west side, I cast off, and she went out like the cork from a bottle. At the right time, I gave the signal for Jack to slip the wire and we were on our way. We fetched Keadby by high water, and after penning into the canal moored for the night.

The next morning Jack went with me to as far as Thorne, on the offchance that he might find another job on a vessel coming down; if not he could take the train from there direct to Hull, which was better than going by New Holland. I gave him five shillings (25p) extra for this, which would just cover his train fare. I made it to Doncaster in good time, then had the sails and the mast ready for going ashore at Mexborough. Bernard James hauled me up from Doncaster to Sheffield and was lucky enough to find the job of hauling a light vessel down to one of the pits. The cement was discharged into the warehouse which spans the basin. I did all the work myself; the sacks had to be put two at a time into canvas strops. I had drawn my first freight for the coal cargo at Beverley, but would not receive the freight for the cement until I returned to Hull, so I used the owner's thirds for the coal freight to finance the third cargo; I would pay the thirds into my uncle's bank at Hull and give him the paying-in slip when convenient.

A page from the cargo book of the keels Waverley *and* Williams *dated 1913, preserved at the Hull Town Docks Museum. Note the phonetic spelling. Leven, about four miles to the east of the River Hull upstream of Beverley, was at the head of a three-and-a-quarter-mile canal opened about 1804 and closed in 1935.* Hull Town Docks Museum

127
Nov 5th
Grain from Levan for Hull
239 qurs at d per qurs £ S D
freight 5 19 0
dues 19 10
C freight 3|4 19 8
Thirds 1 13 2
Settled up
Nov 13th Cement from Hull to Leeds 90 tons
67 tons for 4 0 10 23 tons at 1/3d per ton £ S D
freight 3|5 18 0
Thirds 1 19 1
Nov 27th Coal from Parkhill to Leven 87 tons
at 1/3d per ton £ S D
freight 14 2 6
dues 3 12 6
towing 0 14 6
H B dues 0 1 0
C freight 9 14 6
Thirds 3 4 10
Settled up

128
Dec 11th Grain & Carrots from Leven for Hull grain 6d .. qurs carrots 3d per ton £ S D
freight 6 15 9
dues 1 6 4
Settled up
C freight 3|5 9 5
Thirds 1 16 5½
Dec 29th Coals from Parkhill to Leven
86 tons at 3/3 per ton £ S D
freight 13 19 6
Dues 3 11 8
Towing 0 14 6
Hull B dues 0 1 0
C freight 3|9 12 4
Thirds 3 4 1½
Settled up

I thought I had made a good start with my first two cargoes. The coal freight was at 3s 6d (17½p) per ton clear of brokerage, canal and Beck dues. The cement was 4s 6d (22½p) per ton, also clear of brokerage and canal dues. So my thirds book read as follows:

	£	s	d
Roundwood to Beverley			
Coal 105 tons at 3s 6d clear	18	7	6
One third	6	2	6
	12	5	0

	£	s	d
Melton to Sheffield			
Cement 90 tons at 4s 6d clear	20	5	0
One third	6	15	0
	13	10	0

One third owner's share on the two freights was:	£	s	d
	6	2	6
	6	15	0
	12	17	6

And my two thirds was:	£	s	d
	12	5	0
	13	10	0
	25	15	0

Out of this my expenses were:	£	s	d
Lock pennies (tips) up and down from Stainforth to Roundwood and back to Keadby		1	5
Crane charge at Mexborough for storage and lifting on mast and sail		1	6
Horse hauling from Roundwood to Doncaster at 15s per stage	1	5	0
Purchase-man Thorne to Beverley	1	12	6
Casual labour at Beverley: one man discharging coal 105 tons at 2d per ton		17	6
Purchase-man from Hull to Thorne including payment for loading	3	5	0
Lock pennies Keadby to Sheffield		1	7
Casual help up Tinsley Locks		2	0
Horse hauling Doncaster to Sheffield, 15s per stage plus 5s extra on the top stage	2	10	0
Allowance to warehouse gang Sheffield		2	0
	9	18	6

To this there should be added the cost of feeding the purchase-man and the horse marine, from memory I would say a pound. That sort of money went a long way in the early twenties and thirties. When loading at any of the pit staithes it was the custom for the weigh men at the weigh office to give the person collecting the weigh note one shilling allowance; this was always passed on to the staithe gang.

I was soon to find that my uncle's office regarded the *Guidance* as a bye trader, and only offered work to me when the vessels fully owned by the partnership were not available; my uncle being sole owner of the *Guidance*, I accepted this and looked elsewhere for work. As I made my tour of the brokers and shipping offices I had to face many searching questions about myself and the seaworthiness of my ship; I found that because my uncle had for the last twenty years carried only flour from Rank's mill as his upgate cargo, the *Guidance* was not known to some of the people using keels for transport. However, being Arthur Schofield's son carried weight, and I soon became known to the office runners who would approach me when they were going round the harbour and docks if they had anything to offer. I accepted anything that I thought would show a profit, and this has been my policy throughout my working life; even sulphur and iron pyrites, or copper ore as it was often called. Father would never carry these cargoes while I was with him; after carrying them myself I knew the reason why. Both were unpleasant, and the fumes from the sulphur would hang about for weeks.

I remember two occasions when this policy paid off. The first time I had delivered coal to a trawler in the Fish Dock in Hull, and could see that trade was slack by the number of light keels laid about waiting for work. But it was always policy to have a walk round the offices when livered, if only to lay on and make sure that we would be considered in our turn as work came along. My first call was at the office of Alexander Meek and Sons on Prince's Dock side; they were steamship owners, shipbrokers and forwarding agents, and also owned a fleet of river craft, all dumb vessels. The outer office was full of men waiting for orders. After waiting a while I made to go out. As I went to the door, Percy Andrew, who was the manager, came out of his office and asked if my vessel was light. I said "Yes" and he asked me to wait until he got rid of the crowd. After they had gone he called me from his office, "Come in Joe"—he called everyone Joe. When I entered he said, "I have just one job, if you would like to consider it, I daren't offer it to anyone really; if you turn it down it won't offend. It is so bad that I cannot make any profit out of it myself, so I offer it to you." I said, "It sounds bad. I'd better know what it is." He said: "It's copper ore for Goole alum works, at the usual freight of 1s 9d (9p) per ton; you can load tomorrow ex ship in Albert Dock, but there are only eighty tons. If I do this for myself and pay towing to Goole and back, plus two men's wages, I'll be out of pocket, so I'm offering the

Opposite page: *Keels lying in Princes Dock, Hull, with the old dock offices, now the Town Docks Museum, in the background. The keelman, Tom Bogg, is holding a sounding rod.* Hull Town Docks Museum

job to you." It was then Thursday. I asked about the turnround at Goole. He said: "If you can be alongside at Goole on Monday morning at eight o'clock, I will arrange for your discharge straight away. Goole alum works are to provide all the labour." So I agreed.

I was ready to leave Hull on the Saturday morning tide, and was lucky to have a fair wind. My father came and worked his passage to Goole on his way home for the weekend, so I reached

Keels on the Humber, from a drawing of the port of Hull by W. L. Wyllie engraved by R. Paterson. The keel's topsail is being broken out of the stops as the sail is set; it is the practice to tie the topsail in stops before attempting to set it with any amount of wind. At right is a ketch-rigged billyboy also just setting her square topsail. Hull Town Docks Museum

Goole without any expense. During the weekend I arranged for a horse and marine to be ready to haul me from Goole to Roundwood as soon as the cargo was out. I loaded coal and was back in the Fish Dock at Hull before the keels I had left in the dock had made a move. The freight to Goole was only seven pounds, but it was all clear money and paid the cost of obtaining another and better freight.

The Guidance *in the Royal Dock, Grimsby, lying astern of the steam trawler* Thomas Thresher, *built at Selby in 1917 and owned by the Grimsby Steam Fishing Co. Ltd.* Author's collection

The other time was in the spring of 1932 when competition from road transport was beginning to take trade away from both coasting and inland waterway craft. It was a cargo of barley from Grimsby to Gledhill's at Gainsborough. Road transport had quoted a price door to door which made it hard for water transport to compete. The barley was at Sanderson's malt kiln, and had first to be transported to the dock by rail before it could be loaded into the craft. Grimsby being a seaport, all labour had to be carried out by stevedores; on top of their charges one had to add the cost of rail transport, wharfage, crane hire and dock dues, which left only three shillings and six pence (17½p) per ton for the keel's freight, which was rather on the low side; only by sailing and avoiding any towage charges would I be able to make it pay. We sailed to Grimsby on the Wednesday and tied up on our berth in the Royal Dock. Sutcliffes were the stevedores and their superintendent came down in the afternoon to say they would be ready to start loading the next morning. We penned out on the Saturday morning tide and in a freshening south-west wind sailed to Barrow Roads by night. It was blowing a gale and we remained at anchor until the gale moderated, with the wind veering north-west early Monday morning. We were on Gledhill's berth at Gainsborough ready for work on Tuesday morning. Discharging took two days. A telephone call to Hull confirmed that there was no work on offer there, so I arranged to go up to the Stainforth and Keadby Canal for a cargo of coal.

If anyone had asked me how I was doing in the late summer of 1928 I would have replied "Very well, thank you." But the winter was to be financially the worst of my working life. Early in December, while driving through "No Man's Friend" (a rack on the Trent below Morton bight), Curly Thompson, in charge of the steam tug *Welshman*, came up towing five loaded keels, the last in tow a large dumb oil tanker owned by the Medway Oil Storage Co. Ltd, an unhandy vessel which had recently started to trade on the river. The tug and five keels passed well clear on our port side, but to my amazement the tanker took a sheer to starboard and was on a collision course with our port side. The tanker's mate ran forward to lower the anchor but he was too late, and this anchor stove in three planks on our port side. The *Guidance* was loaded with Trent gravel and settled on the bottom. Darkness was already on us and there was not much I could do except get in the boat with my mate and go back to Morton and find a telephone. John Joe Tomlinson was the only one with a telephone at home and I rang him at Thorne so that arrangements for salvaging the *Guidance* could be made as soon as possible.

The next job was to find somewhere to sleep. The pub landlord directed me to Mrs Cook, who had a shop in the village and was the daughter of a keelman named Barlow. She knew many keel people from Owston Ferry and Stainforth so we were made welcome and comfortable. After fixing up with her we went back on board at low water and ferried ashore what gear we could recover and put up a light that would show above high water level.

On the next afternoon tide Albert Leggett brought his smack from Owston Ferry to ride mark vessel, and left Bob Turgoose to be watch keeper. I agreed to go stand watch with him on night tides and in fog. When traffic was quiet, he would pass the time away by reciting with great relish his imagined sea adventures; he was a bigger glorified liar than Baron Münchhausen. John Will Barraclough was the next of the salvage fleet to arrive with the *Rising Hope*, a small wooden sloop-rigged billyboy. Albert Leggett and his men started straight away to prepare her for lifting the *Guidance* by shoring up her beams and sparrings with large baulks of timber. Albert Leggett's son Tommy was the last to arrive with his sloop the *Salvager A*, a large steel vessel about 68 feet long by 17 feet beam; at

A depressing scene: salvage work begins on my sunken keel Guidance *in December, 1928. The steel sloop* Salvager A *is alongside as preparations are made to dredge out the cargo of gravel.*
Author's collection

that time she was nearly new, about a year or two old, built, I believe, by Dunston's at Thorne.

As soon as the beams had been shored up on both vessels, the hold of the *Guidance* was opened out at low water to make ready for lightening and so make her easier to lift; her hatches and tarpaulins were still in place because she had been battened down soon after loading. The gaff of the *Salvager A* was used for a derrick so that, by means of snatch blocks on the masts of both the *Guidance* and the *Salvager A*, we could dredge out the gravel by the same method as it had been lifted from the bed of the Trent in the first place. Four men heaving on the fore roller of the *Salvager A* supplied the power. When as much gravel as possible had been dredged out wires were pulled under the stern of the *Guidance* and worked into position under the after hold and the fore hold, then passed around both the lifting vessels, hove tight and clamped together. This was all done at low water. As the tide flowed, the *Guidance* was lifted clear of the bottom and warped into shoal water by the lifting vessels' gear; it needed two tides to lift her high enough for the water to be pumped out.

As soon as the *Guidance* was pumped out it was seen that the damage was above light water mark, so the tug, which had come upriver on the flood, towed the four vessels to Leggett's wharf at Owston Ferry. Bob Turgoose went home to his daughter, who was the local postwoman, and I spent the next two nights with Albert Leggett. On the following day we emptied the remaining gravel and transferred back to the *Guidance* the hatches and other gear that had been on board the sloops.

The next day was Christmas Eve. After breakfast I and Bob Turgoose sailed the *Guidance* to Keadby and penned her into the canal. Bob then had to walk the nine miles to Owston Ferry and I caught a train to Stainforth for the worst Christmas that I can remember. We only took time off work for Christmas Day and Boxing Day in those days, so the *Guidance* was in dry dock at the top yard, Stainforth, and ready for survey before the New Year. Fortunately there was no other structural damage than the planks that had been staved in, and these were soon replaced. A far worse job was cleaning out the Trent warp that had gathered in every nook and cranny while she had been under water. Part of the shutts had to be taken up to get it all out.

In February, 1929, I had another setback. I loaded phosphate for Saxilby, and arrived at the tillage works on a Saturday afternoon, with the Fossdyke free of ice. By Sunday morning it was frozen over about an inch thick. On the Monday morning they had to have twelve horses to pull the icebreaker, and it took them all day to go from Lincoln to Torksey. They made it back to Lincoln on the Tuesday, but were only cutting a channel equal to the beam of the icebreaker. I was ready to follow them out on the Wednesday. When we reached Drinsey Nook we found a tug and some Lincoln catches fast in the ice; they had left Torksey following the icebreaker the day before. There was only a single channel in the middle and the sides were several inches thick. After trying to make a passage past, the icebreaker had to give in and the horses were walked back to Saxilby station and put on the train for Lincoln. It was about a fortnight before we were all free—and they had to use fourteen horses to pull the icebreaker.

In the next few months I managed to keep finding enough work to keep me going, but freights were low and there were many out of work. I often thought to myself that I was lucky to be my own master. Plenty of single men were having to exist on dole money, which, if I remember right, was only about twenty-seven shillings and sixpence (£1.37½) per week for a single person. After clearing the ice I made my way by driving and sailing into the Alexandra Dock, Hull, on spec. The morning after arriving in the dock, the dock runner of the Aire and Calder Navigation offered me a cargo for Leeds. The freights from the Aire and Calder office were always less money per ton than any other office because they provided free towing by their own or other tugs, which was an advantage to anyone working by thirds. First I loaded several tons of olive oil in casks, then about a hundred quarters of wheat in four-bushel* sacks, filling up with reels of paper and about one ton of coconuts in net bags, about eighty tons altogether.

* 252lb in each sack of wheat, barley only 224lb.

In the spring of 1929 Jimmy Walker asked if I would like to consider shipping master of the keel *Annie Maud*, owned by Robinson Brothers, the Rotherham flour millers. Jimmy Walker had been forwarding agent and ship's husband for them since the death of John Tommy Rusling, his father-in-law. The *Annie Maud* had been aground on Pudding Pie Sand in the Humber loaded with coal; she was a wooden vessel and her seams opened so that she filled and sank. She then went on Dunston's slip in Thorne for repairs. Herbert Hinchcliffe of Stainforth was her master at the time of her sinking, but he had since joined a trawler bunkering gang at Hull. It was an attractive offer because bulk wheat and coal were two easy cargoes to work, and the agent would see to all the arrangements on the shore end of the job such as lodging bills of lading, the orders of shipping clerks, and making arrangements with stevedores when cargo had to be loaded direct overside from ships. Another attraction was that she would need new standing and running gear except leeboards; the mast, yards and mainsail had been lost or damaged by the salvage contractors. I was keen to take the job, but the next thought was how to tell my uncle; this was going to be difficult. However, he saw it from my point of view and took it very well. The *Annie Maud* would not be ready until late May, so there was time to make arrangements for someone to replace me.

Before leaving the *Guidance* I had the experience of loading a cargo of coal while laid on the foreshore, from the site of the cement works at Chalder Ness. They had closed down and left about two hundred tons of coal in the stockyard which had to be transferred to the cement works at Wilmington on the River Hull. I loaded the *Guidance* first and Joe Robson followed with the keel *Parade T*. We had to hold off to anchor and kedge so that we would float off when we loaded. As soon as we took the ground the trestles were put on the foreshore to carry the planks on which the baskets full of coal were wheeled and tipped into the hold.

I then worked out my notice to leave the *Guidance* by taking a cargo of newsprint from a Baltic trader in Victoria Dock, Hull, to Sheffield Basin for the local papers. They were large reels, but Uncle William Henry took the train to Sheffield and gave me a hand to get them out. Knowing that I had to re-rig the *Annie Maud*, he took the opportunity to give me some good advice on what not to do. Ernest Oglesby, another Stainforth keelman, followed me as master of the *Guidance* for about a year; then he left to take charge of the keel *Amity*, also owned by Robinson Brothers.

During the summer of 1929 my father rather unexpectedly made an exchange of vessels with John "Herrings" Taylor, which was much in my father's favour. Trade was slack and had been so for several weeks when one day while all the keel captains with

Loading and unloading was sometimes done actually on the foreshore. At Barton-on-Humber some vessels loaded from a rickety wooden pier which stretched out into the Humber, as seen in this photograph printed from a glass negative. Hull Town Docks Museum

empty vessels were waiting, as they usually did, on Bishop Lane Staithe to see the brokers as they came to call at the *Pacific*, John Taylor came along with his usual swaggering gait. He was dressed in best suit and trilby hat, a gold albert slung across his chest, and the usual large lighted cigar in his mouth (he was noted for his liking of port wine and large cigars).

After some good-natured banter from all round, talk turned to the present and future prospect of trade. Taylor became despondent and said he was fed up and looking for a buyer for everything he had, except the old woman. After a while he and my father agreed to exchange keels. John Taylor was to have the *Galatea* and six hundred pounds in cash, Father was to take the *Ada Carter* and all the sailing gear then on board the *Galatea*, including masts, yards, sails and leeboards, all standing and running rigging, including gins and blocks; also the sheet rollers, tack rollers, leeboard rollers, and the cogboat. This transfer of sailing gear was done the next day in Alexandra Dock.

I can only think that Taylor must have been desperate for wine and cigar money. The *Galatea* was a wooden vessel over twenty years old and the *Ada Carter* was a steel vessel, then only six years old. She had been built by Warren's Shipyard at New Holland as the *Wanda* for Turner Carmichael of Hull, to replace the keel *Pioneer* which he had lost off Alexandra Dock after being run down by a steamer. John Taylor changed her name to *Ada Carter*, which I believe was the maiden name of his wife. At the earliest opportunity, Father changed her name to *Comrade*, after the steel keel of that name which he had tried to buy from George Robert Scaife before the 1914–18 War. He had been outbid by Ambrose Holt of Thorne, but Ambrose had her only a short while before she was commandeered by the War Department and sent across the Channel; the last news we had of her was that she was working on the Thames as a lighter in the early nineteen-twenties.

When I went to Dunston's yard at Thorne to take over the *Annie Maud* the new mast and yards were already on board waiting for me to rig her out. At that time Dunston's were still mast and block makers as well as shipbuilders and repairers, though they were no longer sailmakers, riggers or ropemakers. The former ropewalk, then a pathway used by the shipyard workers on their way to and from work, is today the access road to a new housing estate, still known as the Ropewalk. The painter had recently finished repainting the *Annie Maud's* cabin, so I went below to inspect his work before going to the stores. The panels had been painted to represent birdseye maple, with walnut surrounds; the

The shipyard of Richard Dunston Ltd at Thorne a few years after I went there to take over the Annie Maud. *A number of steel vessels can be seen under construction.* John Wain collection

mahogany buffet and locker were newly polished and the light to the cabin, coming from a skylight instead of the usual prism in the deckhead, made it appear nice, light and airy, with plenty of locker cupboard space, not so dark as the usual varnished mahogany and oak. The new sails, along with the shrouds and wire halyards, were in the stores, where there was plenty of cordage to choose from, and all the shackles I should need, plus new navigation lights and cabin lamps; also fogbell and foghorn, new signal shapes and hatch covers.

When the crew has to leave a vessel, either through her stranding or her sinking, it is almost certain that some light-fingered person will proceed to strip her of anything that he can transport away by one means or another. If by any chance there should be anything left worth taking away when the salvage contractor takes over, his employees usually contrive to remove it before the vessel is handed back to the owner. The *Annie Maud* was no exception. Only the anchors and cables remained; the rest of the ship was as bare as Mother Hubbard's cupboard.

My mother and father on the Comrade *at Stainforth, seen in a photograph I took late in 1934 when the Comrade was bound for Mexborough with a cargo of bulk wheat. My youngest sister Winifred is standing on the hatches and my wife is seated beside her. In the background is the house built for my grandfather and in which my parents later lived.* Humber Keel and Sloop Preservation Society

So, in addition to the gear already mentioned, I ordered the following items:

Two yards of lamp wick
One vane and spindle
Three yards of red bunting six inches wide
One ball of marline
One ball of whipping twine
One ball of sewing twine
One ball of spunyarn
Two marline spikes
One lignum vitae fid, 1 foot 6 inches long
One lignum vitae fid, 1 foot long
Two cabin hand brushes
Two cabin fire shovels
Two blacklead brushes
One three-pint kettle
One four-pint kettle
One beef kettle (two and a half gallons)
One cast-iron frying pan (10 inch)
One brass tidy
One brass fender and fire irons
One black fo'c'sle fender and fire irons
One tin of blacklead
One tin of Brasso
One white enamel freshwater bucket
One funnel for filling the fresh-water tank
One hold brush and shaft
One dust brush and shaft
One hard deck scrubber
One soft paint scrubber with shafts
Two draw buckets with thimbles on the handle to keep the spliced-on strop in the middle
One axe
One saw
One hammer
Two galvanized padlocks
Two cork fenders
Two bowline pins to secure
Four winch handles
One idle back
Two chain flitters, ¾-inch, for the anchor cables
Two small flitters for the leeboard tail chain and stayfall chain
Spare lamp glasses:
one tall one for the cabin
one short one for the fo'c'sle and stern light
One red cone for the sidelights
One green cone for the sidelights
One hand spike for the windlass
Two grain scoops
Two round mouth coal shovels
Two square mouth coal shovels
One anchor davit and tackle blocks
One 18 feet sounding rod
One 18 feet boathook with grains
Two 16 feet boathooks with grains
Two 22 feet stowers with grains
One 24 feet stower with grain
One mop with shaft
One footing plank 16 feet long, 10 inches wide, 1⅝ inches thick
Two tar brushes
One tar bucket
One gallon of tar in a can
One gallon of black varnish
One two-gallon paraffin can with two gallons of paraffin
Two one-gallon linseed oil cans with one gallon of linseed oil and one gallon of boiled linseed oil
One gallon can with one gallon of Stockholm tar
One stuffing brush
One two-inch varnish brush
One gallon of copal varnish
Four paint brushes from two inch to one inch
Two paint kettles
Turpentine
Dryers
Two books of gold leaf for decoration

- Seven pounds of white lead
- Half a pound of ultramarine blue
- Chrome yellow, green powder, indian red, lamp black
- One 90-fathom cotton line 1½ inches in circumference for a warping line
- Three 45-fathom lengths of 1¾ inches circumference cotton line for horse haulage
- One 30 fathom ⅜ inch circumference cotton line for man haulage
- One canvas seal
- Two pounds of tallow to grease the shroud lanyards
- 30 fathoms of 2¼ inches circumference best Italian hemp for the shroud lanyards
- 15 fathoms of 1½ inch circumference Italian hemp for the backstay and manrope lanyards
- One fine 9 inches circumference coir 30 fathoms long for a tow rope
- One 5 inches circumference coir 25 fathoms long for mooring in Hull harbour
- Two 15 fathom lengths of manilla 4 inches circumference
- One ball of hambro line
- Two stop rope hooks which would also be used as tack hooks
- One snatch block
- Good supply of small hemp and manilla line for tack ends and halyards

The mast and yards were laid on the hatches, just as the carpenter had finished making them, so I gave them a dressing of raw linseed oil. While waiting for this to set, I made a wire grommet with three links to fit on the mast just above the sheave hole, or "hoynins" as a keelman would say; a deep-waterman would say "at the main hounds". The three links were positioned so that the middle one would take the backstay hook and the side ones were on the afterside of the mast ready for the burton pendants. The next job was to remove the nut from the sheave pin, reeve the main tye, then replace and tighten the nut on the starboard side; this was done first so there would be no need to move the shrouds after they had once been put in place. The starboard shrouds always go on first, followed by the port shrouds, which are always made two inches longer than the starboard ones, to allow for them being on top. The forestay fits on top of both pairs of shrouds. The topsail parrels were fitted, and the next stage was to reeve the topsail tye. The sheave hole should be large enough to allow the tye to pass without any bother; it has then to be passed through the thimble on the parrels. The topsail halyard block, with the halyard already rove, was next shackled on to the tye and the backstay hook put in the link on the grommet.

The mast was now ready to be run outboard and the heel put in the lutchet. I had two carpenters to help me with this. While waiting for them I screwed the vane spindle into the plate on the masthead, having already sewn a yard and a half of red bunting on the vane; last of all, the topmast forestay was hooked into the hoop

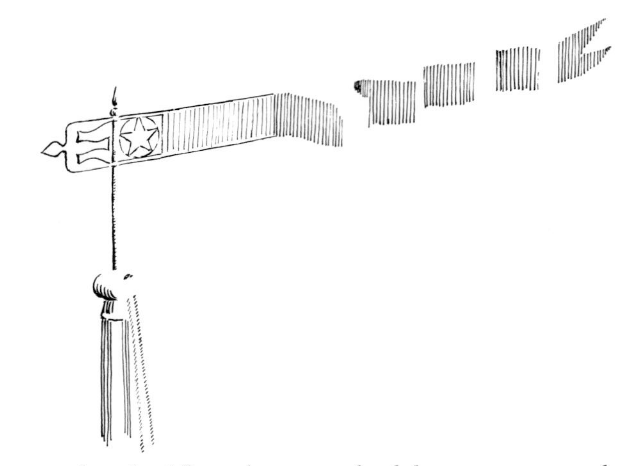

The vane, rotating on a brass spindle, not only showed the direction of the wind but also its strength, which could be judged from the behaviour of the pendant, six inches wide and four foot six inches long.

on the masthead. After the mast had been run out the stayfall blocks were shackled on and the fall rove; when the mast had been hove up part of the way, the mainsail halyard gin could be shackled on to the tye. The next job was to bend the mainsail, after which I stowed the stores while the foreman sawyer made five dozen batten wedges. Lastly I took on board a bag of sawdust, then went up to Stainforth to fetch my personal gear.

The keels owned by Robinson Brothers usually loaded bunker coal at Roundwood staithe for the account of the Kingston Steam Trawling Company on their way down after livering at Rotherham mill. Dunston's yard manager had already sent a laying-on note to the colliery, so I put a letter in the post to George Edwards, who was the coal manager for Kingston's, to let him know of my intention to go to Roundwood. I could have gone to Hull to load wheat, but it was better that I should load coal for the first cargo. The *Annie Maud* had laid empty for several weeks in very hot weather and there was always the risk of a wooden vessel drying out and making some water on first loading, so I went to the pit. It was an open order and no previous arrangement was necessary. Another advantage was that there would be a ready turn; if I had gone to Hull I might have had to wait several days for a ship to arrive before I could load. Before starting to load the coal I put the pump boxes in a bucket of water to soak and swell; after taking about sixty tons on board the pump was tried, but it would not prime, so there was nothing to worry about.

Robinson's mill at Rotherham was a short way up the River Rother away from the main navigation, which made their moorings a nice quiet berth, but difficult to enter when there was any fresh in the river. The horse could only haul the vessel to Ickles New Cut End; then the stowers had to be used to launch the vessel up to the mill. If there should be any fresh running, we had to warp up, using the fore roller with the warping line passing through a block on the neddy so that the vessel could be steered. From Law's wharf up to the Bow Bridge the warping line was fastened to piles which had been driven into the bed of the River Don for that purpose. When one of the keels had a new boat the old one was taken to the mill, so that it could be used for running the warping line ahead. With more than two feet of fresh we could not get back through the Bow Bridge when the ship was empty.

It was rare that one had a quick turnround at Rotherham mill. The rate of intake was usually one vessel per day, 420 quarters (94½ tons). The silo would hold about nine hundred tons, but to safeguard themselves from stoppages through late arrival of grain ships at Hull, through keels not being able to navigate because of fresh in the river, which could occur at any time of the year, or through the possibility of the navigation being ice-bound in winter, Robinson's always tried to arrange to have a good supply of wheat afloat in keels. Demurrage was paid to the master and owners after laying four clear working days, so if possible one made an effort to arrive and have the bill of lading signed before noon. The day of arrival then counted as the first lay day, but if one finished discharging before noon that day was not a lay day. Another compensation was that the freight was always sixpence (2½p) above the wheat freight for Sheffield, which was six miles and fifteen locks further up the navigation, a total of fourteen to sixteen hours' additional working time up and down.

Robinson's keels were managed independently of the mill. When the cargo was out, the full freight was waiting in the office for the master to collect. We always loaded coal as return cargo,

Bow Bridge, Rotherham, through which keels had to pass to reach the Town Mills. When there was more than two feet of fresh in the river we could not get back through the bridge after unloading at the mills. Author's collection

The keel Muriel *discharging bunker coal to a steam trawler in St Andrew's Dock, Hull, about the turn of the century. Her captain, Thomas Shirtliff, stands with his hands in his pockets aboard the trawler.* Miss E. A. Shirtliff collection

usually for the Kingston Steam Trawling Company; again the turnround was dependent on the state of the weather, which could affect the fishing, and the quanitity of bunkers that the trawlers would need. Demurrage was paid after the usual lay days. Having their bunker coal in keels was a great convenience to Kingston's. When landings were heavy and there was a waiting list for a berth at the coaling appliances, Kingston's could have a keel go alongside the trawler and start to fill her bunkers while she was still landing fish. George Edwards of Kingston's would have the freight ready in

The keel Ancholme *alongside a steam trawler in Hull Fish Dock.* Humber Keel and Sloop Preservation Society

Having recently discharged coal into a steam trawler in St Andrew's Dock, Hull, the Annie Maud *has made a two-mile reach on the port tack towards New Holland. We have to get into King George Dock to load grain for the Town Mills at Rotherham. We have just stayed on to the starboard tack, and with a bit of luck we can hope to make King George Dock on this board, having sailed five miles to gain three. I took this picture from the cogboat; the man at the tiller is Ernest Downing of Stainforth, master and owner of the keel* Samaritan, *and the boy is his nephew Bob.* Author's collection

cash by three o'clock on the day we finished livering. When settling we paid him five shillings (25p) brokerage for his trouble, and this was deducted from the gross freight before paying thirds.

In the early nineteen-thirties there were still many grain ships discharging in Alexandra Dock overside direct into keels and lighters. If our cargo was in one of these we might be two or three days before we could have a turn. It was better when we had to pick up a cargo from the silo in King George Dock, or from one of the warehouses in the Old Harbour; we could then expect to be loaded within a few hours of arriving at the silo or warehouse. It was Jimmy Walker's job as Robinson's forwarding agent to lodge the orders with the shipping clerks and others. We rarely saw him until we were loading; he would then turn up with our bill of lading and declaration note, and I would hand over to him the owner's thirds for the last two cargoes, less any amount of money I had spent on ship's stores. He would then sign the thirds and ask if I needed any sub.

Keel Owner 10

I HAD not long been with the *Annie Maud* when Uncle William Henry started to have some trouble with his throat. After seeing several consultants and spending some time in both Leeds and Doncaster Infirmaries, he was told that nothing could be done for him, and after a long illness he died in the spring of 1931. Under the terms of his will, the partnership with J. J. Tomlinson was ended and their keels had to be sold, the money being invested in a trust fund for his wife. My father and his brother-in-law, Luther Dishman, were named as executors.

Tomlinson was given time to find the money to buy the shares of the vessels he was interested in. Walter Barley of Thorne bought the keel *Leslie* and changed her name to *Nita*, George Wilson of Goole bought the keel *Rupert C*. When Father asked me if I would like the *Guidance* I told him I did not think I had enough capital to start on my own. He replied that if I was going to wait until I could afford to buy I would never be a keel owner, so I told him to go ahead and arrange the sale, and the *Guidance* was transferred to me in February, 1932.

I had enjoyed my time with Robinson's. I do not think I could have found a better job, because I had not had the worry of having to find a cargo every few days. That was a considerable advantage in such difficult times as those were. Since the trouble on the New York Stock Exchange in October, 1929, which became known as the "Wall Street Crash", world trade had generally been in a bad way. After the crash, the world price of wool and grain fell to rock bottom, and in Germany the already growing economic crisis quickened in pace until by November, 1929, they had two million unemployed. Adolf Hitler promised to make Germany strong again, and thus were sown the seeds of the Second World War. There were many unemployed in England too; it was so bad that the period became known as the Hungry Thirties. However, with Father's backing, I had to take the chance while it was on offer.

Looking on the bright side, Stainforth pit or Hatfield Main was now drawing coal, and shipping it from a temporary staithe at Stainforth landing until the new staithe and layby was constructed in the Ashfields about a mile below the village. Bramwith Lock was being lengthened and was opened in September, 1932, and work was in hand to straighten the canal at Doncaster and build a new

Opposite page: *The* Annie Maud *at Stainforth in the summer of 1930 or 1931. The sails have been scandalized while I go across to my mother's in the cogboat. The featherings have been removed for painting.* Author's collection

Myself aged twenty-three on the Annie Maud.
Author's collection

wharf and warehouse, opened in July, 1934. Since the end of the 1914–18 War the Sheffield and South Yorkshire Navigation had made steady progress with bank protection and was catching up with maintenance. The Navigation was now in better fettle than it had been for many years.

My first cargo as owner of the *Guidance* was coal from the staithe on Stainforth landing to the Co-operative Wholesale Society's flour mill at Wilmington on the River Hull. The coal was brought from the pit (Hatfield Main) in tip-up motor lorries and tipped down a spout straight into the hold. Discharge at the mill was by grab, straight into the mill bunkers. After discharge, my first visit to the High Street to make contact with brokers could not have been more depressing; five or six old keel captains were there, waiting for something to turn up, and they each in turn told me what a bad time it was to start on my own. I had to wait about a fortnight before I had the offer of a cargo. Then Percy Andrew, who had his office in Hanover Street, fixed me a cargo of sulphur for Furley's wharf in Sheffield. For the next twelve months or so I just about managed to pay my way and was thankful that I had only myself to provide for. The improvement in trade was only slow, but steady.

In the summer of 1934 I married Lilian Atkinson, a Beverley girl whom I had been courting since 1927. When we married in June while the *Guidance* was in dry dock at Stainforth we agreed that we would make our home on board until we found a house that we liked. My wife enjoyed being on board; she soon learned to steer and would take the tiller while I went below for my meals.

We had not been married long before we decided that an engine would be more beneficial than a home ashore. We were thinking of an auxiliary with enough power to take us in and out of a dock and give us about the speed on the canals that we would have when hauled by a horse. The sails were to be used whenever possible; the engine would have to be small so that it could be installed without losing much cargo space. Father had installed a semi-diesel of 40 hp in the *Comrade* two years before; while this showed me the benefits to be gained, it also showed what not to do. After looking at specifications and dimensions, I thought that a small four-stroke diesel of about 20 hp would be about right for our purpose, so in about 1936 we went into dry dock at Staniland's yard, Thorne, to have installed an Ailsa Craig two-cylinder four-stroke diesel engine, rated at 24 hp at 1500 revs per minute, and driving a 28-inch diameter propeller through a 2¾ to 1 reduction gear.

The shaft ran out of the port quarter and was set at an angle so that a straight course could be steered with only slight helm. The aft cabin was not disturbed or altered in any way, and the existing door in the bulkhead, which had previously been the way from the cabin into the hold, was now the way into the small engine room. This was strongly constructed, with a trunk for light and ventilation, so that it was possible to load cargo on two sides and on top. We could still load our usual weight to any place that we were likely to trade to; our full rig of mainsail and topsail was still used and the engine, being regarded as an auxiliary, was shut down when the wind was favourable. The saving in time and money that resulted left me in no doubt that I had done the right thing. The makers of the engine also supplied the shaft and propeller, with all the fittings and copper pipe necessary to complete the installation; I had been able to negotiate with them to supply me at the same price they would have charged a shipbuilder or agent. The cost of labour, dry docking and materials supplied was about £100, and the engine makers charged £190. That engine was not long in paying for itself; trade was picking up and the road haulage people were now causing more trouble to the railways than they were to me.

In the spring of 1938 we were at the South Bullock pump on the Hull, two miles above Beverley, with a cargo of coal. We had arrived on the Saturday morning tide and arrangements were to start discharge on the Monday, so we went to my wife's parents at Beverley for the weekend. While we were out on the Sunday I found that Charles Markham, a builder, was laying out an avenue of new houses in the grounds of Albion House, near the junction of Grovehill Road and Swinemoor Lane. We had a look round and decided that we would try for one. I had to be back on board for work time, so my wife went to make inquiries on the Monday morning, and when I saw her again she told me that she had arranged to rent a house, with the option to buy later if we wished. So, on 1st May, 1938, we were given the key to our first home. We soon made up our minds to buy, and arranged a mortgage with George Dyson Holmes, the shipowner, whom I had known since childhood; he was then living at Goole. It was without doubt the best thing I ever did. The cost of land and building was £450. We stayed there a few months short of forty-three years. We had not been there long when my wife's father said he would like to live next door to us; the house was already let on a monthly tenancy, but the builder paid for the tenant to move to another house so that he could sell the house to my wife's parents. Once they had moved in, father-in-law made himself responsible for both gardens.

After we set up home here on Conington Avenue my wife did not spend much time on board. Our first daughter, Judith, was born in February, 1939, and our second, Audrey, in October, 1941; they all liked to make one or two voyages a year in the summer. Most of the time I now had a youth for mate. While it was

Crane Hill, Beverley Beck, about 1950 with the motor craft Dritan *waiting to unload. This kind of vessel, with a 40 hp diesel engine, usually a Lister or a Gardiner, was built to replace the keels.* Author's collection

understood that I had to leave home to make a living, my wife and family looked forward to my being home at weekends.

Since installing the engine I had been able to carry more tonnage in a given time, and instead of my having to go to the brokers and forwarding agents to find work they were coming to me. When there was a quiet time in Hull, through lack of imports, it was now no trouble and very little expense to make a light voyage to one of the West Riding collieries for a cargo of coal, which was nearly always available. The Beverley Corporation gasworks was taking six thousand tons a year from Denaby and Roundwood, and the tannery needed four or five hundred tons a week to keep going. The Hull and East Riding Co-operative Society's Beverley depot took about ten or twelve cargoes a year from the railway-served staithe at Keadby, while G. N. Bell and Son, the largest coal merchants on the Beckside, bought most of their coal in the summer and distributed it by road over much of the East Riding. Since installing engines in the *Comrade* and the *Guidance* we had been running each summer for Bell's, along with their own power vessels, the *Yare* and *Clyde*, mainly from Hatfield Main and Allerton Bywater. All the house coal had to be filled into baskets and hove out of the hold by hand, then wheeled ashore; and in the case of Bell's coal, it had to be wheeled on top of a heap, fourteen feet high at the end of summer when the yard was nearly full. Later we found an electric winch to do the heaving. Two other coal merchants, "Nigger" Otter and George Freeman, used a horse to pull the baskets out.

Even though we were doing well, there was an air of uncertainty. Adolf Hitler was ranting; how long before the showdown? I was livering flour at the Aire and Calder wharf, Wakefield, when Chamberlain came back from Munich waving the bit of paper that was to guarantee peace in our time. He had been conned. I was at Mexborough mill with a cargo of bulk wheat when war was declared on Germany in September, 1939. The keelman's way of life was never to be the same again.

No movement was allowed on the water between sunset and sunrise, the lights of the floating marks were either extinguished or dimmed, most of the trade was directed to the west coast, and east coast ports became empty and deserted. Even the coal trade was affected by the allocation of coal to merchants. After laying light for three or four weeks, the only freight I could find was forty tons of cement from Melton cement works to Barton to be used for building air raid shelters.

For several weeks the east side of the country was waiting for something to happen and not knowing what to expect; that was the Phoney War. Several of the older keelmen, from Thorne and Stainforth, retired and never sailed again; later in the war they sold their keels for what they would fetch, mainly to be used as open boats in the coal trade on the canals to the power stations. Much later, arrangements were made for bulk wheat to be brought across from the west coast by railway to Sheffield Basin, where it was loaded into keels for onward carriage to those flour mills with the equipment to receive it by water.

In December, 1939, I received an offer for the *Guidance* from Calverts of Goole, who wanted a vessel with some power to carry colliery shale from the West Riding collieries to Goole alum works. The price was right, and because she would be used only on the canal they were to leave me the anchors and cables, mast, yards, sails, winches, leeboards and cogboat. All this gear was put ashore at Stainforth, mainly at my father's place, and the *Guidance* was delivered to Goole in the New Year. We just managed to pass through the New Junction Canal before it became ice-bound for three weeks. The cogboat was sold later for £12 to William Moxon of Hull for use with an old iron billyboy that he used as a lighter; Jack Whitely, the landlord of the *Fox Inn* at Stainforth, bought the winch posts and roller for use on his farm and in the slaughter-house of a butcher's shop that was managed by his son; one anchor and two fifteen-fathom lengths of three-quarter-inch cable were used on the *Comrade*, and the mast and yards made me fencing round some land I had bought at Beverley.

My next vessel was the keel *Vigilant,* a wooden carvel-built vessel owned by my father's cousin, John Schofield, who lived at Thorne, where she had been built in 1923 by Staniland's; she was the last keel that they built. John had told me three months before that he was ready for retiring, but unfortunately he died before I completed the deal and I had to wait until his executors could handle the sale. By that time it was April, 1940, and there was still a bit of ice on the Keadby Canal. The *Vigilant* was in excellent condition, as for several years John had worked only in a leisurely way in the fine weather, laying up for most of the winter; she had a fine set of sailing gear, except for the topmast which John had removed to make her easier to work. The *Vigilant* was laid at Thorne when I bought her, so I arranged to load coal at Stainforth staithe for one of the oil mills at Hull.

By the time that I took that out there was a bit of life coming back into the Humber ports, and I fixed with Bill Weldrick to load wire coils from one of the Ellerman Wilson ships in Alexandra Dock. She had in several hundred tons from Sweden for the Spencer Wire Works at Thornes Lock, Wakefield, so my father came down from Beverley with the *Comrade* to join me, then towed me to Wakefield. After the wire was out we went down together to load house coal at Allerton Bywater for Bell's at Beverley. Until I was able to fit an engine we worked together as much as possible, the *Comrade* towing the *Vigilant* and the *Vigilant* setting her mainsail whenever it would do any good. We helped each other with the loading and livering. About this time we had two rather unusual cargoes as a result of the war, the first being bales of cotton which we loaded out of a Russian ship at Immingham for Goole, where we discharged into railway wagons; then, in another part of Goole docks, we loaded pig iron from railway wagons for House Lock wharf at Tinsley, near Sheffield.

At the start of the war it was not easy to buy small diesel engines because the War Department was taking them for driving electrical generators. After making an appeal through the North East Regional Canal Committee and waiting many months without a reply, I received a circular from the Ministry of War Transport stating that Lister diesel engines of 21 hp could be supplied for installing in inland waterway craft; they could be paid for over a period at only three per cent interest; after another year or so they made a similar offer for larger engines. When I told Father about this he asked me to order one for him as well so that he could scrap the *Comrade's* Ogle rather than spend money on repairs. So I ordered two and in October, 1942, the *Vigilant* was put in dry dock at Staniland's yard to have the engine installed; arrangements were made for the *Comrade* to follow when the *Vigilant* was ready for work. This time I decided to have the engine on the centre line, because at the low price that we were paying for gas oil it was not worth shutting off the power to sail. This was the end of the *Vigilant* as a sailing keel, and of the *Comrade* too until 1976.

One of the first cargoes after putting in the Lister engine was a cargo of flour from the Clarence Mills of J. Rank and Sons, Hull, to Lincoln. It was not a profitable cargo for me, but taking it did me no harm in the long run. John Barlow of North Cave, Rank's broker at that time, knew I had done him a favour by taking that cargo for him, and he put me in for loading flour at Rank's for Sheffield whenever he could. This was handy because I was always sure of a cargo of coal on the return voyage, for either Beverley or Hull, and it also solved a labour problem as Rank's found all labour for loading. As the war progressed and the Navy gained control of the North Sea we began to see cargoes of wheat coming into Hull again. We loaded several cargoes for the Ministry of Food which we took to storage depots at Selby, Castleford and Whitley Bridge near Knottingley. There was also a regular supply of wheat flour imported from Canada which was discharged at Alexandra Dock, Hull, direct overside into keels and lighters for storage at Whitley

A conversation piece: Jack Williamson on the Annie Maud *in the foreground chats with Ernest Swash of Hull and his wife on the* Sympathy *as they lie in St Andrew's Dock tail at low water waiting to get into the dock. I took this picture from the* Annie Maud.
Author's collection

Bridge and other inland warehouses. One such cargo I took direct to the Doncaster flour mill of Thomas Hanley and Sons; after discharging the white flour I loaded, on the same berth, a cargo of the dark National flour for Sheffield. During one of the air raids on Hull, Rank's Clarence Street mills were badly damaged and thereafter we loaded the flour for Sheffield at the Co-operative Flour Mills at Wilmington on the River Hull.

When war materials started to come over from the USA under the Lease-Lend scheme there was a great demand for inland waterways craft of all kinds, and the *Comrade* loaded many cargoes of such materials; but in the *Vigilant* I was fully employed with the flour and coal trades. In April, 1945, Charlie Sheffield fixed me to load five hundred quarters (112½ tons) of wheat at Goole out of the barque *Archibald Russell* for the Wilmington flour mill of the Co-operative Society at Hull. The *Archibald Russell* had been towed to Goole early in the war from Hull and was used for the storage of grain; she was in a bad state when I loaded from her, and a few months later she was towed to the Tyne where she was scrapped.

During the winter of 1944–45 my father became diabetic and had to go ashore. Mother had been a diabetic for several years, but she never complained too much and was always cheerful; suddenly in April, 1945, a few days before her sixty-third birthday, she went into a coma and never recovered; she died in March, 1946. Father,

Tom Puddings, pans or compartment boats were developed from a patent of 1862 by W. H. Bartholomew, the engineer of the Aire and Calder Navigation, to handle the growing coal export traffic down to Goole. On the opening of the New Junction Canal in 1905 the trains of boats could work from the South Yorkshire pits, but this trade did not develop as had been hoped. This is a 1974 scene at Doncaster, photographed from the tug; the linking chains are being tightened as the train leaves the wharf. This trade lasted until 1986. Brian Latham

knowing that he would not be able to look after himself while working on board, decided to retire; my cousin Harry Schofield agreed to work the *Comrade* on thirds and my brother John worked with him as mate.

After the war business began to recover slowly, but the pattern was different, particularly in the grain trade. During the war, when there was a need to turn the bulk wheat carriers round as quickly as possible, the Ministry of War Transport had installed powerful suction elevators on board two Dutch coasters so that the ships could be discharged into lighters and upriver craft while they were at the same time discharging to the grain silo in King George Dock by land-based elevators. This practice continued for some time after the war, and when the stevedore companies tried to return to the old method of discharging grain in Alexandra Dock by hand scuttling, described in chapter two, they had a strike on their hands; it lasted for six weeks. The Transport and General Workers' Union (known as the White Union) was the negotiating union for the Port of Hull, but a number of dockers invited the National Amalgamated Stevedores' and Dockers' Union to open a branch in the port (they were known as the Blue Union). The employers refused to negotiate with them, and for several years there was bitter strife between the two unions; a number of damaging strikes occurred as the Blues fought for the right to negotiate.

My father, Arthur Schofield, outside his home at Stainforth. Author's collection

With most of the grain passing through the silo it could be held in store until it was required at the mills, so fewer craft were needed for onward carriage, and the large shipments of foreign barley that used to pass through Hull to Wakefield and Barton for the malting trade were not resumed. The oilseed trade was not the same because many of the producer countries were now processing the seed themselves, and the seed crushing mill of Barkers and Lee Smith at Beverley closed down for two years while they changed over from seed crushing to compound feed manufacture. When they opened again, trade was resumed with a greater variety of commodities imported through Hull than we had ever carried before to one place; wheat, barley and maize were carried, in bulk and in bags, from the ships at Hull, as well as pollards, sharps, soya meal, fish meal, rice meal, sunflower seed cake, cotton seed cake, linseed cake and groundnut extract.

The coal trade, too, was changing. Oil was cheap and some mills changed from coal to oil for raising steam. The house coal business of G. N. Bell and Sons at Beverley had to close down through the death of the owner, whose eldest son had been killed early in the war while serving in the RAF, and the loss of this summer trade was a blow to us. But I survived the first summer by loading a cargo of palm kernels at Hull for the Selby mill of British

Oil and Cake Mills; I laid in Selby Cut for thirteen weeks on demurrage before discharging, so with freight and thirteen weeks' demurrage I lasted the summer very well.

In 1947 the Labour Government carried out a programme of nationalization which included the coal and gas industries, the ports of Hull, Goole, Grimsby and Immingham, and the inland waterways. This was the biggest blow to the private craft owners engaged in inland waterways carrying since the steaming of George Stephenson's *Rocket*. All the small gasworks were closed down and gas was supplied to the consumers from the bigger works; many of the small gasworks like that at Beverley had always taken their coal by water and the craft owners had been dependent on that trade for a large part of their income. Canal dues and tolls were increased to the point of driving trade off the smaller canals like the Calder and Hebble, until there was no commercial trade left. The Docks Executive at Hull increased their dues and tried to stop the free overside discharge from ships to lighters and river craft which had been the custom since the earliest days of the port; the Hull Rivercraft and Lighter Owners' Association resisted the change, the case going to the House of Lords, with victory for the craft owners.

A bigger blow to the trade of the port and the upriver trade came later when the powers-that-be decided that a National Dock Labour Board should be set up to organize and supply dock labour to the stevedoring companies. Up to then only a few dock labourers had been employed on a permanent basis by the main shipping lines and the stevedores would draw what additional labour they might require on a daily casual basis from the out-of-work dockers who were available. Now each stevedoring firm was to be allocated a given number of dockers to whom they would have to pay a minimum wage each week, even when there was no work for them to do; they could not be dismissed for any cause whatever. The dockers had been given a job for life and began to abuse their new-found power. Their first demand was for a higher basic wage, then for a reduction in the number of working hours. Not that they wanted to work fewer hours per week; oh no, they were quite prepared to work the same number of hours per week, or more, provided there were more hours on overtime rates. Until these demands were met they carried out a series of one-day disruptive strikes at short notice.

Their first demand put them among the highest hourly-paid workers in the country. At first the working week was cut by two hours off the Saturday morning; later Saturday working was cut out altogether. But the dockers expected to be allowed to work until 7 pm on four nights per week, on overtime pay from 5 pm, and also to be allowed to work on Sundays. If they were not awarded these hours on overtime, they worked at a slower rate during the day and the ship was longer in port than she need have been. Even after these demands were met, they were prone to walking off the job at a moment's notice.

The shipowners and transport firms in Hull could not stand for this and began to look for cheaper ports. New private wharves with plenty of under-cover storage were built upriver at Burton Stather, Neap House, Gunness, Gainsborough, Howden Dyke and Selby, and small ships able to by-pass Hull and to discharge at these wharves were employed, while cargoes from many of the deeper draft ships were transshipped into smaller vessels at the cheaper ports on the Continent. All this brought more strikes in the Port of Hull, which did not do anyone any good; commodities that in the old days would have been transshipped at Hull into small craft were now being delivered from the upriver wharves by road transport.

Often when I called to see my father he would hint that he

Grain being delivered from the silo by chute in King George Dock, Hull, in 1952. Many changes were coming to the docks, and some of them were to drive trade away from Hull. Hull Town Docks Museum

would like me to take over the management of the *Comrade*. My brother John was using her in the open-cast coal trade from Rotherham wharf to Goole, but father thought she was not being worked to advantage. I did not want to have to find work for two vessels; there was already talk of the flour trade from Rank's at Hull and Spiller's at Grimsby being lost to road transport, for Spiller's were building a new mill on the Trent side at Gainsborough, which would cut out the need for a depot at Rotherham, and Rank's were planning to deliver all the flour in bulk tank wagons direct to the bakers. I tried to persuade Father to let John have a share in the *Comrade*, thinking it would give him more incentive to find more suitable cargoes for her; John, however, turned down the offer, and Father talked of putting the *Comrade* up for sale if I would not agree to take her over.

There was no ready sale for the *Vigilant* at the time, so after talking it over between ourselves we came to an agreement that both vessels would go to Staniland's yard at Thorne in September, 1953, and have any repairs done that might be needed; a new 31 hp Lister diesel engine, with suitable propeller, should be fitted

Gravel Hill Bridge, a railway swing bridge on the Sheffield and South Yorkshire Navigation, seen from the Comrade *in 1954. Coming through is the* Northcliffe, *one of Bleasdale's keels built at Thorne in 1924.*
Humber Keel and Sloop Preservation Society

in the *Comrade*, the yard taking the old engine in part payment. The Thorne firm of solicitors, Kenyon, Son and Craddock, drew up a partnership agreement between Father and myself under which Father was to take the *Vigilant* off my hands in payment of a half share in the *Comrade* and John was to buy the *Vigilant* from Father, payment to be made as and when he could; I would work the *Comrade* on thirds so that she would provide an income for Father. John worked the *Vigilant* only a short time, for he found himself a job on the surface at Hatfield Main Colliery and sold the keel to a Sheffield man for a houseboat. The partnership lasted until my father's death just over five years later in December, 1958. During that time he derived much pleasure from the knowledge that the *Comrade* was fully employed in the carriage of cargoes that would not be harmful to her, and that she was being cared for as well as he would have done himself.

From the time I took over the *Comrade* in 1953 to 1972 I was as busy as I had ever been since starting on my own account, though it was obvious that inland waterways were losing to roads all the time; the ever-increasing cost of dock labour and dock charges was not helpful. The loss of trade was ongoing. The bulk grain and seed-carrying ships that had been coming to Hull for many years, providing work for upriver craft, were now transshipping their cargoes on the Continent into small coasters that could go upriver to Selby and Gainsborough. Containers were being used more and more, at first as deck cargo, then in specially built vessels. The 20 feet × 8 feet × 8 feet containers were designed for use with road or rail transport in mind and would not fit into river craft that had to be small enough to pass through the locks on the inland navigations.

Carriage of coal by keels had been diminishing since 1939, when nearly all the steam trawlers at Hull were whipped away in a few days to be prepared for war service. The new vessels that were built to replace them in the post-war years were oil burners, and more factories turned from coal to oil. After the discovery of oil and natural gas in the North Sea the changeover from coal became more rapid. I discharged my last cargo of coal for Beverley in March, 1971, and the last coal cargo for Hull at Stoneferry wharf on 22nd December, 1971. The next four years showed a rapidly diminishing trade, and by 1975 all trade by water to Beverley was finished, and there was little anywhere else. As trade was lost we tried to attract fresh, with only limited success. The cost of labour, and the fact that many cargoes had to start or finish their journey by road, was all in favour of direct delivery by road transport.

When I was a boy sail was regarded as the main means of propulsion. Towage by steam tugs or horses was used only when no reasonable progress could be made otherwise, and twenty to twenty-four cargoes a year, plus a few days here and there on demurrage, were considered reasonable. Sometimes the few days on demurrage turned into a few weeks; when I owned the *Vigilant* she was once, as I said, laid in Selby Cut for thirteen weeks, with one cargo of palm kernels. After I installed the small engine in the keel *Guidance* the average year for me was thirty cargoes, and while I had the *Vigilant* I could manage thirty-six in most years. With the *Comrade*, a fully-powered craft since 1942, I carried a greater variety of cargoes; the number per year varied from thirty to forty-three until 1973, when I handled only twenty-three in the full year, and in 1974 only seventeen.

In 1953, the first full year I had with the *Comrade*, I loaded coal from five different places: Dalton Main, Hatfield Main and Water Haigh collieries, and two open-cast mines at Swillington wharf and Malthouse wharf, Wakefield. I had a total of seventeen coal cargoes altogether, one for Hull and sixteen for Beverley. Then there were a few cargoes of tanning materials, solid mimosa extract and myrobalans nuts from the docks at Hull for Beverley, and one cargo of dry hides. We loaded five cargoes of flour that year, three from Rank's Hull mill for Sheffield and two from Spiller's Grimsby mill, one for Laws wharf, Rotherham, and one for the Calls warehouse, Leeds. We also had two cargoes of tractors from the International Harvesters' factory at Doncaster for transshipment at Hull for Sweden. There was one cargo of wheat from Hull to Doncaster mill and one cargo of pigmeal and cattle food for Doncaster wharf from the British Oil and Cake Mills, Hull.

In the year 1954–55 we had two cargoes of wheat from Hull to Doncaster mill, and two more of tractors back to Hull; we could put six tractors in the hold at one time. We loaded our last cargo of flour from Grimsby for Leeds and took five more from Rank's Hull mill to Sheffield. We loaded coal eleven times that year at Hatfield Main, twice at Swillington and once at Allerton Bywater, all for Beverley. We loaded at Hull, ex-ship, for Beverley, one cargo of bulk barley, one of bulk oats, one of cake and one of fishmeal in bags, three cargoes of solid mimosa extract and one cargo of wet hides. From Immingham we loaded for Beverley one cargo of maize ex-silo and one cargo of solid mimosa extract ex-ship. From Wakefield we loaded, at the Spencer Wire Works, coils of copper wire for transshipment at Hull into a Russian ship.

The next year, 1955–56, was a good year. We loaded coal thirteen times at Hatfield Main for Beverley, three cargoes of open-cast coal at Swillington, also for Beverley, and one via Roundwood staithe from Dalton Main Colliery for Hull. We had only one cargo of wheat for Doncaster mill, and one from Hull to Sam Smith's at Sheffield. We loaded nine cargoes of flour for Sheffield at Rank's Hull mill and for the first time in many years we

Between 1953 and 1954 I handled several cargoes of tractors for export from the International Harvester works at Wheatley by Doncaster. The Comrade *could carry six at a time; they were loaded into a ship in the Albert Dock, Hull, for export to Sweden.*
Humber Keel and Sloop Preservation Society

had a cargo for West Stockwith Basin; it was wood pulp for a Chesterfield firm, but instead of transshipping it to narrow boats it was put on to lorries. From Hull to Beverley that year we had one cargo of bulk barley and one of bulk maize, three cargoes of myrobalans, four of solid mimosa extract and 120 tons of wet hides, part of these being discharged at the tannery of Thomas Holmes and Sons on Bankside, Hull, and the remainder at Beverley. From Beverley to Hull we had one cargo (about one hundred tons) of whitening for transshipment in Alexandra Dock to a Yugoslav ship.

To keep working we had to accept anything that could be made to pay. The contract for the coils of copper wire lasted only about two years, but in that short time work was becoming so scarce that the owners of the larger craft were undercutting each other, so that it became unprofitable for small craft. By the end of 1958 Rank's were sending all their flour from Hull to Sheffield in bulk tank vehicles. My share of the coal carriage was still good; in 1958 I

Sheffield Basin remained busy into the nineteen-fifties, at which time it still presented an animated scene with plenty of powered river craft alongside the wharves. The craft in the foreground has a collapsible wheelhouse. R. Frost

had fourteen cargoes from three different pits, Swillington, Allerton Bywater and Hatfield. Hull to Beverley trade was down a little, but I had nine cargoes of paper, ex-ship at Hull, to Leeds and one cargo of copper billets to Yorkshire Imperial Metals at Leeds. We managed to keep going with a few cargoes of ground nuts for Eastwood wharf, Rotherham; zircon sand in paper sacks and cans of tomatoes; things that I would not have bothered with if work had been good. Until the trouble over independence with Rhodesia, there was a steady flow of chrome in drums through Hull to Sheffield Basin and the new wharf at Rotherham, but with the imposition of trade sanctions against Rhodesia another trade was lost from the inland waterways. In July, 1958, I went to Sheffield for the last time; the cargo was four hundred quarters of wheat for Sam Smith's silo.

In December of that year I was at Rotherham mill with 450 quarters of wheat, which we started to discharge late on 14th December, taking out about 150 quarters by knock-off time. About 5.30 am next day, as I was just about to get up ready for an early start, I heard a loud bang which I thought might have been at the steelworks on Sheffield Road. Before I could get on deck the mate came running aft to say that the mill was on fire. I told him to let go the head ropes while I got off the stern ropes; we drove down with the current for about two hundred yards, then made fast to some trees and went below for some breakfast while the mill burned. One of the firemen said that the fire had been started by a dust explosion. By late afternoon the silo and most of the mill was gutted, with hundreds of tons of wheat in the river. We had to take the rest of the cargo to Doncaster mill. It was just nine years before we had another cargo to the new Rotherham mill.

Despite all these setbacks, I managed to put in four more good years' work, discharging thirty-nine times in 1968, forty-two in 1969, thirty-seven in 1970 and forty-one in 1971. In 1972 we discharged only twenty-three cargoes in the year, picking up twenty-four in 1973, and only seventeen in 1974. It was obvious that I was no longer going to be able to make a living. The disruptive practices of the dock labour force at Hull had given the port such a bad reputation that vessels which would in the past have transshipped their cargoes at Hull were now taking them upriver to Goole and transshipping into river craft for carriage back downriver to Hull and Beverley. Indeed, in 1970 and 1971 I myself loaded two cargoes of valerian ex-ship at Goole for Beverley tanners, cargoes which had always before been transshipped at Hull.

From 1965 onwards we loaded the usual coal, grain and tanning raw materials; cocoa beans for Rowntree's at York; also one cargo of gum arabic for Rowntree's; phosphate and canned goods for Gainsborough; canned salmon from Immingham, ex-ship to Hull; Russian cotton from Hull, ex-ship to Knostrop, Leeds; fish meal, ex-ship at Hull for Grimsby; rape meal, copra and linseed from Hull, ex-ship to British Oil and Cake Mills, Selby; iron powder, ex-ship at Hull, for Eastwood wharf, Rotherham; and ferro-silicon for both Eastwood and British Waterways' new wharf at Rotherham. From 1970 until late 1971 I had several cargoes of sugar loaded at Goole, out of East German ships, for the Foss Island warehouse of Rowntree's, and one cargo of cocoa butter; we also had one or two to Queen's staith, York. At Queen's staith we also discharged ground nuts and bales of wood pulp to road transport.

Howden Dyke was an up-and-coming port by the early nineteen-seventies. I discharged there from Hull one cargo of mining concentrates and one of screening pellets, and loaded from a ship one cargo of sponge iron for British Waterways' new wharf at Rotherham. Another job we had for a time was tin concentrates from the South African boats at Hull to Beverley, where they were put on to lorries for transport by road. We also loaded two cargoes of shea nuts from storage at Beverley for British Oil and Cake Mills, Selby, and one cargo of linseed out of storage at Stoneferry for the same consignee.

Cedric Lodge 11

OLDER inland waterways craft were being scrapped as fast as the shipbreakers could take them and the better ones were being sold for houseboats, owing to lack of work, when the Humber Keel and Sloop Preservation Society became interested in the *Comrade* with the idea of buying her for rerigging. The society had been formed in 1970 on the initiative of Cedric Lodge, a Hull engineer, to restore and preserve working examples of Humber sailing craft. A previous attempt in the nineteen-fifties by the Humber Keel Trust had proved unsuccessful.

The society was not at that time in a position to make an offer but in May, 1974, the chairman, John Hainsworth, asked me if I would take the *Comrade* to the Inland Waterways Association's 21st National Rally at Nottingham. Trade was at a low ebb, so I told him to go ahead and make the necessary arrangements. Later in the summer the *Comrade* was put into dry dock at Beverley for survey and bottom fettling while the society members turned the hold into a keel exhibition. On the afternoon of 19th August, with the press and TV crews in attendance, we penned out of Beverley Beck to catch the afternoon tide at Hull for the Trent and Nottingham, calling at Newark for one day on our way.

The rally at Nottingham was one of the biggest ever held by the Inland Waterways Association. Alex McMullen, in *Motor Boat and Yachting*, dubbed it "the Gathering of the 600" and said that the star of the show was a bluff-bowed, slab-sided but beautiful Humber keel called the *Comrade*.

The transfer of ownership to the society was made on 16th December, 1974, an agreement being made for me to work the vessel, on thirds, for the Society until I had fulfilled my trading commitments. I carried three cargoes with the *Comrade* for the society's account. The first was thirty-eight tonnes of fish meal loaded from a South African vessel and forty-four tonnes of sunflower seed loaded from a Russian vessel in King George Dock at Hull for Barker and Lee Smith's mill at Beverley. The last two cargoes were myrobalans nuts for the tannery of Richard Hodgson and Sons Ltd, Beverley, both loaded out of the Indian vessel *Vishva Bhakti* in the Queen Elizabeth Dock, Hull. After a few days on demurrage the *Comrade* livered her last cargo on 19th April, 1975. Within a few months all trade on the Beck was finished. Now all the

Opposite page: *The* Comrade *under sail after her restoration by the Humber Keel and Sloop Preservation Society. She had been down the Humber to Spurn Point and was on the way back when this fine photograph was taken by Mr George Byers.* G. E. Byers

raw materials that had previously been brought to Beverley by water are carried by road transport.

For a retired man, the spring and summer of 1975 seemed to be all go. Two days after discharging her last cargo the *Comrade* had to go to Barton Haven to pick up some gear which the society had stored at Clapson's yard. I took her to Hull and left Alan Hartley in charge to take her across the Humber, with a crew of society members, then went over on the Monday morning to fetch her back to Beverley. Following the sale of the *Comrade* to the society I undertook the job of seeing that she would be correctly restored to

The Comrade's *last cargo being loaded overside from the Indian ship* Vishva Bhakti *at Hull in March, 1975. The cargo of myrobalans, nuts used in the tanneries and dyeworks, was discharged at Beverley on 10th April. I am on the starboard side, Alan Hartley is to port.*
Hull Daily Mail

sailing condition. A pole suitable for making a mast for her was ordered from a local firm, who arranged for it to be imported from Gothenburg, via Gunness on the Trent. In early May I received confirmation from Wharton Shipping Ltd that this had been shipped on board the mv *Marie Everard*; she was expected to arrive at Gunness on the morning tide of 5th May, so I arranged a crew of society members and took the *Comrade* to collect it.

In early June we went to the Lincoln Water Festival, then back to Beverley for an open day to let the public see what we were doing, and on Sunday, 22nd June we had a visit from the Mayor and Mayoress, Councillor and Mrs Sonley, who showed great interest in the exhibition. Our next date was with the South Ferriby Boat Owners' Association at Ferriby Sluice on 6th July, 1975, then we were back at Beverley until 20th August, when it was time for the *Comrade* to pay a visit to the Inland Waterways Association Festival at York. The festival was to be opened by the Lord Mayor of Hull, Mrs Catherine Ellis, and we were asked if we would use the *Comrade* to transport her and the Lady Mayoress from Blue Bridge to the festival site at Clifton Gardens. We were pleased to do this, and, because the Lord Mayor of Hull is, by virtue of the office, also Admiral of the Humber, the *Comrade* was allowed to wear the Admiral's flag while she was on board.

On returning from York to Beverley, the *Comrade* was moored

The Comrade *alongside the* Vishva Bhakti *in Queen Elizabeth Dock, Hull, when taking on board her last cargo. I am on the quayside.*
Hull Daily Mail

on the berth of Beverley Engineers so that we could have a supply of electricity to fit the hold with lights and power for use as a workshop. A start was made on shaping the mainsail and topsail yards and overhauling the windlass. Early in October, the pole which was to be made into the mast was lifted out of the Beck, where it had been all summer, and placed on trestles in Hodgson's yard to dry out. Society member Jim Thompson started to take the bark off about a month later.

On 27th November I was pleased to welcome on board the *Comrade* the Director of the Maritime Trust, Vice-Admiral Sir Patrick Bayly KBE, CB, DSC. He spent about an hour on board having a good look round, then complimented me on the good condition of the ship. At the annual general meeting on board the *Comrade* on 15th November, 1975, the chairman was able to report to the members that a firm order for the sails had been placed with the sailmakers, Jeckells of Wroxham, so that we could take advantage of the cut price offered if the work could be done in the winter months. After much discussion, it had been decided to use a terylene fabric for the sails, as this would be more durable than the traditional flax. The standing and running rigging was ordered

Looking at the pole that is to be the Comrade's *new mast. I am on one side and Bill Wilson and Jim Thompson on the other.*
Humber Keel and Sloop Preservation Society

The Comrade *in Beverley Beck in the summer of 1975, with the pole that is to be the new mast floating alongside.* Humber Keel and Sloop Preservation Society

from Hall's Barton Ropery, on the understanding that the cost would be cheaper if the work could be done in slack periods. The running and standing rigging was ready by the end of May, 1976.

We had the mast stepped by 17th July and the *Comrade* was brought into sailing trim by 12th August, with concrete blocks for ballast. Keels without any motive power other than wind were, with the aid of leeboards, quite able to sail without any ballast when empty. In light condition they would float, or swim as the keelmen would say, about two or three inches by the stern, which is just about the right trim for sailing. But the *Comrade* now has a diesel engine and a tank full of gas oil to run it on which weighs about three tons. These are fitted at the after end of the ship and make her swim 1 foot 6 inches by the stern. In this trim she would not be able to sail to windward, and that is why we had to use ballast to bring her into sailing condition. It would also help her to sail without leeboards, because at the time we could not find the money to buy suitable timber to make them.

We had arranged with the BBC to sail for them on Sunday, 15th August, and on Monday, 16th August, for Yorkshire TV. So on Saturday morning, 14th August, 1976, without a word to anyone, we went down the River Hull to the Humber to have a practice sail before we had to face the cameras. I was the only one on board who knew what to do and how to do it; the crew had not even seen sails set before that day. We cleared the Old Harbour,

The Comrade *returning from meeting the Royal Yacht* Britannia *with the Queen and the Duke of Edinburgh on board. We were in a hurry!*
Hull Daily Mail

and then I fitted the handle to the main halyard roller and hoisted sail. At Hull we found a light easterly wind and slight fog which cleared with the slowly freshening wind before we got to Paull. By flood we were near the Middle Burcom buoy and the wind was quite fresh. She was then sailing nicely with only the mainsail set, but just to show what she was capable of, I set the topsail as well for the run back, which lasted about two hours. Everyone on board was pleased with the outing and many were surprised to find how near the wind the *Comrade* could sail and the speed she could make. We sailed on the Sunday for the BBC for about four hours with light easterly winds, and again on the Monday for about the same time and under the same conditions for Yorkshire TV. As we were returning to Hull on the starboard tack the paddle steamer *Lincoln Castle* crossed our bows, and her captain gave us a salute with his steam whistle which made my day. We managed three more weekends out under sail that year and one open day at Beverley, which was well attended.

During the winter, application was made by the society to the Manpower Services Commission for help towards cleaning and repairing the floor frames and making a well deck over the after hold, so that there would be somewhere for the passengers to sit while the *Comrade* was sailing. The application was granted, and we were able to start two skilled tradesmen on the Job Creation Scheme the following spring (1977). It was early July before the job was through, just in time for the *Comrade* to sail to Grimsby to join the welcome for the Royal Yacht *Britannia* with the Queen and Prince Philip on board. They were to land at Grimsby, and after touring North Lincolnshire, would rejoin the *Britannia* at Hull, passing through Beverley on the way. The Town Clerk of Beverley had sent a letter to the society suggesting that the *Comrade* should be moored at the west end of the Beck at the time that the royal party would pass by. To do this we would have to keep to a tight schedule. Only a short time before, Drypool Bridge over the River Hull had crashed down and it would be months rather than days before they could raise it again. So the *Comrade* could only pass through at low water with her mast down.

The *Britannia* was due in Grimsby Roads on the morning tide of 12th July, and the Queen and Prince Philip were to pass through Beverley on the afternoon of 13th July; it would be just possible to keep time if all went well. On 11th July, 1977, my seventy-first birthday, I found myself sailing a keel to meet the Royal Yacht off Grimsby. Our allocated anchorage was near No 6A buoy and we brought up there for the night. The following morning, 12th July, was damp, with visibility down to about two miles. At 7 am the British Transport Docks Board launch came and laid hove-to a few feet away from us, keeping us informed of the *Britannia's* progress as they received the information on their VHF radio. The *Britannia* came out of the mist at 8.50 am, followed by HMS *Yarmouth*. We weighed anchor and sailed until the Royal Barge, with the Queen and Prince Philip on board, was lost to sight entering the Royal Dock Basin at Grimsby. The *Comrade* was put on to the starboard tack and we headed for the River Hull as fast as we could to reach Drypool Bridge before the tide became too high. On Wednesday, 13th July, I was on board early to dress ship overall with signal flags and burgee at the truck. She attracted much attention and favourable comment. In the late afternoon, Her Majesty the Queen and HRH Prince Philip passed by on their way to rejoin the *Britannia*.

We had two open days in August, one at Ferriby Sluice and the other at Beverley. Then in September, just before the end of our sailing season, we had on board as passenger from Beverley to Hull Mrs Todd, one of the first members and certainly the oldest member of the society; she was at that time ninety-nine.

1978 was a busy year for the *Comrade*, and a profitable one for the society. We made a good start with our first sail of the season on

22nd April, managing to fit in nine months' cruising before the end of the season, as well as other activities. I have pleasant memories of one weekend in May, when on the Saturday I was pleased to welcome on board for a day's sail Frank Carr, the former Director of the National Maritime Museum. We did not have much wind that day, but we did have an enjoyable outing. Then on the Sunday a party of industrial archaeology students and their lecturer came over from Rochdale for a sail. In June we had a party from a camera club for a sail; it rained most of the time they were on board. After that we took the *Comrade* to the Water Festival at Lincoln, and the BBC Brass Tacks team joined us at Torksey for the passage up the Fossdyke to film the *Comrade* sailing on inland waters. Early in July we had a visit from members of the Hull Maritime Society; the following weekend we had a few of them out under sail for the afternoon. On 19th July we set off for a tour of the West Riding, with open days at Leeds, Wakefield, Castleford, Knottingley, and Thorne. We were well received and much interest was shown at all stops. Before we left Beverley, the Mayor and Mayoress of Beverley came on board and handed over letters for the Lord Mayor of Leeds and the Mayor of Wakefield, who each paid us a visit.

We were due at Ferriby Sluice for open days over August Bank

A view on board Comrade *during one of our sails. I was quite enjoying myself.* Author's collection

Holiday. When we sailed from there on the afternoon tide of 31st August, we had another square-rig sailor as passenger, a modern Norwegian Viking called Olaf Envig, with his thirteen-year old daughter Gunn as crew. He had that summer sailed his square-rigged Viking vessel *Hitra* from Oslo in Norway to York, calling at Gothenburg, Copenhagen, Hamburg, Cuxhaven, Amsterdam, Ostend, Dunkirk (Dunkerque), London, Grimsby and Hull. He had taken thirty-eight days on the outward voyage, but from Hull onwards his vessel was going home as deck cargo on board the motor vessel *Domino* at the expense of Ellerman Lines, who had offered to transport ship and captain back home in recognition of his international endeavours and outstanding seamanship. He was writing a research thesis on maritime history, with special reference to the Vikings, their vessels and square-rig sailing techniques. The *Hitra* had been built in 1863 as a square-sailed coastal fishing vessel. Olaf was greatly interested in the *Comrade* and her square sails; he found much in common with his own vessel and showed his appreciation at being invited to sail in her.

On our next outing we had a party of stevedores and their wives as passengers down the River Hull. Then we sailed two days with a party from the Thames Barge Sailing Club, before taking the *Comrade* to York on charter to Kestrel Films Ltd, of Shepperton Studios. They were making a film for young people called "Black Jack", and the *Comrade* was to take the part of an eighteenth-century coastal vessel. It was mid-October before we were laid up for the winter that year.

During the following season (1979), the *Comrade* was invited to visit Grimsby Fish Dock for their open day on 27th July. As this was to be our only engagement for that summer we could push ahead with our crew training, always high on my list of priorities. In June we had another visit from the stevedores, and this time we took them for a short sail. In July ten members of the Thames Barge Sailing Club travelled all one Friday night to work in two days' sailing on board the *Comrade*. Later in the season, we had a party from the Calder Navigation Society for a day's sailing. We started the 1980 season in early May, with a long weekend training in sail for members. In June we had a party from the North West Museum of Inland Navigation for two days, and in July a party from Rochdale for one day. Our main fund-raising event that year was to be a visit to Bridlington at the invitation of the Borough Council, the first time a keel had gone to sea since David Holgate's voyage, also to Bridlington, in 1905. We left Hull on the evening tide of 25th July, with a strong south-east wind, and brought up in Grimsby Inner Roads for a few hours until high water on the morning tide of 26th July. We got under way in poor visibility, which lasted all the way to Bridlington, reaching there by high water on the afternoon tide. We were able to sail into the harbour with main and topsails set; the first keel to do so for over seventy years. On the Sunday we took the *Comrade* out again and sailed for about three hours in the bay. During our stay we had several hundred visitors per day on board. We returned to the Humber on 11th August.

To finish off the season there were two more bookings from members of the society who were also keel owners. The first was Tony Woodward, owner of the keel *Daybreak*, which he used on the Thames as a houseboat. He brought a few friends for the weekend to enjoy the experience of a keel under sail. On the Sunday they had quite a surprise when we sailed the *Comrade* from Grimsby to Hull, against a spring tide, in three hours. The other party, co-owners of the keel *Beecliffe*, came for a weekend in September. At that time the *Beecliffe* was cruising the inland waterways of France.

After laying up for the winter, a start was made on the leeboards, but it was not possible to do any further work on them when the 1981 sailing season came round again. That was another busy year. In early April, I had a telephone call from Peter Dodds, the owner of the spritsail barge *Mirosa*; he was planning to have her

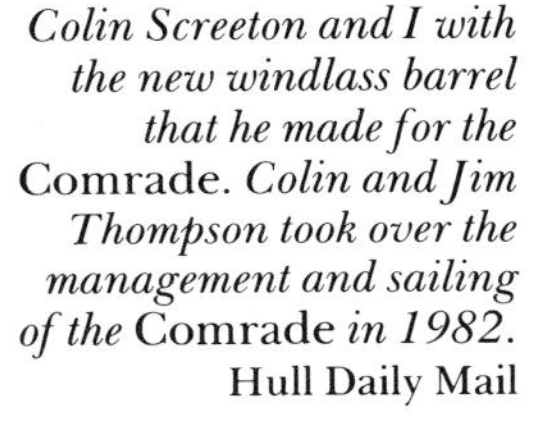

Colin Screeton and I with the new windlass barrel that he made for the Comrade. *Colin and Jim Thompson took over the management and sailing of the* Comrade *in 1982.*
Hull Daily Mail

in Hull by early May to take a party of city councillors for a voyage under the newly completed Humber Bridge, and would like me to give him the benefit of my local knowledge. The *Mirosa* was a wooden barge, built at Maldon in 1892, and had never had an engine. The job was just up my street, and arrangements were made for him to see me as soon as he arrived in Hull. On passage to the Humber, *Mirosa* carried away her topmast, so she had to lay a few days while a new one was made. On 11th May she was moved to Riverside Quay to pick up the civic party.

When they were safely on board, Peter and his mate set the sails while I took the wheel, and we had a pleasant sail through the bridge, with wind our only motive power. Off Chalder (Chowder) Ness I brought her up to anchor, and we had an enjoyable lunch in the hold, which had been prepared by Peter's wife and sister-in-law. After lunch, I again took the wheel, while Peter and his mate weighed anchor and tended the sails. In my early days afloat, spritsail barges were a common sight loading coal at Keadby and Goole, but this was the first time I had had charge of one, and I much enjoyed myself. The following week the *Comrade* was laid on the foreshore at Ferriby Cliff to clean off the growth of weed that she had acquired during the winter. This was followed by a few hours' sailing with strong easterly winds to freshen up the crew ready for our next outing, which was to be with the BBC 2 camera team for them to film the *Comrade* for the "Past Afloat" programme. By this time the society had bought the Humber sloop *Amy Howson*, and much work had been done by members on the south bank of the river to restore her hull and rerig her as a sailing sloop. She was not quite ready for sailing, but she came out with us to carry the cameras. We could have used more wind that day, but managed to give a good account of ourselves. When the film was ready the *Comrade* was given a good write-up in the book published with the series; her portrait is on the cover. The next time out we had a party from Sheffield for the weekend, and this time we had some blustery weather; we hauled two reefs in the mainsail and showed them what the *Comrade* could do.

On 19th June, 1981, the society had a dinner on board the paddle steamer *Lincoln Castle*, laid on the foreshore at Hessle, to celebrate the tenth anniversary of their founding. The Guest of Honour was Frank Carr CB, CBE, an old friend and founder member of the society. At the dinner the chairman was able to announce that the *Amy Howson* had, the week before, been under sail again for the first time since 1939. He also read a telegram from the Duke of Edinburgh conveying to all members his congratulations on the tenth anniversary and best wishes for continued success. 17th July was the day for the official opening of the Humber Bridge by HM The Queen, accompanied by HRH

AMY HOWSON
H407

The Duke of Edinburgh. The ceremony was timed to take place at low water, so on 16th July the *Comrade* was moved from Beverley to Ferriby Sluice for the night. Then, after breakfast on the 17th, we went to a position upstream of the bridge and brought up to our anchor, the *Amy Howson* coming alongside us to wait for a signal from the Harbour Master's launch. We were then to get under way and sail under the bridge as the Queen and Prince Philip were driven over the bridge to Barton. On the next high water both vessels went into Albert Dock for a celebration party. The next day the *Comrade* took a party of members to Spurn, with all sail set, and had to haul out two reefs in the mainsail to return.

The following weekend was Open Day at Ferriby Sluice for both vessels. We lay there until it was time to sail to Leeds for the Inland Waterways Association Rally in early August. For this event our chairman, John Hainsworth, had put himself to a great deal of trouble assembling a collection of ganseys from all over the country, for an exhibition entitled "Historic Ships", featuring maritime preservation around the country. On the way back from Leeds, the *Comrade* was put on the slip at Knottingley so that a party of members could clean and black varnish her bottom. After coming off, we sailed three more weekends, then laid up for the winter.

From my first meeting with the Humber Keel and Sloop Preservation Society I was impressed with the drive and determination of all the members to make the society work. After they bought the *Comrade* each one was ready and willing to use his particular skills to have her sailing again. Right from the first voyage under her new rig, there were two men in particular who showed outstanding ability and an understanding of the theory and practice of working the square sail. Soon they took over as duty mates on alternate outings, and shared in the daily maintenance of ship and gear. At the end of the 1981 season I was sure that they were capable of sailing the *Comrade* on the estuary; by doing so their self-confidence and skill would improve. So I requested the Council of Management to appoint Colin Screeton and Jim Thompson to be relief sailing masters of the *Comrade*. After the first voyage in 1982 I left the management and sailing of the *Comrade* to Colin and Jim. They appreciated my confidence in them and would phone me each time they returned.

I had to take charge again in early August, 1982, when the British Broadcasting Corporation chartered the *Comrade* to take part in a documentary which they were making, to be called "Between Two Seas". The main filming was done over three twelve-hour periods in midweek, sailing between Goole and Hull, followed by about six hours on the following Sunday; then we sailed with the same film crew from Hull towards the North Sea,

Opposite page: *Four veteran ships in Humber Dock, Hull. At extreme left is the sailing trawler* William McCann*; next to her is the* Comrade, *then the sloop* Amy Howson, *and on the outside the Paull shrimper* Venture. Hull Daily Mail

Cedric Lodge at work during the restoration of the Comrade.
Humber Keel and Sloop Preservation Society

until we made contact with the society's sloop *Amy Howson*, returning from Bridlington. Colin and Jim took the *Comrade* out for two more trips before we brought her to Beverley to lay up for the winter. We got the leeboards finished and fitted them in the spring of 1983, and that year I had the pleasure of showing Colin and Jim how to use them.

Since I finished writing the draft of this book the British Waterways Board has tried to attract more tonnage to the Sheffield and South Yorkshire Navigation by building larger locks between Doncaster and Rotherham which are able to take vessels of 400 tons deadweight, but up to now without much success.

All the old trades have been lost to road transport, and there is now no wheat, flour, cement or coal carried on that navigation. The last cargo of coal for the electricity power station at Doncaster passed through Sprotborough Lock towards the end of March, 1981, and the last loaded compartment boats or tom puddings of the Aire and Calder Navigation fleet used the New Junction Canal in February, 1985. The compartment boats have all been scrapped, and the only coal movement on the Aire and Calder is the short-haul trade to Ferrybridge power station. The ships with large cargoes of wheat in bulk which used to transship their cargoes to keels no longer use the port of Hull, and the brickyards of North Lincolnshire are all worked out or closed down, so there is no traditional work for the sloops either.

Only the *Comrade* and the sloop *Amy Howson* remain under sail to serve as a reminder of what used to be. Long may the Humber Keel and Sloop Preservation Society continue its work of keeping them in operation so that future generations may see how we used to make a living under sail.

APPENDIX ONE

Cargoes and Destinations

I HAVE been asked many questions about keels, and most frequently: "Where do you go?" and "What do you carry?" This is my answer, compiled from old cargo books and memory, and it is as complete an answer as you are going to have. It is a list of all the cargoes and places of loading and discharging of the keels *Fanny*, *Confidence*, *Aureola*, *Integrity*, *Amity*, *Galatea*, *Guidance*, *Annie Maud*, *Vigilant* and *Comrade*. The period covered is from 1866 to 1975. Other commodities have been carried by keels at different times; the ones listed here have all been carried in the ten keels mentioned.

Alum

After discharging bulk wheat at the dockside for the mills of Hudson Ward Ltd, Goole, it was often possible to load at the Goole Alum Works of Peter Spence and Co. Ltd small quantities of alum in bags or cases for transshipment at Hull for export.

Barley

Up to the outbreak of the war in 1939, barley suitable for malting was imported into Hull from Australia, California and Chile in bags, and also from the Black Sea in bulk. We received this direct overside from the ships for delivery to Sutcliffe's at Wakefield; also to Gilstrap Heap and Co. at Barton Haven; one cargo only to a firm at Ferrybridge, and one cargo only from the railway in the Royal Dock, Grimsby, for Gledhill's malt kiln at Gainsborough. Barley of a lower quality, suitable for animal feed, came from the River Plate and other areas; this was also loaded direct overside from the ships in bulk or sacks, and from the silo in King George Dock, Hull.

Basic slag

Basic slag, a by-product of the steel industry, is used as a fertilizer. It was loaded by hand from railway wagons at Keadby. At the start of the loading operation, the keel was laid alongside the bank and a gangplank was placed from the wagon on to other planks spanning the hatchway from coaming to coaming. The slag, in one-hundredweight jute bags, had to be placed on a running barrow and wheeled on board. As the vessel became deeper she had to be pushed out into deeper water, and by the time the loading was completed she would be sixteen or eighteen feet out, with the plank now at a steep angle. At Hull the slag was transshipped into seagoing craft for various places. Some was loaded by other keels for delivery to farms near the River Hull. One cargo of basic slag was loaded out of the coastal steamer *Border Firth* in Alexandra Dock, Hull, for delivery to the railway at New Holland; it had to be returned to Scunthorpe for reprocessing after the *Border Firth* had broken adrift from Turner's Wharf at Gunness and damaged herself and her cargo.

Canned goods

"Canned Goods" is the trade description for anything in a tin can. These were usually tomatoes or canned fruit. The tomatoes were from the Mediterranean, loaded ex-ship at Hull, for Eastwood near Rotherham. The canned fruit came from South Africa or Israel, loaded ex-ship at Hull for Gainsborough or Leeds. I also had a single cargo of canned salmon, loaded ex-ship at Immingham, for discharge to warehouses in Hull.

Cattle cake

Cotton seed cake was loaded at BOCM, Selby, for Chambers and Fargus, Oxford Street mill, Wincolmlee, Hull; and from Chambers and Fargus, Oxford Street, linseed cake was loaded for Newark and Lincoln. Linseed cake, cotton seed cake, sunflower cake and groundnut cake were loaded in bags, ex-ship at Hull, for Beverley and Selby.

Cement

Cement was loaded from Earle's Wilmington works at Hull, in one-hundredweight jute bags, for Lincoln, Doncaster, Rotherham and Sheffield; from Earle's Melton works, in one-hundredweight paper sacks, for Doncaster and Sheffield; and one cargo only, from Melton to Barton Haven, in 1939, for the building of air raid shelters.

China clay

In my early days china clay was brought in bulk from Cornwall by topsail schooners and ketches, then transshipped into keels for various destinations. Our cargo was for a place at Sheffield known as Clay Jack's, just above Furley's wharf. It would in those days be used in the steelworks for making crucibles which, until the nineteen-twenties, were used for casting steel.

Chrome

Chrome was usually shipped in boxes or drums from East Africa. We received it direct from ships at Hull or Immingham, for Eastwood wharf or Sheffield Basin. One cargo I carried was loaded from a Russian ship in bulk, and discharged by grab at Eastwood wharf.

Coal

In the late nineteenth and early twentieth centuries, the keel *Fanny* loaded best steam coal at the collieries on the Dearne and Dove Canal: Cortonwood, Elsecar and Manvers Main. It was mainly for bunkering steam trawlers and for the various mills on the River Hull in the Stoneferry and Wincolmlee areas of Hull. Later, the keels *Confidence* and *Aureola* loaded steam hards from Kilnhurst and Roundwood coal staithes for the same purpose, until the outbreak of War in 1914, when our trading ceased while Father was in the Navy, minesweeping. In 1920, trading was started with the keel *Galatea*, loading at Kilnhurst and Roundwood staithes, for

Coal came to the Leeds Tramways generating station by keel by way of the Aire and Calder Navigation. Leeds City Museum

steam trawler bunkering at Hull, and for the tanyard of Richard Hodgson and Sons Ltd, Beverley; while at Aldwarke staithe, gas coal was loaded for Beverley Corporation gasworks. Later, owing to a rise in the water level, which made Aldwarke staithe unworkable, we loaded gas coal at Roundwood and Denaby staithes for Beverley gasworks, until they closed down in 1948 on nationalization; then, until the end of the contract, the coal was delivered to the East Hull gasworks and the British Gas Light and Coke Company's works at Bank Side, Hull.

Steam coal from Dalton Main Colliery (also known as Silverwood pit) was loaded at Roundwood staithe, at the rate of one cargo per year, for the South Bullock pump, until this changed to diesel power. The pump was on the River Hull, two miles above Beverley, and owned by the Beverley and Barmston Drainage Board. When mechanical stoking was introduced, the coal had to be reduced in size and washed to keep down the dust. We then loaded washed singles and washed smalls at the staithes of the following collieries: Roundwood, Denaby, Hatfield Main, Altofts, Allerton Bywater, Allerton Main, (Astley Cut) Water Haigh, for Richard Hodgson and Sons Ltd, at Beverley; for Good, Havercroft, at Stoneferry wharf and Wincolmlee wharf, Hull; for Rafferty and Watson at Scott Street wharf, Hull; for Thomas Holmes and Sons' tanyard at Sculcoates wharf, Hull; and also for several mills on the River Hull. Before Hatfield Main staithe was built, coal was loaded in the *Guidance* from lorries at Stainforth for the CWS flour mill at Wilmington.

Opencast coal for Richard Hodgson and Sons Ltd, Beverley, was loaded at Swillington wharf, British Oak staithe and Malthouse wharf, Wakefield. The *Comrade* loaded opencast coal at Rotherham wharf for transshipment at Goole.

House coal for the Hull and East Riding Co-op's Beverley depot was loaded at Hatfield Main and at Keadby coal staithes from Bentley collieries. House coal, in various grades and five sizes, nuts, doubles, trebles, cubes and large, was loaded for G. N. Bell and Sons, who were house coal merchants at Beverley, from the following colliery staithes: Hatfield Main, Altofts, Allerton Bywater, Fryston, Wheldale and Whitwood. During one winter, when the canals were closed by ice, we loaded house coal from the railway, at the hoist in Humber Dock, for Beverley.

In 1921, when the miners were on strike, coal was imported into Goole and Hull. We loaded at Goole for Pilkington's glassworks at Barnby Dun, and at Victoria Dock, Hull, for the glassworks of Beatson Clark at Rotherham. In 1932, when the cement works at Chalder Ness closed down, there were about 220 tons of coal left in stock; I loaded the *Guidance* with half of it and delivered to the cement works of G. & T. Earle Ltd at Wilmington, Hull.

Cocoa beans

Cocoa beans were loaded ex-ship at Hull for Rowntree's, York, and were discharged at Foss Islands warehouse or Queen's staith; also, for British Cocoa Mills, Hull.

Cocoa butter

Cocoa butter was loaded ex-ship at Hull for Rowntree's, York.

Cocoa cake

Cocoa cake was loaded ex-ship at Hull, for Rowntree's, discharged into warehouses in Hull Harbour and Sculcoates.

Cocoa powder

Cocoa powder was loaded at British Cocoa Mills, Hull, for transshipment at Immingham for New Zealand.

Compound feeds

Compound feeds include pigmeal, dairy nuts, chicken pellets and other animal feedstuffs, and were loaded at BOCM (butter mill), Spiller's and Rank's flour mills at Hull for the warehouse at Doncaster new wharf.

Concentrates

To reduce bulk for transport, some mineral ores were concentrated at, or near, the place they were mined. Tin concentrate came from the east coast of Africa, packed in bags weighing about a hundred pounds. These we received direct overside from the ships at Hull, and took them to Beverley for transport by road to the Capper Pass works at Melton. A wet concentrate, packed in opentop drums, came from Australia. We received the drums direct from the ships at Hull and landed them at Howden Dyke wharf for transport by road to Capper Pass works at Melton.

Copper

Copper plates and ingots were loaded direct overside from ships at King George Dock, Hull, and also at Immingham.

For copper ore see pyrites.

Copperas (Sulphate of iron)

Copperas was carried from Sheffield Basin, and a steel mill at Holmes near Rotherham, to a paint factory at Stoneferry, Hull. It was used for making black paint.

Copra

Copra (dried coconut) was loaded from ships in Alexandra Dock, Hull, for the British Oil and Cake Mills at Selby.

Cotton

During the 1939–45 War one cargo of cotton bales was loaded at Immingham from a Russian ship for transshipment at Goole to the railway. In 1974 one cargo, again from a Russian ship, was loaded at Hull for Leeds, and discharged into warehouses at British Waterway's wharf at Knostrop.

Cotton seed

Both black and white cotton seed was loaded in bulk from ships at Hull and from warehouses, for Barker and Lee Smith's oil and cake mills at Beverley, and for Pearson's Baltic and Ashcroft mills at Gainsborough; also for the Olympia Cake and Oil Mills at Selby, which later became part of the British Oil and Cake Mills group.

Fertilizer

In the early nineteen-twenties before road haulage became so competitive, one cargo of fertilizer, for several farms on the Trent side, was loaded by hand at the Tyger* manure works, Grovehill, Beverley. This was discharged by our derrick and hand winch to farm carts and wagons at Amcotts, Owston Ferry and Wildsworth. About 1944, two cargoes were loaded in Barton Haven for Wakefield and discharged at the Aire and Calder wharf.

Fish meal

Fish meal was imported, packed in jute bags, through Hull in large amounts from South West Africa and Peru, and in smaller consignments from Norway. We loaded ex-ship at Hull for the compound feed mills at Hull, Beverley, Selby and Gainsborough. In 1953, the *Comrade* had one cargo to Goldthorpe's wharf at Grimsby.

Flour

Flour was loaded at Hull direct from Rank's mill, for Doncaster, Rotherham and Sheffield, and discharged to the warehouses of the Sheffield and South Yorkshire Navigation Company. It was loaded for the Aire and Calder wharf at Wakefield and Rank's warehouse at Leeds, and I loaded flour from Spiller's mills at both Hull and Grimsby for their warehouses at Rotherham and Leeds. During the 1939–45 War, Rank's mill was damaged by enemy action; we then loaded at the Wilmington,

* This spelling is as used by a man named Pinnock Tyger, who used the buildings in the early nineteenth century for making paint, see chapter seven.

Hull, mill of the Co-operative Wholesale Society for Doncaster, Sheffield, Rotherham and Lincoln. Leeds was supplied from the two mills at Selby, by river and canal. I loaded at the Ideal mill, Selby, only once. During the war, Canadian white flour was imported into Hull for the Ministry of Food; we took several cargoes to the buffer or emergency depot at Whitley Bridge and one to the Doncaster flour mill of Thomas Hanley and Sons. After discharging, we loaded on the same berth a cargo of National flour for Sheffield. Only once, with the keel *Galatea*, we loaded at Goole from Hudson Ward's for their Leeds warehouse.

Fruit

Dried fruit, mainly currants and raisins, was loaded from ships in Hull and Immingham that were on the South Africa run, and discharged at Trent wharf, Gainsborough.

Fruit pulp

Fruit pulp, in barrels, was imported through Hull from Poland. We received it direct overside from ships and discharged at Hill's wharf, Leeds, for Moorhouse's, the jam makers.

Grass

Dried alfalfa grass (lucerne) came in bags. We handled only the one cargo, imported from America, loaded ex-ship at Alexandra Dock, Hull, and discharged to road transport in West Stockwith Basin, below Gainsborough, for Misterton.

Gravel

Up to the mid-twenties Trent gravel was loaded by dredging from the river bed near Girton and Sutton-on-Trent. We discharged at Hull, Beverley and Grimsby.

The former sloop Spring *in Queen's Dock, Hull, shortly before it was filled in. At this time she was owned by Tommy Claxton, of Castleford, who carried wheat in her from Hull to Allinson's mill at Castleford; Allinson's advertisement appears on the coamings.*
T. E. Claxton collection

Gum arabic

Gum arabic, in two-hundredweight bags, was received from ships overside in Alexandra Dock, Hull, for Rowntree's, York. Derived from certain species of the acacia tree, it is used for making sweets.

Hair

Hair from hides was loaded at Cranehill, Beverley, for export from Railway Dock, Hull.

Hardboard

Hardboard was loaded ex-ship at Hull, and discharged at Beverley to road transport for onward carriage.

Hides

Dry hides, dried in the sun and like boards, were imported from Africa and the eastern countries. Wet hides, salted & slippery, came into Hull from Ireland, Switzerland, Canada and the River Plate. They were loaded direct from the ships at Hull for the Sculcoates tannery of Thomas Holmes and Richard Hodgson's tannery at Beverley.

Iron

Bar iron, pig iron, square moulded dish metal, iron and steel billets and ingots were all loaded at one time or another from ships at Grimsby, Hull and Goole, for discharge at Tinsley wharf, Sheffield, at Sheffield Basin or at the works of George Senior or Dunford and Elliot's at Attercliffe. Bar iron was also discharged by hand to a factory just below Parker bridge at Sheffield; the place was known as "The Hole in the Wall", because each bar of iron had to be pushed separately through a hole in the wall. In 1968 one cargo of iron powder in bags was loaded ex-ship at Hull for Eastwood wharf, and in 1973, one cargo of sponge iron—compressed iron powder—was loaded from a ship at Howden Dyke, for Rotherham New Wharf: this was discharged by magnet.

The sloop Valiant, *owned by G. D. Holmes of Goole—later of Immingham—loading chalkstone, or cliff as we called it, at Levitt Hagg quarry, near Sprotbrough.* Humber Keel and Sloop Preservation Society

Limestone

Two cargoes of limestone were loaded in 1935 direct from Levitt Hagg Quarry, near Sprotbrough and transshipped at King George Dock, Hull, for Australia.

Linseed

Linseed was loaded in bulk direct from ships at Hull for oil and cake mills at Gainsborough, Selby, Beverley and Hull. It was also loaded out of store at Stoneferry for Selby, and one cargo was loaded ex-ship at Hull for a small mill at Grimsby.

Maize

Maize, sometimes called yellow corn or Indian corn, was loaded out of ships or silo in King George Dock at Hull, always handled in bulk for Barker's and Lee Smith at Beverley or Whitton mills, Gainsborough.

Manganese

Manganese, mainly used in steel manufacture as a deoxidizing and desulphurizing agent, was usually loaded in pallets direct from ships at Hull for Eastwood wharf or Rotherham New Wharf (Don Street). Only one cargo from a Russian ship was loaded in bulk for Eastwood wharf and discharged by grab.

Mimosa

Mimosa bark in bales and mimosa solid extract in bags, imported from South and East Africa, was used for tanning leather and making dyes. It was loaded overside from ships at Hull and Immingham for Selby dye works, Thomas Holmes' tannery at Hull, and Richard Hodgson and Sons, Beverley.

Myrobalans

Myrobalans (Myrabs), a dried fruit used for tanning leather and making dyes, came from India. Usually the nuts were left whole for the dye works and crushed for tanning. We loaded both in bags overside at Hull for Beverley, Selby and Leeds.

Nickel

Nickel was loaded ex-ship at Hull for Sheffield and Rotherham, usually packed in drums but occasionally in boxes.

Olive oil

Olive oil in barrels was loaded ex-ship at Hull for Leeds.

Palm kernels

Palm kernels were loaded in bulk, usually in Alexandra Dock, Hull, for British Oil and Cake Mills, Selby.

Paper

All kinds of paper including newsprint were loaded in reels, bales and pallets ex-ship at Hull for Knostrop and Leeds; newsprint only for Sheffield Basin, and at Goole also ex-ship for Newark for transshipment to open Trent catches.

Phosphate

Loaded in bulk ex-ship at Immingham for Lincoln, Saxilby and Howden Dyke, and also in bulk from ships in Albert Dock, Hull, for Hull Bridge, Saxilby and Furley's wharf, Gainsborough.

Pollards

Pollards, a by-product of flour milling, was loaded in bags at Hull from ships in the River Plate trade for compound feed mills at Beverley, Gainsborough and BOCM, Selby.

Potash

Potash in bulk was loaded ex-ship from Albert Dock, Hull, to Hull Bridge near Beverley.

Potassium

Only one cargo of potassium was loaded, from a Russian ship in Alexandra Dock, Hull, for Eastwood wharf. The potassium was in bags of approximately ten stone.

Potatoes

During the time we had the keels *Confidence* and *Aureola* before the 1914–18 War, potatoes were loaded by hand in sacks direct from Trentside farms for transshipment at Hull into ships for export. The main loading berths were Butterwick, Burringham, Amcotts and Meredyke.

Pulp

Wood pulp in bales was loaded ex-ship at Hull in Albert Dock, Victoria Dock and Alexandra Dock. Most of it was discharged at West Stockwith Basin into road transport for a factory at Chesterfield. Smaller quantities were carried to Knostrop wharf, Leeds, and Queen's staith, York, for road transport to a factory at Tadcaster, and the odd cargo to Rawcliffe paper mill.

Pyrites (Sulphide of iron)

Iron pyrites, usually known as copper ore, was loaded in bulk ex-ship at Hull or Goole for Lincoln, Castleford, Hunslet Basin at Leeds and for the Goole alum works of Peter Spence.

A busy scene in King George Dock at Hull in 1922. Hull Town Docks Museum

Quebracha

Quebracha solid extract, which comes from a South American hardwood (*Quebracho Colorado*) known as the axebreaker, is used for tanning leather. It was packed in bags of approximately a hundred pounds weight. We loaded straight from ships at Hull for Richard Hodgson and Sons, Beverley.

Rapeseed meal

Rapeseed meal was loaded from ships at Hull for BOCM, Selby.

Rice

When the *Comrade* was a new vessel, still owned by Turner Carmichael, she was used to load rice in bags overside from a ship in Alexandra Dock, Hull, for Garbutts rice mill just below North Bridge on the River Hull.

Rice meal

Rice meal, which the dockers called "paddy meal", was loaded in bags from ships lying in Hull Docks for Barker's and Lee Smith, Beverley, and BOCM, Selby.

Sand

Trent sand was dredged by hand from the bed of the River Trent below Fledborough railway bridge near North Clifton. One cargo was taken to Rotherham, one to Beverley, one to the River Head Wharf at Grimsby and others to Hull.

White sand

White sand was loaded by grab from ships at Goole. This was a regular trade, but I loaded only two cargoes; one in 1926 with the keel *Galatea* to the glassworks of Beatson Clark at Rotherham and one to Kilner's glassworks at Conisbrough with the keel *Guidance*.

Zircon sand

Zircon sand for the steel industry was loaded in paper bags from ships at Hull for Eastwood wharf, Rotherham.

Shea nuts

In February, 1973, two cargoes of shea nuts (butter nuts) were loaded in bulk in Beverley Lock wharf from out of store and discharged at BOCM, Selby. Later that same year one cargo in bags was loaded ex ss *Ilorin Palm* in King George Dock, Hull. After a few days on demurrage they were discharged at Barton Clay Hole to road transport.

Silicon

Ferro-silicon (an alloy of iron and silicon used in making additions of silicon to steel and cast-iron) in drums, barrels or boxes was loaded from ships at Hull, usually in Albert or Alexandra Docks, for Rotherham Eastwood wharf, Rotherham Don Street wharf, or Sheffield Basin.

Keels and other craft at York; at left is a steam keel. York City Library

Soot cake

Soot cake for use as a fertilizer was loaded in bags by hand from horsedrawn carts at Whitley Bridge for transshipment at Hull for export.

Sorghum seed

Sorghum seed from sorghum grass, a tropical grass, was loaded in bulk ex-ship or silo, King George Dock, Hull, for Barker's and Lee Smith, Beverley.

Soya beans

Soya beans were loaded in bulk ex-ship at Hull for BOCM, Selby.

Soya meal

Soya meal in 100lb bags was loaded ex-ship at Hull for Barkers at Beverley and for mills at Gainsborough. One cargo was taken to York, discharged to road transport at Marygate Landing.

Strawboard

Strawboard was loaded at Goole from ship and warehouse for transshipment at Newark to open Trent catches.

Sugar

Raw brown sugar was loaded in two-hundredweight sacks ex-ship in Alexandra Dock, Hull, for Brigg sugar factory. Refined white sugar in fifty-kilo bags from Poland and East Germany was loaded ex-ship at both Hull and Goole for Rowntree's of York; discharge at York was at Foss Islands Warehouse or Queen's staith. Refined white sugar from the same source was also taken to Sheffield and discharged into warehouses.

Sugar beet

I only had one cargo of sugar beet. In 1936 I loaded by hand with barrows and planks out of a field at Thrybergh, near Rotherham, for the British Sugar Corporation factory at Selby; it was discharged by grab.

Sulphur

Sulphur was loaded ex-ship in Alexandra Dock, Hull, for Sheffield. Delivery would be either at Tinsley wharf, Furley's wharf or Sheffield Basin; it was loaded in bulk and discharged by grab. We also took sulphur to Hunt's at Castleford and to Hunslet Basin, Leeds.

Sunflower seed and cake

Sunflower seed and cake was loaded ex-ship at Hull docks for Barker's and Lee Smith, Beverley, and BOCM, Selby.

Tallow

Tallow was loaded in barrels at Crane Hill, Beverley, from the tanneries for transshipment at Hull for export.

Timber

Several cargoes of timber, in the form of deals and battens, were loaded ex-ship in Victoria Dock, Hull, for Sheffield Basin. In 1936 one cargo of deals, about twenty-eight standards, was discharged at Doncaster to road transport. Several cargoes of plywood were loaded ex-ship at Alexandra Dock for discharge at Beverley to road transport; one only to Goole for discharge to road transport. One cargo of hard timber for cabinet making was loaded ex-ship at Hull for discharge to road transport at Beverley.

Tractors

Six tractors at a time were loaded from the International Harvester Company, Wheatley, near Doncaster, to Hull for export. Discharge was direct to ship.

Valerian

Valerian, from Turkey, much like a horse chestnut, is used for tanning leather. It usually came into Hull in small lots. I did not handle any until the nineteen-seventies when two small motor vessels came to Goole direct from Izmir with about six hundred tons each. I loaded about ninety tons out of each vessel in Goole Docks for Richard Hodgson and Sons, Beverley.

Whitening or whiting

Whitening until 1930 was loaded at Crane Hill, Beverley, by hand-operated crane. It came in jute bags from the Beckside or Queensgate works of the Queensgate Whitening Works on horse-drawn rullies. We took it to the Town Docks, Hull, for transshipment to the weekly coasting steamers which ran a regular service to London, Yarmouth, King's Lynn, Newcastle, Dundee and Aberdeen. Once we loaded a cargo of whitening packed in barrels which we transshipped in King George Dock, Hull, into a steamer for Australia. In the early nineteen-fifties there was one consignment of several hundred tons from the whitening works at Lund, seven miles from Beverley. Along with other keels the *Comrade* loaded one cargo of this consignment from motor vehicles at Hodgson's warehouse on Beckside, Beverley, and transshipped it in Alexandra Dock, Hull, to a Yugoslav motor vessel.

Wire

Coils of steel wire were loaded from ships in Alexandra Dock, Hull, for discharge to Spencer Wire Works, Thornes Lock, Wakefield. Coils of copper wire were loaded at Spencer Wire Works for transshipment at Hull to Russian ships.

Wool

Only one cargo of wool was carried, from a ship in King George Dock, Hull, to a ship in Railway Dock, Hull.

Wheat

Wheat was imported through Hull from Australia, Canada, India, France, Sweden, Black Sea ports and the River Plate. That from Australia and India was in bags of approximately ten stone each, and that from other countries in bulk. Most of the wheat we loaded was carried in bulk, loaded direct from ships or from store, that is from warehouses or after 1914 from the silo in King George Dock.

Until the mid-twenties there were a few mills that could only take their wheat in eighteen-stone sacks. One such firm was Leetalls of Lincoln; we had to heave out the sacks by hand with our derrick and put them on to horse-drawn lurries. Wheat for a mill at Worksop was carried in eighteen-stone sacks to West Stockwith Basin, then transshipped by our derrick to narrow boats for onward carriage on the Chesterfield Canal. The Mexborough mill of the Barnsley British Co-operative Society received their wheat in sacks until 1922 or 1923, when they installed a bucket elevator. There were four small flour mills at Sheffield importing their wheat by keel from Hull; Sam Smith's had their own canalside silo and took their wheat in bulk; the other three, Ibbotson's, Price's and Hazelwood's, continued to use eighteen-stone sacks until 1925, when they jointly leased a warehouse in Sheffield Basin from the Navigation, converting it into a grain silo. Four hundred quarters (ninety tons) was the usual weight for a Sheffield cargo.

Robinson Brothers of Town Mills, Rotherham, were a large user of keels for their supplies of wheat; we could take 420 quarters (94½ tons) to their mill, and 450 quarters (101¼ tons) to Mexborough. To Thomas Hanley's mill at Doncaster we loaded 480 quarters (108 tons). After the 1939–45 War Robinson's and Hanley's came under the Rank Hovis McDougall group, and we loaded wheat for them out of Rank's silo at Clarence mills, Hull; this was often English-grown wheat. There were two flour mills at Gainsborough, both on the Trent side; one was Townrow's, the other Whitton's. I have carried wheat to them both with the keels *Guidance* and *Comrade*. Once after discharging a cargo of wheat from Hull at Whitton's I moved half a mile down the Trent to the Ministry of Food silo and loaded about fifty tons of bulk barley and sixty tons of bulk wheat, for the mill again.

When loading wheat for Gainsborough we usually loaded five hundred quarters in bulk (112½ tons), the capacity of the hold. When loading we could stow some above the coamings and so make up to 120 tons. Five hundred quarters of bulk wheat was our cargo when we loaded for the dockside mills of Hudson Ward at Goole. We took the same quantity when we loaded for Allinson's mill at Castleford and to Leeds for the Leeds Industrial Co-operative Society Ltd. After Barker's and Lee Smith of Beverley changed over from seed crushing to compound feed for cattle we loaded wheat for them from ship, warehouse or silo at Hull and from the silo at Immingham. Once only in the nineteen-seventies the *Comrade* had a cargo of bulk wheat for Timm's flour mill at Goole and one only from a ship at King George Dock, Hull, to Rank's mill at Clarence Street, Hull. In 1930 the *Comrade* loaded wheat in eighteen-stone sacks from a ship laid near the dry docks in King George Dock, Hull, and discharged to the railway in the same dock. It was the largest cargo she ever carried; the weight of the wheat was 146 tons 5 cwts, the sacks two tons more. While I was master of the keel *Annie Maud* I once loaded a full cargo of bulk wheat from a ship in King George Dock between 6 pm and 9 pm and discharged it the next day into the silo.

During the 1939–45 War the Ministry of Food controlled all movements of food and grain. It was expected that there would be times when the east coast ports would be unworkable, so they adopted a policy of moving all foodstuffs away from the ports and built buffer depots at Selby, Whitley Bridge, and Castleford, all accessible by water transport. Selby and Castleford were used all the war for storage of wheat, at first in twelve-stone sacks and later, when they were given suction elevators, in bulk. We had many cargoes of wheat to both places, and of other foods to Whitley Bridge. At the outbreak of war the barque *Archibald Russell*, at that time under Finnish ownership, was sailing from Australia to England. On arrival in the Humber she was towed up to Goole with the wheat on board. When the time came for it to be used I loaded the *Vigilant* with five hundred quarters in bulk for the Co-operative Wholesale Society's flour mill at Wilmington, Hull. Wheat landed at west coast ports was brought to Sheffield by rail and loaded direct to keels for onward carriage. I loaded from there three times with the *Vigilant* after discharging flour from Hull. One cargo was to Robinson Brothers' Town mill at Rotherham, one to Mexborough flour mill (Barnsley British Co-op) and one to King's Mill, Knottingley.

APPENDIX TWO

Sloops

CONDITIONS on the Humber estuary were often difficult for the square-rigged keel, well suited though she was to river and canal work. As early as the eighteenth century some keels exchanged their squaresails for a fore-and-aft rig of mainsail and headsail, giving them a sloop rig, and it was as sloops that they were known. They could work well to windward and their rig was efficient enough for them to make coastal passages. Sloops traded regularly to the Wash ports, to the Thames, up to Bridlington, even to the Tees and Tyne, with occasional visits to Continental ports.

However, the majority of sloops stayed within the Humber, handling the cargoes which the estuary ports offered, farm produce from the Lincolnshire side, bricks and tiles from works on both banks, cement, chalk-stone from the quarries between South Ferriby and Barton, gravel and sand dredged from the Trent at Girton and Clifton, sand from the banks off Paull, gravel from Spurn. Because so much of the traffic was won from the Lincolnshire side of the river, sloops tended to be owned there. Barton-on-Humber was the home of the largest group of sloop men and, until 1926, carvel wooden sloops were being built at Clapson's yard on the west bank of the Haven next to Stamp's wharf, from which W. Stamp and Son ran a regular service of sloop-rigged market boats carrying produce from Barton over to Hull, where they had a berth by Victoria Pier.

Barton sloops found a steady trade carrying coal from the West Riding collieries to the brickyards and house coal merchants at Barton and Barrow. In return bricks and tiles were shipped out in sloops and spritsail barges. On the east side of Barton Haven were the fertilizer works—they are there still—which received large shipments of phosphate and potash imported through Hull and transshipped into sloops for delivery to the works. They had a jetty on the foreshore for receiving these raw materials, while manufactured fertilizer was often shipped outwards from their other jetty in the Haven. During 1943–44 I loaded a few cargoes here with the keel *Vigilant* for Wakefield, entered on our bill of lading as potato fertilizer; we discharged at the Calder wharf, where they were still using a horse to hoist out the cargo.

Clapson's, whose yard had been founded in 1880, specialized in sloops, but many builders turned out sloops as well as keels, at Beverley, Thorne, Stainforth, up in the West Riding at Wakefield, at Mexborough and Swinton, and on the Wash at Boston. In the twentieth century sloop owners, perhaps more than keel owners, turned to steel hulls, well suited to the bulk cargoes which came the sloops' way. Steel construction was the preserve of the larger yards, Richard Dunston's at Thorne, Henry Scarr of Hessle, Joseph Scarr at Beverley, J. S. Watson's at Gainsborough, all of which also built other types of vessel.

E.W. PAGET-TOMLINSON APRIL 1987

Sloop hulls tended on the large size, although many were built to navigation limits like the keels, Sheffield size, Barnsley size and so on. But sloops could go up to sixty-eight feet in length and seventeen feet beam with capacities of up to 130 tons. Lines followed the keel pattern, bluff, almost flat bows, but a fine run aft allowing a good flow past the rudder for working to windward. Leeboards were fitted for the same purpose, and as among the keels there were short-stemmed sloops and long-stemmed sloops, the short-stemmed able to rig a bowsprit to set an extra headsail. As far as hull form went, there was little to choose between a keel and a sloop; indeed some keels became sloops and vice versa. It was the fore-and-aft rig that marked the sloop, demanding a different deck layout.

With a fore and aft mainsail the mast had to be stepped further forward, likewise in a lutchet so that it could be lowered. The mainsheet was rove through a double sheave block on the boom and a single block on a horse on the after headledge, the free end being led to a cleat below. The foot of the foresail was extended by a boom and the sheet secured to a traveller on a similar horse. Fore rollers were fitted for warping and lowering the mast and as in a keel there were leeboard rollers aft, but no tack or sheet rollers. Whereas in a keel the halyard rollers were aft, in a sloop they were alongside the mast, either on the coamings to port and starboard or in a two-hatch ship on deck between the hatches in the space called the sparrings. The port side halyard rollers handled the foresail halyard and peak halyard, the starboard side rollers the throat halyard and the topping lift.

Well peaked up, the gaff mainsail gave a good performance to windward. The canvas was tanned red, unlike the white/grey untanned sail of a keel. Sloop headsails and topsails were untanned, the topsail being rarely set save in light airs. Keel shrouds were set up with heart-shaped deadeyes, of ancient pattern, but the sloops might use the ordinary round deadeyes. Anchor windlass, companions, cabin arrangements were the same as in a keel, likewise the deck equipment, stowers, boathooks, sounding rod, swape, footing plank. Navigation sidelights were mounted on cranked iron stanchions on the stern rail, with the stern light aft on the mainsheet horse, as in a keel, but nothing to do with the sloop's mainsheet.

Sloop handling to windward meant going about smartly, the foresail being pulled over by the mate using a bowline passed round the weather shrouds to bring round the ship's head. Running before the wind was less effective than in a keel, but much of a sloop's work was beating and close hauled sailing in a shoal-ridden estuary. Two men were enough, with all the rollers, to handle a sloop in the Humber, but an extra man would be engaged for a coastal passage so that watches could be stood. Wives occasionally went aboard as mates, but not for long spells.

Ownership was generally a family affair. There were few large sloop fleets, James W. Barraclough of Barton and later of Hull being the main one. Founded in 1890, Barraclough's built up a fleet of some twenty vessels mostly in the bulk trades, coal and grain, owning the last sloops under sail in 1946, the *Ivie* and the *Sprite*; eventually they went over to motor craft, ceasing trading in 1975. Another large owner was G. D. Holmes of Stainforth, later of Goole, whose fleet was founded in the early eighteen-nineties with two vessels; by the nineteen-thirties he had about

Opposite page: *A steel sloop not unlike the* Amy Howson, *now owned by the Humber Keel and Sloop Preservation Society. The* Amy Howson *was built as a keel in 1914 by Joseph Scarr at Beverley for George Scaife of Beverley. Of Sheffield size, 61 feet 6 inches by 15 feet 6 inches, she was in general trade under the name* Sophia. *In 1916 she was re-rigged as a sloop and used on the lower Humber for bank protection work, and then in 1920 she became the* I Know, *owned by Gouldthorpe, Scott and Wright, of Grimsby, passing to W. H. Barraclough, who renamed her* Amy Howson, *in 1922.*

Below: *The port side halyard roller of a sloop.*

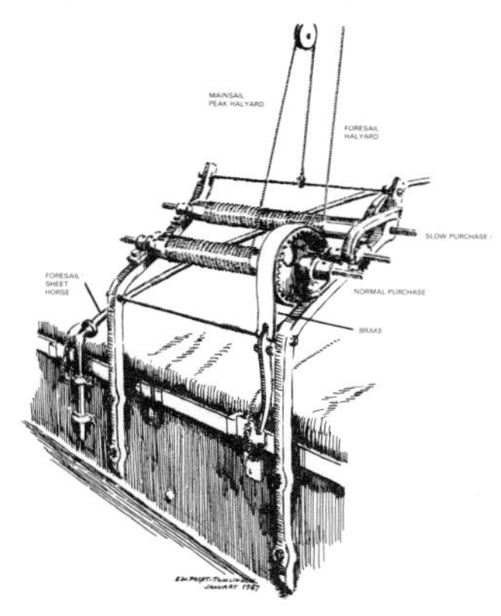

A sloop under sail on the Humber about 1930.
Author's collection

fifteen keels and sloops. They handled bulk cargoes: sand, alum, potash, sulphur, raw wool, and stone for the training walls in the Trent and Lower Ouse. Four sloops were built for this work, bringing chalk from the quarries at Cliff near Barton-on-Humber. Sail survived in the fleet until 1937.

Other owners were the Farmers' Company of Barton, who used sloops to bring in fertilizer and take away farm produce, and brickmaker John Frank of South Ferriby, who carried bricks from his yard on the Ancholme at Ferriby Sluice, returning with coal for the kilns. Earle's Cement had four clay sloops to bring raw materials to their Melton works on the north bank and to Hull, and J. Richardson of Hull had four built with a 14 feet 4 inches beam to go up the Driffield Navigation and the Market Weighton Canal. There were owners at Owston Ferry on the Trent, David Holgate at Beverley had sloops and J. J. Tomlinson of Thorne was in partnership with my uncle William Henry, see chapter nine; the partnership had five sloops. One sloop, the *Anglo-American*, was fitted with tanks to carry paraffin for the Anglo-American Oil Company.

APPENDIX THREE

Billyboys

RELATED to the keel and sloop was the coastal fore-and-aft rigged billyboy, a vessel which could go up the navigations but with her bulwarks was seaworthy enough to cross to the Continent and range south to the Channel ports. Many were owned at Goole and Knottingley, and built there too, others coming from yards at Hull, Beverley, Doncaster, Thorne, Wakefield, Leeds, Castleford, as well as from Wash area builders at, for example, Walsoken by Wisbech.

Some billyboys were too large for inland trading, sixty or seventy feet long by seventeen or eighteen feet beam, others were narrow enough for the canals. The narrow ones were not good sailers; indeed billyboys were sluggish performers whatever their dimensions, slow but safe was their motto. In hull design they were similar to a keel or sloop, although the bow had a more rounded form, often with a clipper-shaped cutwater, while the stern was apple cheeked like a Dutch galleot's. Indeed the billyboy looked Dutch, with the stern bulwarks canted in and a pronounced sheer. Some have regarded the name to be of Dutch derivation, coming from the vessel called the bijlander (by land), but more likely it derives from the adoption of an eighteenth-century term for a Hull sailor, a billyboy. Hull was sturdily loyal to King William III—Dutch again.

A billyboy's bilge was more rounded than a keel's, the planking generally clinker but by the eighteen-seventies usually carvel; by the eighteen-nineties some billyboys were built of steel. One of the last was the steel *Halcyon* built by Henry Scarr at Hessle in 1903 and still operating as a motor vessel half a century later; one of the best known was the *Aimwell*,

Miles from home, the billyboy HH *of Goole is seen at Shoreham, Sussex, with the topsail schooner* Elizabeth *of Bridgwater in February, 1864.*
Commander H. Oliver Hill

wood carvel, built in 1883 at Winteringham Haven on the Lincolnshire side by Routh and Waddingham. The lines of the *Aimwell* were taken off an old half model and are preserved in the Science Museum, South Kensington; two models resulted, one at the Science Museum, the other in the Town Docks Museum at Hull.

Early clinker-built billyboys generally carried a sloop rig, with one or two headsails, two making them cutters in later terminology. Single-masted billyboys remained, but from the eighteen-seventies some were ketch or schooner rigged, often with a square topsail and topgallant and a square course, square sails being set on the single masters too. There was no question of the billyboy imitating the keel rig, they were fore-and-aft vessels with squaresail assistance in a favourable wind. As with the Humber

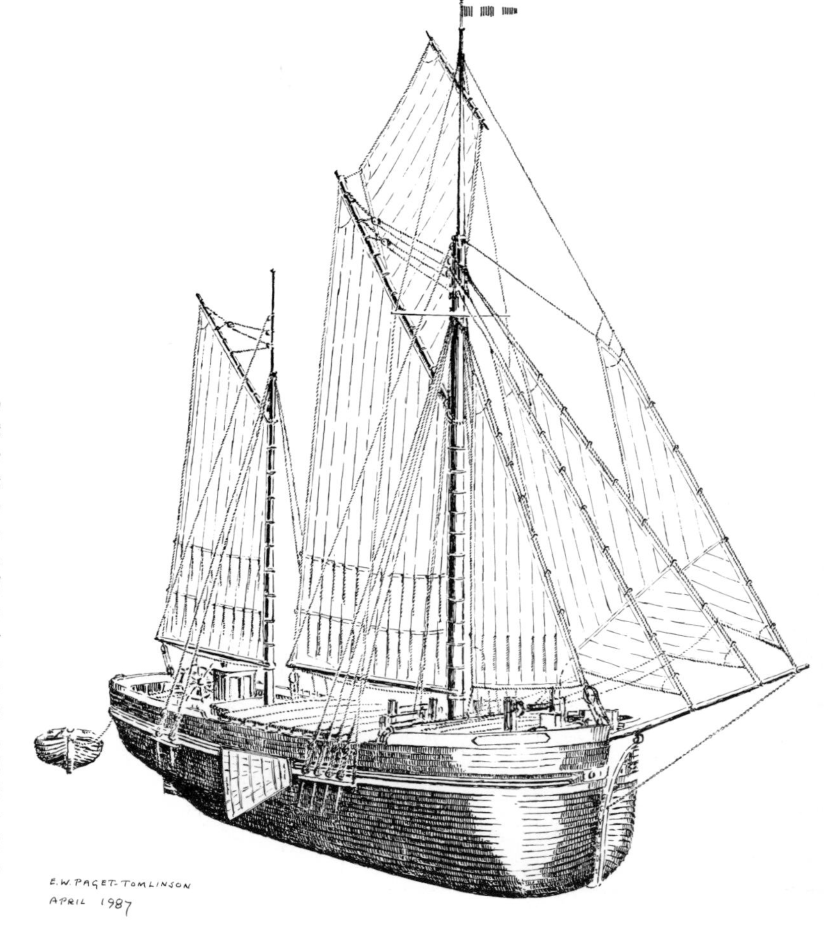

Billyboys came in many shapes and sizes, but universally they were given bulwarks and most were clinker built up to the deck. The ketch rig was common, sometimes with a square topsail and topgallant and even a square course for following winds. The drawing is based on the Aimwell, *built at Winteringham Haven in 1883; she measured 64 feet long by 17 feet beam and 7 feet 6 inches depth of hold. She could carry 100 tons with a crew of three.*

sloop they relied on windlass power for sail handling; the windlasses were grouped by the mainmast between the hatches, in the sparrings, most being two-hatch ships with fore and main hatches. For sea passages the crew could number three or four; some billyboys were family crewed. There were, incidentally, similar but deeper draughted ketches working out of the Humber, without leeboards, locally called dickies.

Leeboards were usual on the billyboys, while many had wheel steering. Some masts were fixed, others stepped in lutchets and were easily lowered for inland work, although the fixed masts could be lifted out if need be. Other features culled from the *Aimwell* plans are the cabin skylight, the pin rail alongside each mast, secured inboard to the bulwarks, the tall after companion, the small hatch aft of the mizzen giving access to the hold. Decoration was evident either side of the hawse holes and along the binds, a painted line with an arrow head at the stem, a white capping rail to the bulwarks, maybe a scraped and varnished strake beneath the binds.

Cargoes were as varied as one would expect, cement, grain, bricks and tiles, fertilizer, coal, oil cake, similar to what the sloops carried, but wider

The billyboy Beverley *of Hull was unusual in having stern windows, not a normal feature of these craft. She had been built in Holland in 1861 as the* Wilhelmina Giezen, *and by 1868 was owned by Edwin Owen of Beverley.* Hull Town Docks Museum

Comparative sizes of sloop and billyboy: Market boat, sloop rigged, Barton to Hull, 57 feet long by 14 feet 8 inches beam, draught about 5 feet with 20 to 40 tons aboard, the usual cargo of a market boat. Sheffield-size steel sloop, 61 feet 6 inches long by 15 feet 6 inches beam; laden draught 7 feet 6 inches with 120 tons aboard. Steel sloop in the Trent gravel trade, 68 feet long by 17 feet 3 inches beam; laden draught 7 feet 6 inches with 130 tons aboard. Market billyboy, Barton to Hull, 57 feet long by 14 feet beam; laden draught 6 feet 3 inches with 85 tons aboard. Ketch-rigged billyboy with square topsail and topgallant, 64 feet long by 16 feet beam; laden draught 7 feet with 105 tons aboard.

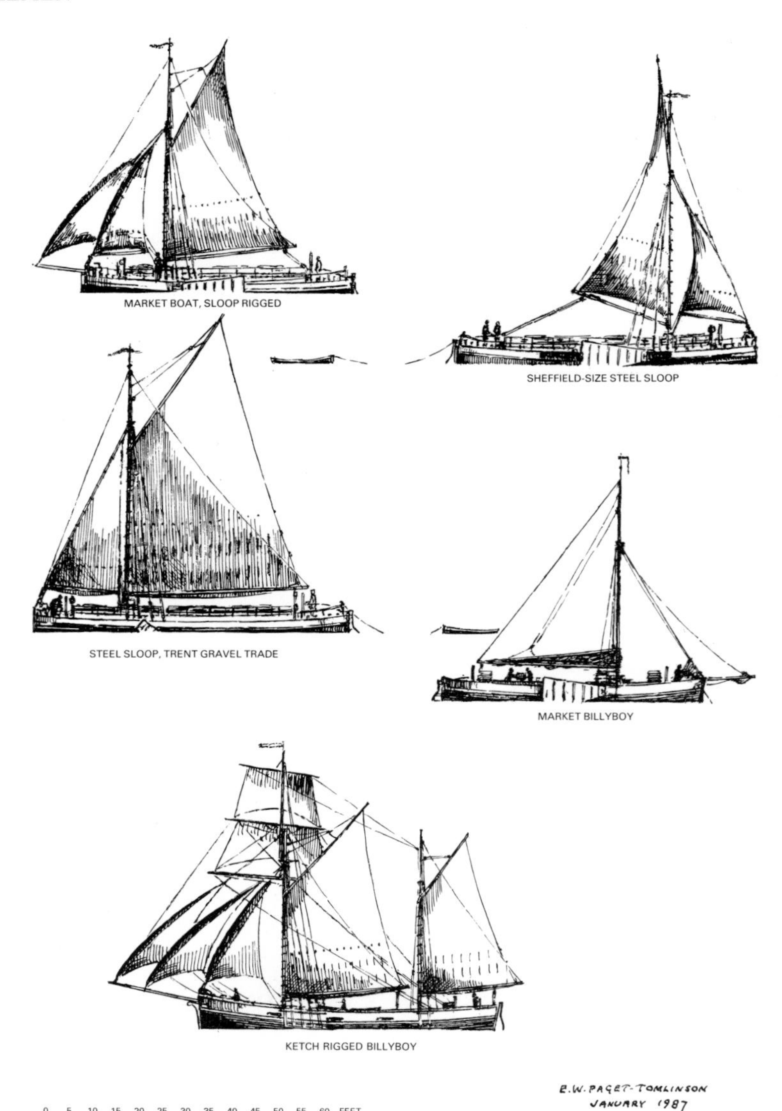

ranging, with voyages to Ipswich, Yarmouth, King's Lynn, South Shields, Rochester, Shoreham and near Continental ports. Unfortunately billyboys could not compete with powered coasters and were slower than many sailing coasters, certainly slower than spritsail barges, so the billyboy died out soon after the 1914–18 War. Like the *Halcyon*, the *Mavis*, built of iron at Beverley in 1896 for Barton owners, became a motor barge and lasted into the nineteen-sixties. She had a crew of four in her sailing days.

APPENDIX FOUR

Steam Keels

STEAM had come early to the Humber. The *Caledonia*, described as a paddle sloop, was in 1814 carrying passengers between Hull and Gainsborough and in 1828 the steam tug *Britannia* of 50 hp was assisting seagoing craft between Hull and Goole. The *Caledonia* was the first of many passenger steamers, running for example from Thorne, Selby, and Gainsborough to Hull. With coach feeder services from Leeds, Sheffield and other places, this would be the most comfortable way of travel before the railways. Connections could be made at Hull with coastal passenger vessels for Scotland, Yarmouth and London.

My mother's father, George Kershaw, and his father had farmed at Westwoodside, about three miles west of the Trent near Owston Ferry, and I have heard my Great Aunt Annie talk about trips to Hull in the paddle steamer *Atalanta*, one of the last passenger vessels on the Gainsborough–Hull run. She had been built of iron at Gainsborough in 1851 and was 135 feet long by 15 feet 2 inches beam. Until the mid-twenties the landing jetties at Susworth, Burringham and Burton Stather were still in place.

Steam passenger vessels had been successful, but up to the end of the 1914–18 War there had not been many mechanically propelled cargo vessels in the upriver trade. With craft limited to the size of the locks and with so many vessels available it was not profitable to sacrifice cargo space for power. From my father I heard of the *Reliance*, a steel vessel built at Gainsborough in 1889 for trading between South Yorkshire and the Louth Navigation. She had an upright boiler supplying steam to a low-powered engine, and carried a small amount of fore-and-aft sail, the mainsail being triangular. When she was on the Sheffield and South Yorkshire Navigation the company would not allow the use of her engine, so the owner contracted with my grandfather for horse haulage when required. The Aire and Calder Navigation was more forward looking. They had one steam tug working on the canal by 1831, a second one in 1832 and a third in 1834. By 1857 they had a daily towage service each way between Wakefield and Goole. When I first went on board to earn my living they had two steam fly-boats working from their wharf in Humber Dock basin at Hull up to Leeds and Wakefield. That was a convenient berth for them. They were never fully loaded on the downriver voyage, so by making an early start on the tide from Goole they could save water on to the berth and start to work cargo in or out all the sooner.

The steam fly-boats were carvel-built wooden vessels, long and narrow, about 70 feet long by 14 feet 10 inches beam. They were worked with three hands, the engine controls being on deck at the after end of the engine room casing, and the accommodation right in the bows. Steering was by a wheel from an exposed position on the fore side of the funnel, which was hinged for the bridges. As was usual with all Aire and Calder

Overleaf: *Comparative sizes of steam keel: Aire and Calder Navigation wooden steam flyboat, Hull to Leeds, Wakefield and Barnsley, 78 feet long by 14 feet 10 inches beam. Aire and Calder Navigation steel steam tug, Goole to Leeds, 85 feet long. Iron steam keel* Swift, *1894, owned by the Farmers' Company of Barton-on-Humber, 67.9 feet long by 14.9 feet beam. Steel steam keel* Eagle, *1905, owned by the Hull flour millers Rishworth, Ingleby and Lofthouse Ltd, 85 feet long by 17 feet beam; laden draught 7 feet with 110 tons aboard. Iron steam keel* Arrow, *1889, owned by the York flour millers Henry Leetham and Sons Ltd, 93.5 feet long by 18.1 feet beam. Trent gravel dredger* Cité de Paris, *built of steel in 1915 as an ammunition carrier, later owned by Lincoln and Hull Water Transport Ltd, 126 feet long by 16 feet beam; laden draught 7 feet with 225 tons aboard.*

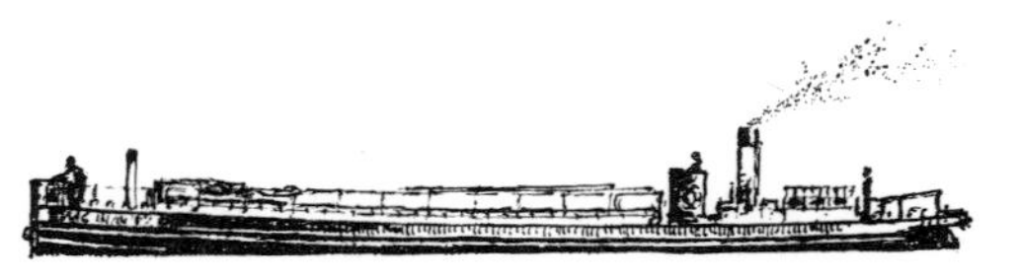

AIRE & CALDER NAVIGATION FLY-BOAT

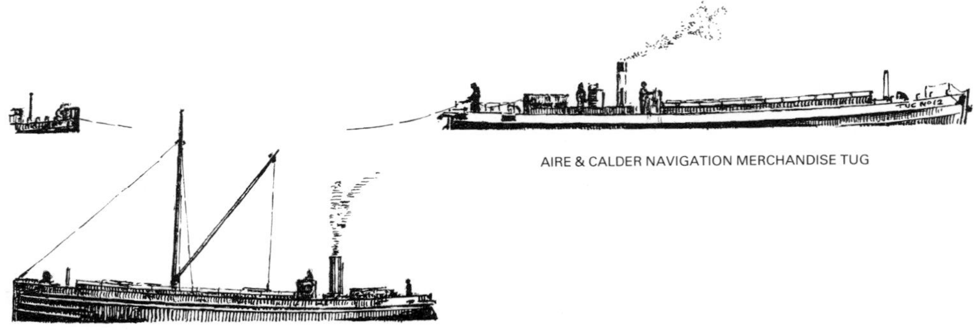

AIRE & CALDER NAVIGATION MERCHANDISE TUG

STEAM KEEL 'SWIFT', 1894

STEAM KEEL 'EAGLE', 1905

STEAM KEEL 'ARROW', 1889

TRENT GRAVEL DREDGER 'CITE DE PARIS', 1915

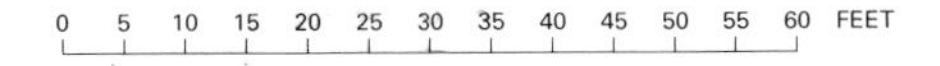

E.W. PAGET-TOMLINSON
JANUARY 1987

Navigation craft, they were not named but numbered. The ACN had two larger, more powerful iron-built steam vessels, combined tugs and cargo carriers, which plied between Goole and Leeds each night towing fly-boats, working cargo in and out during the day.

Rishworth, Ingleby and Lofthouse of the Swan flour mill at Hull owned six steam-powered cargo vessels. The steam keels *Swiftsure* and *Ril* were used in the Hull–Rotherham trade, taking flour and offal from the Swan flour mill to Laws wharf, Rotherham. These two were about Sheffield size and carried three hands each. Engine controls were on deck. Both had wheel steering, the *Swiftsure* from a position on the fore side of the funnel and the *Ril* from amidships. The other four were the *Eagle*, the *Swan*, the *Cygnet* and the *John M. Rishworth*. These were larger vessels, about 80 feet long and 17 feet 6 inches beam by about 7 feet deep, carrying three hands. They had plenty of power to tow two lighters. The *John M. Rishworth* was steered from amidships; the others had the wheel on the fore side of the engine room casing. Being owned by a flour mill all six were spoken of as the "flour packets". They were all built at Hessle between 1904 and 1915 of steel on keel lines.

The ale packet *Gambrinus* was owned by Hewitt Brothers, of the Grimsby brewery. She made two trips each week; one was from Grimsby to Doncaster with beer in barrels and bottles, returning with empties. Built of steel on the lines of a keel with bulwarks all round, she had a steam winch

Built of steel by Henry Scarr of Hessle in 1905, the Eagle *was one of six steam keels owned by the Hull flour millers Rishworth, Ingleby and Lofthouse. She had a Scotch return tube boiler and a compound engine which could be controlled from the deck. Her hull measured 85 feet long by 17.1 feet beam and 7.3 feet depth of hold. With a crew of three, she could carry some 110 tons of flour from her owners' Swan flour mills on the River Hull to Leeds, Wakefield and York.*

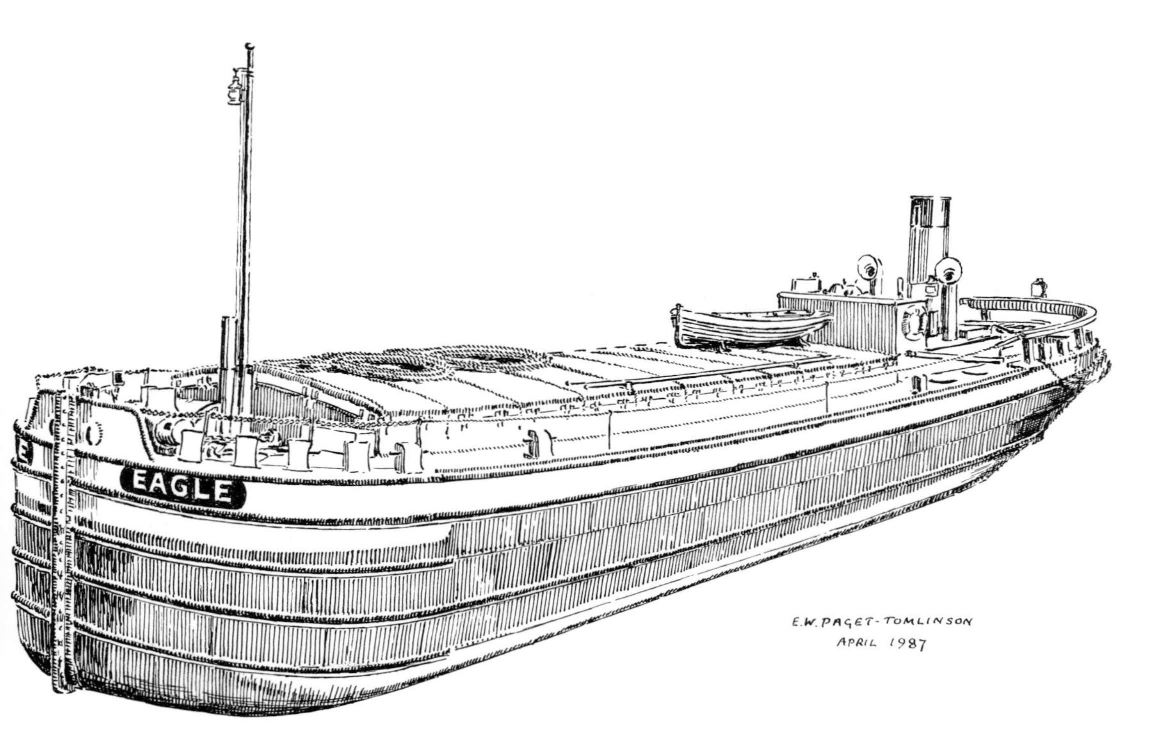

on the foredeck and worked her own cargoes in and out with the derrick. She carried four hands; Brett Middleton was her captain. Having plenty of power, the crew were always ready and willing to make a pound or two on the side by assisting any sloop or keel short of wind. They usually took the Goole and New Junction Canal route to Doncaster, but would divert to the Stainforth and Keadby Canal if there was any chance of a tow.

T. F. Wood and Co. Ltd of York, forwarding agents and river craft owners, owned the *Ouse*, a combined steam tug and cargo vessel 86 feet 8 inches long by 18 feet 3 inches beam and 7 feet 2 inches deep built of steel at Gainsborough in 1898. She had bulwarks right round and was fitted with a strong mast and derrick and a steam winch for working cargo. She often loaded flour at Rank's flour mill, Hull, for York and would tow two lighters. Leetham's, who had a flour mill on the Foss at York and another on the Tees, took most of their wheat from Hull with their own lighters and steam vessels. Working between Hull and York, the ss *Arrow*, built of iron at Hull in 1889, carried cargo and would tow one lighter. *Leetham's Rose*, built of steel at Hull in 1886, was more steam tug than lighter; she usually towed two lighters and could carry cargo, but rarely did so. Leetham's lighters on the York run were of about two hundred tons deadweight, and they had two of 350 tons deadweight working from the Humber to the Tees. One was named *Minster Bell*; the name of the other I believe was *Marteal*. They were towed by the steam vessels *Elizabeth Bromley* (built at Howden in 1912) and *Yendis*; these would carry about 200 tons of wheat and tow one lighter each. I have also seen these two steam vessels going up the river to York.

The steam keel *Swift*, built at Beverley of iron in 1894, was about Sheffield length and beam but rather low, about 6 feet 6 inches. She had the full lines of a keel with bulwarks round bows and stern, and steering was by a wheel just foreside of the engine room casing. She had a mast and derrick for working cargo and a steam winch on the fore deck. Owned by the Farmers' Company of Barton-on-Humber, she traded mainly between Hull, Brigg and Barton; I have seen her a few times at Doncaster. The Farmers' Company also owned a wooden full-rigged keel named the *Britannia*. In the early nineteen-twenties Edwin Bisby, a keel owner of Thorne, had had the *Swift* and put her on a weekly run between Hull and Thorne, loading each Monday at Thorne and each Thursday at Hull. The cargo loaded at Thorne was mainly beer in barrels and bottles from Darley's Brewery there. The Flixborough Shipping Company bought her from the Farmers' Company when the boiler required renewing and installed a diesel engine, then put her to work carrying coal from Denaby to Flixborough and towing one or two other vessels. In 1970 she was lying at Eastwood Low Lock being used as a houseboat.

Finally there were the Trent gravel packets, some large vessels, 118 feet long by 16 feet beam by nearly 7 feet depth of hold. Such were the *Cité de Londres* and her sister the *Cité de Paris*, both built at Dundee in 1915 as ammunition barges to serve the Western Front and coming to the Humber after the Armistice. The *Cité de Paris* was in general traffic up the Aire and Calder, owned by T. E. Claxton and Son, of Castleford, passing to Lincoln and Hull Water Transport Co. Ltd as a grab dredger and salvage vessel. The *Cité de Londres* became a gravel carrier on the Trent, eventually motorized, also for the Lincoln and Hull Water Transport Co. Ltd.

APPENDIX FIVE

Weights and Measures

Grain
63lb = 1 bushel of wheat
60lb = 1 bushel of maize
60lb = 1 bushel of rye
56lb = 1 bushel of barley
42lb = 1 bushel of oats

8 bushels = 1 quarter,	wheat	504lb
	maize	480lb
	rye	480lb
	barley	448lb
	oats	336lb

10 quarters = 1 last, multiply above weights by ten.

Wheat
500 quarters = 112 tons 10 cwt
480 quarters = 108 tons
450 quarters = 101 tons 5 cwt
420 quarters = 94 tons 10 cwt
400 quarters = 90 tons

Rope and wire
Fibre rope is measured by circumference
Wire rope is measured by diameter

6 feet = 1 fathom
100 fathoms = 1 cable

Timber
A standard of timber contains 1,980 board feet, a board foot being a piece of timber one inch thick by twelve inches square; hence a standard is 165 cubic feet.

APPENDIX SIX

Schofield family ships

Keel's Name	*Built*	*Acquired (Sold)*	*Owner*	*Remarks*
Fanny	1866 Joseph Turner, Barugh	1877	John Christopher Schofield (grandfather)	57ft 6in × 14ft 8in × 6ft 6in, wood clinker sides, carvel bottom; see chapter one for description
		(1892)	Half share to William Henry Schofield (uncle)	
		(1904)	To Arthur Schofield (father)	
		c(c 1909)	Sold	
		1921	Bought and sold by Arthur Schofield	
Fleming		c1892	John Christopher Schofield	Possibly iron
City of Sheffield			John Christopher Schofield	Wood, carvel, Sheffield size
Integrity		1904	William Henry Schofield	Wood, carvel, Sheffield size
Guidance	1905 Worfolk, Stainforth	1905	William Henry Schofield	Wood, carvel, Sheffield size; 24 hp Ailsa Craig diesel installed c1936
		(1932)	To Fred Schofield	
		(1940)	Sold to Calvert, Goole	
Sophia			John Christopher Schofield (uncle)	Steel, Sheffield size
Whim			John Christopher Schofield (uncle)	Steel, Barnsley size
Progress			John Schofield (father's cousin)	Iron, sold to Tinsley Rolling Mills as a coal boat
John			John Schofield	Wood, carvel, name changed to *Regent* when John sold her, replacing her by *Vigilant*

James and Mary		1919	Arthur Schofield	Ex-West Riding coal trade to York via the Selby Canal
		(1920)		
Amity		1919	Arthur Schofield	West Country boat bought from Henry Mason, Hull
Galatea (sloop)		1921	Arthur Schofield	Arthur Schofield changed her to keel rig
		(1929)	Exchanged with John Taylor, Hull, for *Ada Carter*	
Vigilant	1923 Staniland, Thorne	1923	John Schofield	Wood, carvel, Sheffield size; 21 hp Lister diesel installed 1942
		(1940)	To Fred Schofield	
		(1953)	To Arthur Schofield and resold to John Schofield (brother)	
		(1954)	Sold to become houseboat	
Comrade	1923 Warren, New Holland		Original owner was Turner Carmichael, who named her *Wanda*; sold to John Taylor and renamed *Ada Carter*.	Steel, Sheffield size; 40 hp semi diesel installed 1933; 31 hp Lister diesel 1953
		1929	Acquired by Arthur Schofield and renamed *Comrade* in memory of the other *Comrade* he had earlier tried to acquire	
		1953	Half shares Arthur Schofield and Fred Schofield	
		1958	Fred Schofield sole owner	
		(1974)	To Humber Keel and Sloop Preservation Society	
		1976	Re-rigged	
Rupert C	1928 Worfolk, Stainforth	1928	William Henry Schofield	Wood, carvel, Sheffield size
		(1931)	Sold to George Wilson, Goole	

The Schofields of Stainforth

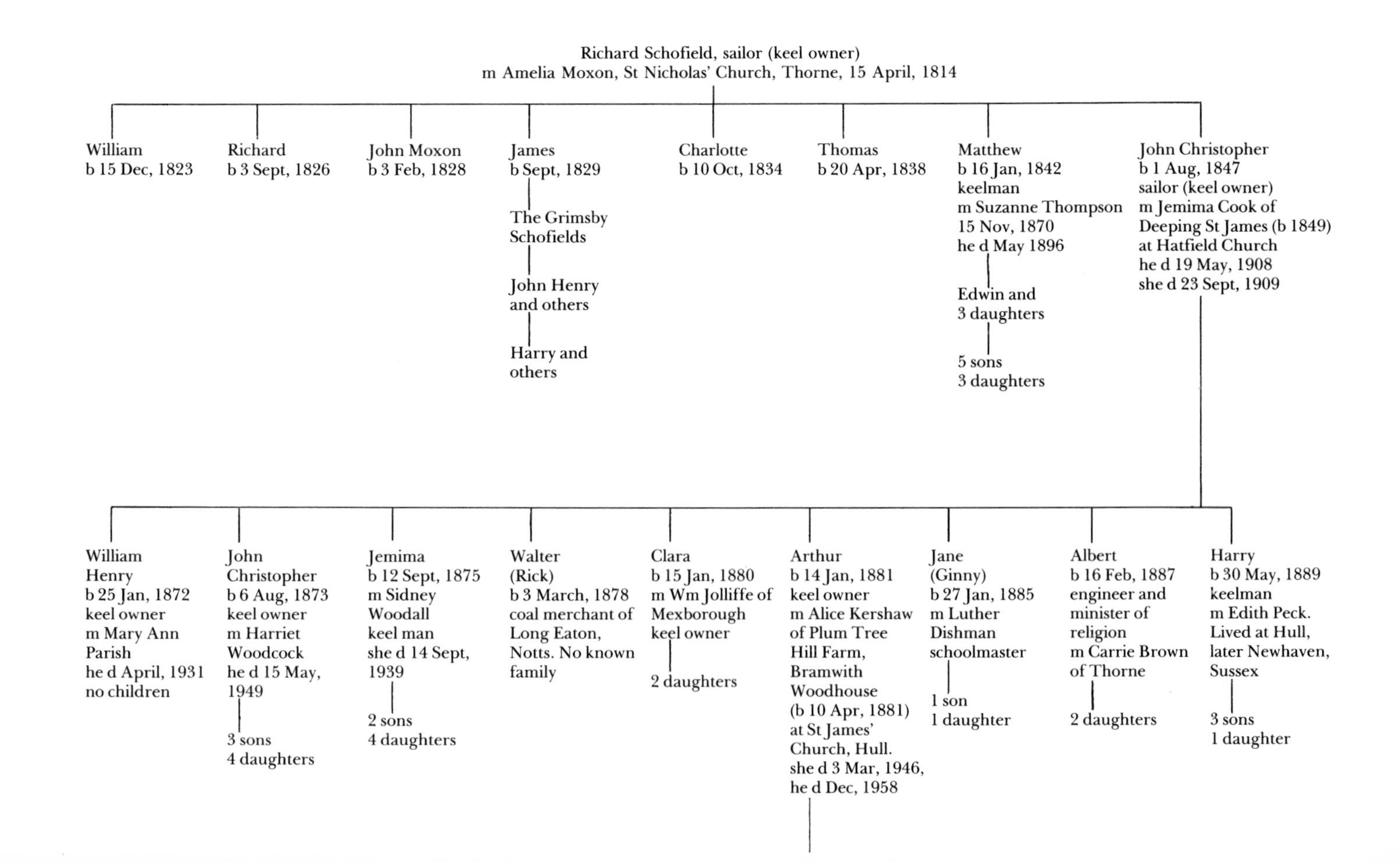

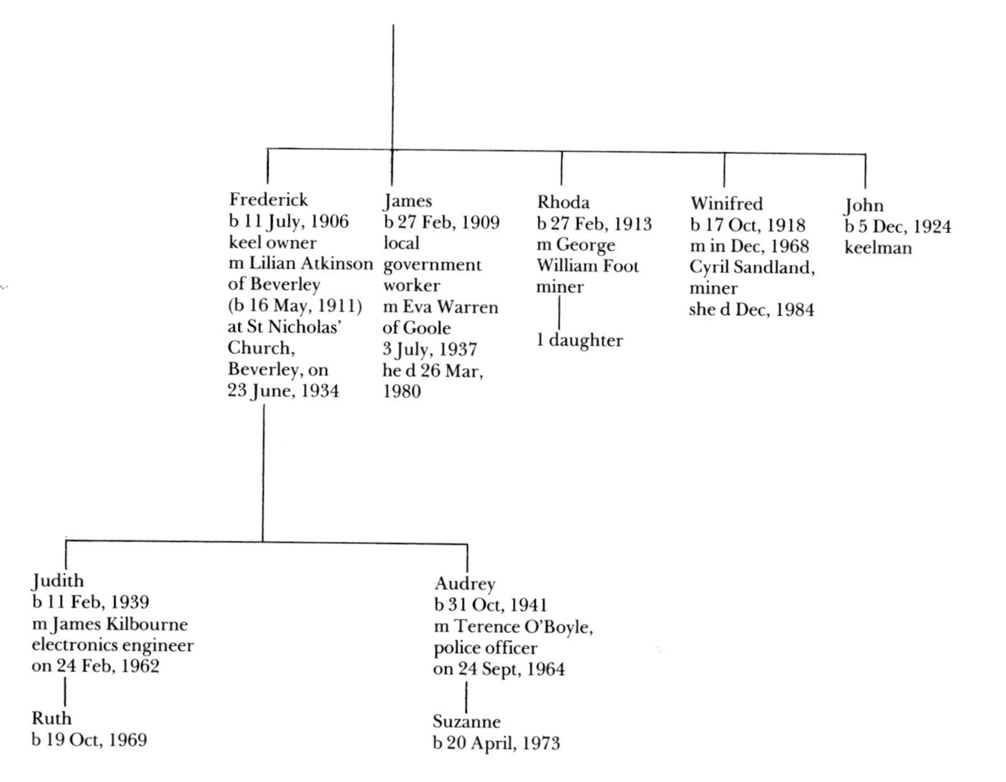
Frederick
b 11 July, 1906
keel owner
m Lilian Atkinson
of Beverley
(b 16 May, 1911)
at St Nicholas'
Church,
Beverley, on
23 June, 1934
James
b 27 Feb, 1909
local
government
worker
m Eva Warren
of Goole
3 July, 1937
he d 26 Mar,
1980
Rhoda
b 27 Feb, 1913
m George
William Foot
miner
1 daughter
Winifred
b 17 Oct, 1918
m in Dec, 1968
Cyril Sandland,
miner
she d Dec, 1984
John
b 5 Dec, 1924
keelman
Judith
b 11 Feb, 1939
m James Kilbourne
electronics engineer
on 24 Feb, 1962
Ruth
b 19 Oct, 1969
Audrey
b 31 Oct, 1941
m Terence O'Boyle,
police officer
on 24 Sept, 1964
Suzanne
b 20 April, 1973

APPENDIX EIGHT

Steel keel specification

THE steel keel *Paul H. T.* was built by Warren's New Holland Shipyard Ltd at New Holland, Lincolnshire, in 1926 for J. J. Tomlinson, of Thorne. Launched on 13th June of that year, she was delivered to her owner on the 28th of the same month.

General arrangement and shell expansion drawings and the original typewritten specification of this vessel, yard no 219, are now in the Hull Town Docks Museum. The following is a transcript of the specification exactly as written.

SPECIFICATION OF ONE STEEL KEEL
built to the order of
J J TOMLINSON ESQ., 26, SOUTH PARADE
THORNE.
by MESSRS. WARREN'S NEW HOLLAND SHIPYARD LTD

DIMENSIONS	Length overall including Gudgeons	74′ 6″
	Breadth extreme	15′ 4″
	Breadth moulded	15′ 1″
	Breadth moulded on Bilge	14′ 9″
	Depth Amidships, top of Keel to deck at sides	8′ 0″
	Sheer aft & Forward	1′ 9″
	Rise of Floor	2″

KEEL — Tee bar 5 × 3 × ⅜ rivetted to Keel plate

STEM — 7 × 1⅛ Bulb bar with Angles 5 × 3 × 5⁄16 rivetted each side.

STERN POST — 3 × 1½ with flanged ⅜ plates each side, three Rudder Irons and Keel pieces.

FRAMES — Steel Angles 3 × 2½ × 5⁄16 from Keel to Gunwale, spaced 21″ apart, about 12″ apart Forward & 15″ apart Aft.

FLOORS — Of Steel Angles 5 × 3 × ¼ straight across from bilge to bilge with 5 No. water course. Floors at ends ¼ plate & 2 × 2 × ¼ Angles on top edge.

CENTRE KEELSON — Intercostal formed of 5⁄16 plate with double Angles 3 × 2½ × 5⁄16 on top edge & connected to Keel plate with double Angles 2 × 2 × 5⁄16.

DECK BEAMS — Of Angle 2½ × 2½ × 5⁄16 connected to Frames with ¼ gusset plates on alternative frames. Beams amidships to have 8″ cambre.

MAIN BEAMS	2 No. of Steel Tee bars 6″ × 4″ × ½″ secured to Frame by gusset plate 15 × 15 × ¼. Aft Main Beam to be portable.
DECKS	at ends to be of ¼ steel plate. Forecastle Deck 8′ long, Cabin Deck 9′ 6″ long.
PLATING	Keel plates, Bilge and Bow plate ⅜″ thick. Remainder of plating 5⁄16 thick. Plate ends on Bilge & Sheer strake to be butted & double rivetted. Remainder of plates to be lapped & double rivetted. Longitudinal seams to be ⅝″ single rivetted. Liners to be fitted instead of joggled.
GUNWALE BAR	2½ × 2½ × ⅜″ from Stem to Stern post, four scuppers fitted each side of vessel.
GANGWAY DECK	Gangway deck 24″ wide coamings 16″ high at each end & 22″ high amidships, gangway decks & coamings flanged plates ¼″ thick. Gangway deck beams on alternative frames 2 × 2 × ¼ & connected to frames by gussets 9 × 9 × ¼. Coamings to lean inboard 2″ at the top & to have 2 × 1 bead rivetted on the outer edge. Rivets spaced 5″ apart C. to Centre. Hatch cleats spaced 19″ apart with pins on every cleat. Iron batten & wood wedges supplied.
BULKHEAD	of 3⁄16 plate, one at each end of Hold, stiffened with Angles 2 × 2¼ × ¼ forward. Bulkhead to be watertight. Recess in aft Bulkhead for stove & Ladder, door in Aft Bulkhead (in halves) on starboard side.
HEADLEDGES	Steel plates 5⁄16 thick to have rise in centre of Fast hatch at each end 5 × 3 bulb Angles. Galvanised tank fitted on Aft Headledge to hold 60 galls.
HATCHES	of 9 × 1 battened together to make hatch 18″ wide. Fore & After 5 × 4½ Red Wood in suitable lengths as arranged. Loose Hatch beams fitted at each end of hatchway.
BEADING	Gunwale edge 2½ × ¾ from stem to stern post. Binns 12″ below of 4 × ¾ between head & stern whiskers. Bilge & half way between, from Binns 4 × ¾ to be carried aft to position arranged.
WHISKERS	3 each side on bow & 1 aft to stop about 12″ from stern post. Whiskers to be 6 × 2½ special rail section.
WINDLASS	Keel's Patent windlass fitted with Monkey, Levers etc. Bitt Heads 12 × 4 oak fitted between ⅜ steel plates connected to deck & Hawse plates by 2½ × 2½ × ⅜ Angles. Centre of Windlass barrel to be 3′ 0″ from Hawse plates.

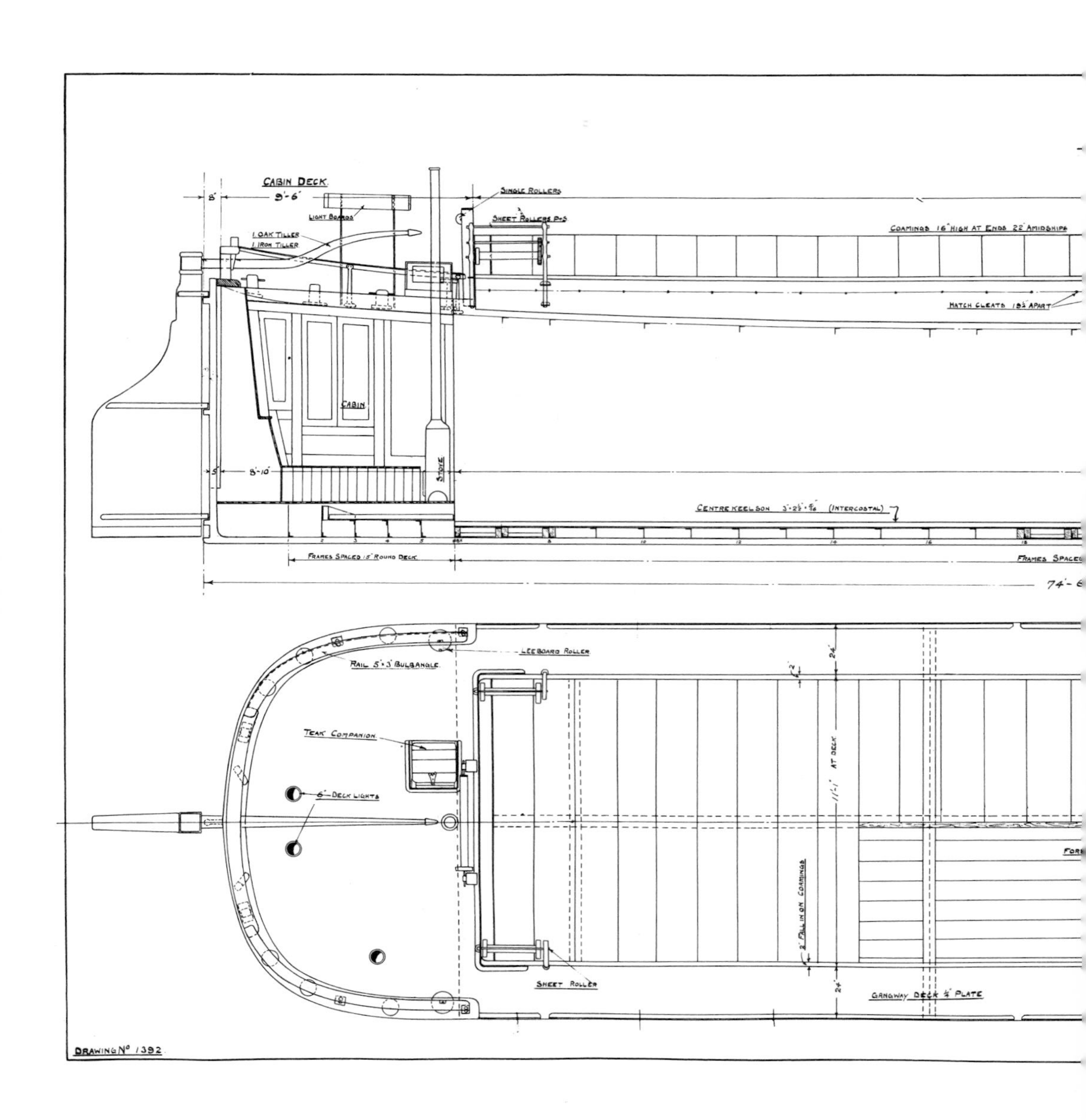
CABIN DECK
9'-6"
8"
LIGHT BOARDS
1. OAK TILLER
1. IRON TILLER
SINGLE ROLLERS
SHEET ROLLERS P+S
COAMINGS 16" HIGH AT ENDS 22" AMIDSHIPS
HATCH CLEATS 18½" APART
CABIN
STOVE
5"
8'-10"
CENTRE KEELSON 3"·2½"·5/16 (INTERCOSTAL)
FRAMES SPACED 15" ROUND DECK
74'-6
LEEBOARD ROLLER
RAIL 5"·3" BULBANGLE
TEAK COMPANION
6" DECK LIGHTS
11'-1" AT DECK
2" FALL IN ON COAMINGS
SHEET ROLLER
GANGWAY DECK ¼" PLATE
DRAWING Nº 1392

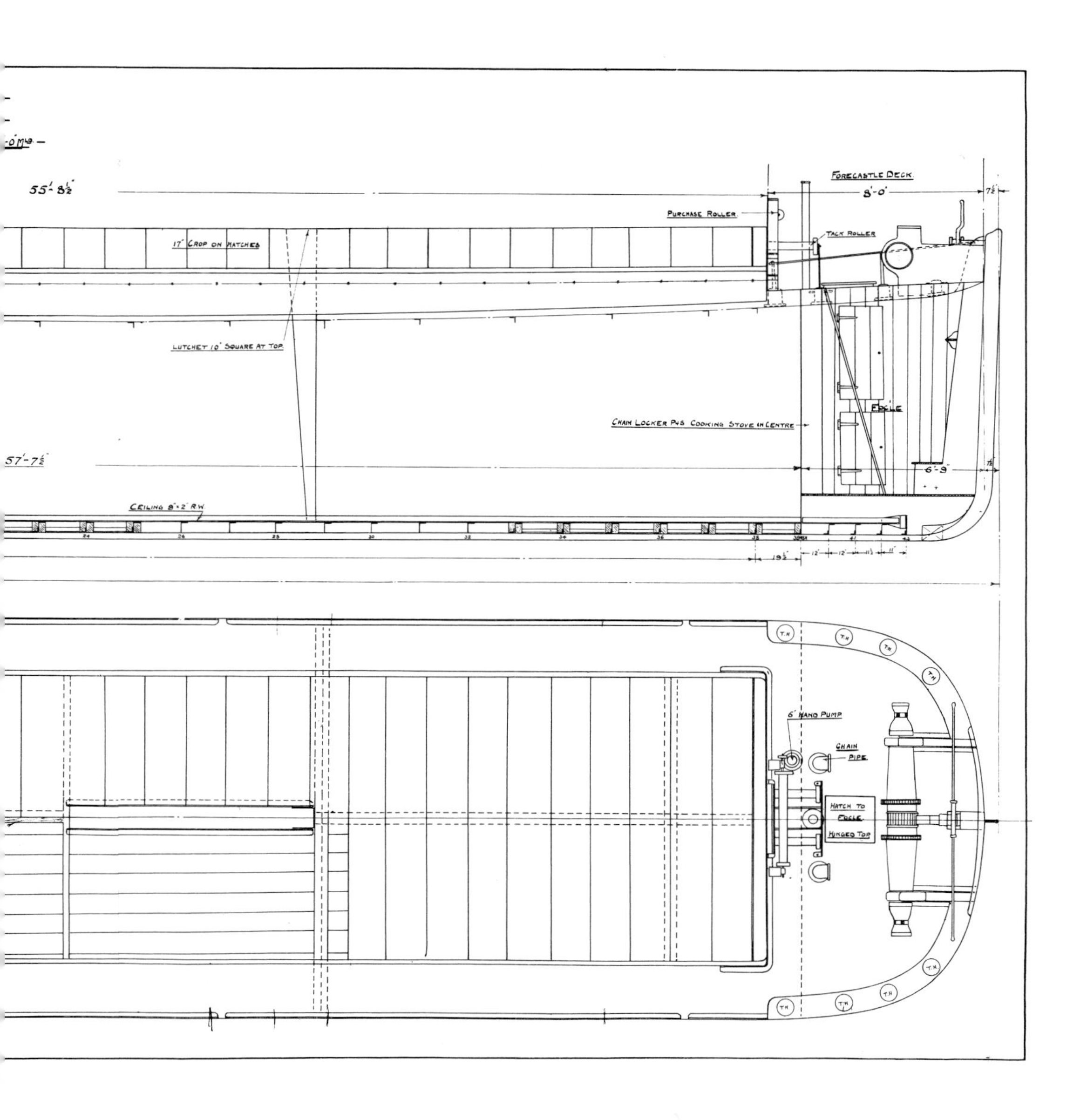
55'-8½"
Forecastle Deck.
8'-0"
7½"
Purchase Roller.
Tack Roller
17" Crop on Hatches
Lutchet 10" Square at Top.
Fo'c'le
Chain Locker P&S Cooking Stove in Centre
57'-7½"
6'-9"
Ceiling 8" × 2" R.W.
19½"
6" Hand Pump
Chain Pipe
Hatch to Fo'c'le Hinged Top
T.H

HORSE	of oak 6 × 6 oak dandy Timbers, rails of Bulb Angle 5″ × 3″ supported on iron stanchions 14½ & 15″ high, iron stanchion to taper from bottom to top. Fore stanchions on Aft rail to have square sole pieces & 4 No. bolts.
HAWSE PLATES	5/16 plates fitted with 2 No 4″ Hawse pipes & 2 No 4″ chain pipes fitted on deck.
TIMBER HEADS	Cast iron 14 No (well canted in) 6 aft & 8 For'd, pin close to top, secured by 4 No 5/8″ bolts. 2 spring timbers (2″ round) fitted each side & bolted to gunwale bar.
COVERING BOARDS	of oak round bow & stern 10″ wide × 3½″ to 2½″ thick.
PUMPS	1 at each end of Hold 6″ dia. & all gear supplied, end of aft pump Tail pipe carried into the 3rd. frame space from bulkhead.
RUDDER	Main Back & second piece of oak, remainder pitch pine, 3 Rudder Irons & bolt.
TILLERS	one of oak & one Iron in two lengths (socket to be 6″ deep)
FORECASTLE	of ¾″ P.T.G. boards fitted up in the usual style with iron ladder, cooking stove & chain lockers. Forecastle Hatch of oak 1′ 10″ × 1′ 10″ with hinged top. 2 batten irons on each side.
ROLLERS	One purchase roller on Fore Headledge, Tack Rollers on Foredeck, sheet rollers on coamings aft. single roller on Aft. Headledge, Lee board rollers fitted to rail.
LUTCHET	of 5/16 plate & angles 2½ × 2½ × 5/16, fitted about 25′ 0″ from the stem, 10 × 10 at the top, & 7 × 7 at Mast step, secured to centre Keelson angles by bolts.
CABIN	cabin Frame work of three ply wood & styles of pitch pine, mahogany Buffets fitted with stained glass doors. Cabin doors of steel in halves fitted inside drying cupboard on starboard side. Ordinary Keel cabin stove with chimney. Teak Companion & 4 No. 4½ deck lights.
CEILING	of Red Wood 2″ thick secured to frames & straight across side to be cemented. Limber boards each side of Centre Keelson.
LIGHTBOARDS	fixed on movable stanchions through rails.
SEACOCK	One fitted in cabin & one in Forecastle.
SUNDRIES	All necessary cleats, handlings, chain plates, etc, supplied.

Glossary

A

Air boards	Removable boards in the ceilings of the hold to ventilate the frame spaces.
Awnings	See "hoynings".

B

Bankfoot	Foot of the river bank.
Beamed up	Swelled up, referring to the planks of the hull, swollen and tight.
Bedside	In the after cabin the main bed is to starboard, the spare bed to port; see also "spareside".
Beef kettle	Large oval flat-bottomed stewpot, made of cast-iron but coated inside with tin, with a collapsible handle.
Bight	Loop or bend in the course of a river, and the middle length of a rope.
Bill of lading	An acknowledgement of goods specified on the bill and a promise to deliver them in the same condition as received.
Billyboy	Yorkshire coasting sailing barge; see appendix three.
Binds or bins	Two thicker strakes of planking below gunwale level to act as rubbing strakes.
Bittheads	Side supports of the anchor windlass with pins through to secure the bowline.
Blopping board	Placed between the coamings and the ship's side to slide stones overboard to make training walls, used more by sloops than by keels.
Boat	In Yorkshire a boat specifically means an open-holded vessel, with coamings and headledges, but no hatch covers.
Boat about, to	To move a keel by manpower.
Bowline	Three and a half fathoms of two-inch rope on the port and starboard sides of the mainsail, twelve feet up each leech from the clew, used for close-hauled sailing. It is passed over the forestay or through a block on the forestay and made fast to the lee side bitthead.
Bow yanking	Bow hauling by manpower; see also "man'sline," "seal".
Bridge running	Passing under a bridge with lowered mast.
Briggage, to give or save briggage	To be able to clear under a bridge; see "crop".
Brighouse fender	An intricately made rope stem fender used on West Country boats.

Beef kettle

Buffet The cupboards across the rear of a keel's cabin; see chapter one.

Burton pendants Tackles on port and starboard, acting as additional "running" backstays and for other duties.

Bushel A dry measure for grain and fruit; one bushel equals eight gallons; see appendix five, Weights and Measures.

Bye trader An independent carrier on a navigation, not linked to a manufacturer or a navigation authority.

C

Cable's length One cable equals a hundred fathoms or two hundred yards (183 metres), one fathom being six feet.

Canal tiller Iron cranked tiller, with detachable extension, which passes over the stern rail, needed in the locks where the rudder has to be put hard over. An ordinary tiller would foul the stern rail stanchions and the lock walls.

Cliff clams

Canch Shoal in mid channel or off a quay berth.

Carlins or carlines Thwartship supports for the deck and the beams supporting the hatchboards of a "carlin hatch"; see below.

Carlin hatch Curved hatch running athwartships from coaming to coaming, the boards running fore and aft, secured to two carlins, making up one hatch. "Lighter" hatches, see below, are flat.

Carpenter's yard A boatbuilding or repair yard.

Catch A Trent vessel, also working up to Lincoln, related to the keel, but with a square bilge, and sometimes setting in addition to the square mainsail and topsail a standing lug mizzen, hence the term catch or ketch; see chapter one.

Ceilings Planking lining the sides of the hold, inside the frame timbers.

Ceol Saxon word for boat, from which "keel" is derived.

Clews Bottom corners of a keel's mainsail or topsail; and the after bottom corner of a fore and aft sail.

Cliff clams Jaws for loading chalk-stone, Cliff being the chalk quarry at South Ferriby.

Clough Pronounced "clow"; a lock paddle or sluice.

Cobble stick Horse's swingletree to which the hauling line was secured.

Cog or coggie boat A keel's or sloop's boat; see chapter one.

Cover up To replace the hatches on completion of loading; see also "open out".

Crag Mast above the topsail tye sheave.

Crop Camber of a keel's headledge to allow clearance under bridges, to give briggage; see "briggage".

Cross pieces Linking timbers, frequently decorated, between the hawse timbers and the long timbers; see chapter one.

Cross ropes Short towropes crossed at the stem of the tow securing her tight up to the tug.

Cut end End of a canal, either the inland terminus or the junction with a river.

Cutwater Extra area of wood at the leading edge of a leeboard.

D

Declaration note A waybill, presented to the navigation toll collector as a declaration of the cargo on which toll should be charged. Originally paid over in cash, latter-day tolls were charged to account.

Demurrage Payment made to a vessel when the cargo is held on board longer than agreed by the charter. In keel and lighter operation demurrage was deliberate, the vessels being used for storage; in other words it was a storage charge.

Dennings Cabin floor planking; see also "shutts".

Derrick pole A thirty feet long rough pole rigged for working cargo.

Dish metal Iron run from the furnace into a square mould, pig-iron being run into an oblong mould.

Dog leg anchor A hook-shaped anchor for bank mooring like the rond anchor of the Norfolk Broads.

Domino See "graving piece".

Downgate Downstream, downriver, see also "upgate".

Draw, to To create a flow of water by raising a lock clough or paddle.

Drive, to To go with the tide, trailing the anchor on the bottom to give steerage way.

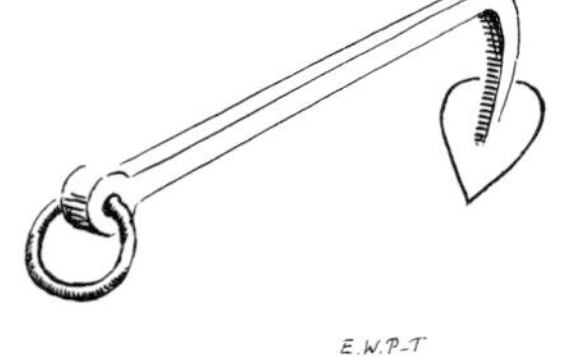

Dog leg anchor

Stem fenders were made of three- or four-part Turksheads. Keels working on non-tidal waters often had three stem fenders, one low down to protect the forefoot from lock cills. One of the two anchors is seen here; each weighed 250 lb.

E

Eakin — A 2½ inch by 12 inch plank immediately under the deck, on the inboard side of the timbers; see also "wiring".

Entrance — The underwater lines at the bow.

Foghorn

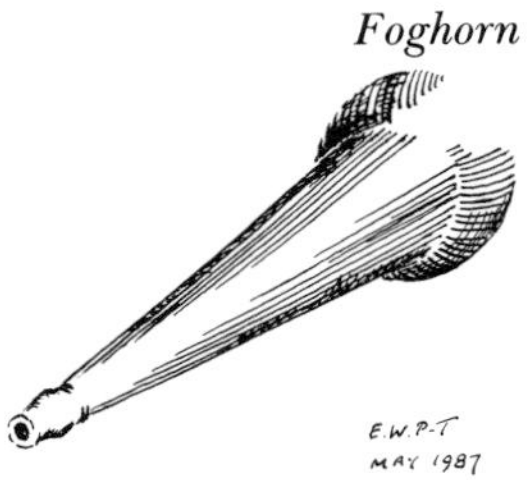

On the forward headledge stood the fore roller, used for raising and lowering the mast, for derrick work and for warping. Beneath were the tack rollers, about two feet off the deck and each just under two feet long.

F

Featherings — The decorated boards flanking the hawse timbers atop the gunwale.

Fettling — Effecting repairs and particularly painting, scraping and varnishing.

Fleeting — Passing out chain cable from the chain locker.

Flitters — Chain dog to stop the anchor chain running outboard while fleeting the cable across the windlass barrel.

Following pieces — Continuations of the gunwale at bow and stern following the edge of the deck.

Fore and afters — Longitudinal supports under the hatches particularly between the lutchet and the half hatch beam (qv) to support the mastway board and half hatches. Also called "partners".

Fore roller — A winch mounted on the forward headledge for raising and lowering the mast and for warping work.

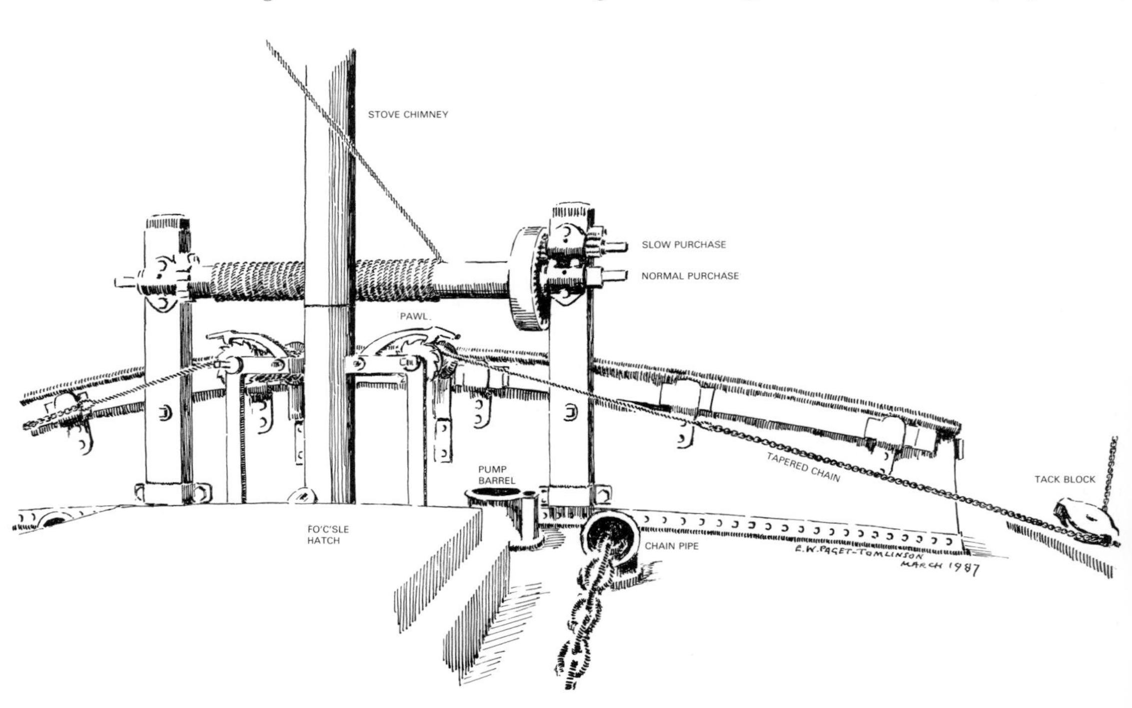

Fother or fodder To pass canvas under the hull to check a leak.
Fresh Land water, storm water, coming down a river.
Futtocks The pieces of timber forming the frame of a ship, secured to each other by overlapping.

G

Graphite and flour A mixture applied to a keel's planking below the waterline.
Graving piece A piece of wood let in to replace rotten or damaged timber or a dead knot; also called a "domino".

H

Hailing port Home port.
Half hatch A hatch spanning the coamings in way of the fore and afters (qv) and mastway board (qv).
Half hatch beam A portable hold beam supporting the fore and afters (qv) and the half hatches.
Halyard roller A small winch mounted on the after headledge of a keel, to handle the mainsail and topsail halyards, the slabline and the braces. In a sloop there are two halyard rollers, port and starboard, foresail and peak halyard to port, throat halyard and topping lift to starboard, mounted on the coamings or on deck on the "sparrings" (qv).
Hand scuttling Filling grain sacks with a scoop or scuttle (qv).
Handling A lock windlass or any crank handle.
Handy billy A ten-foot shaft or boathook.
Hauling Horse hauling with a river line (long) or a "useful" line (short).
Hauling bank Towpath.
Haul out two reefs, to To take in a couple of reefs.
Hawse ports Ports in the hawse timbers for the anchor cable.
Hawse timbers Substantial timbers at the stem pierced by the hawse ports; they are hawse plates in an iron or steel vessel.
Headledge The thwartships coamings of the hold at bow and stern.
Horse marine or marine The horse driver on the navigations, generally also the horse's owner.
Hoynings or awnings In deepsea parlance the hounds; the shoulders on the mast supporting the stays and shrouds.
Huddle The corners of the hold under deck, beyond the headledges.

I

Ice plates Plates lashed to the bows for sailing among ice; in three parts, one for the stem and one for each bow.

Idle back	Made from a flat bar of iron, it fits on the bitt head. When two anchors are out, only one cable can be hove in at a time; the other is secured to the idle back free of the windlass.
K	
Keel	Large family of Yorkshire and Lincolnshire canal, river and estuary craft, decked with hatches, as opposed to open holded "boats".
Kelsey	Keelson.
L	
Last	Ten quarters (qv) of grain; see appendix five, Weights and Measures.
Launch ahead with stowers	To shaft the ship along with the "stowers" (qv).
Lay day	A day allowed under agreement for discharging cargo; generally four clear working days were allowed, after which demurrage (qv) would be paid by the shipper.
Lay on	Put one's name down with a shipper for work.
Laying on note	Note from the repair yard to the shipper that the ship is delayed for repairs but will proceed on completion, designed to avoid losing one's turn for cargo.

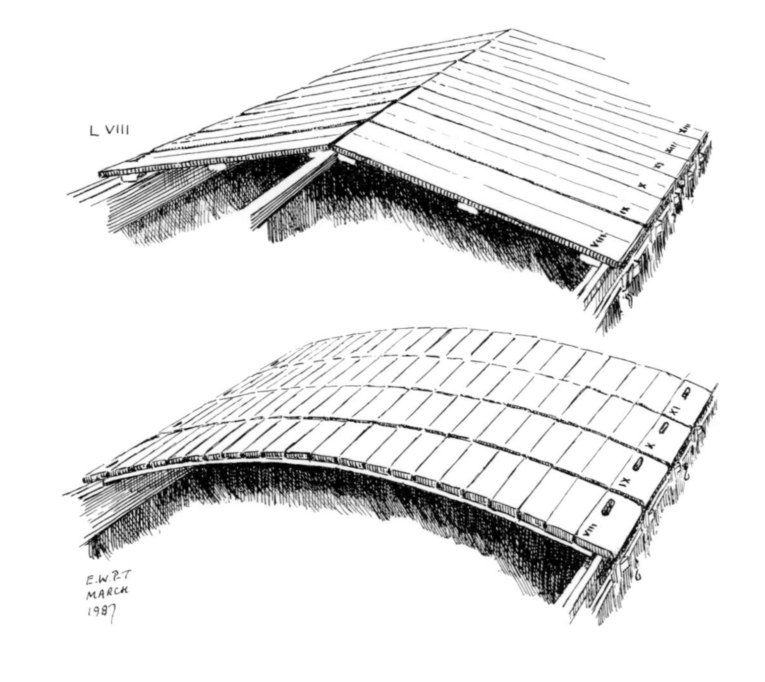

Some keels and sloops had the same flat hatches as lighters, meeting on fore-and-afters like a shallow pitched roof. Each hatch was numbered, I to XXIX with L (larboard) prefix for those on the port side. Carlin or arched hatches reaching from coaming to coaming were numbered on the starboard side, except for the port-side half hatches which had an L prefix.

The leeboard tail chain was handled by a leeboard roller fitted on the stern rail within easy reach of the man at the helm. Some had a slow purchase, the roller barrel being tapered to achieve a lower gear effect as the board became heavier on rising from the water.

Leeboard clamp — The block on the leeboard stanchion through which the leeboard tail chain is passed.

Legs of the sail — Colloquial for clews, the lower corners of the square mainsail.

Lighter — Vessel limited to dock and harbour work. A sailing keel could act as a lighter, handling cargo for local destinations, say from a ship in Alexandra Dock, Hull, to a mill on the River Hull.

Lighter hatch — A flat hatch which lies across half the hold opening, meeting its fellow to form a shallow pitched roof across the coamings; see also "carlin hatches".

Limber boards — Removable boards in the shutts (qv) above the waterways or limber holes in the floor timbers, so that the latter can be cleared.

Livering or livered — Delivering or delivered, discharging or discharged.

Lock head — Head or top gate end of a lock.

Lock penny — Coin thrown to a lock or bridge keeper.

Lock turned round — Either emptied or filled for traffic in the opposite direction.

Long stemmed — Wooden keel or sloop whose stem came to the top of the hawse timbers. Iron and steel ships were universally long stemmed. See also "short stemmed".

Long timbers Taller timberheads alongside the hawse timbers.
Lowance Tea break.
Luffed Brought closer to the wind.
Lurry Horse-drawn wagon; see also "rully".
Lutchet Mast step of a keel or sloop akin to a mast case or tabernacle.

M

Mainsheet horse Rail across the stern bearing the ship's name and home port (hailing port) on the outside and the name of the owner or owner-master on the inside.

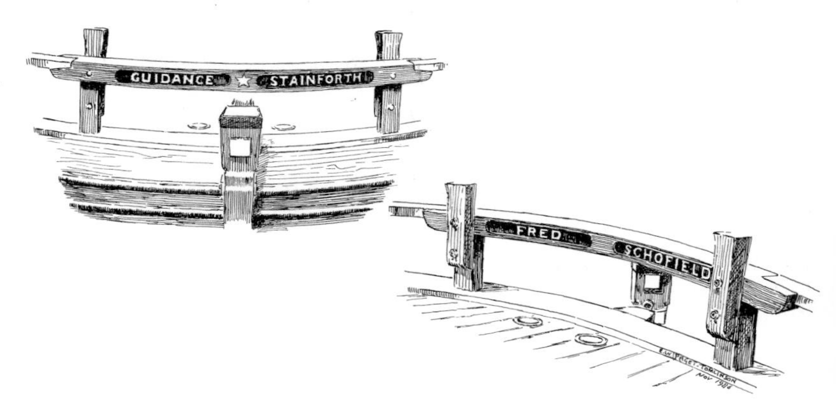

The keel's mainsheet horse, with the name of the ship and the home or hailing port carved on the outside, the name of the owner on the inside. The two bull's eyes give light to the stern cabin.

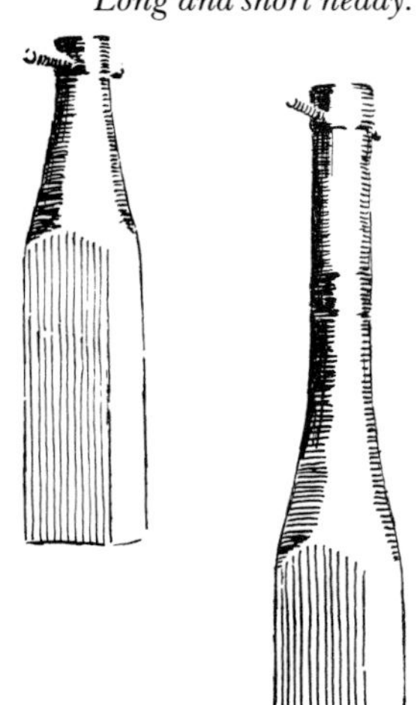

Long and short neddy.

Mangling Warping up to a mooring with the fore roller.
Man'sline Thirty-fathom cotton line about ⅝ or ¾ inch circumference used with the "seal" (qv) for bow hauling or "bow yanking".
Manrope Line from the tack timber to the stern rail set up with deadeyes and lanyard for safety along the side deck.
Marine See "horse marine".
Mastway board Hatchboard aft of the lutchet (qv) in way of the mast when lowered.
Moosey Calm and hazy weather.

N

Nab Point of land.
Neddy Stumpy mast with a pin, stepped in the lutchet of West Country boats and non-tidal keels for canal towage, either short or long, the latter for high loads. Sailing keels did not have them; they would use a pit prop or the anchor stock.
Ness Headland or promontory. On a river it is opposite to a bight (qv), so the ness side is the shallow side of the river. Example Whitton Ness.

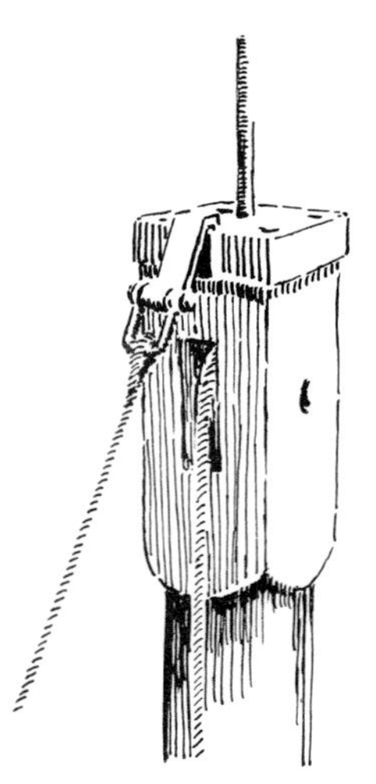
Polka mast.

O

Old Warp Keelmen's name for Read's Island in the Humber.

Open out To remove the hatch covers for discharging cargo; see also "cover up".

Outwent Tidal eddy.

Overside Unloading from ship to keel, sloop or lighter direct; from the point of view of the keel it would be loading overside.

P

Pen and penning To lock in and out; the lock pen, also called lock pit, is the lock chamber.

Pole mast The high mast of a keel, used for regattas, and afterwards often cut down to the shoulders above the topsail tye sheave.

Polka mast A shorter mast than a pole mast, either made by cutting down a pole mast or made new, with a squared top.

Pound Stretch of canal between two locks.

Pulling out Using a horse to work a crane or derrick to handle cargo.

Purchase Remuneration, payment.

Purchase-man Extra hand employed casually.

Purchasing Acting as an extra hand.

Q

Quarter Eight bushels to one quarter; see appendix five, Weights and Measures.

R

Rack Reach of a river, thus Gas House rack.

Registration Keels had to register with a local authority under the Canal Boats Acts of 1877 and 1884. Hull was the usual port of registry and the official number was generally on a board under the mainsheet horse, or on the companion. A keel was also registered as a ship by the Board of Trade, the port of registry being inscribed on the outboard side of the mainsheet horse.

Ricker Rough pole with the bark off.

Ridge chains Chains secured between the long and tack timbers to act as handrails.

Rope board A platform between the hawse timbers and anchor windlass for stowing rope.

Rully Horse-drawn wagon, see also "lurry".

Run The underwater lines of a vessel aft towards the rudder.

Runner	1 Rope from the winch or hoist to work cargo, with hooks, snotter (qv) or strop (qv). 2 Office messenger to ships and berths before the telephone was available to ships in dock.

S

Scandalize	To spill wind from the sails so that the vessel no longer draws ahead. In a keel the topsail is lowered, the mainsail trussed up by the slabline and the yards hauled fore and aft. In a sloop or billyboy the mainsheet is slacked off, the tack or fore lower corner of the mainsail pulled up, the headsails lowered, the peak of the mainsail lowered and the boom centred fore and aft.
Screed	The capping piece on the coamings.
Scuttle	Hand scoop for filling grain sacks. Scuttling was the method of discharging bulk grain described in chapter two, hand filling a sack for weighing and then loading into the keel in bulk or by four-bushel sacks.
Seal	Canvas harness for bow hauling worn round the shoulders; see "bow yanking" and "man'sline".
Seam spike	Square section iron spike fastening for the planking.
Sheet rollers	Winches to port and starboard to handle the sheets of the keel's mainsail, the port roller working the starboard sheet and vice versa.
Ship's husband	Marine superintendent responsible for the stores and provisions and the wellbeing of the vessel.
Short stemmed	A keel or sloop whose stem came no higher than gunwale level, below the hawse timbers; see also "long stemmed".
Shutts	Planking in the bottom of the hold; see also "dennings".
Skating	When the leeboard veers away from the ship's side.
Skirt	Bottom part of any bulk cargo.
Slabline	Light line which pulls up the foot of the keel's mainsail to spill wind or clear obstructions; see also "scandalize".
Sloop	Fore-and-aft-rigged sister to the keel.
Snotter	Two-foot length of light chain for lifting sacks with two-inch diameter rings at each end, one attached to the derrick runner, the bight of chain passing through the second ring to form a loop, put over the sack mouth and drawn tight.
Sounding rod	Eighteen feet long pole, measured in feet by alternate sections of black and white and used to gauge depth.
Spareside	On the port side of the after cabin with the spare bed; see also "bedside".
Sparings or sparrings	Deck space between the hatchways in sloops and billyboys, occupied by the lutchet and halyard rollers (qv) and the derrick winch.

Spring timbers	Sometimes called "lazy timbers" because little used; the timber heads a few feet aft of the foredeck to which mooring springs were attached. "Lazy timber" could also be applied to the last but one timberhead aft.
Staithe	A wharf, mostly spelt with a terminal "e" except in York, where it is staith. The term is applied in Humber, Trent and Ouse ports, on the Yorkshire navigations and in Norfolk.
Start up the main yard	Commence heaving up the main yard and mainsail.
Stayfall	Tackle on the forestay for lowering and raising the mast, using a pair of double-sheave eight-inch blocks.
Stayfall block chock	Shaped piece of timber generally decorated with a carved, painted or gilded star, sited under the lower stayfall block to stop it falling on the anchor windlass when the mast is lowered.
Staying	Tacking head to wind.
Stem chock	Shaped piece of timber, decorated with a carved and gilded motif, set between the hawse timbers of a short-stemmed keel.
Stop rope	Ten-fathom warp for checking the way.

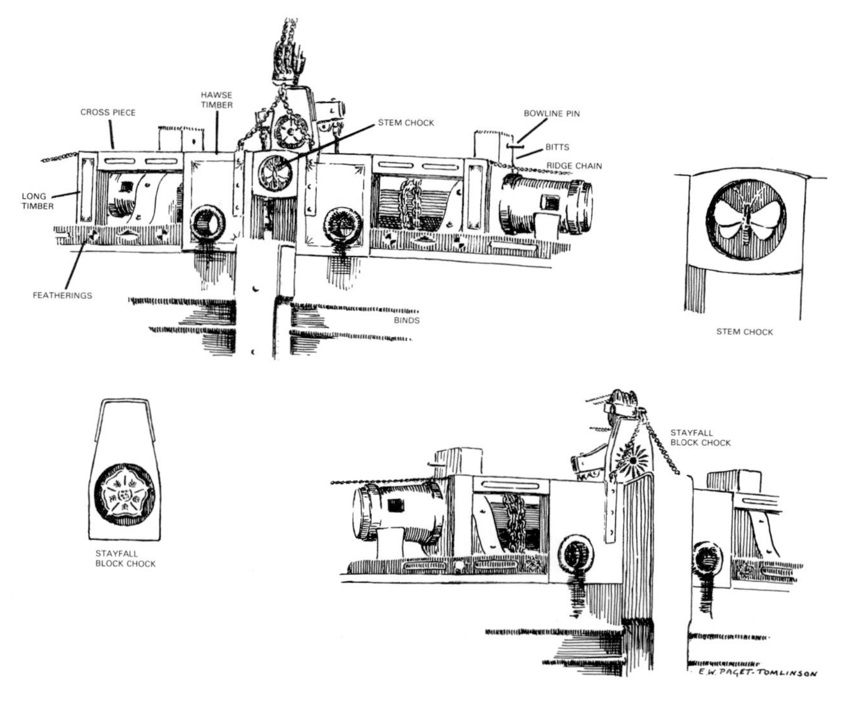

Wooden keels and sloops were either long stemmed or short stemmed, the long stem extending to the top of the hawse timbers, the short to the gunwale. Two decorative but useful pieces of equipment were found at the stemhead: short-stemmed keels and sloops used a wooden stem chock to fill and stiffen the gap between the hawse timbers, while all keels and some sloops had the wooden stayfall block chock to keep the lower stayfall block from falling on the windlass when the mast was lowered. Star or radial patterns were the most popular for both, but there is evidence of a butterfly, and naturally the white rose of York often appears.

Thief bars.

Stopway	Canal term for the abutments grooved to take stop planks or recessed for a stop gate, put down or closed for repairs or in case of flooding.
Stower	Twenty-two- and twenty-four-feet long shafts with two grains or tines. Keels carried one of each size.
Stower dogs	Clog- or shoe-shaped pieces of wood forming rests for the stowers and boat hooks on the hatches.
Stringing	Decorative lining out.
Strop	Short length of rope spliced into a circle for use as a sling or to form the eye of a block.
Sucked in	Stuck in the mud by suction on a rising tide; chains have to be worked round the hull to break the suction.
Swape or sweep	A twenty-four-foot oar to aid steering in light airs.
Swim	Movement of the vessel through the water; a good swimmer is a ship which goes well.

T

Tack rollers	Winches on the keel's foredeck; the two rollers which controlled the tacks to the port and starboard clews of the mainsail, employed when staying (tacking) or working to windward.
Tack timber	Aftermost of the timbers on the foredeck.
Taffrail or taffel timbers	Two timberheads at the extreme stern, flanking the mainsheet horse.
Thief bars	Iron bars securing the companion hatches to the fo'c'sle and after cabin; each companion had two bars, recessed into the wooden framing, forming a cross with a central hole for a bolt and padlock.

Side and stern fenders were made of coir and were hung between pairs of timber heads.

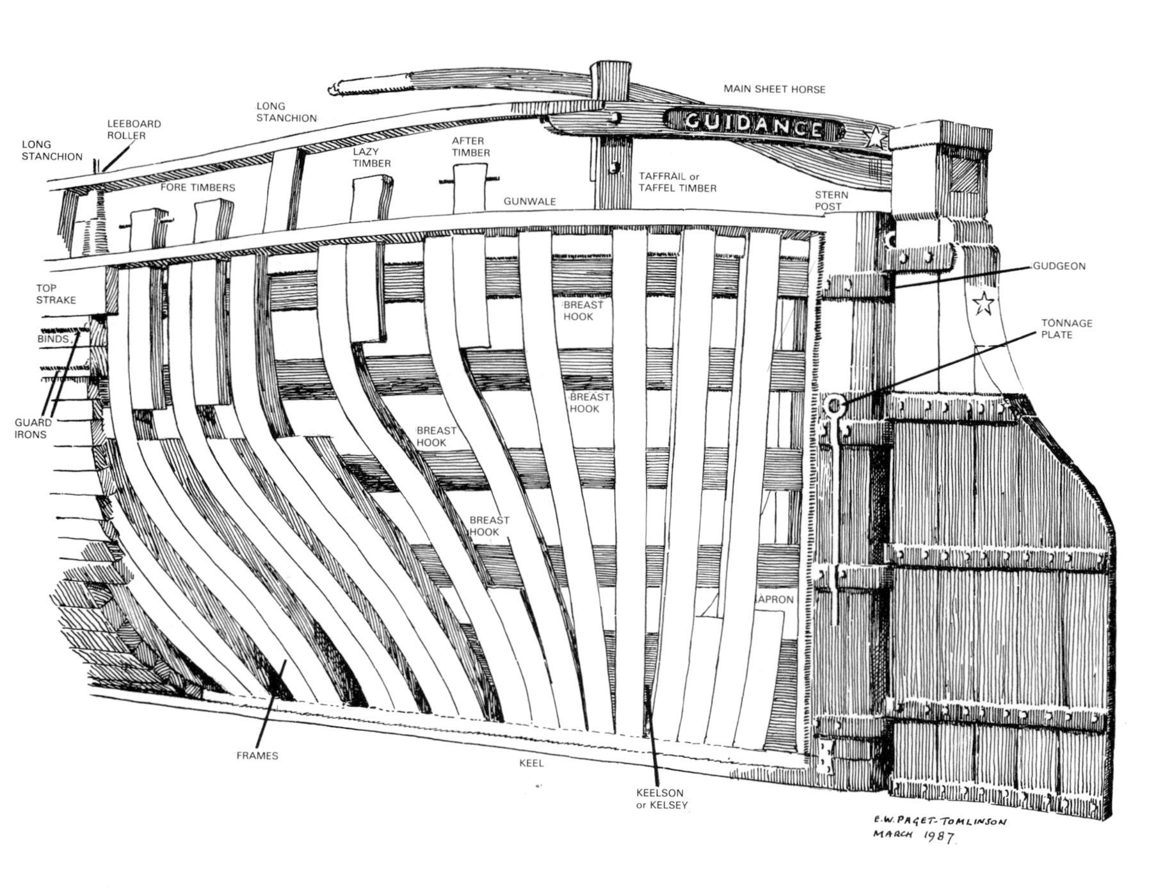

Stern frames in a wooden keel were angled from the centreline to make the shape above the waterline and were bevelled to form the "run", the narrowing of the hull aft to make the ship go well to windward.

Thirds See chapter eight. Briefly the way earnings were shared between owner and captain. From the gross freight the captain would pay brokerage, dock and canal dues, towage charges. The remainder, the net freight, would be divided by three, a third to the owner, two-thirds to the captain. From his third the owner would pay ship maintenance and insurance, from his two-thirds the captain would pay the mate, casual labour and horse haulage.

Tides "mending" Increasing; and "taking off", lessening.

Tidy Ash guard for the stove.

Timber dogs Hooks for securing and lifting baulks of timber.

Timber heads Posts to which mooring lines could be made fast, five a side forward, four a side aft, plus the spring timbers (qv) forward.

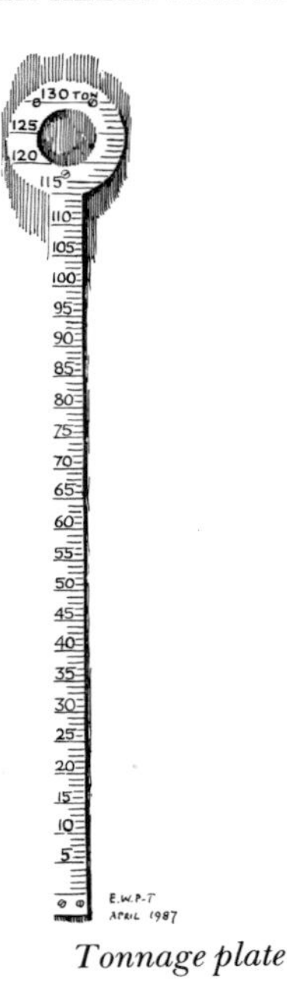

Tonnage plate

Tonnage plates Plates of copper fixed to stem and stern post on one side, the draught marks being cut on the other side in Roman figures. To calculate the tonnage the readings on the fore and aft plates were added together and divided by two.

Top the yard out When hoisting sail the yards were sent about half way up inside the shrouds then "topped out" by heaving down on the topsail sheet (topsail yard) or brace (mainyard) to clear the shrouds. "Topping in" was the reverse process when lowering sail.

Transom locker A locker across the after end of a keel's cabin.

Traveller An iron ring moving on a horse or spar. In a sloop there was a traveller across the deck for the foresail sheet. Both sloop and keel had leeboard travellers, port and starboard, low down on the coamings; they were eighteen inch long bars to which the leeboards were secured by chains, allowing some variation in the setting.

Tye Rope between the halyard and the yard.

U

Upgate Upstream, upriver; see also "downgate".

W

Warp Mud and silt deposited by a river.

Wearing ship Putting the ship about on the other tack by not going into the wind, so keeping the sails full.

West Country boat A vessel small enough for the 57 feet 6 inches by 14 feet locks of the Calder and Hebble Navigation. Although called a boat she would generally have hatches like a keel.

Windhole Wide place for turning a keel.

Wiring Three-inch by nine-inch plank below the "eakin" (qv) on the inward side of the timbers.

Bibliography

Duckham, B. F. *The Yorkshire Ouse*. David & Charles, 1967.

Fletcher, H. *A Life on the Humber: Keeling to Shipbuilding*. Faber & Faber, 1975.

Frank, J. Humber Keels in *The Mariner's Mirror*, XLI, 1955, pp 308–328; XLIV, 1985, pp 218–239.

Hainsworth, J. *Inland Sailers*. Humber Keel and Sloop Preservation Society and the Museum and Art Gallery Service for Yorkshire and Humberside.

Mankowska, J. *Goole – A Port in Green Fields*. William Sessions, York, 1973.

Smith, P. L. *Ethel & Angela Jane – A Brief History of the Commercial Carrying Scene on the Calder & Hebble Navigation*. Published by the author, Wakefield, 1976.

Taylor, J. S. *Two Humber Keels and Their Captains One Hundred Years Ago*. T. A. Tate, Thorne, 1955, 1965.

Ulyatt, M. *Flying Sail*. Bradley Publications, Hull, 1974.

White, E. W. *British Fishing-Boats and Coastal Craft, Part I. Historical Survey*. HMSO, 1950, 1957.

Willan, T. S. *The Early History of the Don Navigation*. Manchester University Press, 1965.

Keel and Sloop Dimensions

KEEL design was governed by the sizes of locks on the various navigations they were expected to work.

In the mid-nineteenth century a length of 57 feet 6 inches, a beam of 14 feet 8 inches and about 6 feet 6 inches depth amidships was a profitable size for a keel, but towards the end of the century many keel owners began to favour the Sheffield size, 61 feet 6 inches long by 15 feet 6 inches wide and a depth amidships of 7 feet to 7 feet 6 inches.

The various sizes of keel and sloop were as follows:

West Country size	57 feet 6 inches × 14 feet 2 inches
Sheffield size	61 feet 6 inches × 15 feet 6 inches
Manvers, Wath, Dearne and Dove Size	57 feet 6 inches × 14 feet 8 inches
Barnsley size	70 feet × 14 feet 4 inches
Driffield size	61 feet × 14 feet 6 inches
Weighton size	66 feet × 14 feet 6 inches
Lincoln size	74 feet × 14 feet 4 inches
Trent size	74 feet × 14 feet 4 inches
Horncastle size	54 feet × 14 feet 4 inches
Louth size	72 feet × 15 feet

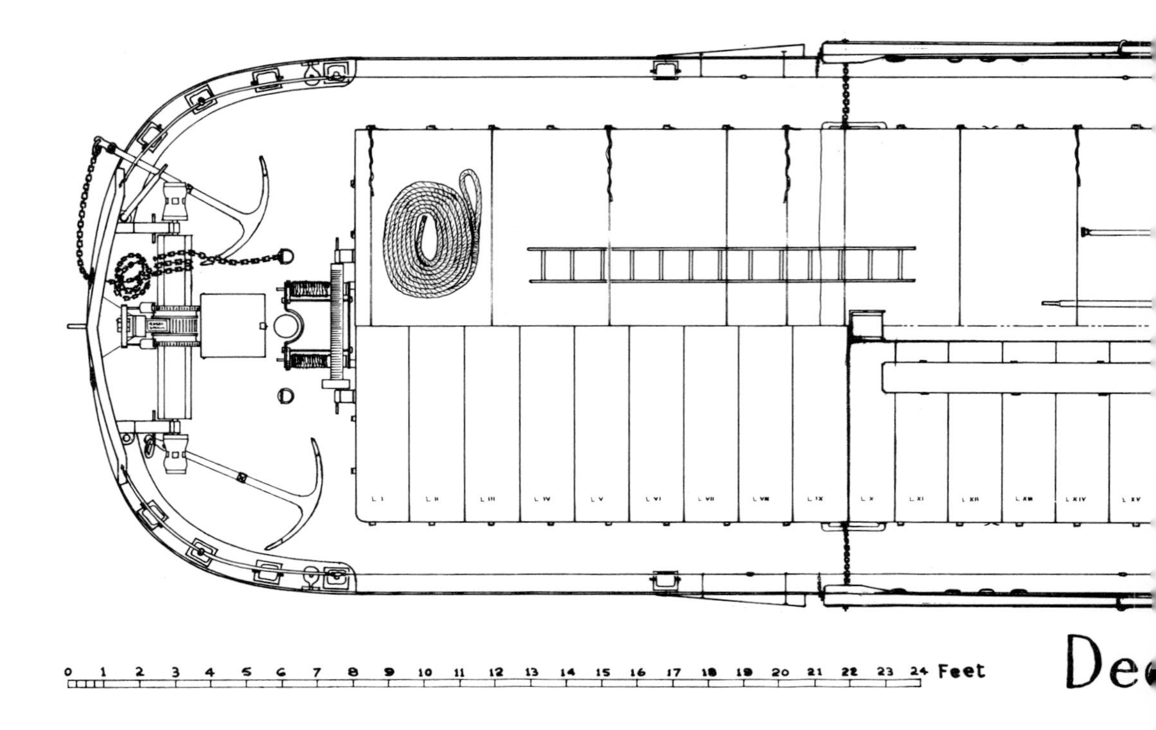
0 1 2 3 4 5 6 7 8 9 10 11 12 13 14 15 16 17 18 19 20 21 22 23 24 Feet

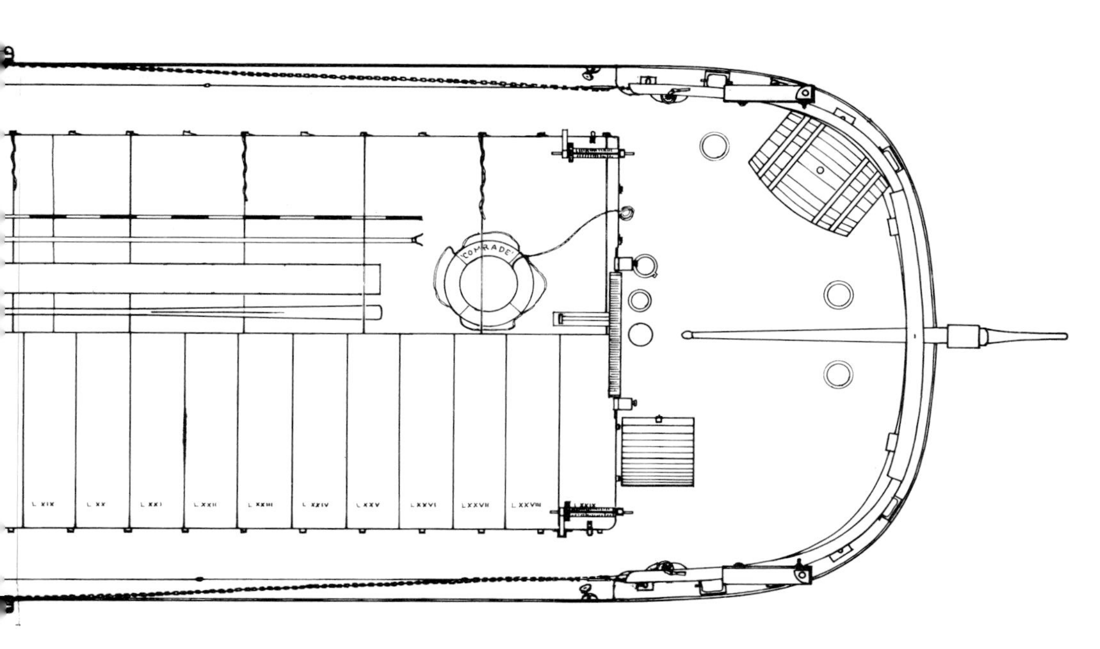

an

Notes - Deck Plan :-

All standing and running rigging, sails and spars have been omitted. Therefore haly'ds, mainstay fall, sheets and tacks are shown wound up on their respective rollers.

The leeboards are hauled up.

Starboard side hatches are shown covered with tarpaulins and lashed down.

Port side hatch boards are shown exposed, with the mastway open and the mastway board alongside.

The fairlead for the sheets is shown displaced slightly to starboard; its correct position is on the ridge of the hatches.

No concession has been made to mechanical propulsion, therefore the keel has been provided with a sweep, a timber rudder and a second anchor.

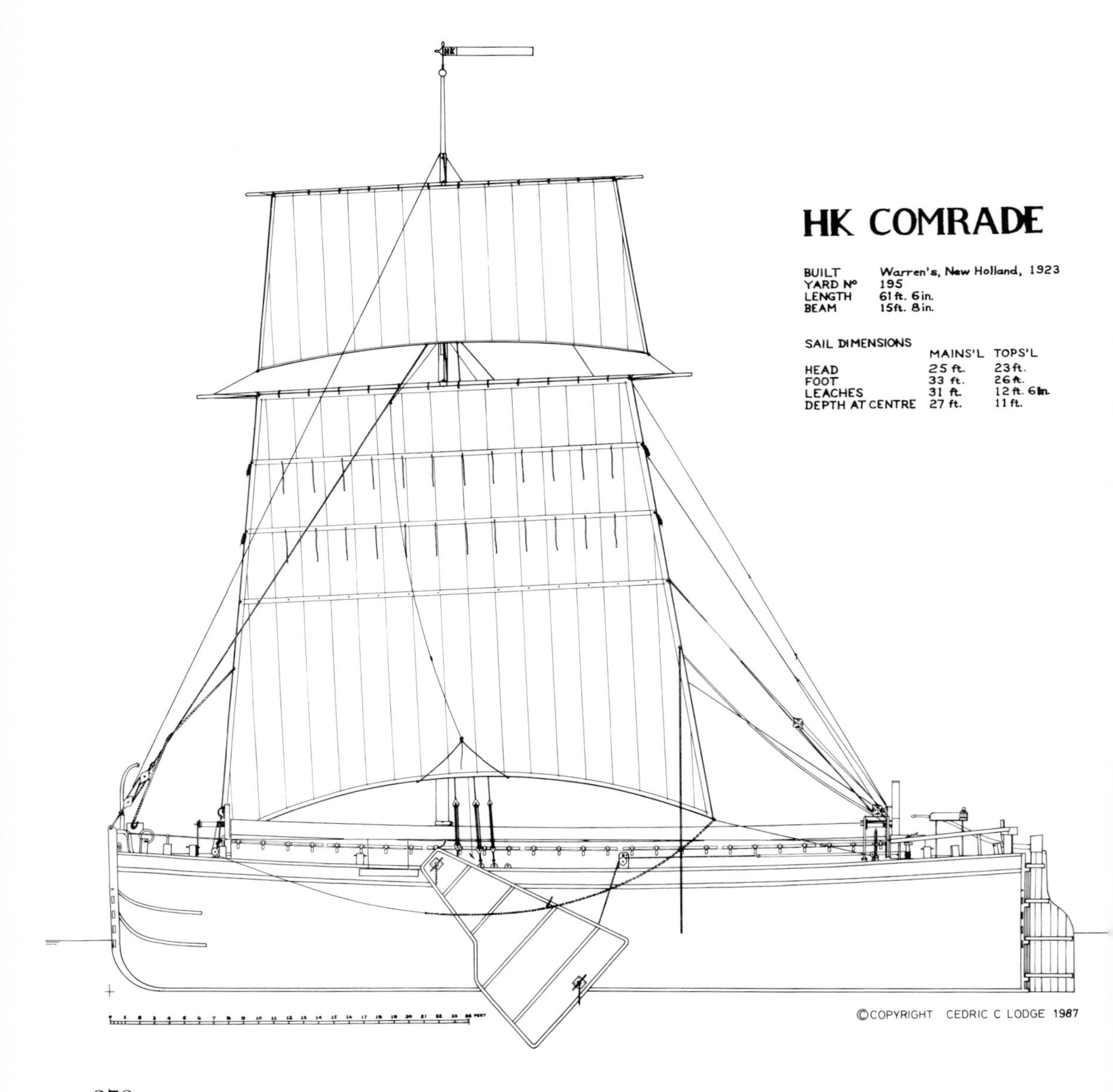
HK
HK COMRADE
BUILT Warren's, New Holland, 1923
YARD Nº 195
LENGTH 61 ft. 6 in.
BEAM 15ft. 8 in.
SAIL DIMENSIONS
MAINS'L TOPS'L
HEAD 25 ft. 23 ft.
FOOT 33 ft. 26 ft.
LEACHES 31 ft. 12 ft. 6 in.
DEPTH AT CENTRE 27 ft. 11 ft.
©COPYRIGHT CEDRIC C LODGE 1987

General Index

Illustrations in bold type

A

Accounts, 170–171
Ackerby, Benjamin, & Sons, 129
Admiral of the Humber, 211
Agents' work, 180, 189
Airboards, 255
Aire, River, 9, 59
Aire and Calder Navigation, 36, 123, 128, 141, **141**, 143, 179, 222, 245, 247
Airship R.38, 133
Aldwarke Colliery and staithe, 87, 112, 149
Allerton Bywater Colliery, 194, 196, 204, 206
Allerton Main Colliery, 128
Allinson's flour mills, Castleford, 128, 236
Alum, 223, 240
Ancholme, 240
Anchors, 23, 27, 261, **261**
Ancotts, 58, 117
Anglo-American Oil Co., 240
Aqueduct, 89
Ashfields staithe, 191
Awnings, *see* Hoynings

B

Barkers & Lee Smith, oil mills, Beverley, 115, 120, 199, 209
Bark, 123
Barley, malting, 127, 142–143, 176, 199, 205, 223
Barmby Dun, 112, 152
Barnsley, 1, 2, 3
  British Co-operative Society, 86, 148, 151, 236
  Canal, 1, 3, 125, 127–128
  size, 49, 125, 239
Barraclough, James, 129, 239
Barraclough, W. H., 129
Barrons glassworks, Mexborough, 85, 156
Barrow-on-Humber, 161
Barton-on-Humber, **142**, 143, 146, 161, **181**, 210, 221, 237, 239, 240, 244, 248
Barugh, 1
Bashforth & Co., 20
Basic slag, 76, 223
Basket, coal, **28**
Bayley, Admiral Sir Patrick, 212
Bar iron, *see* Iron and steel
Beams and beam knees, 257
Beatson Clark glassworks, 87, 138
Bedside, 21, 259
Beef kettle, 21, 259, **259**
Beer, 248
Bell, G. N., & Son, 194, 196, 199
Beverley, 1, 49, 98, 101, 102, 113, 115–129, 131, 136, 204–205, 207, 211, 215, 221, 237, 244, 248
  Albion House, 193
  Beck, 113–115, **114**, **127**, **128**, **194**, **209**, **213**
  Beckside, 115, 127, **127**, 194
  Conington Avenue, 193
  Corporation, 115
  Crane Hill, 113, **114**, 116, 194
  Engineers, 212
  Flemingate, 115, 125
  Grovehill, 115–117, **128**, 166
  Grovehill Road, 128, 193
  Holme Church Lane, 125
  Swinemoor Lane, 193
Bijlander, 241
Bill of lading, 187
Billyboys, 11, 49, 50, 95, 195, 241–243, **242**, **244**, 259
Binds, 7, 243, 259
Binks, 128
Bisby, Edwin, 248
Blacktoft Jetty, 76
Bleasdale, W. & Co, 50, 61, 69–70, 150–151, **150**
Boston, 127, 237
Bowlines, 11, 14, 16, 17, 239, 259
Bowsprit, 239
Braces, 11, 14–15
Bramwith, 11, 59, 78, 82, 108, 112, 191
Bramwith Woodhouse, 47, 51
Breasthooks, 6
Bricks and tiles, 123, 237, 243
Brickyards, 222
Bridges, 7, 25, **58**, 67, 77, 79, 82–83, **84**, 87, 89, 90, 107, 110, **112**, **138**, 152, **202**
Bridlington, 123–124, 217, 222, 237
Brigg, 68, 248
  sugar refinery, 234
Briggage, 7, 137, 259
British Cocoa Mills, 226
British Oak staithe, Wakefield, 225
British Oil & Cake Mills, Hull, 204
British Oil & Cake Mills, Selby, 200, 207
British Transport Docks Board, 215
British Waterways, 50, 125, 200, 222
Brokerage, 146, 148
Buffet, 21, 260
Builders of keels and sloops, *see* Shipbuilders
Bunkering trawlers, 28–29, **30**, 31, 33, 52, 161, 167, 172, 186, **188**, 203
Burringham, 58, 103
Burr's pitch works, Thorne, 82
Burton pendants, 18, 143, 260
Burton Stather, 28, 126, 245
Burton-on-Trent, 4
Bus services, 56, 61, 68, 159
Butterwick, 102, 111
Bye trader, 172, 260

C
Cabin, **19**, 19–21, 239
Cadeby Colliery, 84
Calder and Hebble Navigation, 3, **92**, 118, 200
Calder Navigation Society, 217
Canal committee, North East Regional, 196
Canal tiller, 14, **14**, 260
Canned goods, 150, 207, 224
Capper Pass, Melton, 226
Cargo handling, 57, 138, 144, 154, 194–195
Carlin hatches, 7, 260, **264**
Carlins, 5, 260
Carmichael, Turner, 181
Carr, Frank, G. G., 216, 219
Carvel, 1, 2, 3, 6
Castleford, 120, **126**, 127, 143, 197, 216, 241
Catches, Trent, 3, 96, 104, 260
Cattle foods, 204, 224, 226
Caulking, 98
Ceilings, 6, 7
Cement, 161, 169–170, 195, 224, 237, 243
Cement works, Chalder Ness, 180
Ceol, 1, 260
Chalder Ness, 180, 219
Chalkstone, 126, 237, 240
Chambers & Fargus oil mills, 140
Chartering, 149, **149**
Chesterfield, 205
  Canal, 52, 56
China clay, 75, 224
Christmas, 165–166, 179
Chrome, 206, 224
Clapson's, Barton, **142**, 210, 237
Clay sloops, 240
Clee Ness, 98
Cleethorpes, 57, 93
Cliff (Ferriby), 219, 240
Cliff clams, 260, **260**
Cliff End, 28, **46**, 108, 168
Clinker, 1, 2, 3, 66, 242
Clot Hall, 120
Coal, 2, 28, 31, 50–51, 59, 76, 106–107, 113–117, 121, 127, 137–138, 163, 180, 186, 194, 199, 202, 204, 224–226, 243, 248
  grades, 136, 143, 224–226
  staithes, 224–226
Coaming plank, 6
Coamings, 7, 13
Cocoa
  beans, 207, 226
  butter, 207, 226
  cake, 226
  powder, 226
Cogboat, 11, 13, 38, **38–39**, 131, 260
Collieries, 224–226
Companion, 19, **20**, 22, 24, 239, 243
Compartment boats, 78, 84, 137, **198**, 222
Compound feeds, 226
Conisbrough, 40, 84, **84**, 85, 107, 156
Containers, 203
Cook, Welton & Gemmell, **116**, 117, 120
Cooking and baking, 92
Co-operative Wholesale Society flour mills, Wilmington, Hull, 192, 198
Copperas (Sulphate of Iron), 227
Copper billets, 206, 226
Copper plates and ingots, 226
Copra, 207, 227
Cortonwood Colliery, 51
Cotton seed, 75, 95, 108, 120, 133, 227
Crane barge, 104
Cranes, cargo, 31, 87, 113, 157
Crew training, 217
Crop, 7, 256
Cross ropes, 141
Crowle, 59, 78, **79**, 103
Crow Park Station, 101
Cycling, 56–57

D
Dairy nuts, 226
Dalton Main Colliery (Silverwood Colliery), 87, 164, 204
Darley's Brewery, Thorne, 248
Deadeyes, **8**, 9, 239
Dean, Bill, **109**, 157
Dearne and Dove Canal, 2, 127, 156
  size, 61, 66, 68–69, 118, 156
Decoration and decorative painting, 20, 21, 24, **40–41**, **106**, 159–160, **160**, 183, 243, **269**
Demurrage, 95, 133, 140, 159, 187, 188, 200, 204, 209, 257,
Denaby & Cadeby Colliery Co, 85
Denaby staithe, 2, 66, 78, 86, 118, 136–137, **136**, 194, 248
Dennings, 7, 20–21, 23, 261
Depression 1930, 191
Derrick, 12, 29, 31, **31**, 142, 261
Dickies, 243
Diesel engines, 50, 68, 99, 118, 125, 156, 192–193, 196–197, 202, 213
Dish metal, *see* Iron and steel
Dockers, 200–201, 207
Docks and Inland Waterways Executive, *see* British Waterways
Dog leg anchor, 158, 261, **261**
Don, *see* Dun Navigation
Doncaster, 11, 20, 25, 36, 40–44, 52, 55, 59, 77–78, 83, **83**, 101, 103, 105, 108, 112, 137, 159, 161, 191, 204, 206–207, 241, 247–248
Dredging spoon, 53, 55
Driffield, **58**, 120, **125**, 127
  Navigation, **58**, 120, **124**, 240
  size, 120
Drinsey Nook, 179
Driving, 14, 57, 133, 164, 261
Dundee, 248
Dunford & Elliott, 89
Dun Navigation, 55, 59, 73, 82, 83, 87
Dunston, Richard, **29**, 79, 122, 161, 178, 182, **182**, 237
Dunswell, 165
Dutch River, 59, 61, 68, 136, 137

E
Earle, G. & T., 95, 97, 161, 169, 180, 195, 240
Eastoft, 59
East Point (Trent), 138, 169
Eastwood, George, 41, 77, 111, 112
Eastwood (Rotherham), 40, 43, 87, 112, 206, 207, 248
Ellerman, Wilson, 196, 217
Ellison & Mitchell's pitch works, 86, 155
Elsecar Colliery, 51

F
Fair, June, Thorne, 131
Farmers Company, 240, 248
Farm produce, 237
Feast, Village, Stainforth, 131
Fenders, 259, **261**, 270
Ferriby Sluice, 123, 211, 215–216, 221, 240

Ferro-silicon, 207, 232
Ferry, horse, 43, 87, 164
Ferrybridge, 222
Fertilizer, 227, 237, 240, 243
Fettling, 79, 159, 262
Figham, 131, 164, 165
Film company, 217
Fishlake, 49, 55, 71, 159
  Nab, 60, 70
Fishmeal, 207
Fleetwood, 93
Fletcher, Thomas, & Sons, 122, 127
Flixborough, 118, 120, 248
  Shipping Company, 248
Flood, Louth, 98
Floor timbers, 5, 6
Flour
  and offal, 161, 172, 198, 204, 227–228, 230
  National, 198, 227–228
  packets, 7, 247
Fly-boats, steam, 245
Fo'c'sle, 22, **22**, 23
Food, Ministry of, 199
Footing plank, 7, 239
Fossdyke Canal, 96, 127, 179
Foundry sand, 76
Frames, 5, **5**, 6, 271
Frank, John, 240
Free overside discharge, 200, 263
Freight charges, 148, 171, 172–175, 176
Fruit, 228
  pulp, 228
Furley & Co., 24, 57, 90, **91**, **111**, 125, 148–149, **149**, 155, 192

G
Gainsborough, 24, 39, 51–55, 56–57, 59, 95, **111**, 148–149, 153, 201, 207, 245, 248
  Co-operative Society, 156
Galliot, 75, 241
Garbutt's rice mill, Hull, 232
Garthorpe, 117
Gasworks
  Beverley, 112, 113, 194
  Doncaster, 82, 83, 155, 157
  Hull, 149
General Steam Navigation Co., London, 128
Gilstrap, Heap & Co., **144**, 146
Girton, 96, 101, 108, 237
Gledhill's, Gainsborough, 176–177
Goole, 36, 50, 104, 136–138, 143, 156, 172–175, 196, 198, 207, 219, 241, 245
Goole & Hull Steam Towing Co., 122
Gothenburg, 211
Grab Dredger, 248
Grain, 35, 52, 55–56, 67, 75, 105, 140, 243
  elevators, 199
  measures, 36, 55, 151, 179, and footnote
  silos, 199, **201**
  weighing, 34, 35–36, 142, 146, 199, 259, 264
Granite chippings, 75
Grantham Canal, 4
Grass (alfalfa lucerne), 228
Gravel and sand, 53, 55, 75, 102, 104, 110, 111, 128, 229, 232, 237, 240, 248
  dredging, 53, **54**, 55, 96, **97**, 99, 128, 248
  packets, 248
Gray, Thomas, & Son, 36, 96, 109
Grimsby, 47, 52, 53, 99, 104, 176, **176**, 207, 215, 217, 247
Groundnut extract, 199
Groundnuts, 206, 207
Gum arabic, 207, 229
Gunness, 201, 211

H
Hainsworth, John, 209, 221
Hair (from cowhides), 229
Hall's Barton Ropery, 213
Halyards, 11, **15**, 31, 239, **239**
Hanley, Thomas, & Son, 84, 103, 151, 156, 198
Hardboard, 229
Harker, John, 127
Harrison, Edwin, 117, **117**
Hartley, Alan, 210, **210**
Hatches, 7, 8, 256, **264**, 265
Hatfield, 73
  Chase, 59
  Main Colliery, 59, 61, 71, 78, 159, 191–192, 194, 204, 206
Hauling, horse, 40, 42, **42–43**, **43**, 87
Hauling bank, 42, 43, 263
Hazelwood's flour mills, 90, 151
Headledge, 5, 7, 12, 13, 19, 24, 239, 263
Heaving up, 15
Hessle Sand, 48, 69
Hewitt Bros, 247
Hexthorpe Flats, 84, 107
Hides, dry, 229
  wet, 129, 205, 229
Hinchcliffe, Herbert, Junior, 68, 155, 180
Hodgson, Richard and Sons, 115–116, 127, 164, 209
Holgate, David Junior, 125
Holgate, David Senior, 123–124, **123**, **132**, 217, 240
Holgate, John, 165–166
Holgate, Mark, 126, 127
Holmes, George Dyson, 62–63, 66, 67, 68, 157, 193, 239
Holmes, Thomas, 205
Hook, 120
Horncastle
  Canal, 3
  size, 3
Horse fodder, 41
Horse marines, 41, 42, **92**, **110**, **163**, 259
Horses, 40, 41, 42–43
Houlton, George & Charles, 71, 72, 82
Houseboats, 203, 218, 268
Howden Dyke, 67, 201, 207
Hoynings, **9**, 16, 259, 263
Hudson Ward's flour mills, 104, 140, 144, 151, 236
Hull, 24, 31, 36, 50–51, 53, 55, 59, 67–68, 93, 103, 142, **147**, 149, 192, 200, 201, 204–205, 207, 214–215, 222, 237, 241, 245, 248
  Albert Dock, 31, **74**, 128, 133, 172
  Alexandra Dock, 31, **34**, 35–36, 47, 75–76, 108, 133, 141, 153, 179, 189, 196
  & East Riding Co-operative Society, 115, 120, 194
  Bishop Lane, 148, 181
  Chapman Street, 95
  Daily Mail, 1
  Drypool Bridge, 215
  Fish Dock, 28, **30**, 31, 52, 69, **188**, 197
  Halfpenny Bridge, 169
  Hamilton's Wharf, 95
  High Street, 31, 192
  Humber Dock, 133
  King George Dock, 31, 75, 105, **105**, 106, 122, 138, 189, **201**, 209, **231**

Hull *cont.*
Maritime Society, 216
Old Harbour, 36, 52, **53**, 75–76, 95–96, 133, **168**, 169, 189
Pacific Club, 146, 181
Prince's Dock, 133, 172, **173**
Queen Elizabeth Dock, 209
Queen's Dock, **2**, **3**, 101, 133, **228**
Railway Dock, 116
River, 115, **121**, 122, 133, 213, *see also* Hull Old Harbour
Rivercraft and Lighter Owners' Association, 200
Riverside Quay, 219
Roads, 108
Stoneferry, 102, **122**, 126, 133, 207
Town Docks, 116, 122, 129
Town Docks Museum, 133, 242
Trinity House Navigation School, 62
Victoria Dock, 31, 75–76, **77**, 138
West Dock, 33
West Dock Avenue, 31
Williams Wright Dock, 31
Hull, Goole and Sheffield Transport, *see* Bleasdale
Humber
Bridge, 219
Conservancy Board, 38, 70, 160
Keel and Sloop Preservation Society, 15, 129, 133, 209, 221–222
Keel Trust, 209
Tugs, Hull, 23
Hunter Bros, 118, 153
Hunts Chemical Works, Castleford, 126, **127**

I
Ibbotson's flour mills, 90, 151
Iceboats, 94, 179
Ice on canals, 94, 140–141, 179
Ickles New Cut (Sheffield and South Yorkshire), 186
Immingham, 70, 94, 97, 104, 140 196, 204, 207
Inland Water Transport Division, Royal Engineers, 94–95, 99
Inland Waterways Association, 209, 211, 221
International Harvesters, 204
Ipswich, 244
Iron and steel, 31, 52, 150, 229
Iron and steel construction, 7
Iron powder, 207
Island House Ness, 159

J
Jeckells', sailmakers, 212

K
Keadby, 27, 28, 36, 39, 40–41, 52, 57, **63**, 76, **78**, 96, 103, 107, 117, 194, 219
Keelmen's clothes, 44, 221
Keelson (kelsey), 2, 5, 6, 8, 264
Kendall, Jack, 96, 98
Kershaw, George, 47, 51, 55–56
Ketches, 243
Kilner's glassworks, 85, 156
Kilnhurst, 12, 40, 43, 86–87, 91, 106–107, 112
Colliery and staithe, 2, 41, 43, 86–87, 91, 106, 107, 112, 115, 155–156
Forge, 86
King's flour mills, Knottingley, 236
King's Lynn, 244
Kingston Steam Trawling Co., **30**, 186, 188
Kirk Sandall, 137, 138
Knottingley, 136, 216, 221, 241
Canal, 141

L
Lamp, cabin, 21, **21**
Laneham, 53, **54**, 110
Launch with stowers, 76, 107, 137, 264
Laying on note, 106, 164, 260
Lease-Lend, 198
Leeboard and mast cranes, 25, **26** 27, 40, 42, 60, 82, **82**, 85, 107, 164, **166**
Leeboards, 3, 4, 11, 17, 25, 27, 40, 143, **167**, 213, 218, 222, 239, 243, 265
Leeds, 55, **56**, 67, 118, 122, 127, **140**, **141**, 142–143, 204, 206, 216, 221, **225,** 241, 245
Industrial Co-operative Society flour mills, 67, 142
Leetall's flour mills, 110
Leetham, Henry, flour mills, 248
Leicester, 4
Leith, 93
Leven Canal, 120
Levitt Hagg Quarry, 112, **113**, 155, **229**
Lighter hatches, **264**
Lighters, lighterage, 75, 95, 108, 133, 140, 148, 189, 195, 265
Lights, navigation, 239
Lime, 155, 229
Limestone, 112, 229
Lincoln, 3, 95, 96, 97, 104, **158**, 197, 211, 216
& Hull Water Transport Co., 248
Water Festival, 211, 216
Linseed, 75, 108, 120, 140, 153, 207, 229
Liverpool, 93
Lock "clough", 28, 29
Lock keepers, 28, 78, 81, 89
Locks, 1, 28, **29**, 40–41, 76, **78**, 82–83, 84, 86, 87, 89, 101, 104, 112, 115, **163**, 166
Locust beans, 137
Lodge, Cedric, 209, 222
London, 73, 245
Long Sandall, 101
pitch works, 83
Louth, 98
Navigation, 98
Lower Trent Navigation, 38
Luddington, 58, 117
Lutchet, 7, **7**, 8, 42, 239, 266

M
Mainsheet horse, 7, 13–14, 24, 239, 266, **266**
Maize, 141, 204, 205, 229
Malthouse wharf, Wakefield, **145**, 204, 225
Manchester, 3
Manganese, 230
Manpower Services Commission, 214
Man'sline, 67, **109**, 164, 266
Manvers Main Colliery, 51, 62, 115, 156, 157, 167
Manvers size, 61, 66, 68, 69, 118, 156
Mariners' Society, Beverley, 131
Mariners' Society, Stainforth, 133
Market boats, 98, 103, 120–121, 146, **147**, **244**
Market Weighton Canal, 240
Mast, 8, **10**, **239**, 263
Medway Tanker & Oil Storage Co., 61, 177

Meek, Alexander & Sons, 172
Melton, 169
Meredyke, 58, 120
Mexborough, 7, 40–42, 43, 52, 55, 85–86, 107, 156, 237
Middle Burcom buoy, 214
Mimosa extract, 204–205, 230
Mining concentrates, 207, 226
Mirfield, 118, 127, 142
Misterton, 57
Morton Bight, **102**, 177
Motor Boat & Yachting, 209
Museum
  Science, South Kensington, 242
  Town Docks, Hull, 133, 242
Myrobalans nuts, 204–205, 209, 230

N
Narrow boats, 52, 56, 96
National Dock Labour Board, 200
Nationalization, 200
Neap House Wharf (Trent), 120, 121, 201
Neddy, 43, 262, **266**
Newark, 96, 104, 209
  Dyke, 104
Newbridge, 59
New Holland, 118
New Junction Canal, 55, 68, 83, 136–137, 140, 143, 152–153, 248
Newsprint, 104, 230
Nickel, 230
No Man's Friend (Trent), 177
North Clifton, 110, 237
North West Museum of Inland Navigation, 217
Nose tin, 41, **41**, 112
Nottingham, 4, 36, 104, 209
  Canal, 4

O
Oats, 204
Offal, *see* Flour
Oglesby, Darwin, 40, 68–69, 70
Oil, 199
  Cake, 116, 226, 243
  Seeds, 95, 116, 199
Olive oil, 179, 230
Olympia Cake & Oil Mills, Selby, 120, 133, 138
Open boats, 154, 155–157, 259
Ouse, River, 3, 9, 39, 59, 76, 120, 137, 141
Outboard drive, 156
Owston Ferry, 57, 98–99, **98**, 117, 177–178, 240, 245
Oyster Ness, 169

P
Palm kernels, 199, 204, 230
Paper, 179, 180, 206, 230
Paraffin, 240
Parish, Tom, 61
Parkgate (Rotherham), 64, 87
Parkhill Colliery, 122
Parrels, 27
Pattrick, William, **69**, 137
Paull, 214, 237
Pearson's Ashcroft Oil Mills, 95, 108
Pearson's Baltic Oil Mills, 108
Phosphates, 97, 104, 117, 179, 230, 237
Pig iron, *see* Iron and steel
Pigmeal, 204, 226
Pilkington's glassworks, 137
Polka mast, **267**
Pollards (flour), 230
Potash, 231, 237, 240
Potassium, 231
Potatoes, 58, 231
Power stations
  Doncaster, 157, 222
  Leeds, **225**
  Mexborough, 156
Price's flour mills, 90, 151
Public houses
  Canal Tavern, Thorne, 102
  Dog and Duck, Goole, 143
  Fox Inn, Stainforth, 40, 71, 93, 111, 195
  Half Moon, Gainsborough, 110
  New Inn, Stainforth, 71
  Station Hotel, Stainforth, 71, 167
Pudding Pie Sand, 155, 180
Pulp, *see* Wood pulp
Pump, **104**
Pumping out, 105, 186
Purchaseman, 25, 28, 29, 41, **45**, 167–168, 169, 170–171, 263
Pyrites (copper ore), 117, 172, 231

Q
Quebracha, 232
Queensgate whitening works, 116, 129, 135

R
Railways
  Hull and Barnsley, 75
  Hull and Bridlington, 115
  Isle of Axholme Light Railway, 77
  London & North Eastern Railway, 118
Rank Hovis McDougall, 236
Ranks' Clarence Flour Mills, 68, 127, 161, 197–198, 202, 204, 248
Rape meal, 207, 232
Rawcliffe, 59, 137
  paper mills, 231
Rawnsley, Tom, **110**, **163**
Reads Island (Old Warp), 76, 169
Reckitt & Co., Hull, 62, 63
Redcliffe Channel, 169
Regatta, Hull Keel, 51
Rice, 232
Rice meal, 232
Rigging, 183, 185–186
Road transport, 160, 176, 192, 205, 207, 209
Robinson Bros, **30**, 62, 66, 88, 151, 154–155, 180, 186–187, 189, 191
Rochdale, 216–217
  Canal, 3
Rochester, 244
Roller
  fore, 262
  halyard, **15**
  halyard sloop, **239**
  leeboard, **265**
  sheet, 13, **13**
  tack, **262**
Rollers, 9, 11–13, **13**, 15–16, **15**, **83**, 127, 239, **239**, 262–263, **262**, 268, 270
Rother, River, 88, 186
Rotherham, 41, 52, 55, 64, 73, 87, **88**, 110, 112, 149, **154**, 161, 187, **187**, 204, 206–207, 247
Roundwood staithe, 2, 50, **86**, 87, 91, 112, 156, 164, 186, 194, 204
Routh and Waddingham, 242
Rowntree's Chocolates, York, 20
Royal Navy, 93–94, 120
Rudder, 13
Run, 4, 267
Rusling, John Thomas, 72, 151, 168, 180

S

SLD Market Boat Co., 120, 121, 125
Sacks, 57
Sails, 3, 4, 8, **10**, 11, 15, 239
Saltney, 99
Salvage vessel, 248
  work, 177–178, 183
Sand, *see* Gravel
Sanderson's maltsters, 176
Saxilby, **x**, 96, 179
Scaife, George Robert, 128, 129, 162, 182
Scarr, Henry, 49, 129, 237, 241, 247
  Joseph, 61, 117, 125, 128–129, 237
Schofield
  Alice (née Kershaw), 47, 56, 92, 167, Death, 198
  Arthur, 47, **52**, 56, 93, 95, 102, 133, **133**, 153, 172, 181, 199, **199**, 203, 250–251
  Audrey, 193
  Family tree, 252–253
  Fred, passim
  Harry, cousin, 47, 93, 199
  Harry, uncle, 49, 50, 65, 93, 110
  James, 47, 52, 56, 159
  Jane (Ginny), 47, 50
  John, 159, 199, 202, 203
  John Christopher, grandfather, 47, 48, 60, **60**
  John Christopher, uncle, 49, 60, 61
  Judith, 193
  Lilian (née Atkinson), 192
  Rhoda, 159
  William Henry, 47–49, **49**, 60, 72, 161–162, 180, 191, 251
  Winifred, 159
Schooners, 52, 57, 75, 85, 126, 242
Scotland, 245
Screening pellets, 207
Screeton, Colin, **218**, 221–222
Scunthorpe, 223
Seal, 67, 107, **109**, 164, 264
Seamen's & Boatmen's Mission Church, Leeds, 55
Seamen's Mission, Sheffield, 91
Selby, 120, 123, 136, 140, 197, 201, 207, 245
  Canal, 9, 95, 204
  Warehousing & Lighterage Co., 136
Senior, George, steelworks, 90
Shea nuts, 207, 232
Sheaf Steelworks, Sheffield, 155
Sheets, 9, 10, **13**, 18, 239, 268
Sheffield, 2, 31, 41–42, 44, 50, 52, 55, 59, 76, 89, 90–91, **91**, 126, 149, 161, 198, 204, 206, **206**, 245
  & South Yorkshire Navigation, 11, 25, 36, 40, 48, 50, 52, 55, 59, 76, 83, 98, 126, 143, 192, 222, 245
  size, 2, 48, 49, 161, 239
Sheffield, Charles, 146
Shell Transport & Trading Co., 61
Shoreham, **241**, 244
Shovels, **28**, 114, 163
Shutts, 6, 7, 264
Sicey rack, 164
Sissons' paint works, 104
Slabline, 11, 13, 15–16, 18, 27, 31, 42, 268
Sloops, 11, **121**, 154, 222, 237–240, **238**, 240, 244
Slow purchase, 12, 13, 28
Smith, Samuel, flour mills, 90, 151, 204, 206
Snettisham, 99
Soar, River, 4
Sootcake, 141, 233
Sorghum seed, 233
Sounding rod, 7, 24, 239, 268
South Bullock pump, 193
South Ferriby, 237
  Boat Owners' Association, 211
South Shields, 244
South Yorkshire coalfield, 1
Sowerby Bridge, 3
Soya beans, 233
  meal, 140, 233
Spareside, 21, 22, 268
Sparrings, 239, 243, 268
Spear & Thorpe, 140
Spence, Peter & Co., 172, 195, 223
Spencer Wire Works, Wakefield, 196, 204
Spiller's Flour Mills
  Gainsborough, 202
  Grimsby, 202, 204
Sponge iron, 207, 229
Sports, aquatic, **130**, 131, **132**, **133**
Spritsail barges, 3, 52, 76, 218–219
Sprotbrough, 84, **85**, 222
Spurn, 128, 237
St Leger, 123
Stainforth, 11, **24**, 25, 40, 47, 55, 57, 59–73, **60**, **62**, **67**, **70**, **72**, 82, **82**, 90, 93–94, 101, 102, 111, 131, 133, 136–137, 159, **166**, 196, 237
  and Keadby Canal, 25, 59, 61, 68, 73, 76, 140, 248
  Bridgefoot, **62**, 71
  Briers Lane, 72
  East Bank, 25
  farms, 71
  Finkle Street, 60
  High Bridge, 25, 67, 82
  Landing, 69, **82**
  St Matthew's Church, 73
  school, 73
  shops, 71–72
  Silver Street, 66, 71
Stamp, W., & Son, 146, **147**, 237
Staniland & Co., 50, 82, 106, 192, 196
Stayfall tackle, 11, 12, 40, 269
Staying, 16, 17, 269
Stays, 9, 42
Steamer services, 116, 129, 156
Steam fly-boats, 245
Steam keels, 245–248, **246**
Steel plates, 51
Stemmed, long, 239, 265, **269**
Stemmed, short, 239, 268, **269**
Stone, 240
Stores, keel, 183, 184–185
Stornoway, 93
Stove, cabin, 20, 22–23
Stower clogs, 7, **23**, 270
Stowers and boathooks, 7, 23, **23**, 239, 270
Strawboard, 104, 233
Strikes, 151, 152, 200–201
Sugar, 52, 150, 207, 234
Sugar beet, 234
Sulphur, 172, 234, 240
Sunflower seed, 209, 234
Susworth, 245
Sutcliffe's maltsters, 142, 146
Sutton Holme, 101
Swape, 7, 23, **23**, 239, 270
Swillington wharf, Wakefield, 204, 206, 225
Swinton, 7, 86, 107, 155–156, 237
Sykehouse, 159

T

Tack of sail, 17, 18, **262**, 270
Taffrail timber, 13, 270
Tallow, 116, 234
Tank boats, tar, 82, 155
Tankers, oil, 177, 240
Tanning materials, 115, 116
Taylor, John "Herrings", 180–181
Tees, 237, 248
Television programmes, 209, 213–214, 216, 219, 221
Tetney Haven, **99**
Thames, 237
Thames Barge Sailing Club, 217
Thief bars, **270**
Thirds, 100, 150, 162–163, 171, 179, 189, 203, 267
Thompson, Jim, 212, **212**, 221–222
Thompson, T. W., 37
Thorne, 11, 24, 27–28, **29**, 41, 50, 59, 73, 78–79, 102, 131, 216, 237, 241, 245, 248
Thorne Waterside, 33, 137, **157**
Thorpe in Balne, 59
Tides, 36, 75
Tidy, 120, 267
Tiller, 14, **14**, 260
Timber, 31, **52**, 75, 234
Timberheads, 7, 24, 31, 269, **270**, 271
Timms' flour mills, 236
Tin concentrates, 207, 226
Tinsley, 31, 40–44, 50, 52, 55, 59, 89, 196
  Park Colliery, 89
  Rolling Mills, 50, 154
Tomatoes canned, 206
Tomlinson, John Joseph, 56, 68, 129, 161–162, **161**, 177, 191, 240, 251
Tom Puddings, *see* Compartment boats
Tonnage plate, 272, **272**
Topgallant sail, 9
Topping lift, 239
Torksey, 96, 110, 111, 179, 216
Towage, 3, 36–39, **37**, **56**, 67–68, 96, 108, 141, 143, **157**, 179, 245
Townrows' flour mills, 236
Tractors, 204, **205**, 234
Trades connected with keels, 80, 182
Trade unions, 199
Trent, 3, 4, **4**
  Falls, 169
  Middle Sand, 138
  Navigation, 3, 28, 36, 39, 52, 57, 59, 76, **102**, 111, 120
Tugs, Merchandise, 247
Tye, 11, 42, 272
Tyger manure works, 116–117, 129, 227
Tyne, 237

U

United Towing Co., 37

V

Valerian, 207, 234
Vane, 186

W

Waddington, E. V., 66, 86, 156
Wadsworth, Emmanuel, **92**
Wakefield, 3, 122, 142, 143, **143**, 216, 237, 241, 245
Walker Dykes, 28, 138
Walkley, 154
Walsoken, 241
War
  1914–1918, 25, 44, 50, 58, 60, 68, 71, 73, 93, 129, 131, 182, 192, 244, 248
  1939–1945, 118, 128, 157, 191, 195
  Department, 196
  Transport, Ministry of, 196, 199
Warmsworth, 112
Warping, 12, 38, 39, **38–39**, 187, 239
Warrens' New Holland Shipyard, 161, 181
Washing clothes, 92
Washports, 237
Water cask, **18**, 19
Water Haigh Colliery, 204, 225
Wath Canal size, 61, 66, 68–9, 118, 156
Watson, J. S., 51, 96, 110, 237
Wawne, 165, **165**
Weekends at home, 152
Wells, Norfolk, 99, 118
West Country keels, 3, 95–96, 126, 272
West Stockwith, 52, 56–57, 96, 117, 149, 205
West Trent, 76
West Yorkshire keels, 3
Westwoodside, 245
Wharton Shipping Limited, 211
Wheat, 151, 179, 187, 204, 206, 222, 235–236, 248, *see* Grain
Whitaker, I. H., 70
White sand, 87, 232
Whitening, 205, 235
Whitley Bridge, 141, 197
Whitton Ness, 76, 169
Whitton's flour mills, 236
Whitwood Colliery, 122, 128
Wildsworth, 117
Williamson, Jack, i, **ii**, **45**, 168
Wilsick House, 59
Wilson, Bill, **212**
Wilson, Thomas, Sons & Co., 51
Windlass, 11, 12, **12**, **218**, 239, 259
Winteringham Haven, 108, 242
Wire, copper, 204, 235
  steel, 196, 235
Wisbech, 241
Witham, River, 127
Wombwell Colliery, 51
Wood construction, 4–7
Wood pulp, 205, 207, 231
Wood, T. F., & Co., 248
Wood, 235, 240
Worfolk & Co., 48, 70–71, 82, 103, 153, 161–2, 166
Worfolk, Isaac, 71, 153, **153**, 164
Worksop, 149
Wyllie, W. L., 174–175

Y

Yards, 8, 9
Yarmouth, 244–245
York, 9, 73, 95, **103**, **106**, 207, 211, **233**, 248
Yorkshire Dyeworks, Selby, 123, 129
  Imperial Metals, 206

Z

Zeppelin raid, 94
Zircon sand, 206, 232

Index of Ships

All keels unless described otherwise, and steel keels noted.

A
Ada, **128**
Ada Carter (steel), *see* Comrade
Aimwell (billyboy), 241, **242**, 243
Ainsty, 155
Albatross, 98
Alice, 62
Alpha, 69
Amber (steam trawler), **30**
Amity (Robinson Bros), 180
Amity (West Country), 66, 95, 96, 98, 102, 154–5, 251
Amy Howson (steel sloop), 129, 219, **220**, 221, **238**
Ancholme, 51, **188**
Anglo-American (tanker sloop), 240
Annie Maud, **frontispiece**, **46**, 66, 68, **154**, 155, **163**, 180, 182, 183, 184–5, 186, **189**, **190**, 191, **192**
Archibald Russell (barque), 198
Arrow (steam keel), **246**, 248
Atalanta (passenger packet), 245
A Triumph (motor river craft), 99, 104
Aureola (iron), 56, 58, 137

B
Bayardo (passenger ship), 133
Beecliffe (motor river craft), 218
Bertha (steel), 129
Bessie (steel), 125
Beverley (billyboy), **243**
Blanche, 66
Blessing, 1
Border Firth (coaster), 223
Bowman (tug), 36
Brasso (steel), 62, **63**
Brightside, 69
Bringcliffe, 70
Britannia, 153
Britannia (Farmers' Co.), 248
Britannia (HM Royal Yacht), 215
Britannia (tug), 245
British Oak, 68
Brothers, **128**

C
Caledonia (passenger packet), 245
Calypso (passenger ship), **128**
Carrie, 66
Cedar, 155
Charles William (steel), 62
Charlotte, 125
Cité de Londres (steam keel), 248
Cité de Paris (steam keel), **246**, 248
City of Sheffield, 48, 250
Clara Marian (tug), 40, 68, 157
Clarence T (steel sloop), 161, 251
Clarita (schooner), 93
Clyde (motor river craft), 94
Coalite (steel keel, later sloop), 70
Commerce, 122
Comrade (steel, George Scaife), 129, 182
Comrade (steel, Schofield), **25**, 71, 182, **183**, 192, 194–6, 197, 198, 202, 203, **205**, **208**, 209, 210–12, **210**, **211**, **212**, 213–4, **213**, **214**, 215, **216**, 218, **218**, 219, **220**, 221, 251
Confidence, 52, 55, 58, 75
Cygnet (steam keel), 247

D
Dalesman (tug), 109
Danum (steel), **109**, 156
Daybreak, 156
Daybreak (steel), 156, 218
Dayspring, 156
Daystar, 156
De Brakeleer (motor vessel), 157
Dekar (steel sloop), **127**, 128
Demo (dumb craft), 110
Domino (merchant ship), 217
Don (pitch tanker), 82
Don (tug), 68, **157**
Dritan (motor river craft), **194**

E
Eagle, HMS, 93
Eagle (steam keel), **246**, 247, **247**
Earl T (steel sloop), 161, 251
Eclipse, 69–70, 167, 168, 169
Edith Anne, 62
Edward, **122**
Eleanor B, 63
Elizabeth (schooner), **241**
Elizabeth Bromley (steam keel), 248
Emily, 66
Emily (Ellison and Mitchell), 155
Empress, 127
Endcliffe, 50, 61
Energetic (steel), 70
Energy, **37**, 66, **126**
Essex (steam packet), 109
Ever Ready (market billyboy), 146
Excel, 127
Expedient, 66, 155

F
Fairy, 68
Faith, 62
Fanny (later sloop), 1, 2, 3, 48, 51, 52, **52**, 102, 250
Fido (steel), **114**
Fleetgate (steel), 129
Fleming, 48, 250
Florence, 129
Forward, 63
Frenchman (tug), 36
Friends (iron), 120

G
Gainsborough Trader (motor river craft), 24
Galatea (sloop, later keel), **103**, 103–4, 108–9, 114, 116, 133, 136, 141, 152–3, 163, 166–9, 181, 251

Gambrinus (steam keel, ale packet), 247
Garland, 61, 95
George A1 (steel), 129, 162, 251
George and Eva, 120, **130**
Gertrude, **106**
Girton (steam packet), 99, 104
Glance, 155
Greta, 48
Guidance, 48, **48**, **126**, 140, 161–4, **162**, 166–7, 169, 172, **176**, 177–8, **178**, 179–80, 191, 192, 194, 195, 250

H
Halcyon (iron billyboy), 49, 241, 244
Hall's Avance (sloop), 118
Hanley's Pride (motor river craft), 156
Hannah & Harriet, **69**
Hegaro, **143**
HH (billyboy), **243**
Hitra (Viking ship), 217
Honour, 62, 66, 155
Hope (market sloop), 120
Hope (steel sloop), 125
Humber T (steel sloop), 161, 251

I
I Know (steel sloop), *see* Amy Howson
Immanuel (billyboy), 50
Industry (Albert Hall), 154
Industry (Jack Hinchcliffe), 68
Ino, **85**
Integrity (steel), 48, 56, 250
Invincible, 62, 66, 155
Ivanhoe (steel sloop), 121
Ivie (steel sloop), 239

J
James and Mary (lighter), 95, 251
Jane, 125
Jane and Maria, **117**
Jeanie Campbell (fishing vessel), 93
Jessie, 120
John, 50
John M. Rishworth (steam keel), 247
Junior T (steel), 129, 251
Jupiter, 62

K
Karma (sloop), 51
Kiero, facing **129**

L
Lady Ellen (steel), 96
Lapwing, 62
Leetham's Rose (merchandise tug), 248
Leslie, 161, 191, 251
Liberty (billyboy), 128
Lincoln Castle (paddle ferry), 214, 219
Little John (tug), **4**
Loxley (steel), **102**

M
Mafeking (sloop), 121, 122
Marie Everard (merchant ship), 211
Marteal (lighter), 248
Martha, 155
Marvel, 66
Mary Jane, 9, **9**, 120
Mavis (iron billyboy), 49, 244
May, 129
Mayday, 156
Mayflower, 120
Medina, 66, 137
Minster Bell (lighter), 248
Mirosa (spritsail barge), 218–9
Mizpah, 125
Mog, 51
Muriel, **188**

N
Nita, *see* Leslie
Noble (steel sloop), 161, 251
Northcliffe, **202**

O
Olive, 120
Olive (steel), 129
Ontario (steam trawler), **116**
Onward, 122
Ouse (merchandise tug), **248**

P
Parade T (steel), 68, 161, 180, 251
Paul H. T. (steel), 254–5, **256–7**, 258
Pelican (steel), 129
Pioneer, 111
Pioneer (steel, George Bisby), 156
Pioneer (Turner Carmichael), 181
Powerful (steel), 129
Pride, 122
Primrose, 66
Progress (Tom Parish), **78**
Progress (iron, John Schofield), 50, 250
Progress (steel, George Bisby), 156
Providence (sloop), 128

Q
Queen (buoy tender), 71

R
Radio (steel), 125
Regent, 50
Reliance (steam keel), 245
Rescue (billyboy), 50
Resolute (steel), 120
Ril (steam keel), 88, 247
Rising Hope (market billyboy), 146, 177
Robbie (tug), 120, 136
Robin Hood (tug), 36, 96
Rosalie Stamp (market sloop), 146, **147**
Rupert C, 48, 162, 191, 251

S
Salvager A (steel sloop), 177–8, **178**
Samaritan, **65**, 66
Sarah (iron sloop), 98, **98**
Scindia (tug), 66
Seeker (tug), 123
Sequel (motor river craft), 128
Shamrock (sloop), 67
Skelfleet, 125
Sobriety (steel), 61, **126**
Sophia, 49, 250
Sophia (steel keel, later sloop), *see* Amy Howson
Spider T (steel sloop), 161
Spring, 128, **228**
Sprite (steel sloop), 239
Stephen Gray (tug), 36
Swallow (billyboy), 98
Swan (steam keel), 247
Swift (steam keel), **246**, 248
Swiftsure (steam keel), 88, 247
Sylvia W, 66

T
Thomas Scarr (keel), 123, 125
Thomas Scarr (sloop), 125
Thomas Sugden, **92**
Thorncliffe, 70
Tibby, 68
Triumph, 156

U
Unique, 68
United, 61

V
Valiant (sloop), **229**
Valour (unrigged), 68
Venture (shrimper), **220**
Vigilant, 50, 196, 197, 198, 202, 203, 237, 251
Vine, 151
Viola, 153
Vishva Bhakti (merchant ship), 209, **210**, **211**
Voluta (steel), 68

W
Wanda (steel), *see* Comrade
Warrior, 122
Watchful, **88**
Waverley, **170**
Welfare, 67
Welshman (tug), 177
Whim, 49, **94**, 95, 250
William McCann (sailing trawler), **220**
Williams, 126, **170**

Y
Yare (motor river craft), 194
Yarmouth, HMS, 215
Yendis (steam keel), 248
Yorkshireman (tug), 36

Z
Zelda, 118

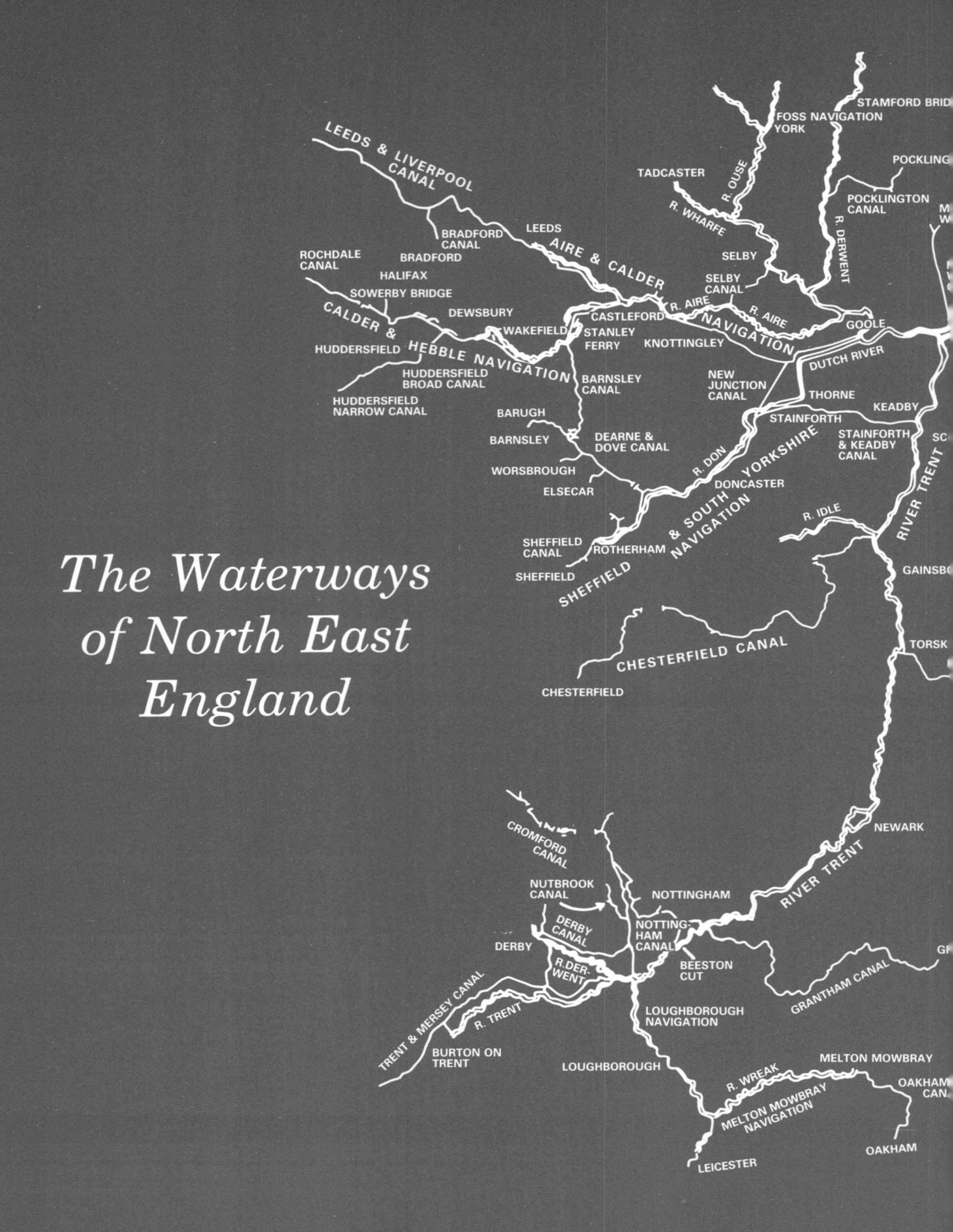
The Waterways of North East England
LEEDS & LIVERPOOL CANAL
FOSS NAVIGATION
YORK
TADCASTER
R. OUSE
R. WHARFE
POCKLINGTON CANAL
R. DERWENT
BRADFORD CANAL
LEEDS
AIRE & CALDER
ROCHDALE CANAL
BRADFORD
HALIFAX
SELBY
SELBY CANAL
SOWERBY BRIDGE
R. AIRE
DEWSBURY
CASTLEFORD
NAVIGATION
GOOLE
CALDER & HEBBLE NAVIGATION
WAKEFIELD
STANLEY FERRY
KNOTTINGLEY
HUDDERSFIELD
DUTCH RIVER
HUDDERSFIELD BROAD CANAL
BARNSLEY CANAL
NEW JUNCTION CANAL
THORNE
HUDDERSFIELD NARROW CANAL
KEADBY
BARUGH
STAINFORTH
BARNSLEY
DEARNE & DOVE CANAL
STAINFORTH & KEADBY CANAL
WORSBROUGH
R. DON
YORKSHIRE
ELSECAR
DONCASTER
RIVER TRENT
SHEFFIELD & SOUTH YORKSHIRE NAVIGATION
R. IDLE
SHEFFIELD CANAL
ROTHERHAM
SHEFFIELD
TORSK
CHESTERFIELD CANAL
CHESTERFIELD
CROMFORD CANAL
NEWARK
NUTBROOK CANAL
NOTTINGHAM
RIVER TRENT
DERBY CANAL
NOTTINGHAM CANAL
DERBY
R. DERWENT
BEESTON CUT
GRANTHAM CANAL
TRENT & MERSEY CANAL
R. TRENT
LOUGHBOROUGH NAVIGATION
BURTON ON TRENT
LOUGHBOROUGH
MELTON MOWBRAY
R. WREAK
MELTON MOWBRAY NAVIGATION
LEICESTER
OAKHAM
0 10 20